Dingle Days

Dingle Days

Eggs and Rashers, Hay and Oats

John O'Connor

GARRAÍ PUBLICATIONS

GARRAÍ PUBLICATIONS
Dingle, Co Kerry, Ireland

A catalogue record for this book is available from the British Library.

ISBN 978-1-0369-2086-9

Editorial and publishing services by Red Hen Publishing
www.redhenpublishing.ie

Typesetting and design by carrigboy
www.carrigboy.co.uk

Printed and bound in Ireland by
Walsh Colour Print

For the descendants
of the children of the shore

Contents

Acknowledgements

I wish to acknowledge the contributions made to this work by some school friends, Temperance Hall friends, and friends of recent acquaintance, all of whom value keeping the history of Dingle alive and recorded for the coming generations.

Appendix 3, which is an index of Dingle businesses, covering seventy-five years, would not have been possible without the help of Noel Brosnan, who has always been a generous contributor to my writings about our town.

Ciarán, a colleague from my boatyard days, helped with information on the boats built in Dingle Boatyard. Thanks to the kind lady (a descendant of Henry Shea) who gave me access to historic ledgers from her ancestor's shop on Bridge Street.

I thank my extended family members who are always supportive of my writings and the things I get up to.

Introduction

In *Children of the Shore – Growing up in Dingle in the 1950s and 1960s*, the story of the life and times of a Dingle family (the O'Connors, my family) was central to the book and mirrored the travails of many poor families in Ireland during those decades. The socio-economic conditions prevailing at the time resulted in a clear split between rich and poor. The less well-off knew their place and many poor children were hungry on most days of the week. Schoolchildren who could not afford pencils and copybooks were scolded by their teachers, more or less for being poor. Fathers and mothers worked nights as well as days to shore up their meagre incomes if, as was the case for some, they had any money at all coming into their home. Fish was the main staple food for people from the Quay area and without it the situation for many families would have been dire. People literally did not know where their next meal was coming from. Going home at suppertime was all about the time and not the supper. A modern family will read this paragraph today with incredulity; the conditions for the poor bordered on being Dickensian; 'I want some more', wasn't uttered as such as that would imply that you already had some.

The children of the shore are still here and it was fortitude that saw them through. The cliché is true: what brings you down makes you stronger. In the mid-1960s, a gradual improvement in conditions for less well-off people took shape. Family members had grown up and many left school after the intermediate or group certificate exams (and some before that) to find employment locally or abroad. Local workers who gave up the bulk of their wages at home were, for the first time, able to keep a little for themselves. Teenagers were gaining confidence which was largely brought about from having their own money to spend. Young people in Ireland were coming out of their shells and becoming aware of the music of the day, and talk of fashion – bell-bottoms and flares – entered their lexicon; heretofore shy and demure youngsters started throwing shapes. Struggling parents got a modicum of relief after the long haul through the drudgery of the previous two decades.

By the end of the 1960s, Dingle Boatyard had a significant workforce and local fishermen started investing in larger boats, some of which were constructed outside of the bustling Dingle Boatyard. In 1968, early scouts from MGM came to Dingle to seek out locations for the filming of *Ryan's Daughter* and the rest, as they say, is history. Several local industries adapted to the needs of a film production company and everyone who had a trade could find well-paid work during the construction phase of Kirrary Village (which was built for the film) and the schoolhouse. Anyone who wanted to, could find work at that time: drivers, cleaners, hospitality workers, stand-ins, property leasers. Every bothán available was gobbled up at lucrative rates by Faraway Productions to house the various departments under its remit. *Ryan's Daughter* was like manna from heaven; it contributed to the enhancement of several local businesses and kick-started a new future for the area in the last three decades of the twentieth century. A small number of local workers moved on with the film company to work on other films worldwide, while some who had come to Dingle to make the story of Rosie Ryan stayed behind and opened businesses.

The 1970s started buoyed up with nest eggs and a store of confidence following the influx from Hollywood. Early in the decade, Neodata Services Limited set up in Cooleen, eventually employing more than fifty people, mostly female. The boatyard got a much-needed extension and doubled its work complement. It looked like the poor days were over and, to an extent, they were. The main businesses in the town had annual 'socials' – ticketed gatherings where a meal and a dance celebrated the year that had gone. In the 1980s, the summer salmon fishing industry was booming and the ripples flowing from it were evident. Tourism was burgeoning and a lone dolphin swimming in Dingle Bay, later named Fungie, would evolve into an eco-friendly tourism industry which would top any preconceived imaginings about the future direction of Dingle as a visitor destination.

Cumann Bádóirí Naomh Bhreannain was established and rowed in with the diving and rowing clubs in seeking a multipurpose building (Dingle Marina Centre) to headquarter their activities. The Department of the Marine took over the running of the harbour and the major developments of the western and eastern marinas pushed back the sea from the town walls, from The Wood to Hudson's Bridge. A gradual shift from fishing to leisure activities was taking place in the harbour. Yacht races finishing in Dingle from coastal clubs in Ireland and *Le Figaro* from France became common.

The harbour and the wider region of Dingle Bay – without which Dingle would be a nonentity – as a resource for tourism has been developed to a high degree at this stage, with boatcraft doing harbour tours, bay trips, along with the popular Blasket Islands tours, dotting the waters on fine days. In the inner waters, sailing dinghies, kayaks, paddleboards and steer-your-own boats vie for domain in one of the most sought-after play areas on the southwest coast. Local fishing boats and lone boatmen have to navigate the harbour environs with more caution, and the sense of ownership and entitlement to the waters and the wild is getting blurred. Malaga-style cruise liners have started coming into the bay (some people think this is great!) and passengers are ferried to the town pontoon on their ship's boats. There are moves afoot to expand the western marina and bring more leisure craft into the mix.

Ashore, a consequence of all that happens on the water and in Dingle during the tourist season is that living accommodation for local workers and people starting out is in short supply. Airbnbs are prolific and have squeezed out the locals from attaining long-term rental accommodation in the town. They are taken by the hordes that want to experience Dingle, including the raucous weekend stags and hens that are a given all year round. Several house-build projects in recent years are beyond the reach of the locals; second homes bought by outsiders are dotting the landscape. The days of the two-month tourist season are gone. Nowadays, eight months of tourism, beginning on St Patrick's Day, is welcomed by the many businesses that cater for the industry while the period has become an inconvenience for some local residents and an endurance test for others. The generation of *Children of the Shore* that left Dingle to find work and raise families away from their hometown return to visit a town they hardly recognise. When they come, they do it during the off-season.

This work is a continuance of *Children of the Shore* with a broader intent to give a flavour of the life and times in Dingle after the 1960s, and especially to show how Dingle has massively transformed from the challenging times of the earlier decades where people without means were trapped in a constant struggle to overcome adversity. In some respects, tourism was the saviour of the less well-off people in the town; more opportunities for work emerged and living conditions improved. But there is a cost to progress, where that brings us and what we lose along the way. Perhaps for Dingle, now, the way forward is back.

John O'Connor, 2025

ONE

Origins

The Garraí (garden or field in Irish), located directly opposite the fishing quay in Dingle is a small street where seven families once lived, including the O'Connors, Brosnans (x 2), Johnsons, Moores, Bowlers, and Morans. The residents called it a lane or laneway rather than a street. In the 1901 census of Ireland, the address of the Garraí was entered as Quay Lane and the main street, now Strand Street, running at right angles to it, was called Quay Street. The Garraí was sufficiently populated at one stage to put together, along with a neighbouring laneway, a Wrenboy group for St Stephen's Day (December 26th) to go hunting for the 'Wran'. The Quay area including the Colony, a small street to the east, was central to the wren day celebrations historically and many of its present-day musicians have antecedents from that part of town. The Colony (off Strand Street) was also the nucleus of the Dingle Fife and Drum Band before the founding families, many of them Flannerys, moved to Ashmount

Terrace (an extension of Goat Street) which then became the headquarters of marching music in the town.

The Garraí inclines upwards to the north and was split down the middle by an open channel (now running underground) which carried water from a spring well at the top. In the early decades of the twentieth century, twelve families drew from the well; in all, upwards of seventy souls relied on the sustenance it provided. The spring was the source of water for households in its environs which extended beyond the Garraí. The top house, Bowler's, was the closest to the spring and had the shortest draw. My grandparents, who were four houses down, had more lugging to do and the detritus thrown out from the upper houses into the channel flowed past their door on its way into Dingle Bay. Advantages existed even in times of hardship with the purest channel water passing by Bowler's door.

My great-grandparents, Jeremiah O'Connor, Strand Street, and Elizabeth Ashe, Reenbeg, were married in Dingle in 1861. One of their sons, James, was my grandfather. My grandparents lived in a whitewashed fisherman's cottage in the Garraí with their children, three boys and three girls – eight people vying for space in the house. Under the pitched and tarred roof, a loft which was accessed by a rustic ladder housed the children at bedtime. The ground floor had a dividing partition which halved the house into two rooms, with the fireplace situated against the northern gable. Mary Deady and James O'Connor, the parents, had their bed east of the fireplace and it was surrounded by a curtain during the day. The cooking was also done in this room as was much of the living during daytime. The southern half of the house had a bedroom and a small workshop where Jimmy (my uncle) plied his trade as a shoemaker. Jimmy served his time at the trade under Paddy Curran (pronounced Craan), his granduncle on his mother's side who was the original owner of the house. Mary Deady was Curran's niece and came to work and live-in as a house girl for her uncle when she was a teenager.

My grandfather James came from Quay Street and married into the house in the Garraí. On All-Ireland day, when Kerry was playing in the football final, a wet-battery radio on the workshop counter attracted a crowd outside the front door. A kitchen dresser stocked with shiny delft, cans of condensed milk and miscellaneous religious icons also acted as a divider of the floor space; beyond that the furniture was rudimentary. A model boat named *Pride of Dingle*, a nobby with a full rig of sails, was also on the dresser, and several fishing households had similar models. Candles and oil lamps were strategically placed and a niche on the west side of the fireplace held what was, presumably, the meagre personal belongings of James and Mary O'Connor.

The three boys from the house (Jimmy, Michael and Jeremiah) stayed in Dingle, while the girls (Elizabeth, Josie and Eileen) left home, as was common with girls in the times that were; the men had the fishing to stay for. My grandfather skippered the fishing boat, *Manx Girl* (owned by Denny Garvey), and his sons Michael and Jeremiah were part of the crew. Three generations of the

O'Connors had the name Jeremiah, including my uncle, granduncle and great-grandfather. Uncle Jeremiah liked to be given the full biblical name though we knew him as Uncle Jerry. He was a well-read man and knew the origin of the name that went back to the sixth or seventh century Hebrew prophet. He was also a bachelor and, as they said in those days, 'he liked a drink'.

While mending nets on the quay, Jeremiah would share stories from the latest book or newspaper he was reading and once, when asked where he got his knowledge, his response was, 'I was reading it last night in the *Wall Street Journal*'. Jeremiah would regularly get copies of the prestigious newspaper from local merchant, Michael F. O'Sullivan, who had the WSJ on subscription and received it in the post. In the three generations on from my uncle, the name Jeremiah is gone from the O'Connor line and that sometimes gives me pause. In 1909, the cottages in The Wood were constructed and one of the new houses went to the O'Connors from the Garraí. My father, Michael, moved into the house after he got married to my mother, Joan Brennan, in 1947.

My father and Uncle Jimmy were hard workers while Jeremiah navigated a more leisurely pace through life. After he gave up fishing for a position in the coast-watching service during the Second World War years, Michael became a postman at the end of the war. After his postman rounds were over, he did any work he could – painting, gardening, filleting fish – to supplement the family income. When Jimmy left the shoemaking behind, he got work with a local merchant and one of his jobs was on a coal delivery lorry where he and the driver delivered coal and carried on their backs 100 cwt (50kg) bags of coal from the street through laneways and round to the backs of houses, work that would not be countenanced today under health and safety regulations. There were sayings in those days such as 'He is a hard man' and 'They were hard men'; alas, for better or worse, the days of the hard men are over. The working week was six days back then which was later trimmed down to five and a half and then to five. As I write, there is talk of further reducing the working week. I wonder what Jeremiah would think of that?

The Garraí was uniquely positioned near the commerce of the fishing industry; the residents had full view of the pier and the comings and goings of nobbies as they landed their catch in the evenings. Four nobbies (fishing boats), including the *Katherine* and the *Brigid* were built in the lower end of the Garraí by Michael Long, a shipwright from the corner of Quay Street and the Garraí, who served his time in the Isle of Man where the nobby design originated. This lower eastern corner of the Garraí was where large boatbuilding in the modern era began in Dingle. The Bord Iascaigh Mhara Boatyard opened in 1952 in Dingle and began the construction of a fleet of fifty-footers, heralding a new design of fishing boat and the end of the nobby era.

The O'Connors and Brosnans had the largest families in the Garraí. The Brosnan family had a newsagency for the *Kerry Champion* and the *Irish Press,* and a son, Paddy, had the franchise for Esso Oil which supplied the fishing fleet with diesel fuel. The four historic industries working out of the Garraí – shoemaking, newsagency, boatbuilding and Esso Oil – had the little laneway to the fore in the commercial activities of the quay area. Corneilius Brosnan, a fisherman from the Garraí, received two bronze medals, one from the Lloyd's Society and one from the Royal Humane Society for saving the life of a young man in Dingle Bay in 1896. In 1921, Corneilius, while crewing on the motor nobby, *Mairéad*, got another medal from the RHS for conspicuous bravery while saving a crew from disaster by fire or drowning onboard the motor boat *Spree* in Valentia Harbour. The other crew members of the *Mairéad* – John Moriarty (skipper), Edward Moriarty, Denis Devane and Corneilius Guerin – also received bronze medals.

Grandparents play a large part in the lives of today's families but the children in our family (while our grandparents in the Garraí were living) never got to know James and Mary and, likewise, the grandparents never got to know their grandchildren. James, a no-nonsense type, was occupied with providing for the house, and Mary Deady O'Connor, a deeply pious woman, was compassionate and open-armed no matter what political side issues might prevail. There is a sense of loss there but it was common then, dare I say, for parents to rear their own children without the help of the previous generation. The times were different, of course, men brought home the bacon and mothers reared the children. Women wore shawls in public as if hiding from the world at large; my grandmother Mary was such a woman. James and Mary died in 1955, three months apart, leaving behind a handful of grandchildren – a handful that has since multiplied, through successive generations, to one hundred and seventy people whose origins are in that small house in the Garraí. The last remaining resident from the Garraí who still lives there, Noel, from the Brosnan family, has seen seven generations of the O'Connor family from the whitewashed cottage.

TWO

Better Times

In *Children of the Shore*, the poverty which prevailed in Dingle in the 1950s and 1960s and how it was part of daily living for the O'Connor family (and many more families) is recounted. In looking back now, long after the trials of those times, there is a realisation that there was also a richness in our lives. Having a home on the harbour, which became our playground, left us with memories of fun, adventure and laughter that are now to the fore, rather than recollections of hardship and want. The positives prevail in our minds. From our bedroom window we could see the harbour spread from the back wall to skirt the south shore at the foot of Carhoo Hill, with Eask Tower standing like a sentinel over our humble existence. A world of our own existed at the back of the house; it was a prized thing despite not being appreciated by hungry youngsters. The only noise to be heard as the day wore on was of children playing in the laneways and on the strand abutting our homes.

Our back door faced south onto the harbour and the stone walls to the front buffeted us from the street where the busy traffic of the time (horses and carts, the odd car and lorry) passed throughout the day. Even then, we were shepherded when going out the front door lest the 'busy' street cause us harm. These days, speedy vehicles continuously suck debris from the footpath into their wake as their drivers rush to keep up with the busy world they live in. We have been driven into a scenario where everybody thinks they have to be in a hurry. Once we had time to stop and talk to friends on the street whereas now it's a case of 'I'm in a rush, catch up later' or 'I must answer this' (the phone, of course). The world of the telegram is long gone, as is the horse and cart, the telephone coinbox, the paperboy and the milkman.

The wedding of Angela, daughter from the O'Connor family, to PJ O'Dowd, in 1973, was the first celebratory occasion where all twelve family members from 122 The Wood came together as a unit to socialise and make merry. Mary and Nuala (who learned hairdressing in Dublin) had already married in England. I was in full-time employment in Dingle Boatyard and some of the younger family members were beginning to make their way in the world. The wedding was the first event where we gathered en masse in public. Following the marriage in St Mary's Church in Dingle, the festivities continued in the Manhattan Hotel in Tralee. The main troupe from the family were driven to the breakfast in a red, windowless Transit van which was on loan; the getting there on wooden benches installed in the back is as memorable now as the main event. Musical instruments, some in the percussion quarter of a makeshift nature, were employed to shorten the road. We were coming out of ourselves and forming our brand. After years of poverty and insecurity, there was a sense of having made it through. Our parents, Michael and Joan, were gradually shedding some of the stress of being responsible for the rearing, with all that entails, of ten children born in a fourteen-year timespan. The responsibility borne by our parents through the rearing years was lost on us; we selfishly thought that all the problems brought about by our poverty were felt by us alone, the young ones. As children, we had not the maturity to take in what was happening from our parents' perspective.

In the early 1970s, things that had been out of reach gradually became attainable to us but it still involved hard work; there was nothing given over freely from mom and dad because they had no more to give. Young people setting up a home saved money to kick-start the process; some were lucky if one of the partners came from a 'bit of land' and got a site but townspeople didn't have that luxury. The beginnings of a family often took shape in two rented rooms and this situation lasted for a number of years while the money for a deposit on a house was painstakingly gathered. Newlyweds got practical wedding gifts such as toasters, electric kettles and sets of cutlery which, if not used right away, were kept stored in their cardboard boxes until the house was built. Getting money gifts for the couple's dream honeymoon was unheard of – a night in the nearest big town with a hotel was the norm.

A modest house to suit the family's anticipated needs would be built from plans in *Bungalow Bliss*. One of my sisters set up home in four different towns while her husband followed the work. When the grandchildren came to visit the house in Dingle, they were all piled into one car; people-carriers didn't exist then. On arrival, the whole complement stacked into one room. Those grandchildren, now grown up, have no qualms about sharing bedrooms with their cousins when getting together. As the generations move on from their roots in Dingle, some don't realise how hard life was for their forebears in the 1950s. A recent young visitor from Dublin to my house thought fish came from fish fingers; during her visit she went boating in Dingle Bay, caught a fish, cooked and ate it, all in the space of an hour. The requisite photos were taken, of course, to inform the world at large that the adventure had happened. For my visitor it was an adventure; for her ancestors it was a way of life.

The spreading-out of the girls from our family began in Co. Clare; two went first and two more followed on. The younger two eventually went to Shannon for work and later headed to Australia where they married and began raising their own families. Carmel reared a prize-winning Irish dancer, Karen, and she herself secured a volunteer role in the 2000 Olympics in Sydney. Bernadette became a chef and cooked for hundreds of Australian soldiers as well as an Australian prime minister. Two boys made homes in London and one in Clare. The house in The Wood was clearing out like the Agatha Christie novel, *10 Little Indians … and then there were none*. After twenty years of having children around the place, our parents were left with the echoes. What were their thoughts on that first night after the last of the children of the shore had left?

Their grandchildren have branched out into the world of commerce and various fields of endeavour that were out of reach to their forebears. Many families that struggled alongside ours are now to the fore in the business and cultural life of the town. The family names that emanated from poorer quarters of the town have members with college degrees and have established themselves as the 'now' people. Dingle has developed to a degree that was unimaginable in the mid-twentieth century when things were bought on the HP (hire purchase) and Green Shield stamps were required to amass household wares and other necessities. The Saint Vincent de Paul charity was to the fore in helping families in need in the town; the reversal is complete and we now bring quality goods to SVP shops. In 1958, a new bicycle for my father was purchased on the HP, in Caball's, Tralee, for £20. 3. 6. (deferred payment price, of course); a £1 deposit was paid and eighteen monthly payments of £1. 2. 5. followed. Coming up with the monthly instalment was challenging and worrying for my mother who looked after the household purse. Her concerns were ongoing as several other items, including furniture and the cooker, had payments due at various intervals. The bike was not for cycling around the west on a sunny Sunday afternoon; rather, it was the means of ensuring my father's bread and butter and an absolute necessity for doing his rounds as a postman. Several workers worked from their bikes in those days, among them the gravedigger, the builder and the carpenter.

Everybody misses out at some stage. We accepted that some things were not always attainable – a square meal every day, the price of a cinema ticket, a good pair of shoes. Pocket money was unheard of for our circle in the 1960s. Schoolbooks were scarce, either handed down, borrowed or shared on the classroom deck. At home, *Ireland's Own* and the *Messenger*, a red-covered Catholic periodical, would be found. Desperate Dan's exploits were found in *The Dandy*, and Dennis the Menace and Minnie the Minx (for the girls) in *The Beano* were regular reading fare. These comic book characters were part of our growing up; they made us laugh and steered our thoughts away from the things we didn't (but should) have had. There was no certainty that the anthological flow of these characters' capers would play out as planned for us because the demands on the household purse could not guarantee the next issue – a small thing but another exasperation to endure, and hearing of the missed instalment from a friend because we could not afford the latest on the shelves didn't compensate.

The sixty-four-pagers, illustrated and captioned comics with war and western themes, were continually swapped among like-minded youngsters seeking distraction. It would be a surprise when our mother pulled a comic out of her hessian shopping bag where also hidden would be a pack of Gold Flake cigarettes for our father. She would produce the fags when our father was reduced to butts as the week wore on. Joan loved shopping when she had the money which was at the weekend when our father brought home his postman's wage and all (as far as we know) was handed over to the bursar. From mid-week onwards, necessities were scarce and the cupboards were bare; long faces abounded as we waited for Saturday. They were the longest days as time goes slow when you are hungry. Comics were read over and over again and swapped repeatedly.

There was a library in Dingle but we were not library-type people. Because of our situation in life, at school we were never encouraged or led to believe that we could join the library and read books. The overriding impression we were left with while attending school was that we would amount to nothing. Today, while young people read the Harry Potter and Lord of the Rings book series, a throwback sense of deprivation is felt – not having had access to books at that stage of our growing up. Bookshelves were not to be found in houses like ours. We missed out on the adventures in books like *Treasure Island*, *King Solomon's Mines* and *Moby Dick* – the book every boy should read. Now we are playing catch-up, devouring books that entertain and those that open our minds about the way the world really works.

A picture won in a pellet gun shoot-out competition at a visiting amusement camp hung in our hallway in the early 1960s; it was a triptych of John Fitzgerald Kennedy, Pope John XXIII and Martin Luther King. It is not surprising that a pope was in the mix, nor an American president whose ancestors hailed from Ireland. MLK was a curious addition, notwithstanding the growing renown for his work with the American civil rights movement. The picture gave a snapshot of that time in Ireland – heroes from church influence and American patronage. The parcel sent from America by Dingle expatriates was a much looked-forward to event. Historically, Irish emigrants headed for the US and many of my ancestors from Dingle sought work in New York, Massachusetts and New Hampshire. 'Tá adharca fada ar na buaibh thar lear' was an often-used Gaelic idiom in Dingle referring to the faraway hills of America being greener and wealthier. In Ireland, and in particular West Kerry, America was considered the next parish, west across the Atlantic. While our nearest neighbour to the east gave work and shelter to our emigrants, empathy was understandably absent, although pictures of the Queen could be found in many houses.

Having a cinema in Dingle gave us a wide variety of American heroes: John Wayne, Gregory Peck and James Cagney were among the favoured. When young and playing in the fields, 'Cowboys and Indians' was our preferred game, hugely influenced by Hollywood films. Toy guns and holsters and felt hats were on the list for boys' Christmas presents. The 1960s, with the emergence of the Beatles and Elvis Presley, opened a new world of would-be heroes. The transistor radio was a wonder and the first one came to our house in 1969, bringing with it Radio Luxembourg. The television came around the same time and introduced us to the world of *Green Acres* and *The Waltons*. 'Good night, Mary Ellen' was often heard in the big room in our house at bedtime, paraphrasing the famous line that was often heard at the end of an episode of *The Waltons*. Everybody needs heroes, it is said. The real, homegrown heroes of our time were the parents who navigated through drudgery in the middle of the twentieth century and steered us youngsters to a world of better times. As is often said about that generation that lived in hard times, 'God, weren't they great people'.

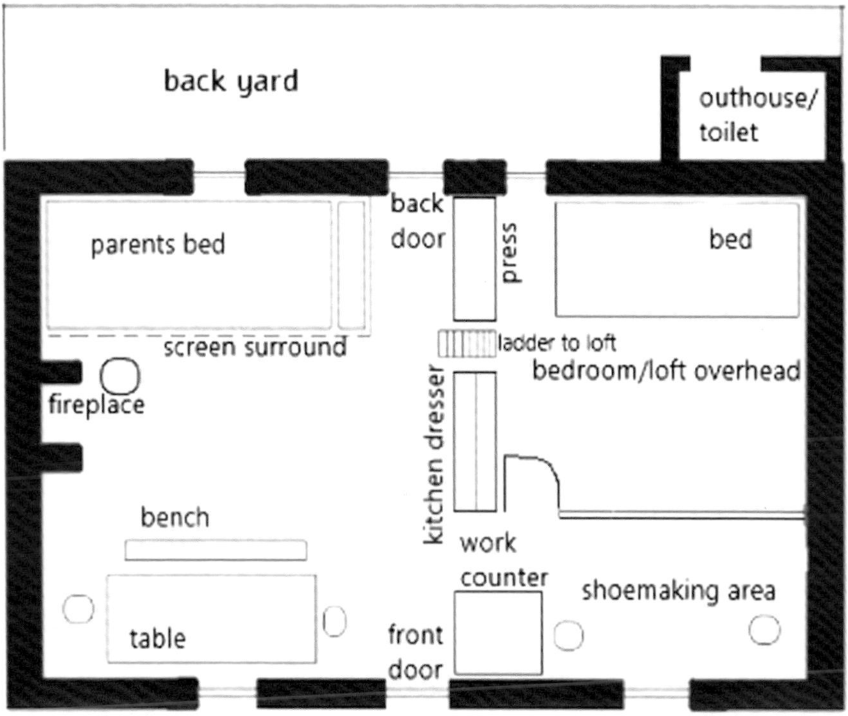

Floor plan of the O'Connor house in the Garraí.

Model of a nobby fishing boat, owned by the Donegan family.

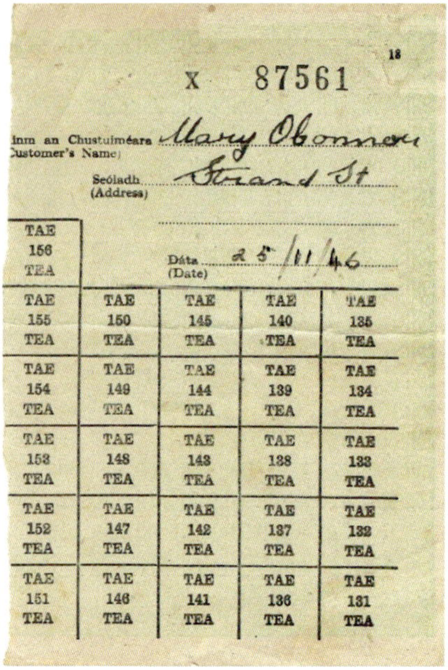

18

X 87561

Ainm an Chustuiméara (Customer's Name) Mary O'Connor

Seóladh (Address) Strand St

Dáta (Date) 25/11/46

TAE 156 TEA				
TAE 155 TEA	TAE 150 TEA	TAE 145 TEA	TAE 140 TEA	TAE 135 TEA
TAE 154 TEA	TAE 149 TEA	TAE 144 TEA	TAE 139 TEA	TAE 134 TEA
TAE 153 TEA	TAE 148 TEA	TAE 143 TEA	TAE 138 TEA	TAE 133 TEA
TAE 152 TEA	TAE 147 TEA	TAE 142 TEA	TAE 137 TEA	TAE 132 TEA
TAE 151 TEA	TAE 146 TEA	TAE 141 TEA	TAE 136 TEA	TAE 131 TEA

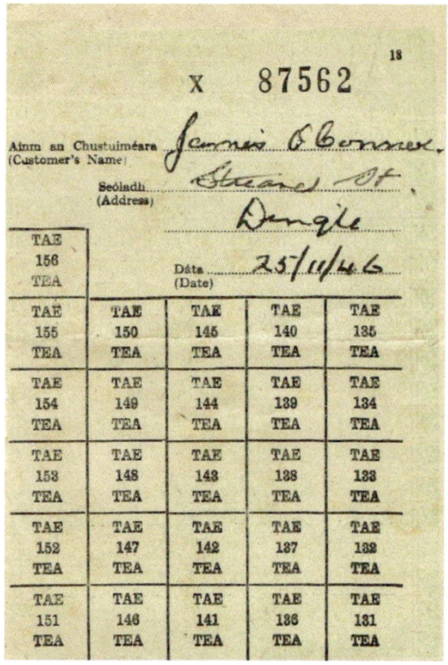

18

X 87562

Ainm an Chustuiméara (Customer's Name) James O'Connor.

Seóladh (Address) Strand St. Dingle

Dáta (Date) 25/11/46

TAE 156 TEA				
TAE 155 TEA	TAE 150 TEA	TAE 145 TEA	TAE 140 TEA	TAE 135 TEA
TAE 154 TEA	TAE 149 TEA	TAE 144 TEA	TAE 139 TEA	TAE 134 TEA
TAE 153 TEA	TAE 148 TEA	TAE 143 TEA	TAE 138 TEA	TAE 133 TEA
TAE 152 TEA	TAE 147 TEA	TAE 142 TEA	TAE 137 TEA	TAE 132 TEA
TAE 151 TEA	TAE 146 TEA	TAE 141 TEA	TAE 136 TEA	TAE 131 TEA

Tea voucher from O'Connor's house in the Garraí.

Top left: Elizabeth O'Connor Kennedy and Padraig Lynch.
Top right: Peggy and James Flahive.
Left: Peggy Flahive, Mayra Duffy, Jimmy Kennedy, Eileen O'Connor.

Dingle pier in the 1960s.

A visiting reporter interviews Pats Brosnan and Timmy Joe Brosnan, 1973.

Paddy Bawn Brosnan pulling a pint in his bar, 1973.

Patrick Garvey, 1973.

A young girl and her dog bring the shopping home, 1973.

New shed under construction at Dingle Boatyard, in 1973.

Paddy Ollie Brosnan and John Paul Flannery having a chat, 1973.

L-r: Mikie Graham, Tomasaín Sheehy and Dernie Graham taking it easy, 1973.

L-r: Michael McCarthy and Johnny Murphy, 1973.

Garda Joe Curran talking with a visiting reporter, 1973.

Names of Dingle-built boats.

A painting by Colleen Duffy of regatta day in Dingle, in 1980.

Tom Fitzgerald (centre) canvassing. Also included are Jimmy Kennedy, Patrick Sheehy, Jimmy Fenton and Paudie O'Shea.

Dingle Regatta Committee and friends. *Front l-r*: M. O'Connor, P. Flannery, – Haughey, P.B. Brosnan, T. Sheehy, J.F. Brosnan, T. Sheehy. *Back l-r*: L. Brosnan, A. Keane, M. Flannery, P. Garvey, C. Cleary, – Haughey, – Haughey, T. Sullivan, V. Noonan, 1980s.

Members of the Quay Wren, *front l-r*: M. Sheehy, M. de Barra, S. Brosnan, T. Sheehy, N. Brosnan, J. Flannery. *Back l-r*: T. Flaherty, D. Donegan, N. Brosnan, I. O'Connor, M. O'Connor, J. Garvey, P. Leahy, J. O'Connor, B. Sheehan, J. Dillon. 1992.

Árd Íde, in Burnham.

Above: The O'Connor brothers John, Michael, Ignatius and Ambrose, with visitors at Slea Head, 1975.

Left: John O'Connor (playing the guitar) and fellow musician, Denis Houlihan, 1990s.

Tommy Flahive beside his horse on Dingle pier, with Paddy Ollie Brosnan at the pier head.

Jeremiah O'Connor, Paddy Bawn Brosnan and John Brosnan onboard the *Ros Dubh*. Note the 50-footer on the boatyard slip and pitched roof on the ice plant.

Michael O'Connor and his sister Liz Kennedy at the Cottages.

Regatta group, 1981. Included are L. Brosnan, J. Boland, P.B. Brosnan, B. Sheehy, T. Sullivan, V. Noonan, J. Dillon. G. Sheehy, P. Curran, T. Sheehy, M. O'Coileán, T. Sheehy.

Photo of Dingle taken before the marina development. Note the seashore touching the main road at Strand Street/The Wood, and the fishing boat *Star Immaculate* on the boatyard slip.

Sign for Dingle Sea Anglers' Club on the harbourmaster's office (now Harrington's Restaurant).

Martin and Peter Flannery crossing the road on Strand Street.

Sign over Thomas Callaghan's pub.

Fisherman Tommy Glouster.

In 1974, the *Star Immaculate* was driven ashore and the sea wall along Strand Street knocked by a storm.

Noel Brosnan and neighbours inspecting a whale on the slip.

Fungie welcoming John O'Connor and cousins.

The Wood cottages centenary celebrations at the Skellig Hotel, 2009.

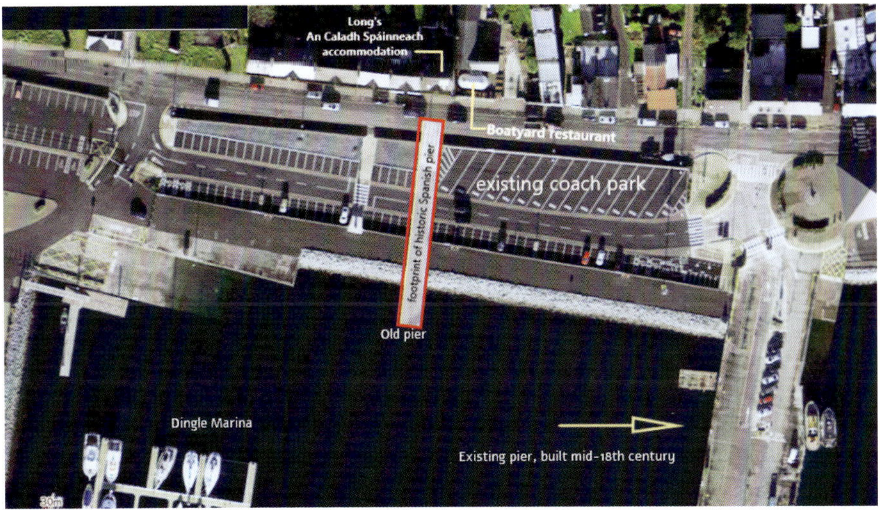

Superimposed image showing the footprint of the historic Caladh Spáinneach (image by J. O'Connor).

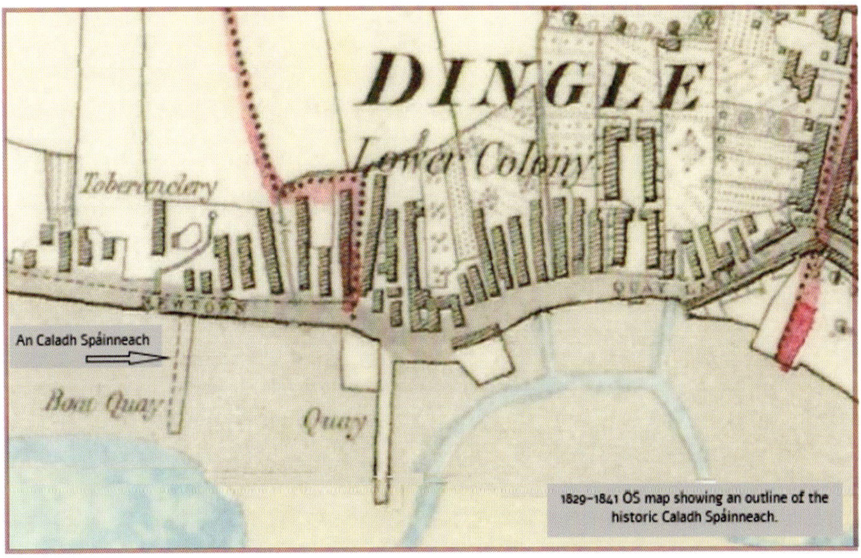

Image of the Caladh Spáinneach on a historic map.

Winch house at Dingle Boatyard.

The Quay Wren take over Strand Street, 2023.

THREE

The Local Shop

Online shoppers have a history of everything they buy available to them in their account section of the online shop; their preferences and the frequency of purchases are held in a digital ledger in the cloud. Historically, merchant shops, large and small, kept ledgers where customer accounts were recorded in neat and meticulous script by studious office workers who dressed to reflect the importance of their position in the chain of employees. In our schooldays, we sat beside some of these neat recorders whose destiny as keepers of names and numbers in straight lines in handwritten Lucinda-like font was inevitable. In smaller shops, a ledger with similar attention to accuracy and orderly detail was kept. For this chapter, I was given access to three three-inch thick hardcover volumes of transactions that cover the decades before and after the Second World War, this by the kind permission of descendants of Henry Shea's shop on Bridge Street.

Before Henry took over, his mother ran the shop and it was locally known as Laois Barry's, Barry being the woman's maiden name. It was common where the man of the house had a separate occupation (away from the shop) to have the woman's character to the fore in the business. I heard an interesting anecdote from a friend who knew Laois Barry. A rambunctious and cocky youngster once asked, 'Give me tuppence worth of sweets, Laois Barry' to which he got the stern reply, 'I am not Laois Barry'. To this, the youngster replied, 'Well, if you are not, you are damn like her'.

Henry's shop was a typically local one; most streets had a similar shop that served the locals within its catchment. Beside our house was Begley's, which served not only the residents but the students in the nearby Technical School and the workers in Keane's fish factory across the road. It was normal in those days to raise a bill (tick) that would be paid off at the end of the week. If tick was not forthcoming near home, the search continued along the street. It can be seen from Henry's books that several of his customers settled up at the end of the week. Henry's customers mostly came from Bridge Street, Holyground, Avondale, The Mall, Station Row, Cooleen and Dygate Lane. He also had a few from further back the town mainly because he was selling *The Kerryman* newspaper (3d, in 1950, 'd' meaning a penny of which there were 240 in an Irish pound) and, of course, because he was an interesting man to converse with.

The stock on Henry's shelves was varied and covered nearly all household needs. It included the following:

> Aspirin, baking soda, beans, biscuits, butter, candles, caraway seeds, cheese, chocolate, Christmas cards, Cleeve's toffee, clothes pegs, cocoa, corn flour, currants, eggs, fruit, jelly, lemonade, margarine, marmalade, matches, newspapers, notepaper, oil, peas, pepper, polish, prunes, razor blades, salad dressing, salt, shoe laces, soap, cigarettes, starch, sugar, sultanas, tea, tobacco, vegetables, washing powder, washing soda.

Henry did not sell bread, according to the accounts. At the time of his ledgers there were several bakers in the town that had their own shops and deliveries by bread vans from outside was not common. His shop was also an agency for a laundry where people dropped off clothes which were forwarded on and picked up days later. The laundry service was availed of mainly by a handful of people who had more money to spend. For their laundering needs, the majority of Henry's customers bought Rinso, the popular washing powder of the time. The shopping habits of his customers tell a tale of people's preferences and, by omission, the things they didn't buy. A nearby woman bought cigarettes regularly while others appear to be casual smokers; it may be deduced that Mrs A, a woman on the same street was not a smoker – she never bought cigarettes. Mr B bought aspirin regularly; Mr C had a sweet tooth and was a lover of Cleeve's toffee and custard.

Plug tobacco was favoured by a number of fishermen. Candles and paraffin for oil lamps were sold regularly. The sales of Mac's Smile razor blades (with the logo of a bald-headed man which, when turned upside down, gave a happy or sad face) gives an indication of the shaving practices of the day. Curiously, a spinster who lived alone bought razor blades from time to time. There was a divide between people who bought butter and margarine, the latter being about half the price of the former. Henry's stock had a range of brand names of the time, some giving rise to the popular saying, 'In Ireland, we have Lambs making jam, Birds making custard and Lyons making tea'.

Henry's entries alternated between pencil and pen and ink. In some entries, he used only first names; these were people he obviously knew well that made regular footfall on his slate-flagged floor. Being a youngster, I didn't know Henry very well but my memory of him is of a precise individual with a distinguished bearing and a defined step whenever he walked out in public. Henry was the cornerstone of Dingle's Saint Mary's Dramatic Society and, by all accounts, he had a great stage presence where he commanded attention and gave gravitas to his performances. Five houses in the street where Henry had his shop, including Henry's, were torn down recently and rebuilt and are now converted into a one-unit block with dozens of Airbnb beds. Where once there were five independent businesses offering diverse services, including a petrol pump service, a music teacher, a barber, mechanic and grocery, now there is one, occupying seventy-one per cent of the street and the product is the turnover of people visiting Dingle, most of whom want to party. The development is an example of the new direction the town has taken in recent years.

There were a number of shops serving the Quay area. Ashe's provided an array of confectionery items and breads which were produced in their own bakery. The Ashe sisters were business-like and proper in their dealings with the public and ran an efficient business. Alice and Mazie presented themselves with a gentle demeanour and were generous in spirit; many a basket loaf (bread) was given on tick to our house. Noan Kennedy (three doors along from Ashe's) was cordial and sat inside the front door on the right where a long wooden-topped counter stretched to the back wall. The street end of the counter housed miscellaneous household items including sweets and buns while the rear end carried stout and spirits and some soft drinks. Noan did a good trade in empty bottle returns which local youths scavenged for on the dumps and on the seashore for pennies. Noan's customers were always sparse somehow; she had a small number of regulars, fishermen mostly, at the back but never had a thriving business at the front grocery section. Nearly every second or third building had a pub licence along with a secondary business, like grocery, drapery or hardware. In those times, Dingle didn't have craft shops.

Noan was an elderly lady living alone in a large, three-storey building – there must have been rooms in the house that she never visited. Unlike some shopkeepers who didn't like to see poor youngsters coming in, knowing full well there was nothing in it for them, Noan would give time to a young fellow trying to sponge a glass of raspberry and a bun with sweet talk and a bundle of sticks for her fire under his arm. Several boys collected wood for Noan, gathered from broken fish boxes and fallen branches and fashioned into a bundle with twine from discarded off-cuts of fishing nets slung over the wall across from her pub. In later years, Noan's premises changed hands and became a busy pub (Murphy's) providing regular music for the next generations. From the street to the back wall, it would be chock-a-block with the new wave of young people who finally had money to spend. A friend I grew up with remarked on opening night as he tried to navigate his way to the toilets, 'Noan Kennedy never had it like this'. Similar could be said of several business premises in Dingle that had large floor space and minimal footfall before the 1970s.

Further along from Noan's, Margaret Long's carried general grocery and ice cream and was a regular stop for people from the Quay. Before my time, cooked crubeens were available there after the pictures. O'Sullivan's on Strand Street (that area of town was also called the Quay) was the first large shop on the way into town. Francie O'Sullivan's was a merchant shop which mainly carried meal, flour and milk from the cows on the O'Sullivan farm. It was the family home to the O'Sullivans and run in the 1960s by Mrs O'Sullivan and her son Michael Francie. It would not be described as a local shop as such; it was mostly a stopover for members of the farming community. Michael Francie also bought and sold periwinkles which were prolific in the adjoining strand in the 1960s. The picking activity was competitive amongst the locals and a welcome source of income for those with little or no money. Michael Francie would also give work to local youngsters on the farm, herding and milking cows, milk delivery, saving hay in summertime and piggery work. Several members of our family worked in various enterprises of the O'Sullivan family. Michael Francie was an avid film fan and, in 1979, he bought the local Phoenix Cinema which he refurbished and modernised.

James Flahive's, also known as Peggy Manning's, was the first pub on the street coming from the west. The premises had the double-counter feature with the pub on the west side and the general shop to the east. The shop was not thriving in my younger years; the pub was the main business then. Our family had celebratory gatherings when cousins were home from America in Peggy's kitchen where her gleaming, highly polished stove inevitably entered the conversation. Peggy always contributed to the celebrations by giving a rendition of one of her favourite songs. She was another from that tranche of businesspeople in the town whose personalities overshadowed the person whose name was over the door. She was popular with the fishermen in the locale and, indeed, with all callers who wished to engage with her. She was famous for having a wide range of cousins and sought out an avenue of connection with all of her customers. On regatta day each August, Peggy's would be packed to the door with visitors to the town, many of whom wanted to catch a glimpse of Charles J. Haughey (when he was Taoiseach) who always called to mingle with the locals in the pubs along the seafront. James Flahive, who had an interesting way of his own, would stay in the background when Peggy was holding court.

Sheehy's (now the Marina Inn) was next door to Flahive's and that was a pub only, no shop, though kippered herrings were processed in the back; that, too, was a business run by the woman of the house. Brigid Sheehy, known as 'Bibit', had her regulars, many of whom shared their custom along the street. The Sheehys were fishing folk and one of the family, Jack, was a shipwright and a Kerry footballer (goalkeeper) famed for his long kick-out from the square. Maud's, Hannie Shea's, Bob's, and Madge's were pubs that were also run by women with strong personalities.

A curious shop/pub in Strand Street was Mikie Long's (now John Benny's). The eastern side of the premises had the pub counter while paint was sold over a counter on the western side to the fishermen for the annual painting of the boats at Easter time when the tides were suitable. The boats were laid over on their sides on the adjacent strand and provided a unique spectacle for all to see with their masts askew and their undersides revealed. As the painting proceeded, extra paint would be required from time to time and on Good Friday (in the days when the pubs were closed on that day) eager painters would go in the side door of Long's for the requisite top-up. Mikie Long was a gentleman and self-taught naturalist and an honorary life member of the Institute of Biology of Ireland. He was noted for identifying rare marine and terrestrial flora and fauna, much of which were brought to his attention by local fishermen who found these specimens in their nets.

The Murdock sisters, who were friendly and amiable, had a shop on Green Street which carried an array of dainty products. It was a shop that our family and set seldom used, as if the glamour of the place and its products were for other people and not for us. Katie Sarah's shop on Green Street was a popular stop for lemonade and Nash's orange. Katie also had a range of buns and sweets that attracted the Presentation Convent school-going students. Calling into Katie's was done on the way home from school as few had the appetite for sweets and lemonade before facing the nuns. Next door to Katie's, Bridge McCarthy operated a similar shop. Bridge was a refined lady compared to the jovial gruffness of her neighbour; she exuded a welcoming attitude and seemed interested in the lives of her younger customers. Bridge's was a popular stop among penny-stretched young men to buy loose cigarettes on the way to the cinema.

Bridge House, known as 'Chocolates' because of the wide range of interesting sweets and confectionaries available to the youngsters in the area, was strategically placed between Main Street and John Street and faced the Mall where the Christian Brothers School drew hordes of students that badly needed sweetening after a day in their charge. In Bridge House, all were treated well, even the sometimes rambunctious and penny-scarce boys from the Quay. O'Connor's, also bakers, sold their own produce and delivered bread to the hinterland. The smell of fresh bread in the shop would instil a craving for better times.

Garvey's shop on Strand Street was a busy spot; it carried newspapers, comics and the bible of the day for film lovers, *Photoplay* magazine. It was a popular stop on the way home from midnight mass at Christmas in the company of our parents. O'Shea's and O'Connor's (the Jukebox) at Holyground sold ice cream and competed with Nell Grandfield's nearby. These shops each had a long bench where one could linger and enjoy ice cream while making plans for the future. Smith's (hairdressers) corner in the vicinity was a regular meeting point for people going to the cinema and the dances. Walter's, a gift shop and sweet shop, carried a range of novelty items and angling gear including reels of catgut, hooks and feathers. Walter was engaging and liked a bit of fun, often demanding of the Quay fellas as they entered the premises to show their money right away.

His mother, Nora, the 'grande dame' of the street, ran the shop in the old days and entertained her customers to the point where customers often forgot what they had dropped in for. Many called in for a chat. Nora had spent time in France as an au pair and, having a command of the French language, was often called upon to translate for French fishermen who docked in the port. Walter's shop was the nearest thing to an enchanted place. Griffin's (Tig an Dearmad), run by Kate Jimeen and located on the way out of town, served the people of The Wood and Milltown and western homebound shoppers who forgot something while in town, thence the name Tig an Dearmad (dearmad: forgetfulness; overlook).

Greaney's on lower Green Street had a small shop, including a bakery that grew and became the first self-service shop/mini-supermarket in Dingle. Mag Begley's at the top of Green Street catered for the Temperance Hall crew. Each street had its own shops and shoppers: Henry Shea's, May Delia's, Walter's and Danny Flahive's were names that rolled off the tongue and are examples of how the owners' businesses and personalities become one. On Upper Main Street, near the convent school, Beedie Keane had a shop where school copybooks, pens and pencils were sold. The shop which carried on the business of catering for the needs of students, Siopa an Chúinne, at the corner of Main Street and Green Street, recently closed after twenty-five years serving the school-going public.

Further up the street, Kennedys had a small shop and pub across the road from the school gates which was ideally placed for anyone with a few pennies to spend after school. Josie Connor, newsagent, had her business next door to the Temperance Hall. Josie was the main employer of young schoolboys doing paper rounds and selling the Sunday papers outside the church after mass. A single-minded lady, she ran an efficient business and treated her young squad of workers fairly, in spite of the odd seller trying to hide a sixpence or thrupenny bit from the returns.

On Main Street, where the labour exchange was once situated, Mary Devane, a descendant from that house, has a seasonally-changing window display which draws scores of people of all ages to her door. It is not a shop but a curiosity-stop for locals and visitors where the window is bedecked with themes reflecting the changing seasons and festivities. In between seasons, Mary's window turns into a photo album of days gone by and a place for commentary on the changing times.

The age of supermarkets put an end to the small shops. The butcher, the baker and the candlestick maker now have their goods under the one roof. The goods to sustain a household can now be bought in the one place. Small shops didn't compete in the same sense as supermarkets: each shop, like Henry Shea's, had its own street to look after and a loyalty existed between owner and shopper. This was reflected at Christmas when gifts were handed to customers for their year-long custom, a system which has been replaced by dropping a ticket into a cardboard box along with your phone number. Your name isn't even necessary; you are a number. A loyalty card system exists in the large chains, a system which, according to research, encourages you to spend more money in that mega-shop. The foreign, large chains have no loyalty to the communities they operate in and, in many cases, draw shoppers away from town centres where community interaction flourishes. In rural areas, the post offices, which were also small shops, are being closed, thereby contributing to the erosion of neighbourly contact. Isolated people living alone will no longer have a chat with the 'man who reads the metre' due to the introduction of 'smart meters'. One wonders what is smart about that?

All shops had a piece of the shopping pie once and their keepers made a living and paid their way. Some supermarkets are now buying up local cottage industries and bringing them under the umbrella of the chain, just like in the tech industries where start-up business ideas are bought up by the Silicon Valley czars. In Dingle, the small shops are now seasonal craft shops that cater for the visitors, unlike Danny Flahive's that was open all year round to serve the population with the requisite seasonal gifts and holy icons. To buy any food item now, a trip to the supermarket is necessary and, while there, shopping can be done and paid for without any engagement whatsoever with the owner of the shop or, in some cases, with another human.

The local shop is long dead and the myriad characters that owned them have, in a short time, become part of the folklore of the town. An integral part of the shopping experience, which was a social engagement, included the exchange of news and views with the owner, talk of the children (from both sides) and their progress at work or school, the latest gossip from your end of town, and inquiry as to the health of your neighbours and, of course, the weather. The experience nowadays in many chains, where you would be lucky to encounter a human at the checkout before you exit, is notable for the robotic 'Hello, thank you, next please', 'Hello, thank you, next please'. Oh, Henry, if only you could see it!

FOUR

Fishing

As predicted by the superior of Dingle Christian Brothers, many of the Quay boys ended up fishing. His sarcastic prediction was always delivered as a slap to keep the poor man's son down, sons who had neither paper nor pencil to validate their presence in his classroom. The pronouncement from the robed one was a stock answer to boys from the Quay who couldn't keep up with the complexities of algebra and the inflections of the classical Latin language. Fishing was the main industry in Dingle during the mid-twentieth century, and long before that, and it was the fate of many boys who came from fishing families to go to sea. That way of life was, by and large, adopted willingly and enthusiastically by the sons, but the CBS Brother threw this industry and occupation, which sustained most of the town, back at the students as if it was an ignoble thing taken up by backward people. The boys – O'Connor, Flannery, Devane, Brosnan, Graham, Flaherty, and Sheehy, among others – knew they would end up passing the Crow Rock to make their living.

They also knew that they were punching in time at school while they gained the physical wherewithal to step and work on the deck of a fifty-footer where their transition from boy to man would be completed. These boys would one day skipper their own boats and acquire skills to understand the workings of a one-hundred horse-power engine and master the art of navigation, drawing from the rudiments of a begrudging education, by the CBS, and an innate understanding of the sea. In the small town of Dingle, these 'rejects' from the CBS created businesses which gave employment and sustenance to hundreds of people. Their descendants have now threaded their way into society and occupy positions as educators, entrepreneurs, craftsmen, doctors, engineers and writers.

In the late years of the twentieth century, a gradual decline in the number of Dingle sons taking up fishing took hold. The town had established itself as a tourism destination and the harbour facilities were remodelled to facilitate passenger ferry boats and sailing yachts. Opportunities for a better life ashore, away from the harsh, tough, inconsistent and physically demanding work of the fisherman, arose. The poverty of earlier decades had subsided and the younger generations from fishing backgrounds found avenues into advanced education and sustained employment. Attendant to this was the belief that the European Union's fisheries policies were not favourable to Irish fishermen. Young people saw no future in fishing and several families at the cornerstone of the industry are now gone from that way of life.

In modern times, fish has become a much-desired thing in Irish restaurants and there is a lot of discussion during the meal – which is invariably expensive – as to the wondrous bounty from the sea. Many families in Dingle were reared on fish and don't see what the big deal is all about. Eating fish in the 1950s and 1960s was an absolute necessity to stave off hunger. My father would often get a bucket of crabs' claws – we called them 'thumbs' – from his fisherman friends and they would be devoured around our table amid the clatter of knives and spoons breaking open the shells. Herring roe, which was known to us as 'paay', was another treat, which came in a clear film-like balloon of ovarian membrane. At the time, the roe was not being exported and the delicacy was freely given to bystanders on the pier when the boats were landing. The boats coming ashore in the evening after a long day's hunt was an event marked by a flurry of activity: horses and carts collecting the catch from the boats, local youths looking for a half-dozen fish to sell to Timmy Griffin, a local merchant, for the price of the pictures or admission to the dance. In the mid-twentieth century, hungry people who had nothing for the supper or the following day's dinner cadged a couple of whiting or gurnet from the boat skippers who were trying to eke out their own living in harsh times.

When the fishing was good, an air of well-being permeated through the community. Onshore workers in fish-processing factories had a pay packet each weekend, publicans along the Quay got in a few extra barrels of porter, tailors got more cloth, and bakers made more bread. My father worked in the 'Scheme' (one of the fish-processing factories) after his daytime work as a postman, and his family ate better for the duration of the good spell and maybe someone ended up with a new pair of shoes as a result of his night-time industry. A single fifty-footer crewed by four men and bringing home a sizeable catch over a weekly period could sustain the crew's family and several ancillary workers ashore for weeks. If fishermen got into debt during a bad spell of weather, they anticipated better days while leaning on the maxim that 'one good haul will pay for all'. A prolonged hiatus from the fishing grounds brought the concomitant downer for crews and dependents. The gas shed at the head of the Quay was a gathering place for fishermen who were forced ashore by strong winds. There they would talk and smoke cigarettes – which were reduced to being horded as butts if the hiatus was prolonged – while waiting out the storm.

In the days when accurate and readily available weather-forecasting wasn't an option, fishermen predicted weather conditions based on cloud formations, the colour of the sky, the behaviour of seagulls and gannets. A cap of cloud on Mount Eagle signified the coming of rain; sun rays cutting into the sea from behind a cloud was a harbinger of stormy weather. The saying went that 'mackerel sky and mares' tails make tall ships wear short sails'. The modern-day fisherman goes to sea with an array of electronic navigation aids and weather charts. The fishing grounds around Dingle Bay were discovered historically and marked by fishermen by aligning characteristics on land and at sea, and by using headlands and mountain tops as reference points. Dangers at sea were marked using the same references such as, when travelling east along the bay to Dingle harbour, if the lighthouse is visible on your heading, you are always clear of the Crow Rock.

Piseógs (spooky beliefs, signs and tales that are harbingers of bad luck) were taken seriously by fishermen. Whistling on board a boat was frowned upon because it whistled up the wind; setting out on a voyage or launching a boat on a Friday brought bad luck, as did meeting a red-haired woman on the way to your boat in the morning. Allowing a red-haired woman on board the boat was a sure harbinger of catastrophe. A lexicon of dos and don'ts at sea was handed down through the generations and revered as gospel by the new young hunters of the catch. The catch and the true extent of it was a secretive thing, too. When inquired of, it often brought the response, 'Very slack today', as if a boast of a large haul would tempt fate; either that or the desire to propagate the 'poor mouth'. A bottle of holy water would be found on every boat; ashore, before their men set out at dawn, the women would sprinkle holy water over them from a bottle, one of which was to be found in every fisherman's house. On the boats, a crucifix would also be jammed in the fo'c'sle between the stem head and the ribs.

Dark greys and browns were the normal colours of the seamen's working clothes, which were topped by a peaked cap. A knitted geansaí was a must for the harsh winter months and the barra baol (a stiff, yellow oilskin dungaree) protected against the elements and the abrasions of the pulling and hauling of the fishing gear. Fish fresh from the sea and cooked on a galley stove was the main staple during the working day at sea. While the boat would have a complement of basic rations, which included condensed milk, it would be rare for a deckhand to bring sandwiches to sustain him during the ten- to twelve-hour day. Most brought their own bread which would have been baked fresh on the hob at home. Cigarettes and tobacco for the pipes were a necessity for many crewmen and skippers, and their skill at lighting-up – with cigarette sheltered in a cupped hand – on a heaving deck in the middle of a howling wind was remarkable. Browned fingers were a common tell-tale of habitual smokers in the days of non-filter cigarettes such as Gold Flake, Woodbine and Player's.

The onshore work of the fisherman was regular and bustling and included mending nets on the pier where deftness in the use of the mending needle came into play. Maintaining the boats and associated gear drew curious spectators. The glass-ball fishing floats of the time would be underfoot on the pier as strollers investigated the progress of the repair work. To equalise the length of the trawl wires, they would be stretched along the main road from the quayside to The Wood, rounding a well-etched strategic concrete bollard at the pier head on the way west to the last cottage. The same operation today would attract a squad of health and safety officers and require a truck-load of traffic cones.

During the lobster season, the pots had to be re-knitted and their buoys (blondies because of their colour, called blandies) securely attached using the skillset of ropework where bowlines and a raft of fisherman's knots were employed. The large wooden crates (tanks) which resided on the top slip for the winter months would be towed to the south shore and anchored to house the new season's weekly catch. The old fishing nets were draped at the end of their usefulness along the stone walls opposite James Flahive's and Sonny Long's. The reward for the day's industry making good the gear ashore would come in the evening in Mikie Long's or Jackie Nell's, where the slate was well worn.

The annual blessing of the boats was a celebration of another year's bounty from the sea and it was a thanksgiving in which the fishing fraternity and the wider community took part. After the last mass on the Sunday, the local people would fall in behind the fife and drum band in the parade of fishermen heading for the Quay carrying oars wielded vertically with blades aloft. At the quayside, people of all ages, classes and persuasion were guided onto the boats by deck hands. They were literally huddled together because of the crowd for the largest community gathering of the year and the odd Christian Brother could be found amid the throng. At the lighthouse, the canon (Lyne and Lynch, in my time) would perform the blessing as the boats – nobbies and fifty-footers (in the 1950s and 1960s) – rounded the mark. The day's proceedings gave recognition to, and showed appreciation for, the huge contribution the fishing industry made to the life of the town.

FIVE

The Kelly Gang

At age fourteen, I started going to the Temperance Hall and for ten years thereafter was a regular there. My brothers joined me in subsequent years, as did my sisters Carmel and Bernadette when the hall introduced table tennis and allowed girls into the male sanctum where snooker and billiards were the main games. At that time (1960s), Mikey Quirke ran the place in a firm and fair-handed manner. Mikey was fastidious and kept the games tables in pristine condition; the green baize cloth was brushed and ironed meticulously every week. Membership of the hall was free; we put our names on a board and queued up for a place at the table. Pakie Griffin was one of the best snooker players in those days and many young newcomers took note of his skills and strategic approach to the game. Mike Sayers and Paddy Joe Connor were also in the rankings as good players whom we couldn't challenge till we graduated to the big table. Both tables were standard size and one was given over to young members. Of the younger crowd, my brothers Michael and Ambrose stood out as great players. There was a cant at the time, 'A good snooker player is a sign of a wasted youth!' John Sheehy, from the Spa Road, would bamboozle you with an ongoing commentary on his strategy as he played and his foreordaining, which was a distraction, made him hard to beat. Kevin Sullivan, a classy player, remarked to one opponent after pocketing the pink and with the black set up as a sure thing, 'I'm afraid the carnival is over'.

Along the northern wall in the snooker room, a dozen green-painted metal tubes hung from hooks. These locked tubes held the personal cues of the exalted and were a wonder to the plebeian newcomers who dared to aspire to be like the local gods of the game. One such skilled player would unlock his cue and peer down along it with his left eye to see if the fluctuating temperature of the building had affected the trueness of the long maple and ebony shaft. This was done with a grin for pure devilment, of course, to let the common players know that he didn't have to settle for one of the bent sticks available to them. Hiding the cue tip chalk from your opponent was another way to cause upset, as was wetting the tip when a player was distracted. The loud crack from the dropping of a cue on the floor when an opponent was taking a crucial shot led to many recriminations and scuffles.

After Mikey Quirke retired, I was asked by Fr Lawrence Kelly to take over the running of the hall. Fr Kelly was newly arrived to the parish and brought with him positive ideas for the (then) boys' club, which he and I implemented. In the early 1970s, under the priest's guardianship, new seating was installed in the snooker room and a maple floor was laid on the ground floor for table tennis. John Boyd, who was head of the ESB in Dingle at the time, was part of our committee and always at the ready to offer his skills when renovations were being made. During the making of *Ryan's Daughter*, the production crew leased part of the building and the income from MGM helped with the costs of installing new toilets, a card games room and a television room. The table tennis was a great addition; Seán A. O'Connor, Peter Lambe and Noel Brosnan were among the top players. My sister Bernadette was without doubt the top female contender. Throughout the year, the table tennis club travelled out to county towns to take part in various competitions. Noel and other car-owners would provide free transport for the excursions.

The activities in the hall were open to all and free of charge. Membership was a given; no names were written down on paper and you came and went as you pleased and were always welcome. It was an unwritten rule that everyone toed the line while present in the hall. I cannot recall any discipline problems during my tenure there, apart from that of a famous and harmless diminutive town 'drinker' who would barge in from time to time and offer to take on the largest man in the place for a fight. As a perk for my input into the hall management, Fr Kelly taught me to drive and would loan me his car to bring members from the hall to the Killarney cinema and to see Chips, a popular band at the time, perform out of town. It was thus that the 'Kelly Gang' was formed; Con Cremin, Pat O'Hanlon, James Malone, Thomas Flahive, Vincent

O'Connor, and James Farrell were regulars in the green Opel Kadett and, following Fr Kelly's departure from Dingle, in Fr Fleming's blue Vauxhall Viva. Fr Fleming carried on the good work of his predecessor.

The Temperance Hall, which was effectively a boys' youth club, was administered by the presbytery and Fr Kelly was committed to his remit. We used have regular meetings about day-to-day activities and discuss ways to enhance the club. Fr Larry, as we called him in lighter moments, also fell in with any heavy lifting required, such as painting and cleaning. In 1969, when I was serving my apprenticeship to the trade of shipwright and giving up most of my wages at home, Fr Larry invited me to accompany him to the All-Ireland football final between Kerry and Offaly. It was my first time in Croke Park and gave me a rare opportunity to watch the great Mick O'Connell in action.

Another perk was that expenses were paid by Fr Kelly personally to show his appreciation for my work with the club. A year later, he topped that when he arranged for me to travel to London with a group from Dingle to see the premiere of *Ryan's Daughter* in the Leicester Square theatre. The weekend away included flights and cinema tickets, all paid for by Fr Kelly from his own pocket. After he moved on from Dingle to other dioceses, I kept in touch with him and kept him apprised of events in my life. As the years passed, my life took a different tack; most of the Kelly Gang went off to college and I lost touch with the hall, apart from when I returned to Dingle 'for the holidays', as they say.

John Michael Graham took over the reins at the hall when I stepped down and ran it successfully for a good number of years. Now, after decades of closure, the hall has been refurbished and is available to local community groups for activities but, alas, its doors are closed most of the time. The days of the games are over. Gone are the times when a crowd waited outside for the key-holder to arrive, jockeying for position to run up the stairs to get their names on the board. Sunday morning after mass had a particular attraction. Members would buy a coloured ball (of which there was a limited number), that came with three lives, and compete on the table by pocketing their opponents' ball till the last man was left standing.

The race up the stairs after the door opened to be eligible for this game (which was called 'pool' for some reason even though it was quite unlike the traditional game of pool that became very popular in bars throughout Ireland) was fierce. Tugging and hauling was merciless and the weak were left languishing on the bottom steps. No prisoners were taken – it was every man for himself. Ah, those were the days.

The snooker tables in the Temperance Hall gave decades of enjoyment to hundreds of boys from fourteen years of age upwards in a time when entertainment for young people was scarce. The hall was a large part of our lives; just like the cinema, it was a place to escape to, a refuge from the uncertainties of the times when many families struggled through poverty, and going to school was a dreaded thing. In the hall, all the boys were participating on a level playing field, unlike at school where disadvantaged students had an uphill battle. In fact, those students from the less well-off parts of town had an edge over the well-to-do boys when it came to 'pool hall' games.

'It takes a village to raise a child', so goes the famous proverb. In Dingle, the Temperance Hall played a large part in the rearing of the town's youth in the decades of the mid-twentieth century. The two snooker tables that saw boys grow to become men and that are imbued with a huge portion of the town's history were dismantled in 2024 and consigned to storage to face an uncertain future. Out with the old and in with the new.

SIX

Marching

In the early 1990s, Dingle was gathering pace as a popular tourist destination. *Ryan's Daughter* had been filmed in the area (1969), Fungie the dolphin arrived (1983) and the sailing club – Cumann Bádóirí Naomh Bhréannain – was formed (1987). Tom Cruise was filming *Far and Away* (1992) in the peninsula and had his star added, alongside that of Julia Roberts, Robert Mitchum and Dolly Parton, on Dingle's own walk of fame – the footpath outside Dick Mack's. A major harbour development was under way with a town marina being built, albeit to the loss of Peggy's Wall (one needs to be a local to understand this one). Peggy Flahive, of James Flahive's pub directly opposite the old sea wall, expressed serious concern and voiced her displeasure to anyone who would listen over the demolishing of the age-old stone wall which had held back the sea from the road for centuries. The east end of wall (opposite Flahive's pub) was also the prime spot for viewers of the Dingle Regatta Festival, held annually in August.

The first real threat to Dingle in modern times from undesired and incongruous development came in the early 1990s. One of Dingle's most popular and scenic walks, right on the edge of town, led from the Rocket House beside the Skellig Hotel to the Banks and the lighthouse. The Banks (from sandbanks) was our summer hangout, the place where townies grew up, socialised and learned to swim in what was our own public playground. It was of our era in the 1960s when anyone with a transistor radio was very popular. The present generation of the town may not know where the Banks is; like the shifting sands of the Banks, opportunities for outdoor activities have moved on within the harbour which now offers a varied range of pursuits, such as rowing, sailing and kayaking.

Swimming is rare now in the Banks because the coastline skirting the area has rock armour installed to prevent erosion of the sand dunes. Further on in Slaudeen, towards the lighthouse, swimming is still popular but not in the numbers of yesteryear. The car has enabled people to travel out to some of the fine beaches around the peninsula. In the 1960s and 1970s, we stayed close to home, walked and discovered the many wonders on our doorstep and that is why the Banks was a prized thing to us. In 1990, the owners of the Skellig Hotel planned to reclaim twenty-two acres from the harbour adjacent to the hotel to build a marina and onshore apartment-style buildings along the shore of the Banks.

Beginning of rape of Dingle

The proposed development of a yachting marina at the Skellig Hotel in Dingle, Co. Kerry, has generated such resentment that local people are "queueing up" to voice their opposition to it, it was claimed yesterday.

Cork Examiner, May 30th, 1991

A public inquiry into the granting of a foreshore licence to the Skellig Hotel to build a marina in the foreshore adjacent to the hotel was held in May/June 1991. At the inquiry the Chamber of Commerce, Dingle Harbour Commissioners and Dingle Tourism strenuously opposed the application and were supported by (approx.) forty witnesses, mostly from the town and including many experts. The Skellig directors attended the inquiry but none gave evidence in support of their application. Only two local people gave evidence in support of the Skellig application.

On 13th of December, 1991, a press release by the Department of Marine stated that the Minister (John Wilson) was granting the licence (in principle) to the Skellig Hotel, subject to a number of conditions. A nominee of the Minister who presided at the inquiry recommended that the licence be granted in principle (subject to conditions) on the (PURPORTED) grounds that it was in the public interest to do so.

Dingle Chamber of Commerce statement, March 1992

The proposed development infuriated local people and united them in opposition to the plan to privatise a large tract of the harbor; action was needed. In mid-December 1991, a small group (of which I was one) of Dingle people got together to discuss the Skellig Hotel plan and the shock prevailing in the town following the minister's decision to grant a foreshore licence for the development, with conditions attached. At our first meeting, it became clear to the group that the people's views articulated at the public inquiry were being trampled on, and that the inquiry was a whitewash that came down on the side of speculators who were allied to Skellig-friendly politicians who were supporting the proposal rather than listening to the people.

From that meeting, the Dingle Citizens Group (DCG) emerged, with a remit to draw up a plan of action to stop this unwanted development. The first event organised by the DCG to draw public and media attention to their campaign was a march on December 29th, 1991, on the streets of Dingle. The march began at Dingle pier, rounded the town and finished at the Rocket House where a stage was erected and several speakers from the town addressed more than 1,500 people (*Cork Examiner* estimate) and called for a united effort in opposing what they saw as an undemocratic decision by the minister. 'Politicians who walk the exalted corridors of power in government buildings should come to Dingle and see democracy at work' was a view expressed from the podium at the gathering at Rocket House which marked the tone of the event. After the long haul of the public inquiry and tireless work done by the Chamber of Commerce, Harbour Commissioners and Dingle Tourism, there was a palpable feeling that the tide would turn in favour of the people following the large turnout and the emotions expressed. It was time for the people to have their say.

> **Dingle marina march gains strong support**
> An estimated 1,500 people, including rock star Liam Ó Maonlaí, yesterday marched through Dingle, Co. Kerry, in protest against a proposal to build a yacht marina at the Skellig Hotel, outside the town.
>
> Organised by the Dingle Citizens Group, the turnout surpassed all expectations and was a boost to those bitterly opposed to a recent decision by Tánaiste and Marine Minister, John Wilson, to give the go-ahead to the controversial project.
>
> *Cork Examiner*, December 30th, 1991

After the big December march of 1991 in Dingle, the usual accusations of 'rent-a-crowd' were voiced by the handful supporting the Skellig Hotel regarding the numbers marching, but the evidence was plain on published video and photos that the people of Dingle, spanning all age groups, were to the fore in this campaign. The march was a huge success and emboldened the DCG, now that it had a mandate from the people to move forward with its efforts to halt the proposal which would take over part of Dingle's playground and make it private property. Years before the Skellig proposal, a local TD (Teachta Dála) predicted that, 'Dingle would one day become a playground for the rich' – this echoed in the minds of many in 1991/92.

Two months later, in February 1992, the DCG organised a march in Dublin, in conjunction with a supporting sub-group made up of Dingle diaspora living and working in the capital, to the offices of Dáil Eireann and the Department of the Marine where, after a short march in the city, a letter outlining the citizens' concerns was handed over. On the day, the early morning train from Tralee to Dublin was crowded with enthusiastic Dingle people on a mission. A sense of unity which lasted throughout the campaign was born and the scenes on the train resembled a group going out of town for a wedding or a football match rather than a gathering of townspeople fighting to hold onto their birthright. The Dublin march, which got good press coverage, including a photo in *The Irish Times*, further solidified the people and buoyed up their resolve to continue in spite of a parallel media campaign by the developers and their allies which denied that such opposition existed. But, in fact, our unity of purpose was a thing to celebrate. It was the first time (in this author's memory) that the people of the town voiced their concerns as one and, by their physical presence at rallies, let it be known where they stood when it came to a private company trying to appropriate a large section of Dingle harbour.

> Nobody owns Dingle harbour. Not the people of Dingle; not the harbour board; not the Dingle Citizens Group; not the government. All are keeping it in trust for the succeeding generations of Irish people and their guests. Consequently, in future decades we, the Irish of this era, will be condemned for our lack of foresight if we allow Dingle harbour to be carved up into lots to be granted to sectoral interests or individuals in return for political, financial or personal patronage.
>
> Quote by a local supporter of the Dingle Citizens Group in its newsletter, March 2nd, 1992

Billheads of Dingle merchants.

PHOENIX CINEMA AND BALLROOM

PROPRIETOR:
JOHN A. MOORE
'Phone: DINGLE 33
'Grams: PHOENIX, DINGLE

Dingle, Ireland
Mar 31 1958

DINGLE, Aug 1st 1956
Co. Kerry

M....

DR. TO
The Dingle Electric Light & Power Co. Ltd.
ELECTRICAL AND GENERAL ENGINEERS
ACCOUNTS DUE MONTHLY

"HOULIHAN, DINGLE."
'Phone 28.

STRAND STREET,
DINGLE, April 8th 1957
Kerry, Ireland.

M
Dingle

BOUGHT OF - - -
J. C. HOULIHAN
DRAPER and OUTFITTER

THE PHARMACY,
STRAND ST.,
DINGLE, 30/4 1957

Prescriptions Accurately Compounded

M

Dr. to
JAMES O'KEEFFE, M.P.S.I.
DISPENSING & VETERINARY CHEMIST
Toilet Requisites, Perfumes, etc., in Great Variety. Horse, Cattle and Poultry Medicines Carefully Prepared. Veterinary Medicines, Sheep Dips, etc.
PURE DRUGS. FINE CHEMICALS. PROMPT ATTENTION.
ALL ACCOUNTS FURNISHED MONTHLY

JOHN STREET,
Dingle 6-4-1957
CO. KERRY.

M

Dr. to
JACK MORAN
MOTORS FOR HIRE

K. C. Ltd.

DINGLE,
CO. KERRY, 28th October 1958

M....

Dingle

DR. TO
KIERAN O'HANLON
SALOON CARS FOR HIRE

ESSO
DEALER

Muinntir Cléirig
An Garáiste
Daingean uí Cúis
Gután 5

M

T. McCARTHY,
GENERAL GROCERY,
BAR AND BAKERY.

Upper Main Street,
Dingle,
Co. Kerry

Date 195

STRAND STREET,
DINGLE March 1st 1958

M

Bought of **JAMES GARVEY**
BOOTS, SHOES, DRAPERY.
HIGH-CLASS CONFECTIONERY :: GENERAL WAREHOUSE.

Head Office
TRALEE
Branches
LISTOWEL & DINGLE

Latchford & Sons
LIMITED

TELEGRAMS: "LATCHFORD."
TELEPHONES: TRALEE 8 & 181; LISTOWEL 15; DINGLE 7

MILLERS, BAKERS, CONFECTIONERS,
COAL, FLOUR & HARDWARE
MERCHANTS,
AGRICULTURAL IMPLEMENTS OF ALL KINDS
LEADING KERRY SEEDSMEN &c

STRAND STREET,
Dingle, 23/4/59
(CO. KERRY)

M..

DR. TO
MICHAEL O'CALLAGHAN
ELECTRICAL CONTRACTOR

AFTON CIGARETTES
first for quality!

M O'Connor

W. MURDOCH & SONS, Mar 22 1958
Grocers,
Ironmongers and General Hardware Merchants
DINGLE.
Telegraphic Address—"Murdoch, Dingle."
Terms of Business:—We buy direct from the Manufacturer for Cash, and sell to the user for Cash at one small profit only.

E. & O.E.

J. J. QUILTER,
THE MALL, DINGLE, CO. KERRY.

M
Dingle

Date, 195

ACCOUNTS STRICTLY MONTHLY

Radio and Electrical Sales and Service

Telegrams: Moore, Dingle
Telephone: Dingle 33

Dingle, 17th April 1957

M
Dingle

DR. TO **JOHN MOORE** M.I.A.A.
AUCTIONEER AND VICTUALLER
COMMISSIONER FOR OATHS

K. C. Ltd.

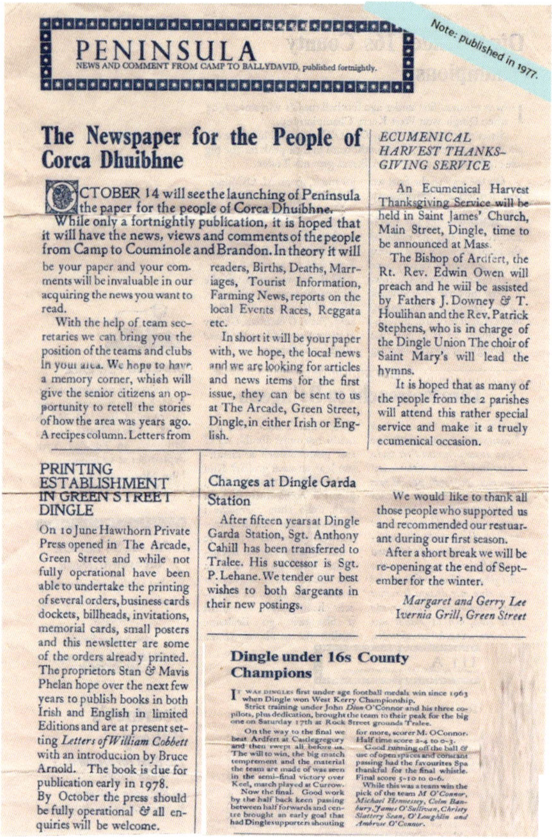

PENINSULA
NEWS AND COMMENT FROM CAMP TO BALLYDAVID, published fortnightly.

The Newspaper for the People of Corca Dhuibhne

OCTOBER 14 will see the launching of Peninsula the paper for the people of Corca Dhuibhne.

While only a fortnightly publication, it is hoped that it will have the news, views and comments of the people from Camp to Couminole and Brandon. In theory it will be your paper and your comments will be invaluable in our acquiring the news you want to read.

With the help of team secretaries we can bring you the position of the teams and clubs in your area. We hope to have a memory corner, which will give the senior citizens an opportunity to retell the stories of how the area was years ago. A recipes column. Letters from readers, Births, Deaths, Marriages, Tourist Information, Farming News, reports on the local Events Races, Reggata etc.

In short it will be your paper with, we hope, the local news and we are looking for articles and news items for the first issue, they can be sent to us at The Arcade, Green Street, Dingle, in either Irish or English.

ECUMENICAL HARVEST THANKSGIVING SERVICE

An Ecumenical Harvest Thanksgiving Service will be held in Saint James' Church, Main Street, Dingle, time to be announced at Mass.

The Bishop of Ardfert, the Rt. Rev. Edwin Owen will preach and he will be assisted by Fathers J. Downey & T. Houlihan and the Rev. Patrick Stephens, who is in charge of the Dingle Union The choir of Saint Mary's will lead the hymns.

It is hoped that as many of the people from the 2 parishes will attend this rather special service and make it a truely ecumenical occasion.

PRINTING ESTABLISHMENT IN GREEN STREET DINGLE

On 10 June Hawthorn Private Press opened in The Arcade, Green Street and while not fully operational have been able to undertake the printing of several orders, business cards dockets, billheads, invitations, memorial cards, small posters and this newsletter are some of the orders already printed. The proprietors Stan & Mavis Phelan hope over the next few years to publish books in both Irish and English in limited Editions and are at present setting *Letters of William Cobbett* with an introduction by Bruce Arnold. The book is due for publication early in 1978.

By October the press should be fully operational & all enquiries will be welcome.

Changes at Dingle Garda Station

After fifteen years at Dingle Garda Station, Sgt. Anthony Cahill has been transferred to Tralee. His successor is Sgt. P. Lehane. We tender our best wishes to both Sargeants in their new postings.

We would like to thank all those people who supported us and recommended our restuarant during our first season.

After a short break we will be re-opening at the end of September for the winter.

Margaret and Gerry Lee
Ivernia Grill, Green Street

Dingle under 16s County Champions

IT WAS DINGLES first under age football medals win since 1963 when Dingle won West Kerry Championship.

Strict training under John *Dion* O'Connor and his three co-pilots, plus dedication, brought the team to their peak for the big one on Saturday 17th at Rock Street grounds Tralee.

On the way to the final we beat Ardfert at Castlegregory and then swept all before us. The will to win, the big match temprement and the material the team are made of was seen in the semi-final victory over Keel, march played at Currow.

Now the final. Good work by the half back keen passing between half forwards and centre brought an early goal that had Dingle supporters shouting for more, scorer M. OConnor. Half time score 2-4 to 0-3.

Good running off the ball & use of open spaces and constant passing had the favourites Spa thankful for the final whistle. Final score 5-10 to 0-6.

While this was a team win the pick of the team *M O'Connor, Michael Hennessey, Colm Banbury, James O'Sullivan, Christy Slattery Sean, O'Loughlin and Ambrose O'Connor.*

Peninsula News, 1977
Dingle newsletter.

Posters for *Shadow and Substance* and *The Playboy of the Western World*, which was filmed at Inch, 1962.

First issue of *West Kerry Live*, published in July 2009.

Postcard of Saint Mary's Church, Dingle, published by Danny Flahive, Dingle. The image shows the church before the gothic arches and granite pillars were replaced with iron.

Sign advertising accommodation for touring cyclists. Benner's Hotel; Fox's, The Mall; Donnelly's, Dygate Lane and Mary Joe Long, Strand St, displayed these signs circa 1950s/60s.

Paudie Fitzgerald, Rás Tailteann winner, 1956.

Robert Mitchum, with Dingle harbour in the background, 1969.

Maggie Brown's dolls.

Ignatius and Mairéad O'Connor and family at the opening of Tig Shiobháin pub in Ballyferriter, 1988.

Carmel O'Connor McNulty greeting the president of Ireland, Mary Robinson, in Sydney, 1992.

Temperance Hall boys, l-r: Vincent O'Connor, John O'Connor, Pat O'Hanlon, Tommy Sayers, James Malone.

L-r: James Malone, Vincent O'Connor, Pat O'Hanlon, Thomas Flahive. Early 1970s.

'DINGLE' on the hill, 2005 (photo by J. O'Connor).

Group at the opening weekend of *Ryan's Daughter* in London, 1970. Included are: Hilary Long, D. Walsh, Paddy McNamara, Agnes Gibbons, Hannah Quilter, John Quilter, Nell McNamara, John O'Connor, Michael O'Dowd, Joanne Baker.

Kirrary village, which was built for the film *Ryan's Daughter*, 1969.

The Rocket House crew. Included are: T. Devane, J. O'Connor, J., Flannery, P. Flannery, J. Rayel, J.J. Murphy, instructor, J. Flaherty, J. Guiheen.

The *Ranga* aground near Dunmore Head, in 1982.

Members of the band Slaudeen. *Front l-r*: Áine Uí Laoithe, Eibhlín Ní tSithigh, Fergus O'Flaithbheartaigh. *Back l-r*: Mary Mazzarella O'Flaherty, Mike Dowd, Mary Greevy, Aoileann Nic Gearailt, Tom Lynch, Johnny Murphy. This photo is from the cover of the album, 'Forever by Dingle Shore', which was released in 1984.

John Joe 'Tipp' Murphy in the foreground, with John O'Connor, David Donegan, Tadhg and Micheál O'Coileán sharing stories about the Wran in Jack Neddy's pub, on December 27th 1994.

Walking on Cars band members, *l-r*: Paul Flannery, Evan Hadnet, Patrick Sheehy, and Sorcha Durham.

Three happy girls at the Cottages centenary celebrations in 2009. *L-r:* Nuala O'Connor Hawes, Angela O'Connor O'Dowd and Elizabeth Hawes.

The motor yacht *Spré* at Dingle marina. *Spré*, which was built in 1928 in Southampton, was purchased by Padraig McKenna and Ciarán Crowe in 2007 and refurbished. The boat was one of the 'little ships' that took part in the evacuation of Dunkirk in 1940.

SUNDAY BUSINESS

Aug. 16, 1992

Murder inquiry to follow McAuliffe's helicopter crash

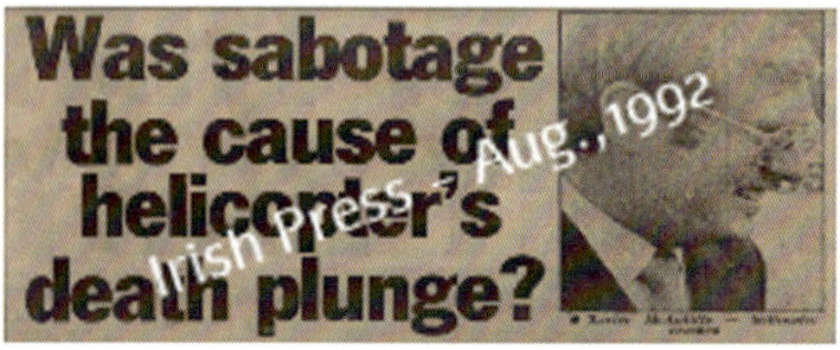

Was sabotage the cause of helicopter's death plunge?

Irish Press - Aug., 1992

Somebody tried to kill the man behind Dingle Marina plan

MURDER HUNT FOLLOWS FATAL CHOPPER CRASH

The Star - Aug., 1992

Tycoon the target of sabotage bid

Press clippings about the Skellig marina controversy.

Dingle Citizens Group with John O'Donoghue, TD, and Minister for the Marine, Michael Woods. *L-r:* John O'Donoghue, Jimmy Flannery, Michael Woods, John O'Connor, Seán Brosnan, David Donegan, Siobhán McKenna, Peter Malone, Rose Brosnan.

Protest march in Dingle in opposition to the proposed Skellig marina, December 1991.

Protest march in Dublin by Dingle people opposing the proposed private Skellig marina in Dingle, 1992.

1992 fundraiser for the Dingle Citizens Group in the Phoenix Cinema. *L-r:* Canon Jack McKenna, Michael Francie O'Sullivan, Fr Pat Moore, Peter Callery, John O'Connor.

Skellig marina campaign, 1992. John O'Connor at the gas shed getting ready for the march.

Site for Proposed Marina and Apartment Complex

1. Size

Reclaimed	7 acres
Enclosed	15 acres
Total	22 acres

2. Proposal

300 Berth Marina
Onshore Facilities
40 Residential Units

3. Funding

Equity	2 million
BES	2.3 million
EC Funds	1 million
Borrowings	.5 million
Total	5.8 million

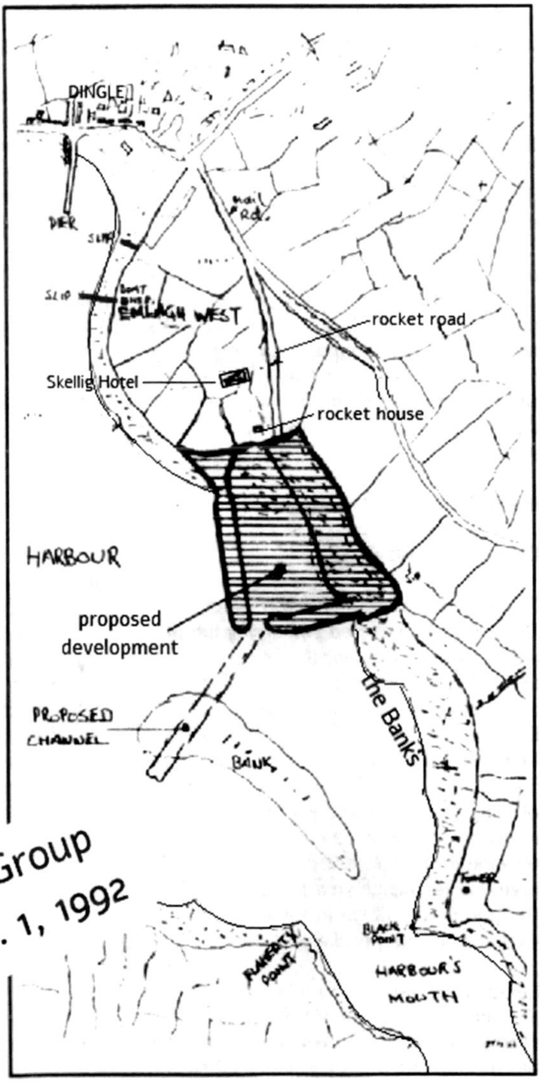

Dingle Citizen's Group
newsletter – Jan. 1, 1992

Dingle Citizens Group newsletter, January 1992.

Skellig Hotel proposal for onshore buildings along the Banks in Dingle, 1991/1992.

Girls at the Dingle Food Festival. *L-r:* Fíona Bailey, Aoife O'Dowd, Mary Russell, Angela O'Dowd, Nuala Hawes, Deirdre O'Dowd.

The DCG and its supporters came up with inventive ways to draw attention to their campaign and kept the people updated and involved by means of a published newsletter. The group anchored a raft in the area of the harbour about to be privatised, adjacent to the Skellig Hotel, with a sign printed in bold capitals, 'HANDS OFF OUR HARBOUR'. It was visible through the hotel dining room windows and curious guests began to enquire as to what was going on. The aim was to embarrass the hotel management in front of their guests. After a number of days, the raft was removed in the dark of night – presumably at the behest of the Skellig Hotel – and placed in the local pound.

The DCG demanded that their property be returned and the group subsequently organised a public march (at short notice) where the raft was shouldered by local people back to the strand at the hotel and secured to the seashore. The march was led by a local woman ringing a bell, like a town crier, to attract attention and show how the people were further emboldened to get their message out there. The Skellig gambit backfired; the removal of the raft from the seashore ignited further anger against the proposed development and led to more publicity for the people's cause.

Funding for such projects as the Skellig marina was available from a European Union fund whose aim was to bring development to, and enhance, regional areas. The DCG and its supporting groups, through the aegis of Pat Cox, a member of the European Parliament, arranged a meeting in March 1992 with the European Commissioner for Regional Policy, Bruce Millan, who was in charge of overseeing such funding. Representatives from DCG, Dingle Tourism and members of Dingle Chamber of Commerce travelled to Strasburg to speak with the commissioner and explain to him that the town of Dingle was in opposition to the proposed marina and made a case that he should deny the developers such funding, which amounted to one million euro. Mr Millan indicated that he would look into the matter of the marina funding but he did let the group know that his hands were tied when it came to domestic decisions about the allocation of funding from the EU. The trip to Strasburg attracted further media attention.

EC to investigate Dingle Marina project

The Kerryman, March 20th, 1992

Fronting the Skellig Hotel to the south, a strip of public land used as a practice ground for the local Coast and Cliff Rescue Service (as it was then known) separated the hotel from the sea, and the hotel dining room looked directly onto this property. Marches along this strip (which the proposed development would privatise) were held by banner-laden locals on a regular basis during the summer. The predominant banners read 'NOT AN INCH', which had become the campaign slogan. It was born at a meeting of the local harbour board of the time when a member – a fisherman – uttered it (with embellishment omitted from the final logo) in relation to the proposed acquisition of twenty-two acres of the harbour by the Skellig company. This ongoing demonstration at the door (as it were) of the Skellig Hotel caused the hotel embarrassment and prompted guests to inquire regularly as to the reason for all of this marching to and fro by people of all ages and occupations. During that summer, the DCG also set up a stall at the pier every weekend to gather signatures and get the message out far and wide.

The DCG was made up of seven people that, individually, had no vested interest in opposing the marina development; they were from that tranche often called the 'ordinary people'. Supporters of the group were the citizens of the town, none of whom wanted Costa del Sol-style developments destroying the charm of their small and scenic town. The campaign was also winning wider support from people around the country and from visitors to the town; hundreds of signatures were collected during weekends when tourist footfall was high. Local politicians (apart from one or two who were allied to the owners of the Skellig Hotel) also fell in behind the people and raised questions in 'higher' places about the proposed private marina which the local people didn't want. After months of successful campaigning, and the huge support that was evident in the town and further afield, the DCG thought that the popular will of the people would be listened to by those in power. How wrong it was!

The Department of the Marine and its minister, John Wilson (appointed by the Taoiseach of the day, Charles J. Haughey), were not for budging on the foreshore licence issue despite appeals from the people and politicians. And then events took a tragic turn. On May 31st, 1992, a helicopter owned by Skellig Hotel director, Xavier McAuliffe, which was making trips from the hotel around the harbour, developed engine trouble and crashed into the water just off Dingle pier, resulting in a fatality. This tragic event would be used to cast suspicion on the activities of the DCG, beginning with, and fueled by, an article in *The Sunday Business Post* on August 16th, 1992. The article alluded to Dingle people being involved in tampering with the fuel of the helicopter. Comments from the Skellig Hotel in the press following the crash were used to distract from the gains made by the people trying to stop the marina development.

> Mr McAuliffe, who was the pilot of the two-seater £80,000 Robinson R22B helicopter, escaped injury when it crashed into the sea off Dingle. However, passenger Siobhan Casey from Sligo drowned when the helicopter sank in about 20 feet of water … The accident happened less than 100 metres from a crowded Dingle pier at approximately 4.50pm on Sunday … Mr McAuliffe praised those who came to the rescue … Jimmy Flannery from the Grove — ironically one of the people who gave evidence at a public inquiry in Dingle exactly a year ago against Mr McAuliffe's plans to develop a 300-berth marina at the Skellig Hotel.
>
> *The Kerryman*, June 5th, 1992

> **EXCLUSIVE: fuel contaminated as marina row raged on murder inquiry to follow McAuliffe's helicopter crash**
>
> Gardaí are set to begin a formal murder investigation into the helicopter crash in Dingle which killed a

young woman. The helicopter, which was piloted by local businessman Xavier McAuliffe is believed to have been sabotaged … A Department of Tourism, Transport and Communications investigation into the fatal crash of May 31st will reveal that "the fuel was contaminated with cleaning agent", according to informed sources.

The Sunday Business Post, August 16th, 1992

Was sabotage the cause of helicopter's death plunge

THE KERRY millionaire whose helicopter crashed last May killing a young Sligo woman has condemned those responsible as "cowards" following the revelation that fuel had been contaminated. Listowel businessman, Xavier McAuliffe, told the IRISH PRESS last night that reports of a murder investigation being launched following the tragedy came as no surprise to him. He had been told by the Department of Transport two months ago that the helicopter's fuel had been contaminated with detergent. "Whoever did this were cowards," he said, insisting that he would not bow to those allegedly responsible by taking extra security precautions in case of another attack.

Mr McAuliffe's plan to build a marina beside the Skellig Hotel, which he also owns, has caused much bitterness and division in the seaside town. Three years ago, a public inquiry recommended granting the application for a foreshore licence. Although the proposal has since been shelved following intensive protests, it is expected that the developers, headed by Mr McAuliffe and Pat Carroll, whose niece was killed in the crash, will go ahead within the next two years.

Irish Press, August 17th, 1992

Somebody tried to kill the man behind Dingle Marina plan.
Murder hunt follows fatal chopper crash

The Star, August 17th, 1992

McAuliffe death crash not yet murder probe
Gardaí have commenced an investigation into reports that the fuel supply on businessman Xavier McAuliffe's helicopter, in which a woman died after it crashed into Dingle harbour on May 31st, was contaminated. Garda Chief Superintendent Donal O'Sullivan this week formally requested a copy of a Department of Transport report into the crash. But, despite confirmation that the helicopter's fuel was contaminated, Chief Superintendent O'Sullivan said that as yet no murder investigation had been launched by his officers.

Department of Transport spokeswoman, Rosaleen Brennan, confirmed this week that the investigation into the crash had revealed that the helicopter's fuel was contaminated. She refused to comment, however, on whether that contamination could have resulted from sabotage or whether it could have occurred innocently. Asked about the possibility of sabotage, she said it would be "purely speculative" of the Department to make any comment on this issue. She added: "What the Press is producing at the moment is speculative in terms of the investigation being carried out by the Department."

The Dingle Citizens Group, objectors to the proposed Skellig Hotel Marina in which Mr McAuliffe is one of the main promoters, this week described suggestions that the helicopter may have been sabotaged and that this may have been connected with the opposition to the marina project as a slur on the people of Dingle. "This has come out of the blue with no formal or even concrete report to substantiate it. There are no charges made and no charges to be answered," said Dingle Citizens Group spokesman Peter Malone. A garda investigation into the crash … will only begin if the Department of Transport inquiry indicates that the helicopter was sabotaged, Chief Superintendent O'Sullivan insisted. He said at present the Gardaí have no evidence to suggest that the crash was caused by sabotage.

The Kerryman, August 21st, 1992

At a recent meeting of the Board of Directors of the Skellig Hotel, a decision was taken to abandon plans for the proposed marina and ancillary facilities on the foreshore adjoining the Skellig Hotel, Dingle, Co. Kerry. This follows an extensive financial reappraisal of the project over the past few months. The directors took a decision to lend their full support to the development and expansion of the marine facilities in Dingle's inner harbour.

Skellig Hotel press statement, October 12th, 1992

Helicopter crash not sabotage

Investigators probing Listowel businessman Xavier McAuliffe's helicopter crash in Dingle harbour — in which … a woman, died — are now satisfied that neither the helicopter nor its fuel were sabotaged, *The Kerryman* can reveal this week. The investigation, which has already established that the helicopter's fuel was contaminated, is now concentrating on the likelihood that the contamination was caused innocently. Investigators are satisfied that sabotage was not involved and that there now appears to have been nothing sinister about the crash or the circumstances surrounding it.

The Kerryman, October 31st, 1992

Helicopter crash report to quell murder rumour

Reports that a helicopter crash in Dingle last May was caused by sabotage were discounted last week when another source of fuel contamination was suggested by government inspectors. The conclusion that sabotage has been ruled out will come as a relief to the people of Dingle. Media speculation about sabotage caused deep anger in the close-knit Kerry resort … The town was awash with rumours, accusations and counter-claims because the crash came after a row over a proposed £5.8 million marina at the Skellig Hotel in which Mr McAuliffe is a director.

Sunday Independent, January 17th, 1993

Xavier McAuliffe for trial on helicopter charges

Listowel businessman, Xavier McAuliffe, has been sent forward for trial at the next sitting of Tralee Circuit Court by Judge Humphrey Kelleher. At the monthly sitting of Dingle District Court, Judge Kelleher said he was sending McAuliffe forward for trial to the next sitting of the Circuit Court on his own bond of £100. McAuliffe is facing a number of charges under the Air Navigation Act. They followed a fatal helicopter crash that took place in Dingle on May 31st, 1992. He is charged with flying his helicopter — a Robinson 22B — while failing to have a certificate of air worthiness and a flight permit granted by the Minister for Transport, Energy and Communications ... on May 31st, 1992 ... He is also charged with failing to have the aircraft maintained in a manner prescribed as appropriate to the aircraft at the same location on the same date.

The Kerryman, November 4th, 1994

Tragic helicopter crash in Dingle

McAuliffe awaits sentence following guilty plea in court

The Kerryman, November 10th, 1995

Businessman loses licence and is fined £8,000 for fatal helicopter crash

A businessman whose helicopter crashed into the sea, causing the death of a woman, has been fined £8,000 and disqualified from holding a pilot's license for seven years. In Dublin Circuit Criminal Court yesterday, Judge Michael Moriarty said it would be wrong to consider the case one of culpable homicide by the defendant, Xavier McAuliffe … He admitted flying the helicopter at or near Cooleen Pier on May 31st, 1992, when no airworthiness certificate was issued or validated, or without a flight permit granted by the Minister for Transport, Energy and Communications. He also pleaded guilty to flying the aircraft when it had not been appropriately maintained. Both charges had been brought under the Air Navigation (Airworthiness of Aircraft) Act of 1964.

The Irish Times, February 3rd, 1996

Reports of murder probe after crash

REPORTS of a possible murder investigation and suggestions of sabotage dominated media coverage to the wake of the tragic accident in which a 22-year-old Sligo woman … lost her life in a helicopter piloted by Listowel businessman, Xavier McAuliffe. *The Sunday Business Post* reported in the months following the fatal accident of May 31st, 1992, that Gardaí were set to begin a murder enquiry into the accident because of suspected sabotage. Gardaí never launched a murder enquiry and this report, and others alleging contamination of the helicopter's fuel, created bad feeling locally.

At the time of the accident, tensions were very high in Dingle because of strong local opposition to a plan being promoted by Skellig Hotel to develop

> a £5.8 million marina and housing development of which Mr McAuliffe is a major shareholder. Those opposed to the marina felt there was an effort being made to smear their campaign of opposition by media speculation that the helicopter had been sabotaged. A foreshore licence has been granted, for the development of the marina — but despite this, the Skellig Hotel consortium abandoned all plans at the time to proceed with the project.
>
> *The Kerryman*, February 9th, 1996

A *Kerryman* article on June 5th, 1992, stated that, 'Mr McAuliffe praised those who came to the rescue'. Among those at the rescue was Jimmy Flannery, The Grove, Dingle, who was, ironically, a member of DCG, the group that would later be called cowards and accused, using innuendo and falsehoods, of causing the tragic crash. It is not the intention of this chapter to open old wounds; the events surrounding the Skellig Marina controversy are a matter of public record. The saga which followed, as the allegations made national news, was prolonged and distasteful. Dingle's reputation was being tarnished. On regatta day 1992, members of our group, DCG, were called 'murderers' while gathering signatures by a friend and supporter (from out of town) of the-then Skellig Hotel owner. This outrageous comment came on the day of *The Sunday Business Post* story.

On October 12th, 1992, and in the face of overwhelming local opposition, the Skellig Hotel abandoned its marina plans. It was a triumph for the community and for grassroots democracy. The timeline of newspaper clippings above shows how the story of the tragic helicopter crash developed and how it concluded with the trial and sentencing of the helicopter pilot. It would be three and a half years before the people of the town got justice for the reputational damage done to them. To this day, no apology has come to the people of Dingle from *The Sunday Business Post* for its uneven and shoddy journalism. That paper was responsible for sowing the vile seeds of malicious innuendo which caused huge upset to the people of Dingle. While other newspapers followed the story of the tragic event and watched it turn and conclude with the truth, *The Sunday Business Post* moved on to the next story.

Some curious questions remain, thirty-two years on from the Skellig campaign. Would there be a united front in Dingle today against such unwanted developments as the Skellig marina proposal of 1991/92? Does that sense of community fellowship and ownership still exist in Dingle? In a recent plan by the Department of Agriculture, Food and the Marine to extend the public western marina in Dingle, which would include a forest of steel piles outside the western breakwater and which would seriously damage the harbour's scenic beauty, it was difficult for the small group that sought to bring the development to the attention of the town to gain traction in its attempts to inform the people. Many of the tourism businesses in Dingle didn't know, or weren't interested, that this proposed development was afoot; they were busy, busy with the latest influx of visitors. Likewise, many local residents seemed unaware of the proposal and some looked on it as something that was going on down by the Quay. Thirty-three years later, it appears that we all fight our own corner.

NOTE: The ownership of the Dingle Skellig Hotel has changed since the Skellig marina controversy in 1991/1992, and no party or individuals connected with the present management and ownership of the Skellig Hotel were involved with the Skellig Hotel in 1991/1992. The Department of Agriculture, Food and the Marine's proposed expansion of the existing marina in Dingle (referred to in the last paragraph here) is presently in the hands of An Bórd Pleanála.

SEVEN

Dingle Now

David Lean and Freddie Young are largely responsible for the Dingle we know today. Lean, the director of *Ryan's Daughter* (1970), and Young, the Oscar-winning cinematographer, captured the scenic beauty of the Dingle Peninsula and put it on the world stage for all to see. During the making of the film, a huge Hollywood star, Robert Mitchum, walked the streets of Dingle and bought his newspaper alongside the locals. Well-established English actors, John Mills and Trevor Howard, and Australian actor, Leo McKern, played leading roles in the saga of Rosie Ryan, played by Sarah Miles who remained a friend of Dingle and visited often thereafter. David Lean was a two-time Oscar-winning director before he came to the town, and screenwriter Robert Bolt also had an Oscar under his belt.

This abundant talent arriving to a small town (with a population of 1,400 in 1969) was bound to get noticed in the world of films and the world at large. The plot of the film (which was panned by some critics) was dwarfed by the sheer magnificence of the canvas on which it was drawn. The film initially enjoyed moderate success but has since gone on to great success among the viewing public, grossing multiples of the initial production costs. It was one of the most successful films of 1970 in Britain and ran for almost two years straight at a West End cinema. A modern reappraisal of the film cites the David Lean 'craft' of film-making.

In the years following the release of *Ryan's Daughter*, tourism was building in Dingle and, in 1983, more manna from heaven descended on the town in the form of a dolphin, later named Fungie and who, according to Wikipedia, was 'named after a local fisherman who was teased for his attempt to grow a beard and who was nicknamed Fungus'. The dolphin became hugely popular with family tourists and got voluminous column inches in the newspapers – even making it into *The New York Times*. The popular John Hurt-narrated documentary, *The Dolphin's Gift* (2008), drew from a diverse section of participants and elicited insightful commentary from people on land and sea while showing the playful dolphin in its natural habitat amid the sometimes-chaotic frenzy of ferry boats jockeying for position to catch a glimpse of this wondrous gift. Fungie would stay for over thirty-five years. Many would say that the dolphin made Dingle; people of *Ryan's Daughter* generation would not agree. Dingle was a brand before Fungie came, thanks to Lean and Young.

Identity is described as a distinguishing character or personality. A town's identity is not a static thing and sometimes it is difficult to pin down what exactly makes any town stand out from others as having something special. Having seen Dingle develop during my lifetime, I find it difficult to describe Dingle's present identity and ponder if it has any at all to describe. Fifty-five years ago, the Hollywoodisation of Dingle changed the trajectory of the development of the town and put it on a track into the unknown; it was an awakening of sorts from decades of privation for a large section of the town's population. The template for a new type of Dingle was forming along with a realisation, and acceptance, that anything could happen in this town. Tourism became the buzzword, and ways of attracting new visitors to a heretofore backwater – where the main event for visitors had been a drive around Slea Head – were explored.

Today, Dingle has arrived where it's at; a tourist town which many long-time residents believe has lost its true character and whose focus is the propagating of commerce though there are a number of laudable achievements and developments which benefit the residential population. If one Googles the word 'Dingle', a list of hotels and Airbnbs are to the fore along with activities for tourists (the first ones constitute sponsored content); next are Dingle Peninsula websites offering detailed information for visitors. The first three pages (I stopped the search then) are all about tourism-related content. And that is the story of present-day Dingle, tourism is its badge, its identity and its raison d'être.

The benefits and the price we pay for having a popular town are part of the double-edged sword. Dingle has laid

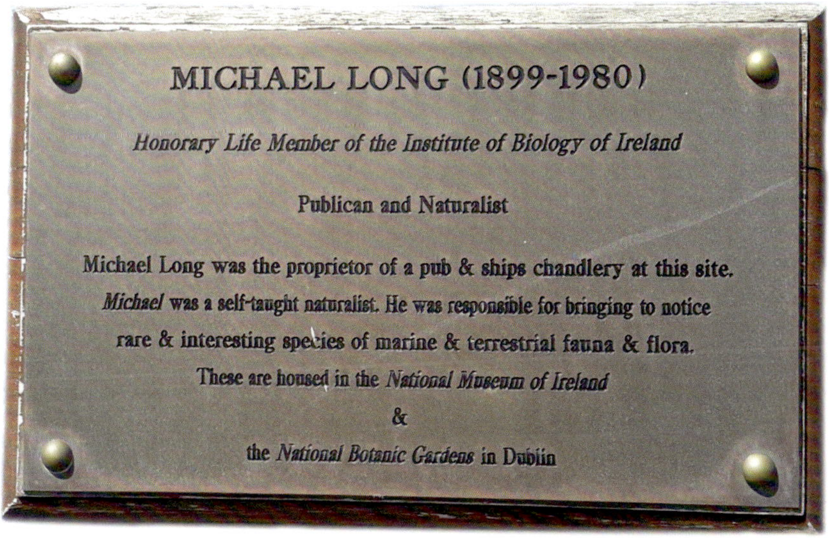

Sign on the wall of John Benny's pub, Strand Street.

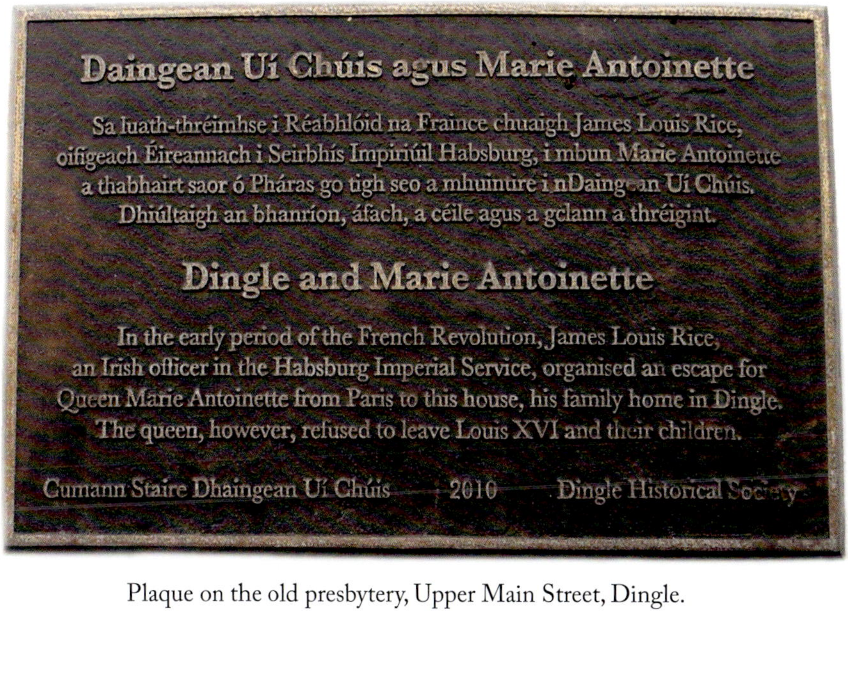

Plaque on the old presbytery, Upper Main Street, Dingle.

Plaque on Fitzgerald's Centra, Main Street, Dingle.

Plaque on the wall of the Temperance Hall, Dingle.

GSWR notice, in Danno's courtyard.

Old ice plant sign, in Danno's courtyard.

Historic road sign, in the courtyard of Adams' bar, Main Street.

Sign in the courtyard of Curran's pub.

(*above*) Concrete plaque on the Presentation Convent, Upper Main Street, Dingle.

Historic carved emblems on Bean, Green Street, Dingle.

Historic stone carving on Maidhchín Fuacht's, Green Street, Dingle.

Carved stone in Begley's (Kanon's Korner), Green Street.

Gate entrance to the Boatyard Restaurant, Strand Street, Dingle.

Dick Mack's Walk of Fame.

Portraits of Robert Mitchum (Adams' Bar, Main Street) and Oliver MacDonnell (Bridge House, Dingle).

Adjoining houses in The Wood, where three numbers are missing from the row of fifteen houses. The missing numbers are on three houses in Goat Street which are in the same style and were also built in 1909.

Sign on Long's (accommodation) house, Strand Street, Dingle.

DINGLE BUSINESSES WITH THE ORIGINAL NAMES FROM THE 1950S ON THEIR PREMISES

J. McKENNA

M.T. MORIARTY

MURPHY

M. NELIGAN

O'KEEFFE
PURE DRUGS
DISPENSING
CHEMIST

O'CONNOR

Ua Flaiṫḃeartaiġ

CHEMIST T. M. WALSH M.P.S.I.

aside some of its historic character and quaintness and has altered the landscape in the pursuit of, let's be honest, the mighty 'dollar'. I doubt if any of the compatriots (those penny-scarce ones like me) that I grew up with would want to return to the hard times of our youth, aside from the adventurous days at play in the open air in a town where we were free to roam and explore unhindered. There was so much we didn't have: shoes – or at least good shoes; money – not a hope; a good suit of clothes – no way; respect – hardly. We were in the gutter, but, to quote Oscar Wilde, '... some of us are looking at the stars'. While it is easy to be glib with such pronouncements, everybody wants to lift themselves up and live, at the very least, a comfortable life. When they get there they, naturally, want a more comfortable life, thus finding themselves in a 'much wants more' situation. The complete quote by Aesop is, 'Much wants more, and loses all'.

When any town, over time, gets a flood of new people who settle and bring new ideas, and in many cases having come from different cultural backgrounds, it is inevitable that this group will not have the same grá for the town and its history as the local resident population with long-standing roots. This lack of awareness of the town's ethos and culture by the new people will put them out of step with the natural sense of protectiveness held by the people who always lived there and who really don't want their way of life, and what they are used to, threatened in any way. While many newcomers will be respectful to the town and what it stands for, there will be an element who won't give a toss about that stuff.

A tourist is a person that travels away from home for pleasure and to experience different cultures; being a transient species, the tourist by definition is supposed to go home again – if they don't, they remain as blow-ins where they settle. This definition of the term blow-in may be found in a selection of English language dictionaries. In the Collins Dictionary, one of the less kind definitions is found: blow-in, noun, 'Australian and Irish informal, an unwelcome newcomer or stranger'. Rightly or wrongly, the term blow-in has entered the narrative in Dingle and in Ireland as a whole in modern times.

The origin of the label, which is felt as offensive in the main, is often debated. It can seem that users of the term may be exerting power and control over others by wanting to keep what they have to themselves and, perhaps, harbouring resentment when newcomers show a different way of doing things. The other side of that coin where 'no one is a prophet in their own land' (paraphrasing from Luke 4.24) is an apt phrase that applies when it comes to new people arriving in any town. Oftentimes outsiders are treated with veneration even when they arrive with half-baked ideas. There is an expectation that local people will (or should, anyway) contribute to their local community and when they do it is often treated as an unremarkable everyday thing that is more or less expected of them. On the other hand, the latest arriving newbie, be they chef, musician, publican, craftsperson or other, is the greatest thing since crubeens and accepted as the latest thing Dingle needs.

This old-fashioned attitude comes from harbouring a reluctance to see our neighbours get ahead or applaud them for the good works they do within the community. The term blow-in was common in the 1970s and 1980s and is used today hesitantly, due, perhaps, to our desire to project an inclusive and cosmopolitan image to our visitors. It would be disingenuous to think that only people born and with ancestry in any town should be considered locals. My mother, who was from Listowel, was treated as a blow-in during her early years in Dingle. When she started rearing a family she was viewed adversely in her neighbourhood for some time.

People come from outside to work in Dingle; they set up enterprises in the area, they marry-in and, while doing so, contribute to the local economic and social life of the town, and their children become Dingle people. These people (grow-ins?) are separate from those who see Dingle as a place of financial opportunity and who want a piece of the pie, as it were. How far back do one's roots in any town have to go in order to be considered a local? A recent visitor let me know he was a blow-in and added, rather impudently, 'Man, nobody really comes from around here anyway'. I reminded him that three generations of my ancestors, going back two hundred years, lived on the street where he stood. I wondered if his perception that locals are scarce on the ground is common with some people when they arrive in Dingle? On further reflection, I concluded that the young man in question, who was blowing sweet-smelling smoke, was seriously misguided and had ended up in the wrong side of town. I haven't seen him back my way since.

Would it be fair to say that people who know where Jackie Nell's, Katie Sarah's, Father Noel's, Maud's and Danny Flahive's were are true Dingle people? The foregoing are, respectively, Bob Griffin's, Bean, Once Upon a Toy, Lord Baker's and Griffin's Gift Shop. I knew everybody in Dingle at one time. I don't say that flippantly; if I didn't know their names, I knew their faces and the part of town they hailed from. For the past decade or more, I encounter people of various nationalities when I go to the shops; strangers serve me and in some shops that come to mind no local people work there. When I discuss this stuff with friends, I often get the retort, 'You can't do anything about that, John'. I agree, of course, but I can still tell it as I see it. I don't recount these observations as a gripe, but as a reflection of the times we live in now. I have no illusions that what I write will change anything and, where would one start anyway? Press pause before *Ryan's Daughter*? A view expressed by a local man in the early years following the release of the film ('It's a pity Ryan didn't have another daughter') sums up the state of delirium the film left in its wake.

A number of local pubs and other businesses are still family-owned and customers can still get served by the man or woman of the house. There are some welcoming Irish pub experiences in Dingle, whether you are local or tourist, such as going into Curran's and meeting James for a chat and browsing through his historic ledgers and records of commerce in Dingle, or sharing banter with

John Benny and debating the ills of tourism and the price of a pint these days. A good number of tourist ventures in the boating, touring and sightseeing areas are still in the hands of local people; we have not reached a point yet where the tourists who stayed are providing for the tourists who arrive. Shopkeepers running tourist-type shops have no idea who their neighbours are and tourists have no hope of getting directions or local knowledge from such places. In some cases, these shops will have new tenants the following year due to rising rents in the busy town.

With help from Google, anyone can research Dingle and its history and begin historic/cultural tours of the peninsula; as I could say, read all about the Giant's Causeway and its geometric wonders and offer similar tours up north. What we offer our visitors should be authentic, and that does happen with many operators offering tourist services. But will tourists come anyway, regardless of what we offer them? Some balance in this regard needs pondering, especially when dealing with the discerning tourist. If one goes to Marrakesh or Florence, the visitor seeks to experience the real flavour of those places: the spoken word, the music, the smell of their food and the banter of their bargaining. I imagine if I am a foreign tourist stepping onto the Blasket Islands, I would like to be greeted there by descendants from that place, which is steeped in island lore, language and culture.

To its credit, the Blasket Centre/Ionad an Bhlascaoid offers a spectacular display to the visitor, featuring island life and culture, at a very reasonable price. The audiovisual displays are at one with the magnificent views from outside that stream through strategically placed windows in the centre. Of the tourist attractions and tours on offer in the Dingle Peninsula, the Ionad an Bhlascaoid experience is one of the best, and value for money.

I would find it strange to go to New Zealand and be greeted and served by somebody from a country at another part of the world. When I have visitors in my house, I like to be there to welcome them (that would perhaps be called old-fashioned). We may be getting a bit jaded and selling lite-tourism because of hubris and presumptive thinking that the tourist will keep coming. In the early 1990s, the harbour in Dingle was developed to provide a marina and enhanced fishing and leisure facilities; the shore along Strand Street was built up and covered with tarmacadam to provide parking for tourist cars and coaches. The footprint of the historic Caladh Spáinneach (Spanish Pier), the original pier which was key to a huge industry of trade between Dingle and Spain in the sixteenth and seventeenth centuries, was unceremoniously covered over.

Apart from a discreet wooden plaque on Long's private house, situated opposite, with the inscription 'Caladh Spáinneach', there is no evidence of that vital part of Dingle's history from whence great wealth grew. It is a betrayal of our past when the foundational imprint of Dingle's history lies under the wheels of tourist coaches. It is still possible to reclaim from the tarmacadam and erect a visual representation of An Caladh Spáinneach, or part thereof, so that our discerning tourists get to know an important part of our history. A bronze statue of

Fungie the dolphin is erected at the pier head, yet there is scarcely a mention of An Caladh Spáinneach. A plaque commemorating the signing of a treaty between Dingle and Spain is on a wall (the Temperance Hall) at the higher end of town and the King and Queen of Spain are due to visit Dingle in 2029 to commemorate the five-hundreth anniversary of the treaty.

> Dingle reached the highest point of its importance in the course of the sixteenth century. It was now established as one of the great trading ports of the south. Continental wine ships and other merchant vessels plied in and out of the harbour, tieing up at the Spanish pier, which stood about one hundred metres to the west of the present pier, and Dingle was numbered among the leading embarkation points for France, Spain and Britain.
>
> From *Dingle,* by Fr Jack McKenna, published in 1985

There has been a creep over recent decades from enthusiastically embracing our visitors to a more casual approach, which comes from familiarity. It is evident when a tourist sits beside you in a pub that they are pleased to be talking to a local, just as they are delighted to be served in an established Dingle drinking house by the owner, and in their native tongue and accent. Admittedly, that still happens in some establishments; the pub/restaurant sector in the main is welcoming. In the 1940s and 1950s, there were reputed to be fifty-two pubs in Dingle. If so, there is now a little over half of that number operating. Fifteen of those have changed hands over recent decades and a dozen are owned and managed by descendants of the original owners from the 1950s. Staff shortages and securing accommodation for summer staff have become a huge issue in Dingle.

The summer job for the local school student is still available mainly because the students can live at home. Properties that were available for hospitality workers have become Airbnbs. Some business owners have bought houses specifically to house their staff. Front-of-house staff in the hospitality sector are largely local but, beyond that, an international brigade of kitchen workers, waiters and bed-makers holds sway. The tourist business in Dingle, as it is now, would not survive without that brigade of workers coming from countries outside of Ireland.

To interact with indigenous people and experience their culture are the reasons many tourists travel. That experience is somewhat watered down when visitors hit Dingle. The bus driver may not speak English, and certainly not Irish. The next port of call is to collect a key to an Airbnb from a coded lock-box. The traditional Irish/Dingle welcome is still there in traditionally established guesthouses and hotels but, outside of that, a quick turnover of visitors, many of whom deal with an agency without the host ever getting to see them, is now normalised in 'Ireland of the Welcomes'. In the early days of tourism in Dingle, there was an excitement in having visitors that now seems to have waned; a more blasé 'here we go again' attitude is creeping in. While visiting Dingle during the tourist season, one could be in any nondescript city in Europe. The character of the town, while not completely eroded, is deeply hidden and the first thing that hits you as you get off the bus is that you have arrived in a tourist town.

Our own language, which is hardly used during the long tourist season, is just another in the melting pot of tongues from several European countries and further afield. While our language and culture are important to many of our visitors, a type of bus tourism is now common where people want a quick stop, a photo opportunity (beside the Fungie statue) and a bite to eat. Another type has a want for quick thrills and raucous pub crawls on weekends, something on offer in hundreds of similar towns. Mingled with many of our welcome visitors are the stag and hen party people, some of whom urinate in public against the walls of residences and into the harbour.

These visitors come off their bus drinking and go from pub to pub carrying alcoholic drinks on the street with them lest the flow of alcohol gets interrupted on their booze cruise. The boys gather in clusters outside some pubs with drinks in their hands and form what must look like formidable and intimidating looking packs to reserved local people going about their day. These revellers, who see Dingle as a place to party unhindered, introduce a crassness which overshadows the good things about the town. They let everyone know they are around as they noisily make their way back to their Airbnbs, many of which are located in residential neighbourhoods. While this behaviour is decried by many, denial also exists for the sake of commerce.

Tourists are often the yardstick used when making decisions nationally about our hospitality industry and their needs are used to justify changes to some of our long-standing cultural observations in order to accommodate visitors (like the opening of pubs on Good Friday). In recent times, we had a leading government minister, who was pushing for extended pub-opening hours in Ireland, state that, 'You can get a drink anytime you want in Berlin'. Well, let them go to Berlin. Discerning visitors are coming to Ireland because we are Irish and have Irish things to offer. Dingle has evolved into a place where tourism reigns for two-thirds of the year. This is obvious in the off-season months when many business doors are closed to the locals. Upwards of fifty shops/businesses in the town rely on tourism.

Some positive local initiatives have taken place in recent decades. In the late 1990s, the Dingle Marina Centre, which houses various water-based activity clubs, was brought about by a group of local people who had the best interests of the harbour and the town at heart. In 1993, Sciuird Archaeological Tours started bringing archaeological sites alive for many visitors. Dingle Oceanworld (1996) has evolved to be hugely popular all year round and attracts family-type tourists. Dingle has some popular festivals, including Féile na Bealtaine, Dingle Literary Festival and Animation Dingle, all of which are valuable assets to the town's arts scene. Dingle is now also a university town; in 2003, Sacred Heart University, Connecticut, USA, set up a campus in the town. This has recently been expanded to allow for larger contingents of American students

The town presents itself well to visitors. The shopfronts are colourful, architecturally pleasing and are well maintained. The streetscapes of Main Street (viewed uphill) and Strand Street/The Quay appear often in internet searches for Dingle town. The much-photographed iconic streetscape along Strand Street and the Quay has been marred by wooden corrals (sheep pens as one local refers to them) – a response to Covid 19 and measures taken to encourage outdoor dining. The unsightly raw-wood constructs, some of which have been painted recently, obscure the traditional image of the street but it looks now that the corrals are there to stay. Outdoor furniture and its surrounds can be done tastefully, as on the continent. The Dingle Bay Hotel, to its credit, went a different route and now has the finest street furniture, which is removed at night and stored for the winter months, outside its premises. Other establishments, like Ashe's on Main Street, followed the attractive European continental (and removable) style. The western Colony (off Strand Street) with the higgledy-piggledy huts and unregulated parking and trading practices is a stand-out eyesore in the Quay area, as is the tourist office, which presents like a crude square block in the way of harbour views from The Wood to the Tracks.

The tourist office, which could have been built in a part of town where the resulting assault on the landscape wasn't an issue, has a huge unused floor space which I have never seen even half-full. The recent opening of Clós na mBád (the boatyard site) is welcome and gets very favourable comment. The marina and pier areas are well managed and have a clean and tidy look, albeit at the loss of the bustling activities of years past when the place was awash with the activity of fishermen repairing nets and maintaining their boats. The area in question is now spick and span, not at all like a working fishing harbour. Improvements along the waterfront are done, in my view, mainly with the tourist in mind and not the fisherman. However, the days are gone when visitors strolled down the pier in the evening to see the arrival of fishing boats landing their catch and to engage with the fishermen about their toil. It is a rare thing now to see tourists walking down the pier; it seems they see no attraction in it.

The term tourism pollution, from both an environmental and cultural standpoint, is gaining traction in some European cities where certain visitor types are not welcome, and a reduction in numbers to historic archaeological sites, because of trampling, waste disposal and pawing of exhibits, is being considered. Amsterdam city council has recently banned cruise ships to prevent over-tourism in certain areas and locals in the city erect 'WE LIVE HERE' signs. 'In Spanish cities, recent protests had hundreds of thousands marching against the housing crisis fuelled by the tourism boom. In Madrid, people rattled keys as they walked through the city's streets and chanted, 'Get Airbnb out of our neighbourhoods' (Sky News, April 2025).

The traffic congestion in Dingle in summertime is often mentioned in local publications, detailing how it inconveniences the flow of commerce in the town. As the tourism season kicks off, local car owners are asked to leave their cars at home to make way for the tourists; shunt the locals to the side for the season. Pedestrian congestion is never mentioned and how the crossing of streets and stepping onto the road because of the jammed footpaths raises stress levels. It is impossible to walk the footpaths unhindered – a small thing which we took for granted but which is now taken from us. A serpentine course invariably needs to be navigated between sandwich boards, street furniture, clusters reading menus and, of course, the screen people talking to themselves and walking straight into your space, oblivious to your existence.

If one articulates these concerns to anyone that matters, little heed is paid to one's 'grumblings' and one is left with the distinct impression that the tourist comes first. I recently remarked to a newcomer trader to Strand Street about a group outside his premises ganged up in the middle of the footpath. He suggested that I should call the footpath police. This is what you get when you complain – sarcasm.

Dingle may indeed be a wonderful place for tourists but local people who need to go about their daily lives have a different view on that. Tourism undoubtedly creates summer employment for people but most of these seasonal employees, who are the mainstay of the industry, will never afford to live in the town they work in. 'Tourism is great for the town' is a phrase that is bandied about ad nauseam, but the people who espouse this sacred dictum don't think about the local young people who cannot set up a home in their own town or its environs because the cost of housing has rocketed due to the influx of moneyed outsiders who want to have second homes in this 'wonderful mecca'. Some domestic properties for sale in Dingle and its periphery have asking prices ranging between €285,000 and €865,000; in a couple of instances prices are comparable with those in Dublin 4. A site (0.20 acres) in The Wood, Dingle, is going for €375,000. The irony is worth mentioning here, that in the early 1970s, many Dingle people were emerging from poverty and young people were able to save money and build houses in their hometown but now, in modern, well-off Dingle, they cannot due to skyrocketing property prices.

A trawl through Booking.com or similar will reveal the high cost of overnight accommodation in Dingle. It is commonly known that holidays in Spain are available at far cheaper rates, at twenty-five per cent less from my own experience. This is not only the case in Dingle, of course, Ireland in general is an expensive place to visit. There are some accommodations that give value for money, and, most of all, have somebody at the door to welcome their guests in the traditional Irish way. More than 650 properties in West Kerry are now active on the Airbnb website (*The Kerryman*, 2023). In 2023, a Bord Pleanála inspector pointed out some key facts in an extensive report; among them were the following:

> Dingle is swamped with holiday homes.
> Hundreds of houses are available for short-term holiday letting.
> No houses are available for long-term letting.
> Dingle has a large social housing demand.
> … figures from the 2016 census indicate that 'the level of holiday homes in some areas (West Kerry) far exceeds the local indigenous population'.

> … the estimated 1,200 holiday and second homes in West Kerry 'requires consideration from a number of perspectives'.
>
> … holiday homes which are unoccupied for most of the year do not contribute to the development of active, vibrant local communities … act as a deterrent to local people wishing to live in the villages … and impact on the Irish language.
>
> … the county council has a responsibility to ensure properties are available for long-term rental … to take due account of residential amenity issues for existing residents.
>
> *The Kerryman*, 2023

In spite of this damning report, Airbnbs and holiday homes continue to proliferate and indigenous people find it hard to secure a home for themselves. Something being 'good for the town' is not the same thing as being good for the people; 'good' in this context is too often equated with wealth and not well-being. Then there's the word 'progress', that old chestnut, often used with a hands-in-the-air gesture signifying that nothing can be done about what's happening to Dingle. You hear people say, 'you cannot stop progress' and 'progress is inevitable'. The word is highly favoured by those who see material profit as a result of the process. Progress happens, but it cannot trample on people's rights and, on its path, bury our history as mentioned above in the Caladh Spáinneach example.

In the off-season, people say, 'Isn't it great to have the town back to ourselves'. For local, non-businesspeople, the tourism industry has become, at best, tiresome and, in some ways, disastrous for the residents who have to endure it and don't recognise their town anymore. Planning decisions for projects in the town frequently come down on the side of business-type developments in spite of vigorous local objections. A recent example is a proposed incongruous leisure development at Dingle harbour, the town's greatest asset and attraction for locals and visitors alike. Residents in some quarters feel frustration at not being listened to when trying to gain improvements, such as safe crossing of roads and safe footpaths, in their areas from the relevant authorities. The encroachment of loud, late-night pub patrons into residential areas is suffered by residents whose pleas are all too often ignored.

Dingle has an ideal template around which a sustainable, resident-friendly tourist industry could be built – the natural harbour, surrounding scenery, significant history, award-winning restaurants and bars, and the Irish language and its culture – but all of these assets are now shaped and moulded for the enjoyment of visitors with little concern for, or input from, the local resident population who have history in the town and who feel they have no say in the direction it takes. There are a few hidden gems that have not been discovered by visitors. I am loath to mention them here lest they become overrun and their calm shattered by busyness and the noise of tourism. We are running out of such places for ourselves, places to call our own. Thirty-three years ago, as detailed in chapter six, the people of Dingle stood together against a proposed development which they saw as a threat to their town. Alas, that collective spirit and pride of place no longer exist in the community and, consequently, Dingle has become a town which could be described as a place where anything goes.

EIGHT

Passing

There is finality in the word 'dead'. Saying someone has died is often softened by saying, 'Jack has passed on' or 'Jack has passed away'. A passing leaves hope for another stage, a hereafter, a soul remaining with us in the ether until all family and friends meet again. Faith is the cornerstone of such beliefs. Some people are great for burying the dead; they turn up, not only for family and close friends, but for distant acquaintances and anyone from their own town. The graveyard is one of the places we meet as a community where we share an event that marks us as being human.

In Saint James' Church graveyard in Dingle, dozens of slate-topped tombs stand above the ground housing family members with old Dingle names, all lying together in the privacy of their hereafter. Several uninscribed stones marking the resting places of forgotten people stand askew amid the grander expressions of finality. Many of the headstones are blurred by centuries of weather, the names and dates ghosted over into the past. The slate slabs, one measuring seven feet by five feet with a thickness of two inches and atop a tomb six feet above the ground, were no doubt hoisted into place using a mechanical aid of the times, like a block and tackle. Once in place, the top, weighing several tons, was there forever and subsequent burials were entered through a side door of the tomb.

The precise chiselling of the names and particulars of the dead on the slate and stone are a testament to the skills of the stone cutters and masons of the day. Identifiable dates from the 1700s are scattered throughout, the most recent date being 1947. There is an air of antiquity in Saint James' Church graveyard of long-ago times and forgotten people shut away in their tombs, a few of which have trees growing through their side walls from roots trapped within the plot from day one – another form of life bursting through to the light from the darkness inside. Some of the inscriptions are revealing and tell the story of an older Dingle: Henry Harris, chief boatman at Brandon station, died 1835; Lt. Thomas Parker, 6th Veterans Battalion, died 1852; Kate Gloster, died 1846; Edward Benner, died 1863; Grece Trigurtil, died 1833.

In Raithín Uí Bhuaigh (Raheenyhooig), on the periphery of Dingle harbour, a mix of names from the town of Dingle is found among the 'locals', people from the catchment area of Burnham where Lord Ventry had a residence, Ballymore, and the surrounding area. When our family members played in the woodlands of Burnham when we were young, we didn't realise that some of our ancestors were interred in the graveyard there. Several seamen are buried there, among them one of my neighbours, a fisherman who died in 1971. Notable inscriptions from times past give evidence of Dingle's association with the sea. 'VENTRY', inscribed in a marble plaque over the slate entrance door with bronze fittings on Lord Ventry's impressively built mausoleum, which dominates the site, remind us of the chasm that existed between neighbours in the earthly world.

Saint Brendan's Cemetery (known as Cill Bhreac in Kerry local authority's graveyard records*), elevated fifty feet above sea level, in Milltown, Dingle, presents a vista of the harbour and the bay beyond which stretches to the next distant peninsula. The spectacular scene can be a forlorn image for the family and friends of the person being laid to rest, and especially by seafaring folk who eked a living from the sea. The cemetery was opened in 1950 and the first two burials were as follows: Georgina Benner, Church of Ireland, from Main Street, Dingle, was interred in November 1950, while in February 1951 the first Catholic, D. McKenna, male, also with an address at Main Street, was buried just inside the cemetery gates, one hundred and ten paces from the lower end of the graveyard where Mrs Benner rests.

For seven decades, the non-Catholic graves, few in number at first, were isolated from the main Catholic cohort. Like a metaphor for the times, Mrs Benner is no longer isolated; the encroachment in her direction from the now-varied strands of believers in the field has narrowed the gap. The surnames of O'Connor, Moriarty, Flahive and Brosnan that were common in the early years of the graveyard are now intermingled with new names that reflect the changing nature of the town as it has grown from farming and fishing to tourism.

The age range of the deceased covers almost a hundred years, from new-born baby to ninety-eight years old. The causes of death, as detailed in the graveyard records, are listed variously as old age, cancer, heart, stroke, natural causes and accident (on land and sea). The occupation of fisherman appears often in the records of the dead, as does that of farmer, farmer's wife, shopkeeper, merchant, fisherman's wife, labourer, and carpenter. In 1955, my grandparents, James O'Connor and Mary Deady O'Connor, died three months apart. James, fisherman, was eighty-two, and Mary, fisherman's wife, was seventy. The cause of death for both was entered as 'old age'. Today we would say Mary was 'only seventy'. In the 1950s, poor people were driven to resignation after living a hard life and this was reflected in their demeanour and the way they dressed, giving up the ghost early, as it were.

At a recent funeral, a neighbour remarked to me that he would not have as large a funeral as that of the man being buried. I asked why not and he replied, 'He played football'. There is that, I thought. Sportspersons and people who have colleagues from work that die are assured of a guard of honour, as are participants in clubs and organisations. The passing of famous local musicians will draw fellow crooners and players who give a musical farewell at the graveside, while many mourners grieve amongst a small group of their own. In Dingle, having a long tradition of Wrenboys, which is celebrated on St Stephen's Day, musicians give a musical tribute at the graveside to former

'Wran' members and supporters. The sound of the fife and drum will be the final farewell to those who donned the colours of their street.

It is a sombre scene at a graveside where a sparse gathering mourns a person who lived a quiet life, away from the hustle and bustle of society. I told my neighbour, a man of great skills, not to sell himself short and that living was not a competition for the greatest turnout at the end of days. It is common at burials, where the deceased is from a part of the peninsula, where long-held customs are observed to have half a dozen shovels on stand-by so that relatives and friends get a chance to say goodbye by laying earth on the remains.

The Irish wake is noted for how it observes the passing of loved ones. The term 'wake' originated in a time when plague and diseases were common and certification of death was not scientific. Often times, the afflicted person would wake up after appearing dead for an extended period, thus, waking the dead was a minimum of a twenty-four-hour vigil. This period of time also gave friends and family the opportunity to say farewell. The passing of a family member is understandably emotionally draining for close relatives, and as a measure to mitigate the sorrow and hurt, songs and music would be introduced along with the telling of stories about the deceased from happier times. This type of farewell is common for people who have lived long lives but the passing of the young, especially in tragic circumstances, can be a truly solemn occasion.

Being commiserated with at a funeral can reveal unexpected reactions and a realisation that one never knows what they mean to people or what people mean to them. There can be awkwardness as you approach the bereaved and you wonder if you should be intruding on their grief; invariably, however, the response is positive and condolences are appreciated. The bereaved family members are to the fore at the graveside with neighbours and friends close by. On the periphery stand many who do not want to intrude or who feel that they don't merit a place up close. Among the attendees will be longtime friends that were particularly close to the deceased. Fellow mourners will often times shake hands with them, knowing that they have lost a good friend. When this happens, it is an acknowledgement that you, too, mattered to the dead person. Looking around the field of mourners at the burial of a local person, the old stock will be seen, turning out for the passing of one of their own. Mourners attending a burial will, no doubt, at some stage reach a stark point where they will be struck by the fact that they have more friends interred than they do still living.

Taking a tour of Saint Brendan's Cemetery is akin to taking a stroll through the social, and sometimes tragic, history of Dingle. A name on a grave can bring to mind an event, a tragedy that befell not only the descendants of the name but the whole town: a mother and son buried on the same day, a child in a small casket being lowered down, three brothers buried in the same year. Deep shock has visited the town a number of times following the passing of young people 'who died before their time'. The names of the young are mingled through the decades of the cemetery's existence; the first child, buried in 1952, was a young girl. Visiting the graves in a cemetery can evoke a mixture of emotions. While sadness is the default reaction, happier thoughts and times come to mind, too. A name on a headstone evokes a happy memory from that person's past, maybe of a song you sang together once, a helping hand given when needed, a realisation that the spirit of the deceased in front of you is still in your thoughts.

In cases where enmity between family siblings exists, the burial of a relative can be straining for the parties involved; a case in point being that of a bachelor 'who took a drink' and who was not allowed to share a plot with his deceased parents. Old wounds come to the fore in times of familial crisis. An evident yardstick of how the dead are revered is the condition of the grave. Fresh flowers and tokens of a person's life are abundant on many of the graves in Saint Brendan's while others remain forgotten, caved-in and unvisited. On some of the older gravestones, the inscribed names are weathered and illegible, with the deceased therein consigned to distant memory. In many cases, evidence of the materialistic worth of the deceased is reflected in the size of a monument. A broken sixty-year-old wooden cross lying askew on the ground belongs to the grave of a poor man and was blown to the spot where it now sits, from whence no one knows.

In old graveyards, vaults belonging to well-off families are common. These burial chambers contain family members spanning generations, all together again, as it were, in privacy. Vaults are not common anymore. There aren't any in Saint Brendan's; the souls buried there share the open ground with all and sundry, lying side by side and finding commonality in the clay. An interesting thought, if one was predisposed to such thinking, is that we know not who will lie beside us in the earth. Will it be friend or foe? My mother is buried in a plot neighbouring a long-time friend of hers in life. A graveyard is a great equaliser; all of its occupants have equal serenity. One is interred today not knowing who will end up beside one tomorrow, but the newcomer may be assured that all will get equal measure of sunshine from that day forth.

> At the blueness of the skies and in the warmth of summer, we remember them.
>
> Sylvan Kamens and Rabbi Jack Reimer

* Cill Bhreac (Kilbrack) burial ground, at another location in the townland of Milltown, west of Saint Brendan's Cemetery, has a cross-inscribed stone from antiquity. Up until the nineteenth century this site was also a burial ground for unbaptised children.

NINE

People, Mungo and Lingo

All of the children in our house had a family nickname. These names were seldom known in the world outside our door; some were affectionate in intent and others were born out of a row and used to rankle. In a family of ten children living in a confined space, clashes inevitably materialised. If any child was perceived as getting preferential treatment from one quarter, a concomitant backlash was inevitable from another. The nicknames within the home would never be revealed outside the circle of family; that was an unwritten code. On the street, everyone was fair game for a nickname, one that had no bearing on the home name. Many managed to escape a moniker, even those that were proficient themselves at the naming game. The street names seldom represented kindly forbearance; they inclined to be derogatory and were rarely designed to make anybody feel good.

The double-barrel names (not quite nicknames), like Mike Daneen, Katie Sarah, Jack Thomas and Skocky Jim, are common in small towns where several versions of a surname exist. It is common for a nickname to span generations; the 'Talls' was a name attributed to a family whose members were renowned for their physical stature. In a particular family, the children were known by their mother's maiden name because of the proliferation of the father's surname in the area. An O'Connor man, a postman who also operated a hackney service, was known as 'The Post'. A local character known for his humorous malapropisms was asked by one of his cronies how he had arrived at a football match in Tralee ahead of the crowd. 'I came by Post' was the reply. My godfather (my father's best friend) was 'Small Georgie'; as it happens there was also another version called 'Big Georgie' who was 'Small Georgie's' uncle. In later years, 'Small Georgie' grew up to be a bigger man.

Some nicknames are born right in front of you, like 'Sam', a name given to a young man because of his constant humming and singing of 'Goodbye Sam, Hello Samantha', a song made famous by Cliff Richard in 1970. 'Chopper' was named after a character in *Chips*, a TV series in the 1980s where motorbike (chopper) cops wore black leather jackets, as our local 'Chopper' did. Kevin, known as 'Hustler', was named after the famous Paul Newman film because of his prowess at playing snooker.

A townsman (another O'Connor) who transported films on his bike in the 1960s to rural Irish-speaking parts of the peninsula had the nickname 'Highfill', which came about because when he ordered stout in a pub, he indicated the volume by keeping his hands vertically apart to indicate the height of a pint – high fill, not a medium fill.

'The Kerryman', from John Street, was generally the bearer of all the latest news; the modern version is a young man known as 'Charlie Bird'. A kindly man in Green Street was known as Maidhcín 'Fuacht' (cold, in Irish) perhaps because he felt the cold easily. Maidhcín's personality was warm and he would often entertain customers and passers-by in his shoemaking shop. At the lower end of Green Street, Jack 'Neddy' (O'Connors abound), an accomplished carpenter-joiner, plied his trade and was part of a quartet of skilled craftsmen (O'Shea, Moriarty, Boland) that rounded the corner onto Holyground.

In Milltown, Dingle, a village of several homesteads in the early twentieth century, there were two kings and a queen reigning at the same time, as one of my neighbours, Edwin, once put it. The village was made up of an eclectic range of characters and one, who was noted for his enterprising stunts, tried his hand at forging a number of florins (two-shilling silver coins), a name taken from a gold coin first struck in Florence. Following that industry, Edwin proclaimed that the Kingdom of Milltown also had its own mint. When the forged lead coin dulled with exposure to the atmosphere, the game was up and the industry closed down. Speaking of royalty, a prince (from a separate kingdom) also resides in the town.

The 'Midnight Postman' was a curiosity for a time in the 1950s. He was a man from Goat Street who would deliver anonymous, accusatory handwritten missives in the dark of night through the letterboxes of neighbours and people of the town with whom he had issue. Another, and more benign, series of letters which were posted to a selection of people circa the mid-1970s came in the form of certificates which deemed the recipients to be award winners in their area of expertise. It was around the time that a local woman won the North Munster regional final of the Housewife of the Year competition.

Every town has a selection of characters that leave an imprint on the place where they live. These are men and women who walk the streets daily, who frequent the pubs and shops, and whose absence on a given day from the social collage would be noticed and a cause for concern. This humanity of characters blend with the regular Joes and Marys to give the town its uniqueness, a brand of its own. Inevitably there will be a spattering of nicknames, some earned and more handed down, in this bunch of stand-out personalities. These include the woman who dresses colourfully and breezes around the town every day and finds the time to stop and chat jovially with people of all ages; Noel, the nonagenarian who takes a daily constitutional and holds his clinic (as he describes it) on a bench on Main Street where others who are doing the daily circuit sit and join him for discourse on the life of the town and Kerry football – no appointment needed! Noel has a vast repository of knowledge and has been a generous contributor to my writings. He was a newspaper boy in Dingle in his youth and can name the residents and businesses that existed in the town (door by door, street by street) when he was a teenager. In recent years, Noel climbed Mount Brandon.

Another daily 'meet' is with a man who voluntarily assists the new construction undertakings in the streets

– directing traffic, strategically placing signs and cones to ensure that the flow of Dingle commerce is least interrupted. Paddy Lambe (now deceased), a returned native and a repository of the town's old history, was an interesting storyteller. Many of his yarns would be delivered with a mischievous glint. Paddy was a fixture in the palette that added colour and individuality to the streets. The pièce de résistance was Denis (now deceased), who possessed a sharpness of wit and a delivery that was always on the mark. His barbs were mostly aimed for fun but occasionally to make a political statement on issues of the day. Denis had a famous nickname that belied his long blonde hair and fair completion – locals will know this one well.

Maggie Brown, from John Street, made dolls out of scallop shells. The painted shells were used to replicate wide flowing dresses on the dolls while a smaller cockle shell was used as an accessory, such as a handbag. This was an original and ingenious idea which would be hugely popular with today's tourists. Maggie's dolls, which became popular as wedding gifts, still adorn mantle pieces around West Kerry but, sadly, are getting harder to find. Maggie's brother, Johnny, was a famous local tin whistle player.

Patrick Cronesberry was a distinctive personality. People would gravitate to him for entertainment as he was a great harmonica player and a lover of the blues. Patrick had swagger and a sense of swing, always imbuing his stories with a colourful tint. His father, Jim, came to Dingle after the First World War and exhibited professionalism playing the big drum in the Goat Street marching band. The attendant sideshow of launching his sticks in the air and retrieving them with pin-point accuracy while on the move was remarkable. Jim was also the town crier in Dingle in the early 1950s.

Patrick had two brothers, John and Henry, and a sister, Mary Ellen, who was, to put it mildly, strongly vocal with her retorts. Patrick and Mary Ellen were famous for their jiving double act in the Phoenix Cinema on dance nights. Henry had his own blend of repartee and was always interesting to chat to. The Cronesberry family and name are gone from Dingle; all are buried in one large grave with an unsecured small plastic sign at the base of an uninscribed concrete cross. The family left an imprint in the town (in my time, in the 1960s and 1970s) and are seldom talked of these days apart from during occasional reminiscences of the good ol' days.

Poggin's (Griffin's) pub on Strand Street (once known a Jackie Nell's) was run by Bob, a well-known streetside character who also set up an outside stall where she sold fresh fish. Tig an Dearmad (house of the forgotten thing) was the last-stop shop on the way west out of town where shoppers stopped for things they had forgotten 'over town'. Kate Jimeen (Griffin) owned and ran the business which was located beside Milltown bridge. The Club, in the Mall, was a pub presided over by an engaging woman named Madge. Here, a regular group of 'clubbers' enjoyed hospitality and jovial repartee with the owner. Foxy John's, a pub which doubles as a hardware shop, is regularly sought out by tourists looking to soak in its quaintness.

Porter is served on the left while, across the floor, rows of shelves containing mouse traps, padlocks and shooting bolts abound. The same pub is also known locally as the University, named for the diverse range of topics discussed there by the knowledgeable clientele that frequent the premises.

The Hole-in-the-Wall was a small pub at the bottom of Main Street, named for its hole in the back wall through which pints would be served to customers in the yard. It was a great gathering place for the Quay Wrenboys on St Stephen's Day. A select group would have it pencilled-in on the lead-up so they could sing their once yearly rendition of their favourite songs. Choruses from 'Brennan on the Moor' and 'The Black Velvet Band' would draw in more to the already chock-a-block floor. A friendly character called The Farmer (who was a fisherman) often obliged with his favourite, 'It was down in the town of old Bantry'. Paguine (O'Flaherty) was historically the owner of Dingle's famous Ua Flaithbheartaigh pub which is one of Dingle's famous traditional Irish music pubs.

Bawn's pub was owned by Paddy Bawn Brosnan, also known as the Gov, who was a fisherman and a famous Kerry footballer. The 'H' of the previous owners, the Houlihan family (who provided electric light to Dingle in the early twentieth century), was inlaid in the terrazzo floor of the porch. Paddy's brothers, Timineen 'Deas' and Mickey Gerard, were a regular fixture around the Quay and the boats. Fishermen were noted for having nicknames and for the invention of same. Another Brosnan fisherman was called 'Waistcoat'. In the fishing fraternity, the surnames

Brosnan, Flaherty, Flannery, Graham, Devane, Sheehy, and O'Connor were prolific, and the bearers obviously needed alternate means of identification. One fisherman skipper found a novel way around the confusion of names and decided to call everybody on board his boat 'John'.

A popular man in the Quay was Paddy 'Ollie' Brosnan. Paddy supplied oil (diesel fuel) to the fishing boats for many decades. Johnny 'Ate-a-Bite', from the upper end of town, was known for calling into neighbour's houses at dinnertime whereupon he would be asked, 'Will you ate a bite?' Johnny 'Peep-out' is self-explanatory. 'Tom the Boy' lived at and presided over the Brewery fair field at the Spa Road. 'Chocolates', O'Connor's shop at Bridge House, got the name because of the popular range of sweets and chocolates it carried. In the female set, 'Pepper' and 'Salt' (one fair and one grey) were a couple of ladies that walked together on Sundays.

Patcheen, Micheáleen, Seamuseen, Seáneen and the like are diminutives (though longer in spelling) of the lead name; the 'een' can sometimes be derogatory and often attributed to crafty know-alls by those who might want to begrudge. More commonly, the 'een' is used to identify the offspring, like Thomaseen, son of Thomas.

During my time as an apprentice shipwright in Dingle Boatyard, I worked alongside an assortment of characters some of whom guided my young mind in directions beyond perfecting the use of an adze or making a spiling for a plank which would eventually wrap around a boat's hull. The workforce included an array of skilled craftsmen and a troupe of ancillary workers, all of whom were necessary to effect the building of a wooden fishing boat from keel to truck. While a plank was cooking in the steam box and the preparatory clamps lay waiting to coax the new addition of a thirty-five-foot-long slab of larch to its resting place, a brief lull would ensue before the frenetic activity and trongalum (there's a word!) of getting the plank to its destination while it was hot.

It was in lulls like these that yarns would be told amongst the waiting group. Paudie was keeper of the saws used in the machinery workshop; the bandsaw blades needed constant sharpening after hours of slicing through four-inch slabs of oak. The circuitous length of a bandsaw could be about twenty feet long and have more than a hundred and fifty teeth that required setting and sharpening on a regular basis. Paudie, while undertaking this work, managed to do it in tandem with yarn spinning and offering witticisms to neighbouring craftsmen on the bench he shared. Paudie and I would meet during the working day and we shared the latest yarn or joke doing the rounds. Our foreman, a kindly man called John, on coming upon us would warn that he would have to find a way to separate us. Paudie would usually finish his story by leaning closer with a whisper when the punchline was at hand – especially if the denouement was risqué.

Maidhc-an-adhmad (O'Sullivan), a teacher and principal in the Technical School, got the name no doubt because he was a teacher of woodwork. A fisherman and later a boatyard worker whom I worked with was called 'Babs'; this name perhaps has its origin in the word baby. 'Mike the Lady' was in the O'Connor ancestry and named for his neatness and deftness at sowing and housekeeping. Two people got the names 'Klondike' and 'Dawson' after being involved in the Dawson City/Klondike gold rush. Mikie the 'Yank' O'Connor' (cousin of the author) was so named after returning from an extended stay in America. People didn't need to travel to faraway destinations to acquire a nickname. The very affable 'Moran from Ballinaboula' is an example. The 'Genius' is attributed to a man who did game hunting and is famous for the pronouncement, 'In the afternoon, I am going shooting peasants'. Here, the appellation speaks for itself. The world of birds (as nicknames) is well represented, too, several species are found within the population.

Brogeen, Pudsy and Puppy are among names from my youth when friendly rivalry existed between different streets in the town when it came to local GAA football competitions, the Wren's Day marching bands, and having the biggest bonfire on St John's Eve. The subtitle chosen for this work (eggs and rashers, hay and oats), comes from rhyming slang of the time when it was common, especially between the Quay boys (Na Piarsaigh) and the streets up town including John Street (Sráid Eoin) and Goat Street to engage in needling and taunting when it came to games of one-upmanship. The full rendering goes: 'Eggs and rashers for the Quay slashers, hay and oats for the Goat Street goats.'

The verse is curious and off-cue in one particular aspect – it implies that people from the Quay ate better (and were better-off) than their uptown counterparts when, in actuality, all were in the same boat. Today, the verse is a metaphor for the changing times of the town where now all have the wherewithal to eat eggs and rashers. The times when these friendly rivalries occurred, and the accompanying sing-song verses that were born with them, give a snapshot of a town living on its own wit and resources, a town which possessed an intrinsic character of its own that has now vanished.

While nicknames can be fun and borne like a badge of honour, some have high potency and are carried with distaste and anger, and the targeted bearers often get hassled more because of the inevitable rise in ire which ensues following the name-calling. The old adage 'Sticks and stones may break my bones but words can never hurt me' as a defence against name-calling never works. Hurt, often hidden hurt, occurs, especially at a young, immature age where the child is not even aware of the origin of the family nickname which may be delivered to unsettle, to rise and to provoke a response. Some such names exist in the town and none was more potent than that which I described in an earlier publication (*Children of the Shore*) about growing up in Dingle concerning a family that lived beside the Barrack Height in the 1960s. I will not, out of respect and compassion for the family involved that suffered ongoing torture at the hands of school bullies, elaborate further on that troublesome saga which is part of the history of Dingle.

As well as having a unique set of names and characters, a town will have words and phrases endemic to it alone; the parlance found on the street stems from occupations and situations common to the town. Dingle, being a fishing town and historically a port that traded with Spain, has nautical lingo that has seeped into common use, including words that would not be found in non-coastal regions. The most common of these is the word 'gallus'. Onboard fishing boats a steel structure called a gallows, which looks like an inverted U and leans out over the gunnel, is used with a swivelled block attached on top to guide the cables from the trawl inboard to the deck of the boat. The gallows (a plural-only word), pronounced gallus, is positioned aft on the vessel, along with a partner forward on the same side. Considerable tongue-twisting ensues when one tries to navigate a conversation when more than one of these items is being discussed.

The gallus is ungainly looking compared to the otherwise clean lines of the hull construct, deck and rigging. With its off-plumb slant it looks as if it was fitted badly, in other words it looks 'gallus' or, depending on pronunciation, 'gallas'. Thus, 'gallus', the oft-used term in Dingle, being a town that built fishing boats, is used to describe something that is 'out of true', trí na chéile, all over the place, fit to fall down. A term as gaeilge that fits is 'go hainnis', meaning 'to cut a poor figure'. The word gallus is explained in some dictionaries as being a variant of gallows, meaning 'fit for the gallows'. Some examples include, 'I was at the dance last night and the music was gallus'; 'the weather is gallus'; 'yer man is gallus'.

Speaking of words where their plurals lend to discombobulation, a tailor's goose was a clothes iron so named because of its curved, goose-like handle. I heard an anecdote about a neighbouring tailor who was ordering one from a catalogue (those were the days) and who was asked by a fellow tailor to order one for him as well. This led to bewilderment when the letter ordering the items was being penned; the writer thought that asking for two tailor's gooses or two tailor's geese didn't sound right and decided to go for 'will you send me on a tailor's goose, please, and while you are at it, include a second one'.

Such is the way of words and phrases that can attach to a town or locality. In general, a lexicon of nautical terms has permeated common usage on land, and terms like 'three sheets to the wind' and the 'cut of his jib' are found in use in sailing/fishing ports. If someone in an inland town uses the term chock-a-block, they probably will not know the origin of the term, which comes from blocks (wooden blocks with a swivel encased) on the rigging of a sailing ship. When two blocks meet, no further movement of the item being hoisted is possible.

It is inevitable that the nautical world would leave its mark on the town which has produced its share of colourful characters through the years, many of whom were steeped in the salt of the sea. Local man David Donegan would describe things with a nautical bent: his floor was a deck; a wall opening was a hatch; a kitchen was a galley. A term used by fishermen is 'able', as in able-seaman, fit for purpose. A term passed from sea to land is 'hand' – give me a hand, lend a hand. Onboard sailing ships, when sailors climbed the rigging to unfurl or reduce a sail, they were operating under the rule that one hand was for the ship and the other for themselves to ensure their safety, thus, the term 'deckhand'. A deckhand who shirked his duties was put 'swinging the lead' – dropping a lump of lead attached to a line (lanyard) to determine the depth of water; the depths were known as soundings.

Being sunk to the gunnels (the edge of the deck on a boat) means you are drunk and in danger of going under; gimballed describes a similar condition. In a storm, no matter how the boat sways and pitches, certain objects (like a compass and a stove) manage to stay upright due to a fitting (a gimbal) which allows the fitment to maintain its normal level orientation. Having your bearings on a walk home from the pub means you know where you are going. Fisherfolk use terms at home which are compass-related: the fridge is west of the dresser; the south bedroom is warmer; the washstand is east of the fireplace. Seeing that a large number of local people have seafaring folk in their ancestry, it is common to hear them refer to the south shore, over east, back west, the near ground (when they take a drink in a pub close to home).

While the vocabulary of the area is spattered with imported 'isms', there are homegrown terms like 'mungo' that are common only to Dingle. The term is an amalgam of money and go – moneygo/mungo meaning money to go – to the cinema, the dance, the concert. (Note: mongo is currency, a sub-unit of the Mongolian tugrik.) The money in question was that acquired from selling a 'strap of fish' (a handful of fish with a cord threaded through the gills and the mouth), given over free from the boats to local youths for their families after landing and sold to a local, small-time fish buyer.

Young boys would voluntarily help at the quayside with the unloading of fish boxes from the boats when they landed their catch in the hope of gaining favour from the skippers and reimbursement in the form of mungo. The mungo was part of the boat's catch kept back from the main fish buyer and used for extraneous purposes. In my days of scrounging for the price of admission to the cinema, the buyer of my mungo was Timmy Griffin. One and three (as it was called) was the price of the cinema ticket in the early 1960s, one shilling and three pence, fifteen pennies of which there were two hundred and forty in an Irish pound. There was gathering in fifteen pennies in those times.

My father would regularly use the term 'put the tin hat on it' and, if damage was done, 'ye'd break iron'. I also heard him say, when describing somebody that was in a hurry, 'he was going like the quarter to one' – a possible reference to the 12.45 train that left Dingle in a hurry with fish to catch the Tralee train for onward transport. In the pubs, a Castleisland 'medjum' (medium) was a half-pint measure, plus a bit extra, put into a pint glass. Following a couple of those, a patron might be heard saying he was going to the 'heads'– the toilet to landlubbers – or the 'jacks'. A 'Jack Tar' was a common slang name for a sailor aboard sailing ships, as was a 'limey' (an English term) due to sailors' dependence on citrus fruits to ward off scurvy.

'Giobals' (another one of those plural-only words) is a hard one to pin down. It appears in an Irish dictionary with the meaning that clothes are in rags or tatters. In English, it can refer to odds and ends of worn clothing trailing about in an untidy fashion, and to similar disarray found in domestic situations where items hang about the house as if looking for a home; things that need to be trimmed may sum it up.

Smashin (without the 'g' at the end) comes, I am reliably told by a Gaeilgeoir, from the Irish phrase, 'is maith sin' meaning, 'that is good'. The confluence of the Irish and English languages as happens in a town like Dingle lends to an interesting mix of words and phraseologies. A well-known former television continuity announcer from Dingle, Máire de Barra, used to close down the night on RTÉ with the words, 'tá sé in ám soip', meaning time for the sop of hay (to lie down on). A similar reference, of Danish origin, 'having a kip', also means having a lie down, kip being a word for animal hide which was used on the ground as a mattress.

Nowadays, the language used is changing due to the proliferation of foreign languages heard in the town. Americanisms have been around for a while. 'Have a nice day' and 'have a good one' are widely used by people working in the shops and hospitality service. And the overuse of the word 'like', especially when a group of girls get together is awesome! 'Hey bro!' uttered by males who address you for the first time, is one of the newer ones. Imported modern-speak has permeated the vernacular and 'tóg bog é', 'slán abhaile', 'conas tá an misneach?' are seldom heard anymore. Workers in the town during the tourist season are welcoming but many struggle with English and the native language is a tough ask of them.

Some prefer not to speak at all for fear of misuse and embarrassment.

Dingle, as part of a Gaeltacht area, has a unique opportunity to offer the visitor something exceptional, something not found in other tourist towns around the coast – its own language, which is seldom heard in the town during the tourist season. In the past, the Irish language was brought to town on fair days and creamery days and could be heard in the shops and pubs when the general trading in the town took place. The local business owners welcomed their customers from the hinterland and enjoyed banter with them in the native tongue. The main business of the town now is tourism and the Irish language is not the language of tourism.

Appendix 1

The following is a timeline of Dingle and its people from 1950 to 2025.

1950 Cill Breac cemetery, now known as Saint Brendan's Cemetery, Milltown, opens. Georgina Benner, Main Street, is the first interred in its grounds.

1950 Dingle Regatta results: Sculling Race, 1. Michael Flannery. 2. David Donegan, 3. Noel Brosnan. Punt Race Snr, 1. T. Brosnan crew. 2. Ml. Moriarty crew. 3. Mce. Moore crew.

1951 Pádraig Ó Siochfhradha (pen name An Seabhac) is nominated by the Taoiseach to the 7th Seanad. Ó Siochfhradha was also nominated to the 5th Seanad in 1944.

1952 Dingle Bórd Iascaigh Mhara Boatyard opens.

1952 Paddy Bawn Brosnan has his last appearance in the All-Ireland Football Championship in the Munster Final between Kerry and Cork. Paddy Bawn won All-Ireland football medals in 1940, 1941 and 1946.

1953 Last journey of the Tralee-Dingle train.

1953 Paudie Fitzgerald competes in the Rás Tailteann (see entry for 1956).

1953 The last remaining inhabitants of the Blasket Islands are permanently evacuated to the mainland and disembark at Dingle pier from the *St Lawrence O'Toole* fishing boat, owned by John Brosnan, Strand Street.

1953 *Ros Glas*, the first boat built there, launches from Dingle Boatyard.

1955 The Phoenix Cinema, owned for more than three decades by the Houlihan family, is bought by John A. Moore.

1956 Paudie Fitzgerald wins two stages and the overall prize in the Rás Tailteann.

1957 Saint Mary's Dramatic Society, Dingle, performs *Shadow and Substance* in the Phoenix Cinema. Members of the committee of the society in the 1950s include Henry O'Shea, Theresa Comyn, John Boyd, Mrs J. Gibbons, M. Quirque. N. Mahony.

1957 Marian Park in Dingle, having twenty-five houses, opens.

1958 Blasket Island writer, Peig Sayers, dies in St Elizabeth's Hospital, Dingle, aged eighty-six.

1959 Moran's Garage opens on Green Street.

1960 Dingle hosts the first national sea angling competition.

1960 *The Story of the Tralee & Dingle Railway* is published by Patrick B. Whitehouse.

1961 Actress Siobhán McKenna, while filming *The Playboy of the Western World* at Inch, attends a prize-giving in the Phoenix Cinema.

1962 Eileen Garvey, Marian Park, is selected as the Kerry Rose for the International Rose of Tralee competition.

1963 Unveiling of memorial in The Mall, Dingle, to honour West Kerry's republican dead.

1963 Turbett's Amusements arrive in Dingle for the first time.

1963 Brother and sister Patrick and Mary Ellen Cronesberry win a 'twist' competition in the Phoenix Cinema.

1964 Dingle Fisherman's Co-Operative Society has its first annual general meeting.

1964 Dingle Regatta, Dingle Races, Dingle Carnival and Sea Angling Festival arc combined as one festival event. Dingle Regatta has a seine boat race under the stewardship of Paddy Bawn Brosnan.

1965 Greaney's Restaurant opens at Holyground.

1965 The Petsounds, Kerry's first boy band, is formed in Dingle. The group is made up of Jimmy Flannery (Ashmount Terrace), Seán A. O'Connor (Upper Main Street), John O'Connor (The Wood) and Brian Scanlon (Chapel Lane).

1965 The first West Kerry Agricultural Show is held in the sports field. Paddy Browne, Burnham, is honorary secretary of the organising committee and the bulwark of the show.

1965/66 Renovation of St Mary's Church takes place; new copper roof and interior alterations; the removal of granite pillars and gothic arches and replacement of same with iron girders forms part of the work.

1966 Michael Begley is elected chairman of Kerry County Council.

1967 President Éamon de Valera travels to Dingle for the commemoration of the fiftieth anniversary of the death of Kerry patriot, Tomás Ághas.

1967/68 Coast guard building is knocked; the Dingle Skellig Hotel is built.

1968 P&T Fitzgerald Hardware opens after the purchase of Latchford's shop on Main Street.

1968 Oscar-winning actor Gregory Peck visits his West Kerry cousins.

1968 Blasket Seafoods opens at The Wood, Dingle, under the management of Micheál Keane.

1969 Michael Begley is elected TD and serves the Kerry South constituency until 1989.

1969 *Santa Maria de la Rosa* wreck found. The Spanish Armada vessel sank in the Blasket Sound in 1588.

1969 The Western Ballroom opens, later evolving into the Hillgrove Hotel.

1969 *Ryan's Daughter* begins filming.

1970 Dingle group travels to London for the premiere screening of *Ryan's Daughter.*

1970 Dingle Badminton Club reopens in the Western Ballroom after a lapse of more than twenty years.

1970 Mazzarello O'Flaherty and Eithne O'Flaherty release the single 'Tomorrow Today Will Be Yesterday'.

1970 Mazzarello O'Flaherty wins the Slógadh 70 solo singing competition.

1970 Dingle Chamber of Commerce is formed. Steering committee: chair John McMahon; hon. sec. Peter J. Callery; treasurer Jack Walsh.

1970 Dana, following her Eurovision win, sings 'All Kinds of Everything' for over a thousand people in the Phoenix Cinema (March 30th).

1970 New 75ft fishing boat, *Star Immaculate*, owned by Paddy Flannery, arrives.

1971 Dingle wins the Junior Gaelic Football County Championship.

1971 Máire de Barra begins working with RTÉ and becomes a familiar face as a continuity announcer on RTÉ television, from 1972 to 1990.

1972 Moran's Garage opens for business on the Mail Road.

1972 Raidió na Gaeltachta goes on air.

1973 Seán O'Connor (Ó Conchubhair), Upper Main Street, is appointed secretary of the Department of Education; retires from the Department in 1975 and becomes chairman of the Higher Education Authority.

1973 Official opening of Neodata.

1973 *Today Show* American production team film travelogue in Dingle for American television.

1973 Dingle Boatyard gets a new boatshed.

1973 Vera O'Keeffe wins the North Munster regional final of the 'Housewife of the Year' competition.

1974 The *Star Immaculate* fishing boat is driven ashore at the upper slip during a storm. The sea wall along Strand Street, west of the pier, is also knocked by the storm.

1974 Doyle's Seafood Restaurant opens on John Street.

1974 Tower removed from St James' Church for safety reasons.

1974 President of Ireland, Erskine Childers, arrives on a state visit to Dingle for the rededication of the Church of Ireland parish church of St James' Church.

1974 P&T Fitzgerald opens for business in the former Atkin's shop on Main Street.

1974 Dingle Mart is founded.

1974 Kerry Group takes over Dingle Creamery.

1975 Mark Kerry opens the Armada Restaurant on Strand Street.

1976 Tim Severin and the Brendan Voyage crew depart from Brandon Creek.

1979 Bord Iascaigh Mhara Boatyard closes and switches to the private sector; reopens as Dingle Boats Teoranta, under the ownership of Joe O'Boyle.

1979 Tom Fitzgerald is elected to Kerry County Council, serving until 1985.

1979 An Café Liteartha opens in Dygate Street.

1980 The Phoenix Cinema, under the new ownership of Michael Francie O'Sullivan and with extensive modernisation, opens with *Kramer vs Kramer.*

1980 T. P. O'Conchúir becomes a member of the first board of Údarás na Gaeltachta.

1981 Dingle's largest industry, Neodata, closes.

1981 Tom Fitzgerald is elected senator (Agriculture Panel), serving for thirteen years in Seanad Éireann, in the 15th, 16th, 18th, 19th, 20th and 21st Seanads.

1981 Dingle Boats Teoranta launches the 73ft fishing vessel, *Ronan Padraig*. Michael Moynihan, TD, attends the ceremony.

1981 Brian de Staic, jeweller, sets up business in Dingle.

1981 Michael Begley, TD, is appointed Minister of State at the Department of Trade, Commerce and Tourism (1981–1982).

1982 The *Ranga* cargo ship runs aground near Dunmore Head.

1982 Publishing company Brandon Books launches in Dingle.

1982 The post office on Strand Street closes and moves to James Shea's on Upper Main Street.

1983 Arrival of Fungie, the Dingle dolphin.

1983 *Green and Gold – The Wrenboys of Dingle* is published by Steve MacDonogh.

1983 Dingle telephone exchange (a 24/7 service) closes. Six operators worked together at a given shift. Fifteen operators were on the full team.

1984 First St Brendan Festival is held in Dingle and runs until 1995.

1984 Dingle Technical School closes.

1984 Fleadh Cheoil Chiarraí held in Dingle; The Chieftains top the list of musicians attending.

1984 Local group Slaudeen launch the album, *Forever by Dingle Shore.*

1985 Fr Jack McKenna publishes the book, *Dingle*, outlining a history of the town spanning several centuries.

1985 Renowned Gaelic Games broadcaster Micheál Ó Muircheartaigh, from Dún Síon, becomes RTÉ's premier radio sports commentator. After six decades of Gaelic Games commentary, Micheal retires in 2010.

1986 Claire Thompson is selected as the Kerry Rose for the International Rose of Tralee competition.

1987 St James' Church on Main Street gets a new gothic front door, constructed by J. O'Connor.

1987 Cumann Bádóirí Naomh Bhréanainn (Dingle Sailing Club) is launched at the Rocket House. Committee: John O'Connor, John Greaney, Eileen Galvin, Dr Finbar O'Shea.

1987 Joe O'Toole is elected senator.

1988 Ignatius and Máiréad O'Connor open their pub, Tig Shiobháin, in Ballyferriter.

1990 Dingle Credit Union is founded.

1990 Máire de Barra, former continuity announcer with RTÉ, opens Maire de Barra's (formerly Mikie Long's) pub on the Quay.

1990 Lord Baker's Restaurant opens in Dingle under the co-ownership of John Moriarty and Tommy McCarthy.

1990 *The Sea Heritage of Dingle* is published by Pádraig Long.

1990 The craft village, Ceardlann na Coille, The Wood, is opened by Taoiseach Charles Haughey.

1990 Joe O'Toole is appointed general secretary of the Irish National Teachers Organisation. He serves until 2001.

1991 Scenes for *Far and Away* are shot in the peninsula. Actor Tom Cruise living locally.

1991 The Marina Inn opens on Strand Street. Formerly known as Sheehy's Pub and Bibit's. The new owners are Jackie and Marguerite Kavanagh.

1991 Dingle Citizens Group is formed. A march takes place from the pier in Dingle to the Rocket House in opposition to plans by the Skellig Hotel to reclaim twenty-two acres from Dingle harbour to build a marina and onshore buildings/facilities.

1992 Opposition to the Skellig marina development continues. Protest march held in Dublin to the office of the Department of the Marine.

1992 Following extensive harbour works, which include harbour dredging and the building of a breakwater, the Dingle marina, located to the west of Dingle pier, opens to visitors.

1992 On regatta day in Dingle (August 16th), *The Sunday Business Post* carries the headline: *EXCLUSIVE: fuel contaminated as marina row raged on.*

1992 On October 12th, the Skellig Hotel abandon plans to build a marina in Dingle harbour.

1992 The Quay Wren is resurrected after a long absence. D. Donegan, J. O'Connor, N. Brosnan and J. Griffin are part of the new committee.

1992 Tom Fox publishes *Dingle Down the Years – A Collection of Old Photographs*. In 1996, Tom publishes *A Second Collection of Old Photographs*. In 2003, he publishes *A Third Collection of Old Photographs*.

1993 Cumann Bádóiri Naomh Bhréanainn (Dingle Sailing Club) and the National Yacht Club, Dún Laoghaire, are joint winners of the sailing club of the year award following the launch of the Dún Laoghaire/Dingle Yacht Race.

1993 A planning application is lodged for a hotel on the boatyard site on the seafront. Dingle Boatyard closes after forty years in business.

1993 *The Dingle Peninsula – History, Folklore, Archaeology* is published by Steve MacDonogh.

1993 Sciuird Archaeological Tours begin operating throughout the peninsula.

1994 First Féile na Bealtaine is held in Dingle.

1995 John Benny Moriarty opens An Conair bar on Spa Road.

1996 Danno's Bar and Restaurant opens on Strand Street. Danno O'Keeffe was previously the manager of Benner's Hotel in Dingle.

1996 Dingle Oceanworld/Mara Beo opens.

1996 Cháirde Choláiste Íde becomes the management body of Coláiste Íde following the withdrawal of the Mercy Sisters who ran the girls' school since 1927.

1997 Orchard Lane, new street off Main Street, opens.

1997 Tom Fox publishes *Ancient Town of High Renown – Rhymes and Poems from Dingle Town and Peninsula.*

1998 Tom Fox publishes *Dingle in the Fifties – The Home Movies of James C. Houlihan* (VHS tape).

1998 Tourist office at the Quay officially opens on the site of the iconic gas shed, historically the store for the gas which fuelled the gas lamps on the pier and the meeting place for shore-bound fisherman for a century.

1998 An Díseart Institute of Irish Spirituality and Culture is founded.

1998 Micheál O'Coileán is appointed Environmental Awareness Officer to Kerry County Council and serves until 2017.

1999 Newly-built Dingle Marina Centre houses the sailing, rowing and diving clubs and provides showers and toilets for visiting sailors.

1999 John O'Connor and Liam Long sail clockwise around Ireland in the yacht *Eibhlís*.

1999 Cumann Rugbaí Corcha Dhuibhne is founded.
1999 Séamus Cosaí Fitzgerald is elected to Kerry County Council.
2000 An Gáirdín Mhuire, West Kerry Care of the Aged Centre, opens on Green Street. Since the mid-1960s, the local care of the aged committee have provided for the needs of senior citizens in Dingle.
2000 Domhnal Ó Loingsigh is appointed president of the Irish National Teachers Organisation.
2000 Murphy's Ice Cream opens in Dingle.
2001 *Other Voices'* first event takes place in St James' Church.
2001 Out of the Blue fish-only restaurant opens.
2001 Le Figaro yacht race comes to Dingle. It comes again in 2003, 2006 and 2009.
2002 John Benny's pub opens on Strand Street; formerly Máire de Barra's, historically Mikie Long's.
2003 Sacred Heart University, Connecticut, USA, opens a campus in Dingle.
2003 Dingle and Santa Barbara, California, sign a twinning charter.
2003 Udarás na Gaeltachta opens headquarters in Milltown, Dingle.
2003 Dingle Bay Hotel opens. Formerly known as Paudie's Bar/ Long's Restaurant. Historically known as Sonny Long's.
2003 Joe O'Toole publishes *Looking Under Stones: Roots, Family and a Dingle Childhood.*
2004 Dingle Historical Society hosts its first lecture.
2005 Dingle/Daingean Uí Chúis campaign begins following a decision by government to name all Gaeltacht towns on road signs (firstly) in the Irish language.
2005 A Dingle sign, in large, white Hollywood-style capitals, is erected on Cnoc a' Chairn.

2005 David Geaney wins his first World Championship title for Irish dancing. David goes on the win four further world titles in different categories over the years, in 2006, 2012, 2013 and 2014.

2006 Amy Winehouse sings at *Other Voices* in Dingle.

2006 Nuala Moore takes part in the Round Ireland Swim Relay; the circumnavigation is 830 miles long.

2007 Pobalscoil Chorca Dhuibhne controversy over its Irish-only policy; parents petition the Department of Education.

2007 The sailing ship *Jeanie Johnston* departs Dingle on a pilgrimage to Santiago de Compostela, Spain. A notable complement of local pilgrims is on the passenger manifest.

2007 First Dingle Food Festival takes place.

2007 An Daingean Fishery Harbour Centre is transferred to the Minister for Communication, Marine and Natural Resources.

2007 Colonel David Ashe, formerly of The Mall, Dingle, is promoted to Brigadier General (see entry for 2011).

2009 Dingle Cottages at The Wood celebrate 100 years.

2009 First Dingle Marathon held.

2009 Dingle group Lumiere is formed by vocalists Pauline Scanlon and Éilís Kennedy.

2009 West Kerry Live starts business in Hannah Rayel's, Main Street.

2009 An event to mark the four-hundred and eightieth anniversary of the signing of the Treaty of Dingle (between Ireland and Spain) is held by Dingle Historic Society.

2010 West Kerry Community Hospital opens on the Mail Road on land kindly donated by Shane and Máire O'Connor. The donation was described locally as a magnificent gesture. Official opening takes place in 2012 by Dr James Reilly, Minister for Health.

2011 Dingle band Walking on Cars forms.

2011 Dingle Brewing Company is launched on the site of the old Dingle creamery and produces Tom Crean's Fresh Irish Lager.

2011 Major General Dave Ashe, Deputy Chief of Staff (Support), retires from the Defence Forces.

2012 Dingle Distillery is launched on the site of the old Dingle mill at Milltown, historically a corn mill and later converted to a timber saw mill.

2012 Maritime Heritage Weekend launches to celebrate local man Mikey Long, an honorary member of the Institute of Biology Ireland.

2013 The Blow-Ins (a self-named duo) play their first Dingle gig in the Dingle Bay Hotel.

2013 Séamus Cosaí Fitzgerald is elected mayor of Kerry.

2013 Coláiste Íde is listed sixth in the *Sunday Times* league table of the nation's top schools.

2013 Dingle group Lumiere performs at Carnegie Hall, New York.

2013 As a member of the Bering Strait Swim relay, endurance swimmer Nuala Moore swims across the Bering Strait from Russia to the USA. In the following years, Nuala participates in endurance swimming competitions in Finland, Ireland, Argentina and Russia.

2014 John O'Connor publishes a sailing memoir, *More Than a Voyage*.

2014 Pobalscoil Chorca Dhuibhne are Hogan Cup winners, and again in 2015.

2015 Largest ship to dock in Dingle, *Wilson Dublin*, takes 3,500 tons of gravel from Lispole quarry to the UK.

2016 Carl O'Flaherty publishes *Dingle Before Fungie Came to Town*. In 2018, Carl publishes *Dingle People*.

2017 Thomas O'Callaghan records the CD, 'Dingle Bay'. In 2023, Thomas releases the album, *Outside the Box*.

2017 Pat Neligan publishes *The Knave of Trumps*.

2017 John O'Connor publishes *Craftsman Furniture from a Dingle Workshop*.

2017 John O'Connor publishes *Dingle Coastguard Station* (2017); *Boatbuilding in Dingle* (2018); *Phoenix Paradiso* (2019); *Ryan's Daughter in Dingle (*2020) in the magazine of the Kerry Archaeological and Historical Society.

2018 Dr Conor Brosnan publishes *Smuggling in Dingle in the Eighteenth and Nineteenth Centuries* in the magazine of the Kerry Archaeological and Historical Society.

2018 Dan Graham publishes *District Inspector Michael John Hunt of the Royal Irish Constabulary* (2018); *John Francis Marshall Miles, Dingle Doctor, Magistrate and Humanitarian 1847–1912* (2019); *Outpost of Empire – The Dingle Royal Constabulary Barracks, 1886–1922* (2019) in the magazine of the Kerry Archaeological and Historical Society.

2018 Nuala Moore completes the Meeting of the Oceans swim from the Pacific Ocean to the Atlantic Ocean in the Drake Passage off South America.

2019 Maxim O'Sullivan, The Wood, representing Pobalscoil Chorca Dhuibhne, wins the Ireland Junk Kouture award, with a cinematic theme design.

2019 The Ireland Coastal Rowing Championship finals are held in Dingle. The event is held again in 2023 and 2024.

2019 Dingle Literary Festival is founded.

2019 Breandán Fitzgerald is elected to Kerry County Council.

2020 Fungie, the Dingle dolphin, disappears.

2020 John O'Connor publishes *Children of the Shore.*

2020 *War in The West 1918–1923* is published by Noel Ó Murchú.

2020 Ted Creedon publishes *The Coast Guard on the Dingle Peninsula* in the magazine of the Kerry Archaeological and Historical Society.

2021 After existing for centuries serving as a store, a fisherman's co-op and an ice plant, the building locally known as the ice plant is demolished.

2021 After one hundred years of cinema, the Phoenix Cinema closes. The last picture show, *Parasite*, is screened in 2020.

2021 The Gregory Peck – Dingle Classic Film Society is founded.

2021 Dr Conor Brosnan and Kieran Murphy publish *Tralee Imports and Exports of Food through the Port of Tralee during the Great Famine* in the magazine of the Kerry Archaeological and Historical Society.

2021 Dingle jockey Jack Kennedy wins the Cheltenham Gold Cup on *Minella Indo.*

2021 Caroline (Danaher) Lynch sets up the Dingle Food Company; in 2022, Caroline wins the Local Food Hero award in Munster for sourcing local produce.

2022 Pat Lawless takes part in the round the world Golden Globe Race.

2022 Research vessel, *Tom Crean*, is commissioned in Dingle.

2022 Dr Conor Brosnan publishes *The Massacre at Dún an Óir, 1580* in the magazine of the Kerry Archaeological and Historical Society.

2023 WAVE (Wild Atlantic Virtual Experience) Dingle, opens at The Wood.

2023 Nuala Moore, endurance swimmer, publishes *Limitless – from Dingle to Cape Horn, finding my true north in the earth's vastest oceans.*

2024 *Dingle, Lispole, Fionntrá/Ventry* is published by Carl O'Flaherty.

2023 The Dingle Food Company wins the national catering service of the year award.

2024 John O'Connor publishes *Building the Tearaght Lighthouse* in the journal of the Kerry Archaeological and Historical Society.

2024 Dingle jockey Jack Kennedy is crowned champion jockey in Ireland at the end of the 2023/2024 season.

2024 Robert Brosnan is elected to Kerry County Council.

2024 First double-decker bus operates in Dingle.

2025 The Dingle Food Company wins the Munster catering service award for 2024 at the Irish Takeaway Awards.

2025 Dingle open-top tour bus begins operation.

2025 Sacred Heart University open its new campus at the former CBS site in Dingle.

2025 Rugbaí Chorca Dhuibhne are the Martin O'Sullivan Cup winners for the first time.

2025 John O'Connor publishes *Dingle Days – Eggs and Rashers, Hay and Oats.*

Appendix 2

Following is a list of businesses, large and small, existing in Dingle during the 1950s and onwards; some of the businesses included precede 1950; bed and breakfast/guesthouses are not included in the list except for historical context.

Cloosemore, Milltown

Barry – Jimmy – blacksmith.
[**Griffin** – John – garage. **Solar Beo** – Murphy – electrical/solar energy.]
Uí Fhlaithearta – petrol, grocery.
Milltown House – accommodation, falconry experience.
Pitch and Putt – J. O'Connor.
[**Latchford** – timber mill. **P&T Fitzgerald** – timber mill. **Dingle Distillery**.]
Griffin – Kate Jimeen's (Tig an Dearmad) – grocery, ice cream.

The Wood

de Staic – Brian – jeweller. Established in Dingle, 1981.

[**Ceardlann na Coille** – miscellaneous crafts/industries, including: **Maintín, Luibín, Seódóir an Daingean, Stephanie – Fiodóir, Nóinín – Ceard na mBláth, Bréidín, Dingle Linen, Bistro an Daingean, Dingle Chocolates, Cookery School.**]

Murphy – (last Cottage) – fish (scad), paraffin oil.

Lynch – Maurice and father, Patrick – tailors.

Murphy – Mary – paraffin oil.

ESB depot.

Kennedy – Minnie – small grocery.

O'Sullivan – Michael F. O'Sullivan – piggery. Hostel.

Fanning – **Sméara Dubha** – vegetarian restaurant.

Mace – Ireen – **Singing Salmon** – restaurant.

Begley – Michael/Bruiser – small grocery, curran tops.]

[**Keane** – **Blasket Seafoods** – **Ó Catháin Iasc Teo** – fish processing. **Wave Dingle. Fish Factory Restaurant.**]

Ó Catháin Iasc Teo – fish shop.

Strand Street, left-hand side, going east

•●•

Oceanworld – sea life – tourism. Formerly the site of Dingle Technical School. Craft shop, books.

[**Griffin** – John Poggin – small shop. Formerly McKenna's house. **Marina Hostel.**]

[**Savage** – Donal – doctor. **Sheehy** – (John) – accountant.]

Long – Mary Joe – hostel for cycling club. Now the 'Caladh Spáinneach', in recognition of the original (Dingle) Spanish pier which was situated opposite on the strand.

[**O'Sullivan** – Michael Francic – bought and sold periwinkles. Bicycle hire. **Waterfront Café. The Boatyard Restaurant.**]

[**O'Sullivan** – Michael Francie – milk deliveries, flour, grocery. **Cunningham** – cufflinks, crafts. **The Bay Restaurant**.]

Devane – Johnny, off Strand Street – shoemaker.

Out of the Blue – fish restaurant (originally the stable for Dolly, the milkman's horse).

[**McCarthy** – Michael, Jim Long's Lane – blacksmith. **Irish Adventures**.]

[**Flahive** – James – pub, shop. **Dingle Boat Tours**.]

[**Sheehy** – Bibit's – pub, kippered herring. **The Marina Inn** – J. and M. Kavanagh. Gavin O'Grady. J. Kavanagh.]

[**Long** – James – pub. S. Kennedy. **James Long's**.]

[**Long** – Michael, The Garraí – shipwright, builder of nobbies, at the rear of Harrington's Restaurant.]

O'Connor – Jimmy, The Garraí – shoemaker.

Brosnan – The Garraí – newsagents for the *Sunday Dispatch*, *Kerry Champion*, *Irish Press*.

[**American Express** – J. and R. Harrington – restaurant. Previously the harbour office. **Harringtons** – G. and E. Boyle – restaurant, takeaway. Established in 1979.]

[**Long** – Mikie – pub, paint, grocery (rations) for fishermen, fish merchant. **Máire de Barra's** – pub, restaurant. **John Benny's** – pub, restaurant.]

Griffin – Timmy, in Mikie Long's Lane – fish buyer/seller.

Kennedy – Jerry, in Mikie Long's Lane – cabinetmaker.

[**Ashe** – Alice and Mazie – pub, bakery, confectioners, coal merchant. The **Star Inn Bar** – Paddy and Martina Flannery. J. Flannery – leased. Walter Ferber – new owner. Mark Kerry – new owner. B. McKenna – new owner. **Armada Restaurant**, upstairs – T. Coffey. **Danno's Bar and Restaurant. Dingle Woollen Company. McCarthy** – crepes, coffee.]

[**Ashe** – originally a store for fishing gear; fish box repair by Captain (Flannery). **Asgard Restaurant** – T. and K.

Moynihan. **Armada Restaurant** – Mark Kerry. **Highways** – Michael O'Connor – grocery shop, ice cream. **Murphy's Ice Cream.**]

[**Brosnan** – Ina's – fish and chips. **Leac a Ré** – bookshop, gifts.]

[**Long** – Sonny – fish merchant, pub, confectionery, grocer. **Fish shop** – John Paul Flannery. **Long's Bar and Restaurant/ Paudie's Bar. Dingle Bay Hotel.**]

[**Murphy** – John, shipwright – pub, second-hand clothes, salted fish, cooperage. Later, games arcade, under Michael Murphy. **The Linen Chest. Cosaí. Chocolate shop. The White Room. Blasket Sea Life Tours.**]

[**Kennedy** – Noan – historically a pharmacy; pub, grocery. **Murphy's Pub.**]

Turbett – western Colony – amusements, seasonal.

[**Cois Farraige** – Eileen Mary – restaurant. **Crafts,** tourist shop.]

Art gallery – Liam O'Neill, The Colony.

Dingle Music Shop – Michael Herlihy, The Colony.

[**Johnson** – Bridgie – fishmonger, The Colony. **Anchor Down** – restaurant, The Colony.]

Callaghan – Mikie – electrician, The Colony.

[**Kavanagh** – pub historically. **Telephone exchange. Lynch** – Padraig – insurance. **Strand House** – clothes, shoes, café.]

[**Griffin** – Poggin's/Bob's – formerly Jacky Nell's Flaherty – pub, fishmonger, barking nets. **Bob Griffin's Bar.**]

[**O'Connor** – Margaret Long – grocery, sweets, crubeens after the pictures. **Kool Scoops** – ice cream. **Tapas** – restaurant.]

Post Office, now **GS&L.**

[**Callaghan** – Tomás – pub. **Ramble Inn** – D. Geaney, 1967 – pub. **Garvey's** – pub. Now **GS&L.**]

Garvey – James – boots, shoes, clothes, grocery, newsagents. **GS&L. Garvey's Sport and Leisure** now encompasses three original business premises.

[**Sheehy** – Walter – gifts, fishing (angling) tackle, key cutting. **Dingle Goldsmiths** – jewellers.]

[**Sheehy** – on the corner – **Aishling Gift Shop. Flower Shop. Original Kerry Crafts.**]

Strand Street, right-hand side, going east

•●•

[**Chandlery. Dingle Boat Tours.** Marina Centre. **Coco and Pol** – café. **Cassidy's** – café/restaurant. **Fish** – restaurant. **Lily Mai's** – clothing. Marina Centre.]

[**Gas shed** – gas, for the lamps on the pier; oil/fuel for the fishing boats (administered by Paddy 'Ollie' Brosnan). **Tourist Office. Dingle Dolphin Trips. Sea Safari.**]

[**Dingle Fisherman's Co-op** – (**The Scheme**) – centuries-old building used by Devanes as a warehouse for nets, fishing paraphernalia; fish processing, ice plant. **Dingle Bay Fisheries Ltd.**]

Dingle Boatyard – Bord Iascaigh Mhara (BIM). **Dingle Boats Teoranta** – Joe O'Boyle.

[**Lovett** – Bridgie Sheehy – small shop, sweets. **Juice for Thought. Kerry Views** – prints.]

Moriarty – Johnathan – pub, grocery, clothes, shoes, wool merchant.

[**Flahive** – Danny – gifts, holy pictures, religious icons. **Griffin's** – gift shop.]

Griffin – Tadhgeen – bakers.

[**Fenton** – formerly O'Donnell's. **ESB depot. Butchers. Dolphin Shop.**]

[**Houlihan** – of the cinema Houlihan's – draper and outfitter, pub. **Paddy Bawn's Pub**, established 1958.]

[**Grandfield** – (Nell's) – ice cream, small grocery. **Murphy's Ice Cream.**]

[**O'Keeffe** – formerly Dr Moriarty – **pharmacy**, opened in 1946. **Pure Pharmacy**, 2023 (after seventy-seven years O'Keeffes cease operating).]

The Tracks

•●•

Fitzgerald – auctioneer; **West Kerry Properties.**

[**Kingdom Fresh** – fruit and veg. **Olde Sweet Shoppe.**]

Cathríona's – hair salon.

An Cupán Tae – café.

NOTE: The preceding businesses (along with one other, Quayside B&B) occupy what was historically a farm building, including a wool store loft, owned by merchant Johnathan Moriarty.

Turbett – amusements, seasonal. Initially immediately east of the boatyard, on the Tracks opposite Murphy's pub and also in the western Colony.

Holyground/Avondale/Grey's Lane

•●•

[**Long** – Tom – pub, harness maker. **Garvey** supermarket.]

[**McKenna** – corn mill, merchants (grain from Ukraine). **Faraway Haven** – B. Moore – pub. **Garvey** supermarket.]

[**Martin** – Jamie – pub. **Garvey** supermarket.]

[**Sullivan** – shoemaker. **Garvey** – supermarket, bakery.]

[**Greaney** – chip shop, restaurant. **Browne** – bookmakers.]

Reel Dingle Fish.

Mrs Smith – hairdresser.

[**Shea** – Mike – carpenter/wheelwright, ice cream, grocery. **The Diner.**]

[**Moriarty** – ice cream, small grocery. **Mad Hatters** – fashion, gifts. **Seed and Soul. Hair Therapy.**]

O'Connor – Juke Box – small grocery, ice cream. First juke box in Dingle, mid-1960s.

[**Boland** – carpenter/wheelwright, tableware. The **Dingle Framer. Green Lane Gallery.**]

[**Barry** – Tommy – blacksmith. **The Forge** – restaurant. **Internet Café. Shirt Shop. Uisce Saddlery** – leather goods.]

My Boy Blue – café.

Flahive – Tommy – undertaker. Bridie, hairdresser.

Houlihan – Vin – veterinarian, Avondale.

Hand – Johnny and Mrs Hand – barbers, Avondale.

Cashen – Tim – tailor, Grey's Lane.

Sullivan – Denny – shoemaker, Grey's Lane,

Grey's Lane Bistro.

[**Nail Studio. Little Cheese Shop**. Grey's Lane.]

Bridge Street/Mail Road/Cooleen

[**O'Shea** – Henry – general grocery, newsagent for *The Kerryman*. Agent for laundry. **Vittles** – restaurant. **Tig Líse** – café/restaurant. **Base Dingle.**]

[**Cleary** – petrol, bicycle repair. Guns, cartridges. **Amusement** – games arcade. **Base Dingle** – accommodation.]

Griffin – Kathleen – music teacher, ballad sheets, tin whistles.

Cleary – garage, to the rear in the Tracks.

Enright – Danny the barber.

NOTE: the preceding five houses/businesses have been knocked and rebuilt. All now operating as **Base Dingle** – accommodation.

Moriarty – Foxy John. **Ua Flaithbheartaigh** (1958) – Paguine – pub. Music shop (Molly O'Flaherty) agent for Walton's.

O'Sullivan – doctor; known as the Lady Doctor.

[**Blasket Craft Shop. O'Donnell** – optician.]

[**Moriarty** – Paddy – shipwright, (the black shed). **River God** – restaurant. **Chart House** – restaurant. **No. 3.** Café.]

[**The Dingle Elf. Irish crafts. Christmas Shop** – Mary Moore. **Penny's Pottery. Kerry Woollen Mills. The Coach House** – gifts, interiors.]

[**Cleary** – Mail Road – garage. **Moran** – supermarket, garage, petrol, delicatessen. **Dingle Cleaners. Moriarty** – butcher.]

Neodata – Cooleen.

Flannery – Jimmy, Cooleen – boat construction.

Hand Electronics – Cooleen.

Pitch and Putt – at corner of Mail Road and Station Row.

Keane – Tadhg – veterinarian.

Skellig Hotel – formerly the site of the coast guard building.

O'Connor – Donal – undertaker. Formerly Dingle train station.

The Mall

O'Loughlin – veterinary surgeon.

[**Gibbons** – Mrs – church organist, music teacher. **Dingle Medical Centre.**]

Fitzgerald – Ned – beside the grotto – garden produce.

O'Connor – garage, petrol pumps, undertakers.

Ryle – Joe – metalwork products, engineering.

Walsh – dressmaker. Clothes shop.

Fitzgerald – set back from The Mall – carpenter/wheelwright.

Fox – cycling club hostel/accommodation.

O'Sullivan – Seán accountant.

Devane – Paddy, the Bridewell – curing fish.

Sullivan – Paddy Dan – building contractor.

T. and J. Ashe – Guinness agents, bottled lemonade and orange producers.

Neill – Billy – shoemaker.

Clinic Cois Abhainn – Fanning – medical doctor.

[**Barrett** – Madge – pub. **Courthouse pub.**]

[**Spillane** – shoemaker. **Cuchulain** – R. Riordan – restaurant. **Simple Pleasures.**]

Curran – butcher shop. Café.

Rayel – John – tailor.

Moriarty – O'Toole's – sweet shop, ice cream.

[**Quilter** – John – radio and electrical sales and service, wet-battery charging. Announcer at the Dingle Races. **Shamrock Restaurant** – Ignatius and Máiréad O'Connor. **Mike Kennedy** – auctioneer, valuer.]

[**Four in One Restaurant** – Johnny Whelan. **Chip Shop,** run by Jerry O'Connor.]

Green Street, right-hand side, going uphill

•●•

O'Connor – Jack Neddy – carpenter/joiner, pub. **Hannie Agnes.**

Devane – fish/general merchant. Stationery, magazines. **Dentist** – Mrs Fenton.

Devane – solicitors, Burke/Callery. Dr O'Shea.

[**Greaney** – John Joe – bakery. First self-service supermarket in Dingle. **Subway. Tig Maya** – leather goods, jewellery, crafts. **Heritage Crafts.**]

[**Murphy Electrical. Kathleen McAuliffe** – fashion.]

[**Mitchell** – drapery. **Crinkle Stores** – crafts.]

La Bohéme – clothes, fashion items.

[**Munster and Leinster** – bank. Burke/Callery solicitors.]

[**Murphy** – Tipp – grocery, chip shop. **Bácús** – bread. **Hedi O'Neill Pottery. Kelly Marie** – jewellery.]

Dillon – dressmakers.

[**Moore** – John – auctioneer/valuer, cinema owner, commissioner for oaths. **Beginish Restaurant. Tír na Rí** – restaurant. **Áras de Staic** – jewellers.]

[**W. Murdoch & Sons** – (Mercy and Eunice) – general hardware, ironmongers, grocery, ice cream, sweets. **Lisbeth Mulcahy.**]

[**Griffin** – Katie Sarah – homemade sweets, lemonade. **John A. Moore** – auctioneer. **Bean in Dingle** – coffee house.]

[**McCarthy** – Bridge – sweet shop. **Candle shop.**]

Dingle Crystal.

[**Reidy and Fitzgerald** – television repair, satellite dishes. **Dingle Pottery.**]

[**MacDonnell** – Dick Mack's – pub, leather goods. Established, 1899. Arcade: **Courtney's Bakery. Keogh's Art Gallery. Barbershop. Brewery. Ivernia Grill** – Jerry Lee. **El Toro** – restaurant. **Blue Zone** pizza. **Printing** – Stan and Mavis Phelan. **Dingle Record Shop** – Mazzarello O'Flaherty. **Strawberry Beds** – linen, quilts.]

[**Moriarty** – Patty Attie – butchers. **Irish Artman Gallery. The Fish Box.**]

Garden Café and Wine Bar.

Leary – holy pictures.

[**O'Connor** – Tom – harness maker. **Windle's Barber Shop.**]

Carol Cronin Gallery – laneway.

[**Scully** – doctor. **The Dingle Bookshop.**]

Out West – clothing.

[**O'Connor** – Ted – auctioneer/valuer. **O'Connor** – John Diony – auctioneer/valuer.]

Moriarty – Foxy John – bicycle hire, general hardware.

[**Moran** – Jack – garage, petrol pumps, undertakers. **Classic Hair Design. Celtic Gift House.**]

[**Begley** – Maag – sweets, loose cigarettes. **Kanon's Korner** – chips, burgers.]

[**Reen (Mrs)** – sweet shop, cigarettes. **Tripster** – travel retro Irish posters.]

Green Street, left-hand side, going uphill

• ● •

Sheehy – John Joe – supermarket.

Fenton – restaurant.

[**Fenton** – **Dingle Linen. Reidy and Fitzgerald. Betting shop. West Kerry Live. Sweet Pea** – crafts.]

Devane – yard – net storage, fishing merchandise, coal.

[**Curran** – Michael Lovett – butchers. **Surf Shop.**]

Carnegie – library.

Walsh – pharmacy, MPSI (established 1930).

[**Nelligan** – Ellie – draper. **Brian de Staic** – jeweller.]

O'Sullivan – Maidhcín Fuacht – shoemaker.

[**Moore** (originally). **Paddy Curran's** – butcher; first to make sausages in Dingle. **Weldon** – jewellers.]

[**Moore** – building with window display of film stills of upcoming films. **Dingle Artworks.**]

[**Fitzgerald** – dentist. **Dingle Bog Oak** – exhibition.]

The Coach House – Gráinne Kavanagh – gifts, crafts. Beside the old presbytery.

John Street, right-hand side, going uphill

• ● •

Unique Ireland – phone and gift shop. New hotel under construction, 2024.

[**Houlihan** – tailor, later **Michael Horgan,** who was apprenticed to Houlihan. **Curtain Call. ACME** – blinds.]

[**Dowd** – Ned – pub. **Idá's** – restaurant. **Bull Head** – restaurant. **Land to Sea** – restaurant.]

O'Connor – grocery, bakery (prior to Bridge House).

[**O'Connor** – Jamie Highfill – taxi driver, film projectionist. **Granville** – paint shop.]

Kennedy – Muirishín Cool – butcher.

Stay Dingle – accommodation/property rental.

Hoare – Julia – midwife.

Moran – Jack, Barrack Height – garage, car repair, motors for hire.

Moriarty – Skocky Jim, Barrack Height – wheelwright.

John Street, left-hand side, going uphill

O'Connor – Bridge House, Chocolates – baker, grocery, chocolates/sweets. **Dingle Bridge House** – pub, restaurant (opened 2024).

Martin – Johnny – pub.

[**Farrell** – Debbie – pub. **The Half Door** – restaurant.]

[**Malone** – John – pub, grocery. **Doyle's Restaurant**.]

Griffin – pub.

[**Lynch** – Eileen – pub. **O'Súilleabháin** Bernard – agri-merchant, construction materials.]

[**McDonald** – George – butcher, vegetables, milk. **O'Sullivan** – Muirish Dan – grocery, butcher, pub. **Muirish Dan's** – Tommy Griffin – pub.]

Galvin – Tadhg – pub, travel agent.

[**Rohan** – pub. **Riordan's** – supermarket, bar. **Barrack Height Pub.**]

Harrington – milk deliveries.

O'Sullivan – Dawson's – pub; owner returned from the Dawson City/Klondike gold rush.

Sullivan – Tom the Gabha – blacksmith, Brewery Lane.

Image and Design – Brewery Lane.

[**Grandfield** – shoemaker. **Foley** – solicitor.]

McMahon – small grocery shop, sweets.

Casey – Casey's Hotel, local slang – lodging house for travelling balladeers, people in transit. A shilling a night which included the use of the fire for cooking.

Dygate Lane

•●•

Ma Greaney – corner shop – sweet shop, for cinemagoers.

[**Dingle Electric Light & Power Co. Ltd** – Houlihan, electrical and general engineers. **Phoenix Cinema: Houlihan, Moore, O'Sullivan** and **Murphy**, Cillian.]

[**Donnelly** – Cycling Club Hostel. **Dillon** – Mary – hairdresser.]

[**Sullivan** – Johnny the Gabha – blacksmith. **Elaine Kennedy Photography. Blas na hÉireann** – food awards.]

[**Dingle Bay Restaurant** – Carol O'Connor. **Random** – restaurant.]

Dánlann – gallery, musical instruments, crafts.

Begley – Jack – tableware.

[**Moriarty and Bambury** architects/draughtsmen/planning advice. **Diggin** – Patrick – solicitor.]

Marian's – hair studio.

Lyne – Carol – flower shop, laundrette.

[**Sullivan** – shoemaker. **Tele Chorca Dhuibhne** – Michael O'Connor – phone services.]

[**Tigín Bán Gallery. Thyme Out** – café, delicatessen. **Púca** – café.]

[**Whelan** – Stan – printing. **Bespoke Letterpress** – printing (Bóthar an Uisce).]

Fitzgerald – dentist; operating in the house next to the Café Liteartha. **Dispensary** (discontinued).

Café Liteartha – café, bookshop (established 1979).

[**Moriarty** – Hannah – bakery. **Paddy's Bike Shop** – bicycle shop.]

CompuCara – computer/technology advice.

Grapevine – hostel.

McKenna – tea house, grocery. **Café Liteartha** – café, books.

McKenna – drapery, clothes, bedding.

Spa Road

[**Shea** – Hannie – pub. The **Mill Wheel. Donaleen's.** An **Droichead Beag.**]

O'Connor – peace commissioner, carpenter/wheelwright.

Farrell – pub.

[**Fitzgerald** – Tommy – general contractor, pub. The **Spa Well. An Conair.**]

[**Carroll** – Dermot – café, meat pies. **Veterinary Clinic.**]

[**Sheehy** – Fred – pub, hackney. The **Brewery Gate. Nelliefred's.**]

[**Brewery** – (run by Tom the Boy). The **Fairfield.** The **Mart.**]

Grogan – pharmacy.

Dingle Doc.

Dingle Cleaners.

Lidl.

Brosnan – Jim – doctor.

Kerry Agribusiness – farm store.

[**McCarthy** – The **Western Ballroom. Hillgrove Hotel. Dingle Linen Service.**]

[**Dingle Creamery** – milk, cream, eggs, butter, turkeys at Christmas. **M. Brosnan**, Dawn Dairies depot. **Dingle Brewing Company.**]

Noonan – Vincent – building contractor.

McKenna – Padraig – construction contractor; established 1932.

Lynch – Tommy – Ballinasig – engineering.

Dingle Food Company – Caroline 'Darcy' Lynch – food catering.

Main Street, right-hand side, going uphill

•●•

[**O'Connor** – John J. – pub, butcher, grocery, cattle dealer. **Droichead Beag.**]

[**Neligan** – pub, grocery. The **Mighty Session.**]

[**Phelan** – lodgings. The **Droichead Beag.**]

[**Begley** – meat pies. **Whole Food Café. Justin** – barber.]

[**Moriarty** – Jim – tableware. **Pantri. Ashe's.**]

Ashe – pub, seafood restaurant, Guinness agents.

Moriarty – **Foyle's Library**, privately run library.

[**The Medical Hall** – (Paddy Bowler) – pharmacy. **Dingle Pub** – off-licence.]

[**Griffin** – Maud – pub. The **Dingle Pub.**]

[**Shea** – Mamie – pub. The **Dingle Pub.**]

[**Sullivan/Annie Higgins** – drapery, pub. **Paul Geaney** – pub.]

[**Griffin** – general merchant, milk, flour, shoes. **Whelan's Restaurant. Sizzlers** – restaurant. **Land to Sea** – restaurant. **Hare's Corner** – café.]

[**Martin** – Pat's – grocery. **Hannah Rayel. WKL** (West Kerry Live). **Music Shop** – M. Herlihy. **Chop Central** – hair salon. **The Wicked Shop. Shoebox.**]

[**O'Connor** – shoes, boots. **The Lantern.**]

Provincial Bank – now **AIB**. Formerly, Lee's Hotel.

[**Barrett** – Margaret – clothes. **An Gailearaí Beag** – West Kerry Craft Guild.]

[**Neligan** – pub, general warehouse. **13 Bandon** – arts, crafts. **Piglet Siopa.**]

[**Neligan** – Mae Delia – gift shop. **Dingle Candles. Kennedy** – Mike – auctioneer, valuer.]

Lynch – Mrs – school books/copybooks.

[**Moran** – pub, drapery. **Adams' Pub**, established 1852.]

[**Neligan** – Sweet Pa (formerly private secretary to Padraig Pearse) – **Labour Exchange. Dingle Health Foods.**]

[**Sullivan** – pub. **Dry Cleaners** – Sayers. **Pure Beauty** – salon.]

Curran – Joe – pub, wool merchant, coal, grocery, drapery, wellingtons.

[**Curran** – John – clothes, shoes, newsagent. **Callaghan** – Jerry – electrical. The **Global Village** – restaurant. **Surf Shop.**]

[**Ashe** – Peggy. **O'Shea** – James – pub. **Post Office. Credit Union.**]

Main Street, left-hand side, going uphill

•●•

[**O'Connor** – grocery. The **Old Smokehouse** – restaurant. **Tír na Rí**, Chinese restaurant.]

NOTE: the original smokehouse was used to smoke bacon for O'Connor, butchers, across the road.

[**Novo Cento** – pizza.]

[**Fitzgerald** – Hole in the Wall – pub. **Walker's Bar.**]

[**Phelan** – hotel, pub. **McKenna** – drapers. **Artisan Hair Studio.**]

Enright – Danny the Barber – at corner. **McKenna.**

[**Griffin** – grocery. **Fiadh.**]

[**Dowd** – Hannah – grocery. **Kay's Hairdressers. Nature's Knowledge.**]

[**Kennedy** – Jack – drapery. **Commodum.**]

Bank of Ireland.

Benner – hotel.

Hennessy – Fadó – antiques, picture framing, artworks.

[**Sheehy** – Maud's – formerly Baker's pub and believed to be the oldest licenced premises in Dingle, established 1890. **Lord Baker's** – restaurant.]

[**Latchford** – hardware. **P&T Fitzgerald** – hardware, household. **Post Office** (Lundon). **BoyleSports.**]

[**Griffin** – builder. (Fr Noel's). **Mrs O'Neill**, hairdresser. **Rita Lynch** – boutique. **Once Upon a Toy.**]

[**Grommel** – tailor. **Pig and Leaf** – coffee/tea shop.]

[**Dillon** – butcher. **Fitzgerald Centra.**]

[**Atkins** – (historic building) – general hardware, flour, meal. **Fitzgerald Centra. Fitzgerald Homevalue** – (P&T, at rear) – general hardware, timber, construction materials, household, Euronics; also, with a depot in Ballinaboula, Dingle.]

Post Office, at rear.

Devane – formerly the labour exchange. Now having a **famous window** (by Mary) displaying images of local interest and seasonal themed displays which attract hundreds of children throughout the year.

Moriarty – Benny – clothes shop, drapery.

McKenna – pub. **Moriarty** – Foxy John – pub, hardware, household, bicycle hire. **Foxy John's.**

Siopa an Chúinne – Mary Dowd – school/office supplies.

Orchard Lane

•●•

[**Darcy's** – Café. **Deirdre's** – café. **Vincent's** – charity shop.]

Little Italy – restaurant/pizzeria.

The Beauty Lounge.

Wave Length – hair salon.

O'Connor – fruit and veg.

[**Apple Tree** – cafe. **Cístí Chorca Dhuibhne.**]

[**Kennedy** – butcher. **The Dingle Butcher.**]

NOTE: Orchard Lane first opened in 1997.

Goat Street/Upper Main Street, right-hand side, going uphill

•●•

O'Connor – Josie – newsagent, employer of paperboys.

[**Donoghue** – pub. **Dr O'Shea.**]

Ferriter – Jack – tailors, father and son.

Kennedy – pub, grocery.

Dental practice – L. Corkery.

Declan Noonan & Associates – architectural/engineering.

Frank O'Connor – solicitors.

[**Lynch** – Jimmy Tom Dick's – pub, shop, bus stop. **Barr na Sráide.**]

Dingle Dental – B. Long.

Foley – Paddy – tailor, at Holy Stone.

Scanlon – Padraig, Chapel Lane – tailor.

[**Mahony** – Richie – builder. **Farrell** – Ned – garage. **John Griffin** – garage.]

Falvey – John – undertaker.

Murphy – (number 125) – shop.

Goat Street/Upper Main Street, left-hand side, going uphill

•●•

[**O'Connor** – Beedi Keane, Johnny the Post – pub, taxi, schoolbooks. The **Goat Street Café**.]
McCarthy – Danny – pub, grocery, bakery. Established 1867.
O'Connor – Tom – shoemaker.
West and Mid-Kerry Live – advertising/news magazine.
[**Dispensary** – O'Halloran's, discontinued. **West Kerry Care of the Aged** – charity shop.]

Breakdown of businesses/trades/goods in existence over the period outlined

•●•

Bakers: 8
Blacksmiths: 5
Books: 6 (3 dedicated)
Butchers: 11
Clothes shops: 11
Craft shop/gift shops: 35
Drapers: 9
Engine fitters: 7 (in Dingle Boatyard)
Fishmonger/merchants: 10
Garages: 6
Grocery/small groceries: 32
Ice cream outlets: 8
Pubs: 51
Shipwrights: 43 (40 in Dingle Boatyard, spanning four decades; 3 private operators). Dingle Boatyard also had a fleet of general workers along with painters, electricians, welders and office personnel.

Shoemakers: 9
Tailors: 9
Wheelwright/carpenters: 5

Businesses with the original names on the premises

Ashe – in porcelain – pub, Guinness agent, Main Street.
Benner's Hotel – on concrete plaque.
Curran – in porcelain – pub, Main Street.
Ferriter – in concrete – tailor, Upper Main Street.
Flahive – painted on the fanlight – pub, now ceased operation.
Kennedy – in concrete – pub/shop, Upper Main Street (not quite the original; a remnant of the original name is visible in the background plaster).
McKenna – in concrete – drapery, clothes, Dygate Street.
Moran – painted on the fanlight – pub, now known as Adams, Main Street.
Moriarty – in porcelain – pub, grocery, wool merchant, Strand Street.
Murphy – in concrete – pub, Strand Street (now a gift shop).
Neligan – in porcelain – pub, Main Street.
O'Connor – in porcelain – juke box, Holyground.
O'Keeffe – sign, hung on fanlight – pharmacy, Strand Street.
Seán Ó Béoláinn – in concrete – carpenter/wheelwright, Holyground.
Ua Flaithbheartaigh – hand-painted sign – bar, Bridge Street.
Walsh – in concrete – pharmacy, Green Street.

Appendix 3

Dingle Boatyard

Before Dingle Boatyard came into existence in 1952, Michael Long, Strand Street, Dingle, built four nobbies at the bottom of the Garraí laneway. The nobby fishing boat originated in the Isle of Man (where Michael served his time) and preceded the fifty-footers which were among the first boats built in Dingle Boatyard.

One hundred and four boats, ranging in size from 26 ft to 75 ft, were built in the boatyard during its existence. Forty qualified shipwrights worked in the yard over the period, along with engine fitters, office personnel, painters and general workers. During its peak in the 1970s there were approximately fifty people working in the yard.

Some of the skilled workers from Dingle Boatyard would later play a significant and leading role in the building of the *Jeanie Johnston*, a replica of a three-masted barque that was used as a transport during the Great Famine in Ireland. The keel was laid for the *Jeanie Johnston* in Blennerville in 1998. In 2003, the *Jeanie Johnston* sailed from Tralee to Canada and the United States on her maiden voyage.

List of boats built at the Bord Iascaigh Mhara Dingle Boatyard

1953 *Ros Glas*, 50 ft
1955 *Ros Arcan*, 50 ft
1955 *Ros Mult*, 50 ft
1955 *Ros Buí*, 50 ft
1956 *Ros Cré*, 50 ft
1956 *Brother's Hope*, 50 ft
1957 *Maria*, 50 ft
1957 *Naomh Iud*, 50 ft
1957 *Three Flowers*, 50 ft
1958 *Maura*, 50 ft
1958 *Dún Nariogh*, 50 ft
1959 *St Jude*, 50 ft
1959 *Sancta Maria*, 50 ft
1959 *Naomh Cailean*, 50 ft
1960 *Rath Osan*, 50 ft
1960 *Rath Chormaic*, 50 ft
1961 *Rath Connla*, 50 ft
1962 *Dún Riabhbhac*, 38 ft
1962 *Beal Árd*, 32 ft
1962 *Cill Caingin*, 26 ft
1963 *Beal na Carraige*, 32 ft
1963 *Beal Choinnigh*, 32 ft
1963 *Cill Droichead*, 26 ft
1963 *Cill Caithne*, 26 ft
1964 *Ros Beithe*, 50 ft
1964 *Guiding Star*, 56 ft
1964 *Cill Mor*, 26 ft
1964 *Gaoth Daile*, 26 ft
1964 *Cill Carna*, 26 ft
1964 *Cill Glas*, 26 ft
1964 *Cill Caisil*, 26 ft
1964 *Cill Croine*, 26 ft
1964 *Cill Carthac*, 26 ft
1964 *Cill Manach*, 26 ft
1964 *Cill Leac*, 26 ft
1965 *Cill Einne*, 26 ft
1965 *Cill Ice*, 26 ft
1965 *Cill na Mona*, 26 ft
1965 *Cill Fenora*, 26 ft
1965 *Cill Coiee*, 26 ft
1965 *Cill Maoile*, 26 ft
1966 *Cill Batha*, 26 ft
1966 *Loch Saile*, 26 ft
1966 *Loch Claoin*, 26 ft
1966 *Loch Con*, 26 ft
1966 *Loch Corrib*, 26 ft
1966 *Loch Iasg*, 26 ft
1966 *Loch Cultra*, 26 ft
1966 *Loch Dubh*, 26 ft
1966 *Loch Garman*, 26 ft
1966 *Loch Finne*, 26 ft
1966 *Loch Cuan*, 26 ft
1966 *Loch Eirne*, 26 ft
1966 *Maco*, 26 ft
1966 *Loch Dearg*, 26 ft
1966 *Loch Aluinn*, 26 ft

1966 *Loch Gara*, 26 ft
1967 *Beal Inse*, 32 ft
1967 *Beal Linn*, 32 ft
1967 *Beal na Sionnaine*, 32 ft
1967 *Loch Fada*, 26 ft
1967 *Loch Rí*, 26 ft
1967 *Ocean Star*, 32 ft
1967 *Loch Gull*, 26 ft
1967 *Loch Measg*, 26 ft
1968 *Fionntragha*, 30 ft
1968 *Lios Dairbre*, 30 ft
1968 *Loch Caoin*, 26 ft
1968 *Scellig*, 26 ft
1968 *Beal Bocht*, 32 ft
1969 *St Peter*, 50 ft
1969 *Saint Anne*, 50 ft
1970 *Saint Colette*, 50 ft
1970 *Foyle Fisher*, 52 ft
1970 *Arctic Swan*, 52 ft
1971 *Silver Fern*, 52 ft
1971 *Midnight Star*, 53 ft
1971 *Favourite*, 56 ft
1972 *Sean Óg*, 58 ft
1972 *Bountiful*, 58 ft
1972 *Miraculous*, 58 ft
1973 *Assumpta*, 54 ft
1973 *Darnette*, 65 ft
1974 *Sharon Rose*, 58 ft
1974 *Autumn Glory*, 65 ft
1975 *Onedin*, 65 ft
1975 *Roving Swan*, 65 ft
1975 *Saint Oliver*, 65 ft
1976 *Silver Spruce*, 65 ft
1977 *Sea Eagle*, 60 ft
1978 *Aelindrew*, 65 ft
1979 *Speckled Fort*, 65 ft

Dingle Boats Teoranta

In 1980, BIM ceased operations in Dingle Boatyard. The following boats were built by Dingle Boats Teoranta under the management/ownership of Joe O'Boyle. In 1990, Dingle Boatyard ceased operations.

List of boats built by Dingle Boats Teoranta

Marber Therese, 56 ft
Paul Stephen, 56 ft
Atlantic Fisher, 60 ft
Girl Bríd, 60 ft
Ronan Pádraig, 72.5 ft
Resplendent, 75 ft
Ború, 45 ft
Passenger boat for Jeddah, Saudia Arabia, steel, 50 ft
Mussel farm work boat, steel, 40 ft
Tricia Anne, 45 ft
Silver Harvester, 75 ft, largest boat built
Cathy Angela, steel, 50 ft

Historic fishing boats of Dingle (pre-Dingle BIM Boatyard) and the families that owned them

Nobby boats, 45 ft approximately

Angelus Bell – Griffin
Brendan – Flaherty
Brigid – Flaherty
Madonna – Walsh and Quinn
Majestic – Flaherty
Manx Girl – Garvey brothers
Mary – Devane
Mary Bernadette – Flaherty brothers
Ocean Star – Flaherty
Petro – Devane
St John – Graham

Sea Fisheries Association (Scheme) nobby cruiser-stern boats, 40 ft approximately

Colm – Flannery
Elsie Mabel – Brosnan
Naomh Diarmuid – Griffin
Naomh Enda – Moriarty
Pride of Ballinacurra – Guiheen
Pride of Dingle – Flaherty
Pride of Kerry – Flannery
Pride of Ventry – Curran
Pride of Wicklow – Sullivan
Rory – Brosnan
St Lawrence O'Toole – Brosnan
St Peadar – Flaherty

OTHER BOOKS BY JOHN O'CONNOR

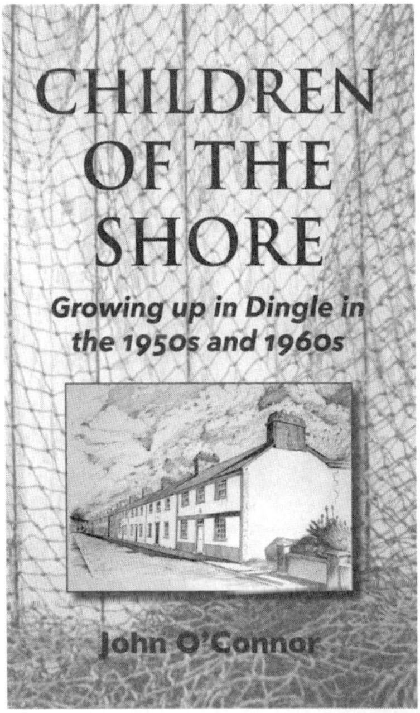

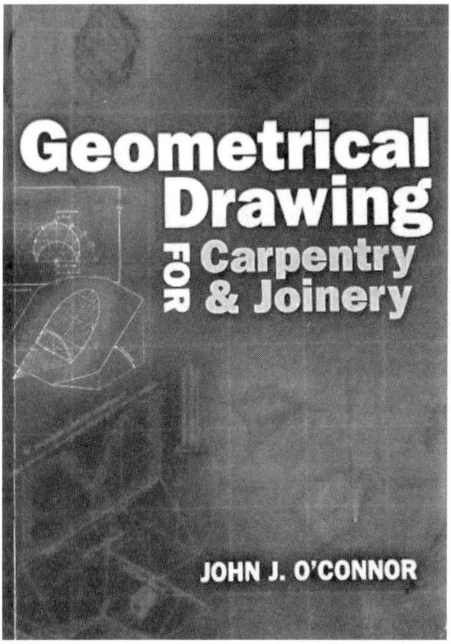
Geometrical
Drawing
FOR
Carpentry
& Joinery
JOHN J. O'CONNOR

MORE THAN
A VOYAGE
Stories of Voyaging in Ireland,
Cornwall and Brittany
John O'Connor

Contents

Introduction

Murray A. Rae

I

There have been two major periods in the history of the Christian Church in which the doctrine of the person of Christ has been at the forefront of theological controversy. The first spanned roughly the period between the Councils of Nicaea in 325 and Constantinople in 553. The second we are now in the midst of. The points at issue in the patristic controversy were first, whether and how it is possible to speak of the man Jesus as fully and properly divine, and second, if he is divine, how should the relation between the divine and the human natures be construed? The points at issue in our own time are essentially the same. That sameness ought to banish the frequently heard suggestion that it is the peculiar conditions of the modern world that require us to abandon the naïve and outmoded confession of the divinity of Jesus of Nazareth. There are, to be sure, distinctive characteristics of modern disbelief, but in both the modern and the ancient worlds theological controversy arose because of the incapacity of then current philosophical assumptions to accommodate the news that God was in Christ.

It might be argued that, in the ancient world, the divinity of Christ was resisted for God's sake, that is, in an effort to safeguard the transcendent sovereignty of God who, by definition, could not be found in the figure of a weak and suffering human being. On the other hand, the modern objection to the confession that Jesus is the Christ is typically advanced, so its proponents say, for the sake of humanity. It is in the light of modern advances in knowledge and in defence of the supposed omni-competence of human reason that we are urged to resist the claim that an other-worldly

God should miraculously appear in the midst of the closed causal continuum of human history.

Whereas the ancient disbelief had a precursor in Origen's rather too accommodating relation between Christian theology and the surrounding Greek modes of thought, and came to fruition in Arius and the Arians, the modern rejection of the divinity of Christ has its beginnings in the likes of Reimarus, Lessing and Kant, and finds contemporary expression through those who speak of the *myth* of God incarnate, and in the work of the Jesus Seminar whose members insist that 'Christology' must not transcend the bounds of what may be known through historical-critical inquiry. In both cases – ancient and modern – the boundaries of Christological confession are determined by a set of philosophical assumptions that render the Christian gospel impossible. In both cases those assumptions are taken to be self-evident. None of this is surprising. The Christian gospel, then, now and always, is not a modification or refinement of existing philosophies but *news* that the world is not as we thought it was. It is to be understood, not in the light of our own conceptions and observations, but in the light of Christ in whom is revealed the creative and redemptive agency of God. Old wine skins won't do for the containment of this new wine. The conceptual conveyances for holding and handing on this news must be fashioned anew under the impact of the Christological reality itself.

Such fashioning is the task of theology. It is a fashioning that begins with attentiveness to what has been said and done before us. This is meant in two senses; first and foremost, and new every morning, it means attentiveness to the speaking of God's own Word, that triune event of the Father, the Son and the Holy Spirit, in which God addresses us and claims us as his own. As it is put later in this volume by Douglas Knight, 'We are preceded by a conversation, the conversation of the Father, Son and Holy Spirit'. Theology's task then, as Knight further points out, is to set out some of the logic of that conversation. Theology begins thus with attentiveness, with 'silence before the Word'.[1]

The requirement of attentiveness to what has been said and done before us applies secondarily to the tradition of the Church. As the community of Christ gathered by the Spirit into communion with the Father, the Church spends its life attending to the Word, and is itself a conveyance for the news of the gospel. The conveyance takes shape, first of all, as the story of a community, gathered by Christ himself, and re-gathered by the risen

[1] The matter is put this way by Dietrich Bonhoeffer, *Christology*, trans. John Bowden (London: Collins, 1966), 27.

Christ after being scattered by his death. As the community grows and spreads, its story is safeguarded and passed on through testimony both oral and written. It is to these words too that theology must be attentive, not first because they are binding – although an account may be given of the ways in which we are bound to them – but rather because these testimonies of the community are themselves a part of the story of God's creative and redemptive work that theology seeks to interpret.

Attending to these words then – of God, and of scripture and tradition – the essayists in this volume are engaged in interpreting what has been said and done, and in fashioning a testimony for our own time to what has been said and done in Christ. They are not persuaded by the contrary testimony of those who say, in the name of modernity, or even of postmodernity, that the gospel in the form once given to the saints can no longer be believed.

II

Because it is generally easier to say one thing, rather than several things, at a time, the work of Christology has often proceeded with a distinction between the person and the work of Christ. In treating person and work distinctly, however, it has not been supposed that these two aspects of Christology are independent of one another. Indeed the question of who Jesus is was prompted throughout Jesus' career in Palestine by what he did. 'Are you the one who is to come?', John the Baptist enquires, and Jesus responds, 'Go and tell John what you hear and see; the blind receive their sight, the lame walk, the lepers are cleansed, the deaf hear, the dead are raised, and the poor have good news brought to them' (Mt. 11.2–5). The implication of this Matthean report is made explicit in the Gospel of John: '. . . even if you do not believe me, believe the works, so that you may know and understand that the Father is in me and I am in the Father' (Jn 10.38). Likewise in the early Church, it was because Jesus was confessed as saviour that the question of his identity and of his relation to God had to be tackled. It was one of Athanasius' key arguments against the Arians, for instance, that it made no sense for them to worship Christ as saviour if they would not also confess him as truly God from God.[2]

That the title of this book refers to the person of Christ and not to his work therefore indicates a focus on the question 'Who is Jesus?', but does not entail that the *work* of Christ does not also come within its ambit. It is a book that focuses upon Christ's person, rather than upon salvation, or the

[2] See, for example, *Contra Arianos* 2.23–4; cf. 2.12.

atonement, or upon his work in the creation and consummation of the world. However, the essays themselves reveal that the person of Christ is made known through his work, which in turn has its saving efficacy only because it is he who does it. To put it simply: what Christ does belongs to the description of who he is – the saviour, the crucified, the risen one, the ascended one, and so on. That relationship is consistently apparent in the essays comprising this volume.

III

We begin with prolegomena, with the attempt, that is, to articulate the basis of the Christological task and the manner by which it ought to proceed. As John Webster's essay in this volume makes clear, however, pro-legomena, the beginnings of what we may say, arises out of Theo-legomena, out of what God himself says in uttering his Word. The identity of this Word, however, is not simply past, nor is it finished. The basis of Christology is the presence of Christ – God's Word – who is known, as Webster argues, 'by virtue of the movement of his being in which as Lord and reconciler he freely gives himself to be known . . . '. This movement of Christ's being is the reality with which Christology is concerned, and to which, through faithful witness, it seeks to be responsible. The concept of 'presence' here needs further examination, however. Christ is not present, Webster explains, as an object among others. Christ's presence is divine presence, and is, as such, both antecedent and eschatological, eternal and majestic. It is the presence of the *Lord*.

It is by virtue of his presence that Christ is known by us, and that knowing is – again, *because* of Christ's presence – a joyful and reverent science. Webster speaks here, not of the pious disposition of Christology's practitioners, but of the means by which the object of Christology is appropriately construed. The joy and the reverence of Christology are engendered by the reconciling presence of Christ himself. That presence, in turn, renders redundant any prolegomenal demonstration of the viability of the Christological task. Prolegomena becomes instead, as seen in Webster's essay, a matter of testimony to (not demonstration of) what is already accomplished.

To speak of the presence of Christ implies a sphere of his presence in which he can be and is known. 'As he presents himself', Webster writes, 'he establishes a domain and gathers a community which he authorizes and empowers for knowledge of himself'. Christology is thus a positive science of this fellowship; it is a science of the church. And the instruments of Christ's presence within this ecclesial domain are Scripture and the

Sacraments. Holy Scripture, under the inspiration of the Spirit, is to be understood, accordingly, as the 'fitting servant of the self-presentation of Jesus Christ', and is the norm to which all Christology is subordinate.

From prolegomena, therefore, we move to a more explicit focus on Scripture itself, and, more particularly, to the testimonies to Jesus received and fashioned by the writers of the gospels. Those testimonies have been variously handled in recent times. Indeed the question of *how* these testimonies should be handled has been at the forefront of the Christological controversy in which we are presently mired. To what extent, if at all, are these testimonies reliable? Are they not so much fashioned as fabricated, not so much a crafting of the material of Jesus' career itself, but creations more or less *ex nihilo*, brought about in service, not of truth, but of the early Church's own interests? Many have argued so, and thus conclude – or have they presupposed? – that the confession of Jesus' divinity can no longer be sustained.

Or perhaps the gospels are not deceptions but rather testimonies whose fault is only that they are shaped by a world-view that is outmoded and naïve. In that case, we are urged, by those seeking nevertheless to make something of Jesus' good name, to separate out from the gospel testimonies the chaff of primitive cosmology and to salvage from them the genuine grain of a gospel that can be confessed today. Typically, this gospel has to do with the exemplary humanity of Jesus. He is properly revered – it is utterly unclear why he should be worshipped – as one who lived life as it should be lived, according, that is, to the will of a God who remains remote and uninvolved. The balance of wheat and chaff varies enormously among scholars who adopt such an approach, as do also the resultant pictures of Jesus. George Tyrell's celebrated summation of the nineteenth-century Quest of the historical Jesus remains apposite for those who adopt similar approaches today. The Jesus that they see, looking back through twenty centuries of history, is only the reflection of their own faces, seen at the bottom of a deep well.[3]

Among those who retain allegiance to a more orthodox Christology, however, there has likewise been debate about how best to handle the testimonies of scripture. Richard Burridge, in the second essay of this collection, offers a survey of this methodological diversity and argues that,

[3] See G. Tyrrell, *Christianity at the Cross-Roads* (London: Longmans, Green & Co., 1909), 44. Albert Schweitzer had earlier reached a similar conclusion in remarking that, 'it was not only each epoch that found its reflection in Jesus; each individual created Him in accordance with his own character'. See Schweitzer, *The Quest of the Historical Jesus* (London: A. & C. Black, 2nd edn, 1936), 4.

despite earlier rejections of the idea, especially by Rudolf Bultmann, the gospels really ought to be seen as biographical accounts of Jesus' life. We must not presume by this, however, that the gospels are like *modern* biographies. They are rather to be compared with ancient 'Lives' in which the accounts given of their heroes are not arranged chronologically but take the form of collected anecdotes, have a strong focus on the hero's death, and often serve an underlying apologetic, polemical or didactic purpose. The gospels, Burridge contends, were composed by their authors and understood by their first audiences according to the conventions of Graeco-Roman *bioi*. The focus of our attention, too, must therefore be on their particular subject, Jesus of Nazareth, rather than on, say, 'presumed problems in their hypothetical communities'. The gospels are about a person; they are Christology in narrative form. The narrative form is important here. It is improper to proceed in Christology by exclusive attention to the titles given to Jesus, or to the sayings of Jesus, or to particular passages, isolated from the whole story. That whole story is essential to the Christological testimony being offered through the particulars. One important result of Burridge's argument is that particular passages are properly to be understood in the light of the 'Christological key' that is revealed through the narrative as a whole. A theological lens, as it were, is not necessarily distortive, as has commonly been claimed, but is the *conditio sine qua non* of faithful attention to these words of testimony to Christ.

Faithful attention to the testimony of Scripture has given rise in subsequent tradition to the confession that in Jesus Christ we are encountered by one who is both truly human and truly divine. The conceptual development of this confession, however, has not been a simple matter. Yet the church has felt constrained by the reality of Christ himself to persist with this confession even while acknowledging that it places our conceptual resources under strain. One strand of the debate about how we are to conceive together the humanity and the divinity of Christ has focused on the doctrine of the *communicatio idiomatum*. This matter is taken up in this volume by Robert Jenson and Stephen Holmes.

One of the first matters to be attended to in employing the doctrine of the *communicatio idiomatum* is to say what one means by such a communication. Robert Jenson sets out what others have meant – especially the Lutheran theologians of the late sixteenth and early seventeenth centuries, identifying, in particular, three classic forms of the *communicatio*. Jenson himself then offers his own 'minimal' statement: 'the one Christ lives his life as God and as a man, divinely and humanly, and his doings and sufferings cannot be sorted out into two differing sorts of doings and sufferings'. Jenson's deliberations about this matter are directed then to two questions: 'What does the *fact* of the mutual communication of divine/human attributes mean for our understanding of the Trinity? And what is the trinitarian import of doctrines *about* the fact?'. What is at stake here, for Jenson, is the self-determination of God, and the point he argues is that the narrative of 'Jesus-in-Israel ... is God's self-determination as the particular God he is'. The eternal Son is not other, that is to say, than the human life he lives. 'The man Jesus is one of the Trinity.' Unless we hold to a form of the *communicatio idiomatum* that allows us to say this, Jenson concludes, then we open the way for the story of triune life 'to be determined by stories other than the biblical story'.

Whereas Robert Jenson draws especially on the Lutheran development of the doctrine of the *communicatio idiomatum*, Stephen Holmes examines the Reformed tradition, in part, thereby, to defend the proposition that there is in fact a distinctively Reformed Christology. Calvin, of course, is the starting-point, and Holmes argues of Calvin's Christology that there is a determined and careful effort to maintain the distinction of the two natures in Christ while not succumbing to Nestorianism. Not all commentators have been convinced that Calvin succeeded in this latter intention, but Holmes shows that Calvin's allegedly Nestorian formulations, particularly in treating Christ's birth of the Virgin Mary where he appears to steer away from the term *Theotokos*, are not a compromise of the unity of the natures but, rather, are designed to preserve the distinctive identity of the divine Son. Mary is the mother of the Son alone and not of the Father and Spirit. What is essential in the Reformed tradition, especially so when the debate spills over into eucharistic theology, is the proper distinction of the two natures of Christ within the hypostatic union, a distinction not properly preserved, allegedly, in the Lutheran opponents.

From Calvin, Holmes moves on to the Reformed Scholastics, and first to François Turretin, in whom he finds a careful refutation of both Eutyches and Nestorius and a continuation of the concern for a proper articulation of the distinction of the natures within the hypostatic union. A form of the *communicatio idiomatum* is proper according to Turretin's account, but only that form which asserts a communication of the distinct properties of the natures to the one person of Christ, and not (against the Lutherans) between the natures themselves. Thus the attributes (*idiomata*) of each nature belong to the person of Christ, but each nature retains its own *idiomata* so that the attributes of one do not become the attributes of the other. At stake for Turretin is the reality of the incarnation itself. If this distinction between the natures is not maintained in this fashion then it cannot be truly said of the Son that he was human as one of us.

An exploration of the Christology of John Owen provides occasion for Holmes to spell out the implications of Reformed Christology for the doctrine of sanctification, pneumatology and the *extra calvinisticum*. Owen maintains the line that the only admissible version of the *communicatio idiomatum* is that which posits the communication of the attributes of each nature to the one person of Christ and not between each other. Holmes concludes his discussion by taking us back to the Christology of Cyril. He argues that a continuous line may be traced between Cyril and Owen, passing through Chalcedon too, and that in following this line we may find the resources to safeguard the proper concerns of Lutheran and Reformed alike.

The theme of person and nature is continued in the essay by Douglas Farrow, but here attention turns to the Greek orthodox theology of John Zizioulas, and particularly to the necessity-freedom dialectic in Zizioulas's concept of the person. Drawing on the existentialist background to his thought, Zizioulas reverses the traditional association of being with necessity and conceives necessity as a threat to authentic personhood. In contrast with the persons of the Trinity, who are uncreated and thus unconstrained by all manner of creaturely mechanisms of cause and effect, human persons are bound by their finitude, their biological nature and by self-centredness. The incarnation of the second person of the Trinity is seen in this context as the advent of free and authentic personhood, overcoming nature, necessity and death. Jesus Christ, in Zizioulas's account, generates free persons 'by the power of his own prior personhood, that is, by virtue of the eternal relation (*schesis*) to the Father which constitutes him as a person'.

So far so good it may seem, but Zizioulas's explication of this theological anthropology is not without its problems, Farrow contends. In particular, Farrow raises questions about whether Zizioulas's scheme is sufficiently Chalcedonian. Nestorianism is avoided clearly enough, but Farrow wonders whether in vesting the personhood of Christ so emphatically in his relation to the Father, Zizioulas is not in danger of a Eutychian neglect of the human nature. The incarnation, as such, appears to have 'no bearing on Christ's personhood'. There follows, in Farrow's essay, a detailed inquiry into what precisely is meant by personhood in Zizioulas's theology. Farrow, for his part, wants a distinction to be made between human personhood and divine personhood. At stake here, he argues, is the proper distinction between the divine and the creaturely, which even in redemption, reconciliation, and indeed *theosis*, has still to be maintained.

The next essay, by Brian Horne, is also a study of a particular theology, that of the poet Charles Williams. Williams's theology is certainly idiosyncratic, as, for instance, in his description of theology itself as 'the measurement of eternity in operation', but it warrants attention, Horne argues, on account of its originality – though Williams himself laid no claim to the description – and because Williams develops the connections between the various elements of Christian doctrine in ways that are thought-provoking at least, and often profoundly illuminating. Horne singles out for attention the relation Williams develops between the incarnation, the atonement, and the doctrine of creation. Echoing the position famously associated with Duns Scotus, and advanced also by B.F. Westcott, Williams holds that while the particular circumstances of the incarnation were due to sin, the idea of the incarnation itself 'was due to the primal and absolute purpose of love foreshadowed in Creation'[4] and would have taken place, therefore, quite apart from the need occasioned by sin. More controversially (and idiosyncratically), however, Williams 'postulates creation as a kind of by-product of God's primary intention, which is to take matter to Himself in the personal union of the Son with human nature'. Creation merely serves that end.

At the foundation of Williams's explication of the incarnation lie the twin principles of co-inherence and exchange. 'All genuine human life operates on the basis of exchange. That is simply a definition for him; an irreducible fact'. In the incarnation, accordingly, there takes place an exchange between divinity and humanity, the purpose and outcome of which is simply 'joy'. Joy is the purpose of God, and joy is accomplished through this glorious exchange. Therefore there must be incarnation, and for this, in turn, the 'stage set' of creation is made ready. The fall, for its small part, determines only the particular circumstances in which the incarnation is brought about. Other things are associated with this conception of the incarnation, notably a high valuation of the body which is held to be 'an instrument for the communication of heavenly beauty'. Horne considers briefly here the possibilities for theological aesthetics and draws an interesting comparison with the defence of Icons proffered by John of Damascus. We find in Williams, Horne concludes, 'a sensibility that was incapable of separating religion from life, theology from aesthetics, Christology from art, theory from practice' – thought-provoking and illuminating indeed!

[4] Charles Williams, *The Epistles of St. John* (London: John Murray, 1886), 317–18. Cited by Brian Horne in this volume.

From the fact of the incarnation we move to three essays that examine in more detail what is accomplished through the work of Christ and what is revealed thereby about the *person* of the Son. Murray Rae investigates the baptism of Jesus by John and considers why it should have been that 'the one who was without sin' should submit to John's baptism of repentance for the forgiveness of sins. Rae begins by noting the reticence of the gospel writers to enter upon this question, but finds a clue to its resolution in Matthew's contention that Jesus is baptized 'to fulfil all righteousness'. The theological tradition is largely agreed that Jesus stood in no need of baptism himself, but several different accounts are offered as to why he should have gone through with it nevertheless. After surveying these accounts, Rae follows a line of thought that is found in the homilies of John Chrysostom according to which the baptism is central to the event of the incarnation itself in which the Son of God takes upon himself the whole mystery of our human nature, a nature that is marred by sin. This is a line of thought that leads eventually to the cross, for it is there that the full consequence of the incarnation – Christ's assumption of sinful flesh (σάρξ) – is redemptively worked through.

The theologies of Edward Irving, Karl Barth and John Zizoulas are called upon as the implications of this position are further explored. In particular, it is observed that this account of the baptism requires a relational ontology of personhood in which Christ acts as the representative of sinful humanity, and reconstitutes our fallen humanity by bringing it into reconciled relation with God. This is a work of divine love and so reveals the one who does it to be God's beloved Son.

The action of the Son is further explored in the essay by Douglas Knight, and the focus here is upon the Son's confession. There are, Knight argues, four 'moments' in the theo-logic of God's speech. The Father speaks; the Son receives that speech 'so it comes to its proper place and is vindicated'; the Son answers the Father with his obedience; and the Father receives the Son. In and through this act of conversation and communion, creation is brought into being, is completed and perfected, and offered back to the Father for his approval and joy. That conversation between Father and Son is sustained by the Spirit who continually gives the future, completed world to the church.

This four-fold speech-act constitutes the economy of God through which the world receives its being. More than that, however, this economy of God is also the means by which we are made both hearers and speakers of God's Word. The action of God is an action that enables humanity under the leadership of the Son and the enabling of the Spirit to join in the Son's work of presenting the world to the Father in thanksgiving and praise. It is in confessing Jesus as Lord, finally, that 'we, for the first time, freely and really act ... We are not the Lord, and so we can thank God'.

Worship is also the theme of the essay by Sandra Fach, who explores the role of the ascended Christ as mediator of our worship. Drawing particularly on the work of Josef Jungman, Fach argues that the mediatorial role of Christ in worship has long been neglected. Of crucial importance here is the neglect of Christ's humanity in the ascension. Far from leaving his humanity behind in the ascension, it is precisely in the unity of his person as human and divine that the ascended Christ *continues* his mediatorial work.

Attention is focused initially on the mediatorial doxology, 'Glory to the Father *through* the Son and in the Spirit'. As the tradition of Christian worship progressed, however, we find the mediatorial 'through' increasingly replaced by 'with' so that the role of Christ as mediator is lost. Fach offers a detailed account of this linguistic alteration, noting in particular the increasing separation between God and humanity that the doxological change effects. If Christ is not the mediator of our worship, then we are left to direct towards God only our own pitiful expressions of praise. Little wonder then that God should appear remote. There is desperate need, therefore, for a recovery of emphasis on the priestly mediation of Christ. Fortunately the tradition has not left us bereft of the means for such a recovery. Fach mines deeply the theologies of Basil and Nicolas Cabasilas, of Calvin and Charles Wesley, along with the more recent work of James and Thomas Torrance, and Douglas Farrow. To worship the Father *with* the Son certainly preserves Christ's divinity, but to worship the Father *through* the Son, maintains in much better balance the *humanity* of Christ as well. More yet to the point, we are thus enabled to worship God in spirit and in truth.

The volume concludes with a response to all of the above from Christoph Schwöbel of the University of Tübingen. In characteristically masterful style, Schwöbel provides a clear articulation of the key themes treated in the volume and adds his own constructive contributions to the debates engaged in by the earlier contributors.

IV

The conference at which these essays were first presented was planned by Professor Colin Gunton before he died. As always with Colin, he was looking forward with great enthusiasm to the gathering of his colleagues and friends at yet another in a long series of successful conferences of the Research Institute in Systematic Theology at King's College, London.

Sadly, Colin was not to be with us at the conference in September 2003 as he died very suddenly in May of that year. As it turned out, therefore, many friends and colleagues gathered at that conference who would not otherwise have been there, some of whom wrote papers for the occasion in honour of Colin himself.

Although these papers are not, for the most part, a direct engagement with Colin's theological work – there is plenty more time for that ahead of us – they are, nevertheless, gathered together as a modest tribute to him. Colin's contribution to theology during the course of the past three decades was both prolific and incomparable. It is not just a matter of *what* he said and wrote – although that legacy will serve us richly for many years to come – we have much reason to be grateful also for the timeliness of his theology. Colin helped a great many people to recover confidence in the intellectual coherence and explanatory power of the Christian faith at a time when it has been under siege. He did this quite simply because of his own confidence that the gospel of Jesus Christ is the truth about God and about the world, and that it is the good news of the world's redemption. That meant for Colin that every part of the world, and every facet of its life was a proper object of theological investigation. His own interests were broad, from music, to literature, to art, and, of course, to nature in his beloved horticultural endeavours, and he brought all these to bear in the theological task of bearing witness to the love and the glory of God.

It is in appreciation of Colin's theological gifts, as also of his friendship and collegiality, that this volume is dedicated to him. It begins therefore with a tribute to his theology, penned by Christoph Schwöbel, and first delivered at a memorial service in the chapel at King's College in September 2003.

A Tribute to Colin Gunton

Christoph Schwöbel

Giving thanks for the life of Colin Gunton, the theologian, the teacher, the colleague, the friend, means remembering and celebrating what we have received from Colin and through Colin. It means remembering a particular person with particular gifts and characteristics whose achievements are all shaped by the person he was and by the particular personal characteristics that made him the person we remember with respect and affection. Colin would have been the first to remind us that what we received from him was not his to give but is ultimately rooted in God as 'the giver of every perfect gift', as the King's College Prayer has it, and who is the fount of all goodness that can be found in created beings. In expressing our gratitude to Colin we trace the lines that relate what we receive from other persons so that being grateful to Colin entails being grateful to God for Colin.

Colin was first of all a theologian. Although he started his career in this college teaching philosophy of religion, which for him remained a lifelong conversation partner, theology was always his primary calling. Colin was a theologian, in a very specific sense of the word, who understood all theology as part of the human response to the message of the gospel. The gospel was for him not an extra piece of supernatural information that guides us beyond the capacities of our natural reason. It is the way in which God personally, as Father, Son and Spirit, relates to us, gives himself to us and lays claim to all dimensions of our existence so that theology is a response to this event, the response that is enabled by God's address to us. If this is the case that theology is ultimately rooted in God's triune self-giving, then the primary question for all theology is that of the identity of this God who so relates to us. 'Who is God if the message of the Gospel is true?' is the one question that guides the whole theological enterprise.

Colin was a trinitarian theologian. The doctrine of the Trinity was for him no optional extra to theology. It was simply the way in which theology can remain true to the gospel. Doing trinitarian theology is the manner in which a theology can be a Christian theology. This conviction can already be found in his doctoral thesis, written under the supervision of Robert Jenson and published under the title *Becoming and Being*,[1] and it later developed, very much in conversation with John Zizioulas, into the major focus, the organizing centre of his theology. *An Essay Toward a Trinitarian Theology* was the subtitle of the little book *Enlightenment and Alienation*[2] that he published shortly after becoming Professor of Christian Doctrine at King's College. It could have been the subtitle for every one of the dozen further books he published later.

If God is not simply 'a sea of essence, infinite and unseen' but first of all this particular God, the Father, the Son and the Spirit whose story begins with Israel, culminates in Christ and involves us in the dynamics of the operation of the Spirit of truth, the particular must have a paramount significance in theology as well as in every other dimension of created life. Every created being is called to be particular just as humans are called to be persons. If we still followed the ancient custom of venerating the great doctors of the church by a particular title, Colin Gunton would have to be the *doctor particularitatis*, the teacher of the significance of the particular who was never content with abstract generalities. This applies as much to his theology as to the other passion in his life, his gardening. Gardening was for him the activity of cultivating particularity so that the garden could reflect the rich diversity of particularities that characterizes the creation of this particular trinitarian God.

Colin Gunton was, secondly, a theologian in communion. His theology always needed to be rooted in a particular community. First of all, in his family, which provided the secure foundation of his work and was always the first instance of what Colin thought about when he talked about the significance of particular communities. The dedications of his books say more about this than anything that can be said here. Secondly, his theology was rooted in his church, Brentwood United Reformed Church, the church he served for many years as associate minister, elder, interim-moderator,

[1] *Becoming and Being: The Doctrine of God in Charles Hartshorne and Karl Barth* (Oxford: Oxford University Press, 1978).

[2] *Enlightenment and Alienation: An Essay Toward a Trinitarian Theology* (London: Marshall, Morgan and Scott; Grand Rapids: Eerdmans, 1985).

occasional violinist, member of the recorder group and master of ceremonies at the Christmas celebrations. This is by no means the usual thing. Theologians may write extensively or even excessively about the church without ever really belonging to a local church. This was different in Colin's case. He has reciprocated what he received from Brentwood by making it one of the most well-known churches on the theological scene through his collection of 'Sermons for Brentwood': *Theology through Preaching*.[3] And there is the community of King's College to which he remained faithful for over thirty-four years, an almost unique exception in modern academic life.

Being a theologian in communion meant, for Colin, to be a theologian in conversation. Teaching theology and doing research in theology meant creating spaces for theological conversation in which knowledge and wisdom could be cultivated. He loved to talk, but he could also listen. When, now fifteen years ago, a younger colleague came forward with the proposal of establishing a Research Institute in Systematic Theology, he immediately agreed and helped to develop the minimal organizational structure that was needed. Since then the Tuesday Seminars, the Day Conferences, and the International Conferences have become a fixture in theological life. The five volumes of papers presented at the International Conferences with topics such as *Persons Divine and Human*, *Trinitarian Theology*, *God and Freedom*, *Creation*, and *Reconciliation*, mostly edited by Colin Gunton, can be found on the reading lists of the most important institutions of theological learning in the world. Many of the former student participants of the conferences now return as speakers.

Colin liked to listen. All of his books since the classic *The One, the Three and the Many: God, Creation and the Culture of Modernity. The* 1992 *Bampton Lectures*[4] were discussed by colleagues and research students in the Tuesday Seminars before publication. His elegant prose reflects the conversation in which the author involves the reader and echoes the many conversations behind the text. The traces of these discussions and of remarks made by those who read his manuscripts before publication can be found in numerous footnotes in his books. I know of no other leading academic who attributed so many significant points to conversations with students and colleagues. The international invitations Colin received and followed, always accompanied by his wife Jenny, to America, Australia, Canada, Germany, the Netherlands, Romania, Singapore (to name but a few) in

[3] *Theology through Preaching. Sermons for Brentwood* (Edinburgh: T&T Clark, 2001).

[4] *The One, the Three and the Many: God, Creation and the Culture of Modernity. The* 1992 *Bampton Lectures* (Cambridge: Cambridge University Press, 1993).

recent years when he was recognized as the most significant voice of English systematic theology, were for him simply extensions of conversations which first began in his cramped study in King's College, London.

Of course, the conversations were not always about theology only. A Tuesday Seminar would have no proper conclusion without lunch in the Riverside Restaurant and the inevitable fish and chips. And at the Annual Conferences of the Society for the Study of Theology which Colin served for ten years as Secretary and later as one of its Presidents, he enjoyed 'associating with the young' as he called it, in the bar after the conference sessions where the transition from serious theology to jokes accompanied by loud laughter – his sense of humour was not always very refined – seemed as easy as it was pleasant.

Thirdly, Colin Gunton was an uncompromising theologian. A declared enemy of all kinds of reductionism he abhorred nothing more than the compromise of theological thought with the fleeting moods of the culture of the day. He was not afraid to appear dogmatic, for he was too well versed in the history of the concept of dogma, knowing that before it became a technical term for the agreed conciliar teaching, it denoted – as, for instance, in its use by the Stoics – the view of reality which can account for the origin, destiny and meaning of all there is. Dogma in the Christian sense means interpreting reality theologically. In this sense, Colin Gunton was fond of being dogmatic, demonstrating that being dogmatic is not the opposite of being critical, as Kant supposed. Every critique has its dogmatic foundation, and dialogue only becomes possible if these presuppositions are declared.

It was this uncompromising approach to the theological task that simply accepts no predefined boundaries for theological discourse that made this dogmatic theologian an acute observer and interpreter of the cultural situation of today. The astonishing range of his writing, from the most intricate problems of the interpretation of the Fathers to the meaning of *The Lord of the Rings*, from problems of the modern understanding of health to the conceptual problems of modern cosmology or to Mozart, all these are relevant questions if 'God and the world', 'this God and this world', is indeed the overall theme of a theological interpretation of reality.

For Colin Gunton this uncompromising approach to theology required discipline, the particular discipline of the methods and criteria of systematic theology. Today, systematic theology is a well-established discipline in English universities. When Colin started his academic career it was seen more as something one did elsewhere – in Germany or in the United States. In the course of his career he established the discipline almost single-handedly in English universities, and the 'King's approach' has become one of the most respected species in the garden of theology. In 1980, when Colin Gunton became the first Lecturer in Systematic Theology in King's College, nobody would have guessed that from 1999 one of the most respected journals in the field, the *International Journal of Systematic Theology*, would be produced by Blackwell of Oxford and edited by Colin Gunton and John Webster, along with Ralph del Colle, and that, even earlier, an English theologian, Colin Gunton, would become a co-editor of one of the established competitors on the Continent, the *Neue Zeitschrift für Systematische Theologie und Religionsphilosophie*. It was the uncompromising persistence of Colin Gunton that effected the change.

Uncompromising was also Colin's attitude to his own work, and uncompromising were the demands that he laid upon himself. The restless energy which everybody could see when he paced the corridors of King's, the impatient creativity which could lead to his sketching a new paper while listening to another that had not quite caught his interest, were never motivated by personal ambition, nor simply by a Puritan work ethic. When the academic honours came – the honorary doctorate from Aberdeen, the DD from London and now Oxford, the named lectureships, the visiting professorships – he accepted them proudly, but also with a sheepish grin as if to say, that's not the real thing, is it? He was too much of an English nonconformist ever to consider himself a pillar of the establishment. What propelled his apparently boundless energy was his passion for theology, the passion to offer the best response to what he understood to be the best promise that humankind ever received. The uncompromising character of his style of doing theology was never more apparent than during the few months at the Center of Theological Inquiry in Princeton when within a space of three months the draft of the first volume of the planned *Systematic Theology* was completed. Colin returned weary, but satisfied, and eager to go on, to rework the first and start on the other three volumes. Uncompromising was also his final reflection on the title: 'Ah well, I think I'll call it "Dogmatics" after all.' This uncompromising style of doing theology was not only Colin's way of living dangerously; it also had a particular enjoyment. I remember quite a number of occasions when we came home on the same train or returned to Brentwood after one of the Conferences of the Research Institute and he would say, 'That was a wonderful discussion. And imagine, we're being paid to do that.'

Let me add one last point that perhaps only a foreigner, albeit an Anglophile, could make: Colin Gunton was a particularly English theologian. To find an English style of doing systematic theology was his life's project. He never ceased extolling the virtues of being English to me, the foreigner, knowing full well that he was preaching to one of the converted. Englishness was the only context in which he would find a constructive use for the term 'religion' which he, whose theological stance was shaped by Karl Barth and Robert Jenson, was accustomed to use only critically. How often have his friends heard him quote: 'The English are such an irreligious race that they invented cricket to give them a sense of eternity.' Cricket was a religion he adhered to and one that marked a clear cultural boundary to cultures which in other ways he admired. I never dared ask about the relationship of this particular religion to the Christian faith, afraid that the answer would point to the batting of some long-forgotten Essex cricketer as an example of the operation of the Holy Spirit. And I am sure it would have turned out that this cricketer was a member of the Congregational Church. There was nothing ideological about this, at least not often. Rather, it was part of the theology of this particular English theologian that these particularities matter. This was never a nationalistic nor an insular attitude. Colin had learned too much from the theology of Israel, Cappadocia, Germany, Switzerland and America to see an English systematic theology as an exercise in theological isolation. Quite the opposite; in the last thirty years the English contribution to the international theological discussion was to a very large extent Colin Gunton's and that of the people he encouraged and influenced.

In giving thanks for the life of Colin Gunton we are comforted by the hope that he shared fervently that our life here on earth and our conversations here are only a beginning, because God wants to converse with us eternally as we shall participate in the conversation which is the life of the triune God. We are grateful for all Colin has given us. And we are grateful for the gift that Colin was for us and continues to be for us. Therefore our gratitude must be directed toward the triune God who is rightly addressed as the Giver of every perfect gift – albeit in created, human, imperfect form which waits to be perfected by God. Thanks be to God.

Chapter 1

Prolegomena to Christology: Four Theses

John Webster

I

Antecedently present in his effulgent majesty as the eternal Son of God, Jesus Christ is known by virtue of the movement of his being in which as Lord and reconciler he freely gives himself to be known by us, and not otherwise.

In Christology, at least, the method may not be arbitrary, for Christology is determined in a fundamental way by the fact that its 'object', that towards which its attention is turned and by which it is led, is the personal presence of Jesus Christ. Jesus Christ is present; his identity is not simply past. His identity, that is, is not located in a temporally remote sphere, nor is it 'finished' in the sense that it can be docketed as a closed, achieved reality which does not initiate active encounter with us but possesses only the passivity of a past reality which we summon into our presence. He is, and is present. Jesus Christ's identity as one who is present to us is, of course, inseparable from his past, a past which has a definite, unalterable sequence and shape, summarized in the church's confession through the key moments of birth, suffering, crucifixion, death, burial, resurrection and ascension. But, as the last two events in that sequence indicate, the trajectory of Jesus Christ's identity stretches inexorably into the present, his past being gathered into his present identity as one who cannot truthfully be spoken of only in the past tense. His past is not mere contingency, but an integral part of his identity as the one who was and is and is to come. He is risen from the dead; and his resurrection is not simply a retrospective declaration – an indication, perhaps, of the unity of purpose between Jesus and his heavenly Father signalling the Father's vindication of his cause – but rather the actuality of his participation in the aliveness and comprehensive presence of God. Moreover, as the present one, Jesus Christ is not absent. His temporal 'presentness', that is, is not only actual in a sphere remote from us. He is our contemporary, not in the sense that his time as it were runs parallel to ours in some other region but does not enter into our own and remains inaccessible, but in the sense that he is *with* us. Risen from the dead, he ascended into heaven and sits at the Father's right hand in glory. But though his presence is no longer in bodily fashion, he is not thereby separated from us: ascension and enthronement are not mere withdrawal, but express the lordly freedom with which he enters into relation with and, indeed, binds himself to those to whom he presents himself in the power of the Holy Spirit.

The 'matter' of Christology is this present one. How is his presence to be characterized? He is present *antecedently*. His presence precedes our self-presence, and fashions it into a counterpart to itself. That is, the presence of Christ is not an extension or modification of our presence to ourselves; it is not some presence-to-hand towards which we are entitled to dispose ourselves as we will. The presence of Christ is divine self-presence, and as such becomes a human present autonomously, in spontaneous fulfilment of its own determination, by virtue of the action of the Holy Spirit, and not by human acts of projection or reconstruction. Accordingly, our presence to ourselves is not a stable and settled disposition of ourselves by which all other presences are measured, and before which Jesus Christ may be summoned to appear as a further object for our attention. It is 'eschatological': our human self-presence is a function of the fact that as Jesus Christ presents himself to us in the Spirit's power, he creates a human present as the auxiliary of his presence, overcoming our pretended self-sufficiency, and making us into the new creatures of God who confess that he is before them. The paradigm of his antecedent presence as the risen one is thus the effortless, unfettered and wholly effective coming of Jesus Christ: 'Jesus came and stood among them' (Jn. 20.26).

Jesus Christ is present as God is present, and so *present in his effulgent majesty as the eternal Son of God*. As the *eternal* Son, he is not Son by adoption or annexation, drawn into the life of the Godhead from outside and ennobled, but ingredient within the immanent life of God. No less than the Father, he is in the beginning; were he not, the Father would not be who he is. The Son is God from God, light from light, sharing in the substance of the Father, and so fittingly praised as God. He does not merely symbolize God or present a particular concentration of the divine presence; he is divine person and agent, to be confessed as Lord. As such he is God's *only* Son. His sonship is wholly unique: he does not exemplify some more general relation of creatures to God, but as the 'only begotten' Son of the Father he is distinguished from all creatures because his origin lies wholly within the inner life of the Godhead; 'begotten of his Father before all worlds', he is the repetition of the being of God, antecedently God's Son. As true God and only Son of the Father, in short, he is Lord, intrinsic to the divine essence, sharing in its might, majesty, dominion and power. And for this reason the Son is – as the *Te Deum Laudamus* puts it – *venerandus*, worthy of all worship, the fit object of the creature's praise of God because he shares in the eternal glory of the divine nature.

The presence of this one is his presence in *effulgent majesty*. It is a majestic presence, because in his presence he is and acts as one who is infinitely superior, disposing of himself in utter liberty. As he comes to us, he does not place himself in our hands, ontologically or noetically; he cannot be converted into a function of our intention, thought or action, but comes as the one he is, in boundless majesty. His presence, though it is real, reliable and constant and not merely asymptotic, has the character of proximity, of a coming to be near rather than of that which can be held and manipulated.[1] Yet this majestic presence is not dark, something whose form we cannot discern. It is radiant; in it the divine glory is manifest (Heb. 1.3; 2 Cor. 4.4). God is in himself glorious and therefore resplendent. His glory is not self-enclosed but self-diffusing, a light which, because it is *light*, sheds itself abroad, freely and majestically imparting and disclosing itself. The presence of Jesus Christ is this divine effulgence: radiant presence, presence which enlightens and so establishes knowledge of itself.

Once again, this radiance may be characterized more closely. The light which Jesus Christ is, his effulgent majesty, is not simply a state but an action and movement. In his majesty as the eternal Son, he is not inert and passive, resting in a separate and secluded glory. Rather, the majesty of Jesus Christ is known in and as the action or movement in which he imparts himself. He himself moves towards us; he *comes* to us; his being is a being-in-coming which is equiprimordially a being-in-giving. This

[1] In this connection, Hans Frei's worry that talk of the presence of Christ – at least in its nineteenth-century idealist exposition – almost inevitably subjects Christ to the believer to whom he is present might be countered by a more dogmatically robust articulation of the freedom of Christ's presence – something which Frei's alternative concept of 'identity' does not fully succeed in doing because of its formality. See H. Frei, *The Identity of Jesus Christ* (Philadelphia: Fortress Press, 1975), vii–x.

movement is the movement of the one who is *Lord*. It is a free movement, not an action under constraint; in his self-bestowal, Jesus Christ does not give himself away. To be accosted by this movement of his presence is not to encounter something accidental, a process wholly within the economy of human temporal causality and sequence, but rather that which is the fulfilment in time of the eternal resolve of God. The origin, energy and mobility of this movement all derive from the divine purpose which is 'set forth in Christ' (Eph. 1.9), and so that which is to be discerned in Christ's presence is 'the purpose of him who accomplishes all things according to the counsel of his will' (Eph. 1.11). Further, this movement is the movement of one who is *reconciler*. The particular path of this movement, that is, is one along which the Lord faces and overcomes the creature's opposition. As he moves along this path, he directs himself to the evil reality of creaturely defiance and repudiation of the human vocation to live in the presence of God – defiance and opposition which trap the creature in ignorance and idolatry. The presence of Jesus Christ as reconciler simply abolishes this human hostility; it outbids it by its sheer radiance, scattering the darkness and restoring creatures to fellowship, and so to knowledge.

In sum: the movement of the being of Jesus Christ is presence, radiance, reconciling self-bestowal. In this movement is the *Sache* of Christology. What are the consequences of this for the knowledge of Christ and therefore for the manner in which the Christological task is to be approached? Our proposition states it in these terms: *Jesus Christ is known by virtue of the movement of his being ... and not otherwise.*

Knowledge of Jesus Christ flows from the movement of his self-presentation which we have just described in summary form. What is the fundamental ground of the knowledge of Jesus Christ? The judgment of some dominant strands of modern theology has been that knowledge of Jesus Christ is subject to a dynamic which is immanent to the human knower, and which can be formulated in general, content-neutral principles of human cognition. Christology is therefore to be preceded by an epistemology, a hermeneutics or a phenomenology of human knowing and interpreting as modes of being in the world. If such a procedure is Christologically problematic, it is because it entails a basic compromise of the character of the object of Christology: it cannot be shown to be fully coherent with the church's confession that Jesus Christ is Lord. If Christology is erected on this basis, that is, at some point or other there will become visible the fact that this strategy regards the knowing or interpreting human subject as the *fundamentum inconcussum veritatis*. This coheres ill with intellectual deference to the lordly movement of Jesus

Christ's own being, since it involves a fatal exchange of subjects in which knowledge of his presence is subordinated to the conditions of the knower. Tucked inside this strategy there is often an assumption about creaturely competence in the matter of knowledge of Christ. This may be a prideful assumption (Jesus Christ, like everything else, is subject to the dictates of universal reason), or it may be a very insecure and anxious assumption that we can rely on nothing other than our fragile selves. But both pride and fear construe acts of knowledge as lying outside the sphere of Christ's lordship; and it is precisely into this construal that Christology must at all costs not betray itself. The lordship of Christ is his non-comparable, self-grounded and axiomatic sovereignty. In the matter of the knowledge of himself, the corollary of his lordship is that there is no access to him other than that which he himself affords. If there were any such access, if parallel to the movement of his self-presence there were a creaturely movement which could anticipate, evoke or even compel Christ's appearance, then Christ would no longer be Lord, for he is not Lord if he is not the agent of his own becoming known. This is simply the extension of the principle *solus Christus* to the *ordo cognoscendi*. In formal terms, what is spoken of here is 'revelation'. But to speak of revelation is to indicate how knowledge of Jesus Christ is rooted in the teleology of his being, his turning to us in which he is known, not because we can draw him into our sphere but because he himself reaches out, anticipating us by being already on the way to us as the risen one in the Spirit's power. Only he can do this; only he has authority and competence to establish knowledge of himself; and only he has the mercy and the determination to act with such authority and competence. Moreover, to speak of revelation is at the same time to speak of reconciliation. Revelation is a term for Jesus Christ's merciful outreach in which he creates fellowship with lost sinners, and 'revealed' knowledge is that knowledge which occurs in the course of the reconciliation of sinners to whom it has been given to perceive the glorious self-movement of the reconciler.

As a result of this free, gracious movement of his, Jesus Christ is *known by us*. He bestows himself, bridging the gulf (historical, moral, experiential) between himself and us, and thereby granting a specific permission and establishing a specific prohibition.

The permission is permission to know him. Knowledge of Jesus Christ is possible and legitimate because of his antecedent, gratuitous and utterly real self-presence. Setting himself forth, expounding himself as the present one who encloses and orders all things, Jesus Christ makes himself known, and thereby excludes the possibility of legitimate, well-founded ignorance of himself. He is, and therefore he is present, and therefore he is known.

There is a negative inference to be drawn here, namely that this given presence of Christ excludes ways of approaching the task of Christology in which there lurks the assumption that Jesus Christ is not, or may not, or cannot be present to us. Jesus Christ's givenness sits ill with, for example, those Christologies which make historical scepticism or probabilistic reasoning the first principle of the knowledge of Christ. More seriously, it cannot be made to cohere with ascetical or negative Christologies which so fear making Jesus Christ into a possessed object that he is pushed into extreme transcendence. Scruples along these lines may be motivated ethically (a desire to counter ideological abuse of a theology of Christ's presence) or metaphysically (a desire to extract Christology from ontotheology). But the diagnosis is incorrect, in that it assumes that the Christian confession of *Christus praesens* is an instance of a degenerate ideology or ontology; and the cure – an assertion of the elusiveness of Christ as the first principle of Christology – kills the patient.

Jesus Christ can be known, and known *by us*. The knowledge which is authorized by the self-presence of Jesus Christ is a genuine human knowing. What his risen presence creates are forms of thought and speech which are a human counterpart to his self-declaration. The gift of his presence is thus not simply an utterly objective and self-enclosed *perfectum*, but a matter for human knowing and language. Alongside and in strict subordination to 'revelation' there is 'revealedness', the human fruit of the Spirit's regeneration of the work of creaturely knowing in which Christ is not only glimpsed from afar but genuinely known by those whom he illuminates with his presence. Because this creaturely work can at no point be considered in abstraction from the work of the Spirit, it has a particular character; both the identity of the knower and the activities of knowing are transformed as they are subject to the Spirit's realization of the regenerative work of Christ. This knowing and its human subjects are in Christ, and therefore they are a new creation. Their newness is especially visible in that the knowledge of Christ which the Spirit realizes is not an act of *positing* but of *confession*. There is certainly a genuinely human knowing which can properly be characterized as a knowing *by us*. But 'by us' does not entail 'put forward by us': we are not authorized or competent to make any such proposal, once again because that which is the matter of our knowing is Jesus Christ's reality as Lord, the one whose majesty and spontaneous freedom wholly precede us. The deity which is his and in which he presents himself to us is antecedent (otherwise it would not be deity). As such, it cannot be ascribed to him, perhaps as the fruit of some process of theological deduction; nor can it be an evaluation of him reached as the terminus of a consideration of his moral or experiential impact. He is Lord, and therefore knowledge of him cannot be derived from anything other than his own being and action. But this does not disqualify knowledge of him as authentic human knowledge; it simply specifies it as confession – as an act of hearing, obedience and allegiance in which the church bows before the presence of the one by whom it has been found, and gives voice to his sheer prevenience.

To draw the threads together: in the sphere of reality whose resplendent centre is Jesus Christ himself, God the Father has willed a knowledge of the Son of God which God the Holy Spirit has effected. The God of our Lord Jesus, the Father of glory, has given to his church a spirit of wisdom and of revelation in the knowledge of him (cf. Eph. 1.17). This permission carries with it a prohibition: that *Jesus Christ is known by virtue of the movement of his being* entails *and not otherwise*. The fact that in the Spirit's power Jesus Christ gives himself to be known in this way, creating this very specific reality and the corresponding capacity, entails an exclusiveness of access. The rule by which Christology must be governed is: he is Lord in the knowledge of his lordship, and can therefore be known only as he moves towards us. Only as the one he is and in the movement of his being can he be known. Because he is who he is, and because he acts as he acts in his majestic self-presentation, he cannot be 'sought'. That is, he cannot be approached as if he were an elusive figure, absent from us, locked in transcendence or buried in the past, and only to be discovered through the exercise of human ingenuity. Christology cannot creep up on him and catch him unawares. Nor is it at liberty to decide that his self-presence is so indefinite or fogged over by the distortions and incapacities of his human witnesses that theology must run its own independent checks in order to reassure itself that he really is able to present himself. All such strategies, whether in biblical scholarship or philosophical and dogmatic theology, are in the end methodologically sophisticated forms of infidelity. Their assumption is that he is not present unless demonstrably present – present, that is, to undisturbed and unconverted reason. But to such demonstration he will not yield the mystery of his person.

II

'God sets among men a fact which speaks for itself.'[2] We may sum up what has been indicated so far by saying that as there is a sphere of reality over which Jesus Christ presides as the enthroned Lord who is before all things

[2] K. Barth, *Church Dogmatics* IV/2 (Edinburgh: T&T Clark, 1961), 221.

and in whom all things hold together, so there is also a sphere of knowledge of him. He establishes that sphere in the act of his self-bestowal; his reconciling presence sets aside the estrangement and hostility of mind of corrupt creatures, and brings into existence a place in which he makes himself known. The knowledge which he creates is legitimate; it is not wholly imperilled by the vacillation and pride of all human projects, but calmly, soberly and lawfully constituted as true, reliable knowledge of Christ. Its legitimacy, truth and reliability do not derive from its human subjects (whether in the form of epistemological sophistication, critical awareness, historical learning or experiential finesse), but solely from the turning of Jesus Christ. That movement of his being is always gracious; it cannot be arrested, or considered a movement which is complete and can be set behind us. As a consequence, there is always a measure of human insecurity in this knowledge. But what is humanly fragile is divinely secure, authoritative and lawful, because of the self-giving of Jesus Christ. In that movement of his, he is supremely indifferent to human ignorance, unbelief and anxiety; he does not remain at a distance or keep silence, but he simply comes and speaks (cf. Mt. 28.18), declaring the promise which is the unshakeable basis of knowledge of himself: 'I am with you always' (Mt. 28.20). Before proceeding to discuss the character of the sphere of the knowledge of Christ – the sphere of the church and, more particularly, of the church's hearing of Holy Scripture – we pause to consider the consequences of the cognitive ground of Christology for the understanding of the Christological task as positive science.

Within the sphere of knowledge established by Jesus Christ's self-bestowal, Christology is a joyful and reverent positive science whose prolegomena performs a didactic but not demonstrative task.

Christology is a positive science, in that it is the repetition, elucidation and explication in human words and concepts of the axiomatic reality of Jesus Christ. Because of this, Christology may not proceed as an *a-priori* inquiry into the creaturely conditions for knowledge of Jesus Christ: such inquiry cannot but subvert Christology's attention to its object by treating it as a possible state of affairs, so holding at bay its lordly actuality. Rather, as a positive science the task of Christology is an *a-posteriori* depiction of that which has been given. Certainly both terms, 'positive' and 'science', are stretched when deployed in a Christological context. This *positum* has its own determinate character as the presence and action of Jesus Christ in which by the power of the Holy Spirit he sheds abroad the knowledge of his reconciling person and work. His 'givenness' is not that of a worldly entity but of a history of willed divine activity: only in this sense is Christology positive. Moreover, this givenness determines the mode of *scientia* which is appropriate to itself: the operations of Christological science are at every point determined by the lordly movement of Christ, and Christology will always in some way struggle against the confines of existing conceptions of science. Christology is a special science of a special object. However, the designation 'positive science' can still serve to indicate how in the circle of knowledge established by reconciliation and revelation, questions of the existence and availability of its *Sache* have already received an answer in the church's confession of the mystery of Christ's presence.

Christology is *a joyful and reverent* science. Such terms are not merely accidental descriptions of the subjective states of its practitioners; rather, they identify Spirit-generated dispositions which are properly 'objective', that is, fitting and necessary if the work of theological reason is to act in conformity to its given matter. Joy and reverence are not simply ways of talking of the atmosphere of piety in which Christological thought is undertaken. They determine the operations of theology in a direct way, shaping its procedures by enabling it to construe its object appropriately, to adopt a proper posture before that object, to pursue certain modes of activity and to refrain from others, to articulate goals, and to establish criteria by which judgments of adequacy can be made.

Christology is a *joyful* science because thought and speech about Jesus Christ really are made possible by his presence. Finding itself in the sphere of knowledge which he brings into being and maintains, Christology is not harassed by anxious scruple. It is not, for example, overwhelmed by concerns that talk of 'presence' can slide into all manner of idolatry, or that may be tied to a leaden metaphysics of substance, or that it requires some foundation other that that of the sheer self-presentation of Christ as Lord. Christology can be joyful in the face of these anxieties, not because it fails to register that there are real threats to its purity, still less because it considers itself amply equipped to overcome them. Christology's joy derives instead from the fact that it is undertaken in the sphere of Christ's presence and promise. Only in abstraction from that sphere does Christian thought and speech seem a joyless task, condemned to an unending search for reassurances which can never be had in the manner in which they are sought. Yet the joy which is to characterize positive Christological science is *reverent* joy: not brash confidence but the astonished gratitude of the reconciled at the goodness of the one into whose presence they have been called. Joy may be displaced not only by anxiety or irony, but also by a very human and ungodly assertion (orthodox or unorthodox) which replaces the spiritual *positum* of the presence of Christ. A Christology in which this is the case will betray lack of reverence, because it will be forgetful of the movement of mercy which is its founding condition and constant accompaniment. If Christology is to guard itself at this point, however, it will not be by adopting more strategies of self-inspection, more mechanisms to regulate trust. What is required is a certain spiritual vigilance, that fear of the Lord which fastens on the very specific calling and hope given to theology by the presence of Christ, and which looks to him not only to judge but also to sanctify and perfect its work.

In the light of this characterization of the positive science of Christology, what is to be said of the task of formal prolegomena? First: positive Christology requires no prolegomenal demonstration of its viability, because what such a work of demonstration seeks to achieve is already accomplished by its object, Jesus Christ himself in his lordly self-demonstration.

In more detail: Jesus Christ is comprehensively Lord and therefore Lord in the knowledge of his lordship. Because of this, Christology proceeds illegitimately if it attempts to deduce Jesus Christ as a conclusion from some premiss other than his own luminous reality, from something supposedly anterior to him, and more firmly established or evident. Jesus Christ is only and always the beginning, not the end, of a process of thought; his reality is analytic, not synthetic; basic, and never derivative. Thought and speech about him may not be set within some more comprehensive context or considered from some higher vantage-point – a theory of history or religion, some sort of philosophical theism, an ethics of justice. He is not a conclusion to be drawn from some other reality; we cannot look behind him to discover something more fundamental. Christology, therefore, does not labour towards him, but moves easily and freely in the light of the fact that he has already posited himself and established the sphere in which he can be known.

Accordingly, prolegomena conceived as independent *demonstratio* of the reality of Jesus Christ is not a defence of him but a narrowing of the range of his effectiveness, even, perhaps, a covert attack on his sovereignty. To defend his majestic self-presence by some prolegomenal strategies is to risk standing against the free clarity, power and truth of his giving of himself, by acting as if we had competence to tender our assistance to complete his self-manifestation and render it persuasive. Why press this point? The ground for this refusal of prolegomenal demonstration is not a principled rejection of apologetics or foundations: theology is unlikely to be served by over-interest in such issues of general epistemology. What calls into question independent demonstration of positive Christological science is not epistemological theory but an ontological matter: Jesus Christ is the embodiment of the divine omnipotence. He has no ground of reality except in himself, the Son who proceeds from the Father; and there is, therefore, no ground of the knowledge of him except his own spontaneous and effective self-exposition in the Holy Spirit. Put formally: the law of thinking must be the law of the object. The object is 'law' in that it is a formed and self-communicative reality, an authoritative presence which commands, empowers and directs our acts of recognition. Prolegomenal demonstration subjects that object to an alien law (epistemological, phenomenological, metaphysical). In so doing, it has to evade the fact that the object of Christology is, indeed, *in se* formed, self-communicative, authoritative and present, and has to operate as if form, communication, authority and presence were bestowed on him by a reality more fundamental than Jesus Christ himself. This a well-ordered Christology will not allow.

In this light, Christological prolegomena has a more modest, *didactic* task. Its aim is to outline basic characteristics of Christological thought and speech, and to indicate something of the requirements under which Christology stands by virtue of its subject matter. In an important sense, it is retrospective, in that it seeks to draw attention to that which is already established, namely Christ in his self-demonstration, and to trace what that self-demonstration entails for the intellectual activity of Christology. Its limited concern is with the character and modes of operation of Christology in the face of the given reality under whose tutelage it stands. It is a low-level undertaking, presenting a preliminary map of the Christological terrain and offering guidance on how best to move through it. It orients Christology to the nature of its object (Jesus Christ's majestic self-communication); it indicates the sphere of his presence in the fellowship of the saints; and it identifies the instrument of his self-communication (Holy Scripture) and speaks of the manner in which that constitutes the norms of Christological thought and speech. In this way it serves orderly instruction. Beyond this – in prefacing Christology by some pre-theological discussion of methods, norms and sources, or in articulating a better rationale for confession of Christ than that known to the confession itself – it will be reluctant to go.

III

Christology is a positive science in the church, the fellowship of the saints which knows Jesus Christ.

Christology is church science, the orderly explication of the knowledge of Jesus Christ which is already present in the church because Jesus Christ is present to the church. It has, therefore, a twofold 'positivity'. It is a positive science because of its object, Jesus Christ, who presents himself to the church in lordly freedom. But it is also a positive science because, as Jesus Christ presents himself by the power of the Holy Spirit, he posits a sphere in which he can be and is known. As he presents himself, he establishes a domain and gathers a community which he authorizes and empowers for knowledge of himself. Theology is the positive science of that fellowship.

These two aspects of the positivity of Christology – that which derives from its object, and that which derives from its social locale – exist in strict and irreversible sequence. Christology is positive church science because and only because it is positive science of Jesus Christ; its churchly positivity is wholly derivative from the positivity which it has by virtue of its object. This is so for two reasons. (1) The churchly positivity of theology is not an instance of a general rule that *scientia* is always embedded within particular forms of common life. Application of this rule has been standard in criticism of modern ideals of universal reason and their purported elision of the local or traditional character of rational practices; as such, it has often found a welcome from those who have sought to recover the churchly character of theological work. One of the weaknesses into which these theologies may be betrayed, however, is that of slipping into an immanentist ecclesiology in which churchly positivity far outweighs Christological positivity. Appealing to general principles of sociality, the accounts of churchly existence which are produced are often only secondarily theological. Frequently lacking in much by way of direct deployment of language of Jesus Christ's self-presentation, and frequently giving prominence to the historical visibility of the church, they construe the churchly positivity of theology primarily in terms of its existence within this social domain. This is often coupled with a view of the church as a stable, consistent set of practices which it is the task of theology to describe. But the church is not simply a visible form of common life: as the fellowship of the saints it is in a very important sense 'invisible', that is, visible and knowable only by virtue of the act of Christ's eschatological self-presence in the Spirit. Only as such is it a *positum*, and only as the science of such a community is Christology a positive churchly science. (2)

The churchly positivity of Christology does not entail a claim that Jesus Christ attains to wholeness of being in the sphere of the church, or that the church bodies forth or completes him. Such a claim is both Christologically and ecclesiologically inadequate. Its Christological inadequacy is that only with difficulty can it cohere with a sense that Jesus Christ is *a se*, and that he is an ontological *perfectum*. It construes his giving of himself to the church as in some way his generating of himself. His sufficiency, his majestic repose at the Father's right hand in which he is head over all things, is not easily coordinated with any affirmation of the coinherence of Christ and the church. Certainly he is 'head over all things for the church' (Eph. 1.22); certainly the church is his 'body' and 'fullness' (Eph. 1.23): but always and only because of his immanent and sovereign power as the one who 'fills all in all', who alone is properly and in himself 'fullness'. Furthermore, the ecclesiological inadequacy of talk of the church as bodying forth Christ is that its expansiveness misconstrues the character of the church as *creatura verbi divini*, failing to catch the passivity of the church's existence as elect fellowship, called, justified and made holy for praise, confession and testimony. That is, any account of churchly positivity has to respect the fundamental ontological law of the church, namely that as God's 'workmanship', the church is what it is by virtue of 'the immeasurable greatness of his power in us who believe' (Eph. 1.19). With this qualification, we turn to explicate how it is that Christology is church science.

First, the church of Jesus Christ is the fellowship of the saints, the holy church. The church's holiness is its election by God. Holiness is not a property which the church has in and of itself, but a relation into which it has been adopted, and a summons which it is called to obey. The church's holiness is alien: it is holy, not because of any inherent worth or dignity, or on the basis of moral or religious performance, but because of the absolution which it has received from the work and word of Christ. He makes the church holy, calling it into fellowship with himself, cleansing it from its sins by his death and resurrection, and through the Spirit uniting it to himself so that it becomes the gathering of those who are 'saints in Christ Jesus' (Eph. 5.25b–27). The church's holiness consists, therefore, in the fact that it is set apart by the triune God. By the will of God the Father, the church is destined to live in holiness – from all eternity, 'before the foundation of the world', the church is chosen to be 'holy and blameless' (Eph. 1.4). The Father's will is acted out in the saving mission of God the Son, in whom the holy church has 'redemption' and 'forgiveness' (Eph. 1.7). And the church is renewed in holiness by the action of God the Holy Spirit, whose work it is to bestow God's life upon 'the saints who are also faithful in Christ Jesus' (Eph. 1.1). Holiness is thus the gift of the Holy Trinity. It is precisely this that prohibits theology from developing an account of the church's life (and of the churchly character of its Christology) primarily in terms of its visible sociality, for the fellowship of the saints is first of all vertical, and only by derivation horizontal; the saints' *koinonia* is defined by its object (Jesus Christ in his active self-presence) and only thereafter by the co-presence of social actors.

Second, this fellowship of the saints is, *inter alia*, a sphere of knowledge. The acts of the Holy Trinity in electing, reconciling and sanctifying the community continue in the work of enlightening the church about the truth of its existence. The church is therefore a fellowship in which it makes good sense to pray 'that the God of our Lord Jesus Christ, the Father of glory, may give you a spirit of wisdom and of revelation in the knowledge of him, having the eyes of your hearts enlightened, that you may know ...' (Eph. 1.17f.). The saints' knowledge may variously be described. It is (1) a triune work. It is not the hesitant or bold self-reflection of the community, but knowledge that must be talked about by speaking of the God of our Lord Jesus Christ, the Father of glory and the Spirit who bestows understanding. Such knowledge is, therefore, (2) knowledge by gift. It is Spirit-derived wisdom, the fruit of revelation and enlightenment in which human folly, ignorance and darkness are set aside in order that the church may know. And it is (3) knowledge that has a definite object, namely the condition in which the church stands. It is knowledge of 'the hope to which he has called you ... the riches of his glorious inheritance in the saints, and ... the immeasurable greatness of his power in us who believe' (Eph. 1.18f.). It is not exploratory or arbitrary knowledge, but the cognitive repetition of the divine work which engenders and upholds the church. In a culture for which historical process is axiomatic, the immediacy of the way in which Ephesians describes the church as a sphere of knowledge is startling. Are we committed thereby to describing the saints' knowledge of Christ as somehow 'pure' – non-contingent, unsullied by time and the processes of learning, segregated from other spheres and acts of knowing, simply given? The commitment of a good deal of historical theology to deny that the church's knowledge of Christ is uncontaminated has certainly sometimes been a wholesome affirmation that creaturely knowledge of Christ is just that – *creaturely*, and therefore not independent of creaturely modes of reception. But more needs to be said: the church's knowledge of Christ, because it is the knowledge of the *holy* church, of the saints, is a sphere in which human knowing is in transformation. It is not simply caught up in the tide of human process, but is also set under the sign of Christ's victory. That victory includes his victory in the sphere of knowledge. In him, there is given to the saints not an indefinite word overlain with all manner of accretions, but 'the Word of truth' (Eph. 1.13). And because of him, the apostle's prayer 'that you may know' (Eph. 1.18; cf. Col. 1.10) is a prayer that looks towards a very real possibility, one for which the saints are authorized and empowered, and one under whose promise the work of Christology is to be undertaken.

IV

As an exercise of sanctified reason in the fellowship of the saints, Christology assists in the Spirit's work of edifying the church by orderly explication of the knowledge of Christ which is already present in the church because he himself is present to the church. Jesus Christ is present to the church as the Word of God. As the eternal divine Word he is in himself eloquent, and he now addresses himself to the church, setting himself in the midst of the fellowship of the saints clothed with his gospel. The instruments of his self-presentation as Word are Holy Scripture and the sacraments. Through these creaturely auxiliaries he bears witness to himself and so edifies the community. The theological work of the church has a particular relation to the canon of Scripture, because through Holy Scripture Christ exercises his governance of the church's intellectual acts, moulding the saints' thought and speech into conformity with himself by reproving invention and arbitrariness, and enabling truthful articulation of the gospel. Hence a final proposition: *The norm of Christology is Holy Scripture, the sanctified and inspired instrument through which Christ speaks his gospel to the church and which, as the sufficient and clear attestation of the reality of Christ and as the subject of ever-fresh exegesis, is to direct the church's Christological thought and speech.*

As a positive science, Christology is a normed science. Because it does not posit itself but is posited in and with Jesus Christ's self-presence, Christology derives its law *ab extra*, and is legitimate and edifying to the degree to which it does its work in submission to that law. Christological *ratio* is subordinate to *lex Christi*. Jesus Christ is himself the proper and final norm of Christological science; all other norms (creedal, confessional, traditional) are relative to him. His direction of the thought and speech of the church is, however, exercised through the creaturely auxiliary of Holy Scripture.

To put the matter in telegraphic form: Holy Scripture is a fitting servant of the self-presentation of Jesus Christ because it is sanctified and inspired in order to perform this service. The sanctification of Scripture – that by virtue of which it may be called holy – is the work of the Spirit whereby this collection of creaturely texts is, without forfeit of its creaturely integrity, so ordered, shaped and preserved that it becomes capable of the task to which it is appointed. As a sanctified reality, Holy Scripture is not divinized; rather its course – from pre-literary tradition through authorship, redaction, reception and canonization – is overseen, and it is made sufficient for its calling. Inspiration is a more restricted category, a way of indicating the work of the Holy Spirit with regard to the words of Scripture. Scripture is inspired, not simply because its authors or readers are illumined, but because – again without prejudice to the integrity of creaturely occurrence – the Spirit generates a *text*: not simply a 'message' within a text, or a response from its readers, but a fitting linguistic form of the substance of the gospel in which Christ addresses himself to the saints. The viability of such an account depends, of course, on a variety of other factors: a non-dualist, non-competitive understanding of the relation of divine and creaturely activity, a carefully constructed account of divine self-mediation, a direct and operative theology of resurrection, ascension and Spirit. Here, however, these matters must remain unexplored, and the main point secured, namely that, so construed, Holy Scripture is the means through which Christ speaks his gospel to the church, so attesting his own reality and presence. This complex though unified collection of texts serves the presence of Jesus Christ by indicating or bearing testimony to his address of the saints.

This event – Jesus Christ's act of eloquence – through this instrument – the canon of Scripture – is the norm for the church's Christology. Christology is a normed science; because it is church *science*, knowledge in accordance with the inherent law and movement of its object, it is not an arbitrary but a ruled exercise of the church's mind. This means, consequently, that Christology has a definite subject matter about which it is required to think and speak. That subject matter is not something which the church's theology is free to create or manipulate *ad libitum*, perhaps in response to the demands or limitations of its culture. Jesus Christ presents himself in this definite form, through the testimony of the prophets and apostles; he is radiant *here*, in a way that requires Christology to discover in Scripture the clarity that he already has, rather than to cast around for some other kind of clarity (such as the clarity of historical evidences or philosophical foundations). And in the light of this very definite subject matter which presents itself in Holy Scripture with radiant force, Christology is subject to very definite limits beyond which it is prohibited to go. To the *clarity* of the gospel of Christ in Scripture there corresponds its *sufficiency*: the thought and speech of the church in the matter of Jesus Christ do not require some supplements to Scripture, for the instrument through which Jesus Christ announces himself is, by virtue of the Spirit's work, adequate for the task that it is appointed to undertake.

Normed in this way by the canon in its clarity and sufficiency, Christology is required to make a definite act of submission. Holy Scripture is Christology's norm. But respect for that norm involves a good deal more than formal acknowledgment of its authority; Scripture's normativeness is not abstract, but a concrete directive, namely, a requirement that Christological statements both derive from and promote attention to the biblical attestation. The seriousness with which Christology takes up its position beneath the canon will be shown less in formal statements of biblical authority (and still less by efforts to establish Scripture's veracity through historical apologetics) and more by constant exegesis. This is because the normativity of Scripture is not merely statutory, something that can be accorded recognition but then left to one side, to be invoked only in cases of transgression. Scripture is norm because it is the *viva vox Christi*, a movement of revelation requiring not merely acknowledgment but a corresponding movement of active subordination. How is that subordination demonstrated in the work of Christology? Christological science attempts to explicate the self-presence of Christ to which Scripture testifies. That explication has characteristically involved the fashioning and refinement of a (relatively small) number of concepts such as substance, person, nature and their corollaries, mostly borrowed from the vocabulary of late antique metaphysics. Those concepts have acquired authority in the church by incorporation into its confessions, which act as a further, subordinate norm for Christology. The fruitfulness of this conceptual equipment, its capacity to act as a fitting norm, depends upon its being deployed in such a way that it demonstrates deference to the biblical testimony. This deference requires a careful employment of abstraction. Abstract concepts such as those created in the dogmatic tradition of the church are not intended to replace or improve upon what is set out in Scripture, but simply to gather together what Scripture articulates to assist its orderly explication. The concepts are valuable only to the extent to which they are lightweight, informal and transparent to the biblical witness which they serve to indicate. The conceptuality of Christology must therefore emerge from and promote attention to Scripture; its end is to demonstrate exemplary submission to the canon and so assist in the church's hearing and speaking of the gospel of Christ.

V

Christology is a special science of a special object. Hegel's worry – that such a theology condemns itself to become the last relic of pre-critical realism, busily portraying a world of timeless supersensible objects – has by now acquired canonical status. Critical theology sought to dispose of the danger by refusing to allow that there are any special-status sciences: if coherent claims to knowledge of Jesus Christ are to be advanced, they must be defensible as instances of a more comprehensive science. More recent deconstructive theology has sought to dispose of the danger by a more extreme measure, namely abandoning both 'science' and 'objects'. What is attempted here is certainly closer to the tradition for which Kant had only contempt, and over which Hegel lingered before making a final rejection; but there are some important differences. It places much emphasis on the divine 'movement' or 'turning', and so its understanding of the fit between concepts and reality is historical, not static. It sees this movement as one of reconciliation, a history of repentance, rebirth, justification and sanctification, and not as abstract coordination of minds and objects. And its idiom is that of the personal presence of Jesus Christ in the power of the Spirit and in fulfilment of the Father's resolve. Christological science is the science of this movement. To trace that movement is not to busy oneself with a comfortable science of being, but to be brought into crisis – not the pretentious crisis of dissonance from cultural norms, but the crisis that derives from the fact that to encounter Christ in thought is to be encountered by one before whose feet we fall as though dead (Rev. 1.17). Yet the one who slays also addresses us: 'Fear not'; and in that is the promise under which Christology may stand.

Chapter 2

From Titles to Stories: A Narrative Approach to the Dynamic Christologies of the New Testament[1]

Richard A. Burridge

It is commonplace within literary theory to talk of texts as windows and mirrors. To read a text as a 'window' is to look through it to that which lies 'beyond', 'behind' or 'on the other side' of the text. With regard to the New Testament, especially the gospels, this approach uses the text to gain access back behind the period when they were written in order to reconstruct the historical Jesus, or to test out hypotheses about the early Church communities. It is a method that has dominated tradition-historical critical study of the New Testament over the last century or more. From a doctrinal point of view, such an approach can also be used to reconstruct early New Testament Christologies lying behind the text, such as early belief in Jesus as Son of Man or a prophet.

The problem is that we just do not know anything about what lies 'on the other side' of the gospels. At least with St Paul's letters, we know who wrote them and usually those to whom they were addressed – except, of course, that both authorship and recipients of many epistles are disputed and the dates of all of them are open to debate. With the gospels, we know

[1] Having first met Colin Gunton at the Society for the Study of Theology in 1994, when I gave a paper on the Christology of the gospels, I am glad to offer this paper as a tribute at the RIST (Research Institute in Systematic Theology) conference dedicated to his memory.

even less about the authors, methods of production and delivery, original audiences and so forth. Thus, while we may think we are looking *through* the text as a 'window' to what lies 'behind it', in fact we may be catching a reflection *in* the text as a 'mirror' of what lies 'in front of it' – namely our own presuppositions or prejudices. Thus exegesis becomes eisegesis and the hermeneutical circle collapses into a vicious circle. It is not surprising therefore that many literary theorists have given up an authorial intention and moved instead to reader-response approaches, concentrating on the meaning found in a text by its audience or reader today. If this is using the text as a 'mirror', at least it is an honest attempt to recognize that this is what we are doing. Systematic theologians and doctrine specialists have always used the New Testament texts to enable them to 'reflect' upon Christian doctrines, especially Christology – and this is another example of such 'mirror' approaches.

Neither treating texts as windows nor mirrors really does justice to the nature of the New Testament books, since they fail to ask questions about the nature of the texts themselves. What kind of glass do we have here? How is it meant to be used? Increasingly, narrative approaches have been adopted by biblical critics over the last decade or two, and these may provide a better direction for the use of the New Testament in Christology in general. Furthermore, such narrative approaches demonstrate that there are a wide variety of differing Christologies within the books of the New Testament which may be more use to systematic theologians and doctrine specialists than more usual 'synthetic' approaches. This essay will explore traditional approaches to the New Testament as a 'window' through titles and historical reconstructions, followed by a consideration of recent alternative approaches, especially those arising from the interpretation of the gospels as biographical narrative.

Christology through Titles

The History of Religions approach to the New Testament, *die religionsgeschichtliche Schule* – from its early German proponents, particularly from the University of Göttingen, through to Bultmann and others – tended to see an evolutionary development in early Christology, beginning with Jesus as a wandering Palestinian teacher or Jewish rabbi, going through various stages such as healer and prophet within the early Jewish church; and then increasingly he was seen as a divine man or saviour figure within a Hellenistic context, until finally he becomes the Lord of a mystery cult, otherwise known as the early Christian church. This is, of course, best laid out in Bousset's magisterial treatment, *Kyrios Christos*.[2]

Oscar Cullmann stressed that early Christian theology is Christology. God is identified as the 'Father of Jesus Christ'.[3] He also pointed out that the later Christological controversies were all about the 'person of Christ' or his 'nature', in terms of his relationship to God and within the Godhead, or in terms of his divine and human natures. However, the New Testament 'hardly ever speaks of the person of Christ without at the same time speaking of his work' (p. 3); the concern is not so much about the nature of Jesus, as about his function. Cullmann was cautious about the comparative religions approach, suggesting that 'Christology had necessarily to conform to the conceptual scheme already present in Judaism or Hellenism' (p. 5). Rather, he saw Christological debate as arising, even during Jesus' lifetime, with the questioning at Caesarea Philippi, 'Who do people say that I am?' (Mk 8.27–29). Since the response includes theological titles such as 'prophet' and 'messiah', Cullmann sets out to examine all the various possible titles in turn. He divides them into titles that refer to Jesus' earthly work (prophet, suffering servant, high priest), to his future work (messiah and Son of Man), and to his present work (Lord and Saviour), before finally considering those that refer to his pre-existence (Word and Son of God). In each case, he looks first at the meaning of the title within Judaism, then at whether Jesus saw himself in terms of this title, and what it might have meant in his life, before going on to analyse the New Testament material about each title. As a result, he argues that New Testament Christology did not arise out of a contemporary mythology, but out of the facts and events about Jesus and through the reflection of the early Church upon *Heilsgeschichte* (pp. 315–28).

Hahn followed a similar approach of concentrating on the titles of Jesus, though he linked them to the evolutionary history of religions concept and contended that the highest ideas of pre-existence and divinity came out of a Hellenistic background.[4]

Moule protested against all of this.[5] He compared the history of religions approach to an evolutionary process, such as the evolution of *homo*

[2] Wilhelm Bousset, *Kyrios Christos: A History of the Belief in Christ from the Beginnings of Christianity to Irenaeus* (ET; Nashville: Abingdon, 1970); German original, Göttingen: Vandenhoeck & Ruprecht, 1913.

[3] Oscar Cullmann, *The Christology of the New Testament* (ET; London: SCM Press, 1959); German original, Tübingen: J.C.B. Mohr, 1957.

[4] F. Hahn, *The Titles of Jesus in Christology* (London: Lutterworth Press, 1969); German original, Göttingen: Vandenhoeck & Ruprecht, 1963.

[5] C.F.D. Moule, *The Origin of Christology* (Cambridge: Cambridge University Press, 1977).

sapiens from a lemur or ape (p. 2), with a radical change between the early stages of Jesus being seen as a revered master within a Jewish Palestinian setting and then being worshipped as divine Lord by Hellenistic Christians. Rejecting this schema, Moule argued instead for a 'developmental approach' in which the later stages are construed not as new additions but rather as a 'drawing out' of what is already there, analogous not to the evolution of a new species but rather to the unfolding of the flower from a bud, or the growth of fruit from the flower (p. 3). He also criticized as too clear-cut a chronological sequence from early Palestinian Jewish Christianity, through the diaspora into Pauline and later Hellenistic Gentile communities. Nonetheless, Moule still follows the same basic approach by studying titles – first Son of Man, Son of God, Christ and Kyrios – and other descriptions such as corporate phrases or concepts like the Body and the Temple. Further consideration of Paul, the rest of the New Testament, the scope of the death of Christ and the theme of fulfilment, lead him to conclude that his developmental model is a better approach, and he finishes by arguing that all the later Christological ideas are rooted in Jesus' own understanding.

Dunn also follows this method of studying titles.[6] He looks at Son of God, Son of Man, the last Adam, spirit or angel, the Wisdom of God and the Word of God. It is probably the most thorough treatment of the title-based approach and it still repays careful study, especially in the second edition with Dunn's extended response to his critics in a new foreword (pp. xi–xxxix). Dunn's conclusions go against the history of religions approach by arguing that there was nothing in the Jewish or Hellenistic worlds that would have given rise to the idea of the incarnation; while we cannot claim that Jesus believed himself to be the incarnate Son of God, this later development was 'an appropriate reflection on and elaboration of Jesus' own sense of sonship and eschatological mission' (pp. 253–54). It was the resurrection that was the real catalyst, followed by the growing 'backward extension of Son of God language', with Paul's use of Wisdom language bringing the process to the crucial point where John then developed the idea of the pre-existent Word. It is important to note that Dunn does see a really significant break and change with the Johannine doctrine of the incarnation – yet nonetheless views this as an 'appropriate reflection'. Therefore Dunn can still refer to this as an 'evolutionary process' (p. 261), though in his later work he prefers to talk of it as 'unfolding'.[7]

[6] J.D.G. Dunn, *Christology in the Making* (London: SCM Press, 1980; 2nd edn, 1989).
[7] J.D.G. Dunn, 'The Making of Christology – Evolution or Unfolding?', in J.B. Green and M. Turner (eds.), *Jesus of Nazareth: Lord and Christ* (Grand Rapids: Eerdmans, 1994), 437–52.

Whatever term or metaphor is used, we notice that all of these treatments concentrate on the titles and descriptions of Jesus within the New Testament; they try to study each one separately and then relate them to an overall chronological sequence for the evolution, development or unfolding of New Testament Christology. Thus all of them have a concern for an overall process of Christology within the New Testament – whether that is seen against a background of the history of religions, or as a temporal sequence being traced back to Jesus, and down through the history of the early Church. They all imply that one can talk of 'New Testament Christology' as a single enterprise, and they use New Testament texts as a 'window' onto it. Whether in fact they are merely catching reflections of themselves or their presuppositions in a mirror remains to be seen!

Christology from Below: Historical Reconstructions

Both historical sequences and a consideration of titles feature in the various Quests for the historical Jesus: the original Quest, which started from Reimarus and progressed through the works of Strauss, Weiss and Schweitzer;[8] secondly the so-called New Quest beginning with Käsemann's lecture of October 20, 1953 and leading into Bornkamm, Jeremias and Robinson[9] (which is the background for Cullmann's, Hahn's and Moule's treatments) – and now, with what is increasingly seen as the Third Quest, through the work of E.P. Sanders and Tom Wright in their debate with the Californian school of the Jesus Seminar, represented in particular by Robert Funk, Burton Mack and Dominic Crossan.[10]

Obviously, the attempt to provide an historical reconstruction of the life and ministry of Jesus must lie at the heart of any such quest – but it usually involves, or leads into consideration of, the extent to which Jesus saw himself as a prophet, teacher, or Messiah and what he considered his relationship to God and his mission to be. Thus E.P. Sanders's

[8] A. Schweitzer, *Geschichte der Leben-Jesu-Forschung* (Tübingen: Mohr, 1906); ET *The Quest of the Historical Jesus* (London: A. & C. Black, 1954).

[9] J.M. Robinson, *A New Quest of the Historical Jesus* J.B. Green and M. Turner (eds.), SBT, 25 (London: SCM Press, 1959).

[10] B. Mack, *A Myth of Innocence: Mark and Christian Origins* (Philadelphia: Fortress Press, 1988); J.D. Crossan, *The Historical Jesus: The Life of a Mediterranean Jewish Peasant* (Edinburgh: T&T Clark, 1991); R.W. Funk, R.W. Hoover and the Jesus Seminar, *The Five Gospels: The Search for the Authentic Words of Jesus* (New York: Macmillan, 1993).

reconstruction of *The Historical Figure of Jesus*[11] sets out clearly the Palestinian context of Jesus' life and ministry, depicts him as a miracle-worker and teacher–healer, and calls him a 'charismatic and autonomous prophet' (p. 238); it then goes on to discuss all the Christological titles such as messiah, Son of God, Son of Man, and so on. Sanders concludes, however, that 'we do not learn precisely what Jesus thought of himself and his relationship to God by studying titles' (p. 248). Instead he argues that Jesus saw himself as 'having full authority to speak and act on God's behalf' and coins the new description of 'viceroy'.

Tom Wright's massive treatment, in three volumes so far, follows a similar line of argument.[12] In *Jesus and the Victory of God*, he entitles his main historical reconstruction 'The Profile of a Prophet' (Part II, pp. 145–474), while Part III attempts to reconstruct 'The Aims and Beliefs of Jesus' (475–654). While Wright uses titles such as Prophet and Messiah, he also argues, like Sanders, that Jesus' self-understanding is crucial; that while Jesus did see himself as a prophet and in messianic terms, Wright concludes that we should 'forget the "titles" of Jesus, at least for a moment'. It is through Jesus' 'vocation' and intimacy with God whom he knew as 'father' that his ideas of sonship make sense, as he enacts the return of God to his people, the 'returning and redeeming action of the covenant God' through his ministry and death (p. 653). Wright has put forward similar arguments in his various more accessible and popular books.[13]

Markus Bockmuehl's response to the Jesus debate uses titles in its subtitle: *Martyr, Lord, Messiah*.[14] He too attempts an historical reconstruction of Jesus' life, ministry and death, and his messianic self-understanding, and relates this to later Christological development and the debates of the early Church. He concludes that 'the emergence of Christology can be seen as an authentic and consequential expression of the Apostolic faith in the risen Jesus' (p. 166).

[11] E.P. Sanders, *The Historical Figure of Jesus* (Harmondsworth, Penguin 1993); this is the most accessible treatment of Sanders's work, using his large monographs such as *Jesus and Judaism* (London: SCM, 1985).

[12] N.T. Wright, *Christian Origins and the Question of God*: I. *The New Testament and the People of God* (London: SPCK, 1992); II. *Jesus and the Victory of God* (London: SPCK, 1996); III. *The Resurrection of the Son of God* (London: SPCK, 2003), leaving two more volumes still to come.

[13] N.T. Wright, *The Original Jesus: The Life and Vision of a Revolutionary* (Oxford: Lion, 1996); *The Challenge of Jesus: Rediscovering Who Jesus Was and Is* (London: SPCK, 1999); and his debate with Marcus Borg in *The Meaning of Jesus: Two Visions* (San Francisco: Harper, 1999).

[14] Markus Bockmuehl, *This Jesus: Martyr, Lord, Messiah* (Edinburgh: T&T Clark, 1994).

Perhaps the most thorough book on the historical Jesus is the *Comprehensive Guide* by Gerd Theissen and Annette Merz.[15] After all the detailed background and setting, this too has a titles-based approach for its main sections. It offers studies of Jesus as a Charismatic (pp. 185–239), Prophet (pp. 240–80), Healer (pp. 281–314), Poet (pp. 316–46), Teacher (pp. 347–404), the Founder of a Cult (pp. 405–39) and Martyr (pp. 440–73). The book concludes with sections on the Risen Jesus (pp. 474–511) and discussion of the beginnings of Christology, again looking at titles such as Messiah, Son of Man, Son of God and Kyrios (pp. 512–68). In the end, however, Theissen and Merz attempt 'a short narrative about Jesus' since 'narratives form the basis of identity' 'The narrative about Jesus is the basis for Christian identity' (p. 572).

Finally, we return full circle to Bousset and *Kyrios Christos*. Central to the history of religions approach was the development of Christology from a Palestinian setting for Jesus as a rabbi through to his worship as Lord arising from a Gentile, Hellenistic context. Larry Hurtado has been working for many years on this area of devotion to Jesus and worship of him.[16] His enormous and detailed study, *Lord Jesus Christ: Devotion to Jesus in Earliest Christianity* has recently appeared.[17] The whole book is a careful reappraisal of the history of religions approach and its claims, with detailed study of Jewish monotheism, the earliest forms of Judaean Jewish Christianity, Pauline groups, the writing of the gospels and other Jesus books, Johannine Christianity, and on to the second century with its radical diversity and proto-orthodox devotion. After some 650 pages of painstaking research and argument, Hurtado concludes that devotion to Jesus as 'Lord' is neither a later, nor a Hellenistic development; rather, worship of Jesus as divine 'erupted suddenly and quickly' in the earliest Jewish Christian circles (p. 650). It was the struggle to work out this devotion and belief within monotheism that led to the diversity of approaches within the New Testament and in the first centuries of Christian history. Devotion to Jesus was central then – and today the key question remains: 'Who do you say that I am?' (p. 653).

Thus the consideration of titles, especially 'Lord', has dominated Christological studies of the New Testament for over a century, returning

[15] Gerd Theissen and Annette Merz, *The Historical Jesus: A Comprehensive Guide* (London: SCM Press, 1998).

[16] Larry Hurtado, *One God, One Lord: Early Christian Devotion and Ancient Jewish Monotheism* (Philadelphia: Fortress Press, 1988; Edinburgh: T&T Clark, 2nd edn, 1998).

[17] Larry Hurtado, *Lord Jesus Christ: Devotion to Jesus in Earliest Christianity* (Grand Rapids: Eerdmans, 2003).

full circle with Hurtado's homage to, but refutation of, Bousset. Yet increasingly, it has become clear that titles alone will not suffice; they always need to be placed within a narrative – both in terms of a reconstruction of the historical narrative of Jesus himself and the early Church, as well as the narratives about Jesus told by the early Church and contained within the New Testament.

Protests and Different Approaches

One of the first protests against such a traditional approach to New Testament Christology came in Leander Keck's Presidential address to the Society for New Testament Study (SNTS) at Trondheim in August 1985.[18] Keck's interest in Christology is well known and long-standing. Here, he argued that the preoccupation of scholarship with historical analysis of Christological materials and motifs has produced impressive results – but that the time was at hand to take up an explicitly theological approach to New Testament Christology, for only that can renew New Testament Christology. The formal structure, grammar or syntax of Christology consists of three key relationships or correlations – to God (theological); to the created order (cosmological); and to humanity (anthropological). The last links Christology with soteriology: 'soteriology makes Christology necessary; Christology makes soteriology possible' (p. 363) – and the different Christologies within the New Testament reflect different understandings of the human condition and need.

The problem with the early work of Wrede and others culminating in Bousset's *Kyrios Christos* was that the New Testament was replaced by 'early Christian literature' and Christology was supplanted by history – as is evidenced by the concern about titles: 'probably no other factor has contributed more to the current aridity of the discipline than this fascination with the palaeontology of Christological titles. To reconstruct the history of titles as if this were the study of Christology is like trying to understand the windows of Chartres cathedral by studying the history of coloured glass' (p. 368). Concentrating on titles misses 'christologically-important passages in which no title appears', and cannot deal with the plurality within the texts; furthermore such study misses the whole point of the Jesus-event. Because the study of titles bypasses the syntax of Christology, New Testament Christology must be 'liberated from the

[18] Leander E. Keck, 'Toward the Renewal of New Testament Christology', *New Testament Studies* 32 (1986): 362–77.

tyranny of titles' (p. 370). Instead, we must focus on the texts themselves, including giving attention to their genre, and to their subject matter – 'the construal of Jesus' identity and significance' (p. 372). This will involve a different approach to the 'plurality and diversity of the Christologies in the canon' and the way they are juxtaposed, requiring 'a sustained conversation with fundamental and systematic theology' (p. 374).

It is a pity that this important clarion call is not better known – but Keck has himself tried to carry out some of the things for which he was calling. It is significant that his contribution to the 1999 Festschrift for Jack Dean Kingsbury is placed after eleven separate studies of the Christologies of Jesus, and of each of the New Testament books or authors.[19] Keck draws attention to the different understandings of Christology in the New Testament and shows how study over the last century was dominated by the direction set by Wrede and by Bousset's *Kyrios Christos*, especially through the study of titles. Yet 'the Christology of a text cannot be grasped by concentrating on christological titles used in it'. This is especially true of 'extended narratives like the Gospels ... concentrating on the titles tends to rupture the inherent nature of Christology as bipolar discourse, in which the person and work must be thought together' (p. 196). Thus he again concludes with a call for 'interpreters to think as theologians' (p. 198). He has attempted to answer his own call in his book, *Who is Jesus? History in Perfect Tense*.[20]

Meanwhile, R.E. Brown gave a somewhat different direction to his *Introduction to New Testament Christology*.[21] After a brief introduction for his more general readers, he attempts to reconstruct Jesus' own self-understanding as Christ, and then looks at the different 'Christologies of New Testament Christians', grouping those to do with his Second Coming or Parousia, those expressed in terms of his public ministry and those concerned with his pre-ministry. He concludes by taking the story on into the early Church controversies, arguing in the process that Nicaea is 'faithful to a major direction in New Testament Christology' (p. 147). What is significant for our purposes here is the recognition once again of

[19] Leander E. Keck, 'Christology of the New Testament: what, then, is New Testament Christology?', in Mark Allan Powell and David R. Bauer (eds. *Who Do You Say That I Am?, Essays on Christology in honor of Jack Dean Kingsbury* (Louisville, KY: Westminster/John Knox Press, 1999), 185–200.

[20] Leander E. Keck, *Who is Jesus? History in Perfect Tense* (Columbia: University of South Carolina Press, 2000).

[21] Raymond E. Brown, *An Introduction to New Testament Christology* (London: Geoffrey Chapman, 1994).

different Christologies within the New Testament – and the absence of titles, replaced by consideration of different periods of the Jesus narrative.

Other recent treatments have followed similar paths. Christopher Tuckett discusses the traditional approach through titles in his introduction to *Christology and the New Testament*,[22] arguing that the 'protest against an over-concentration on christological titles has been well made by several scholars in recent debates' (p. 11). He considers, however, that they still 'constitute an important part of the evidence for the Christology of the New Testament', continues to use them, and offers discussion of such titles as Messiah, Lord, Son of God and Son of Man, and also of angels, and divine attributes such as Wisdom and Word. He then considers the titles in the epistles, gospels and Johannine literature, separately, before concluding with a discussion of the earliest material and Jesus' own self-understanding.

In contrast, Ben Witherington III argues that such title-based approaches are wrong, being 'synthetic in character and synchronic in assumption' (p. 6).[23] Instead of synthesizing all the material about any one title together, regardless of its context or date, we need to realize that all Christological ideas are grounded in historical events. Thus Raymond Brown's attempt to move away from titles to different periods of the Jesus-event 'is so helpful'. Witherington stresses that 'there is a narrative character to much of the Christological discussion in the New Testament' (p. 4). Thus his treatment is diachronic, starting with the earliest Christologies of Jesus himself and the pre-Pauline Jewish churches through the Christologies of Paul and the gospels and the other New Testament books – and concluding with a discussion of how all of this led to the great debates of Nicaea and Chalcedon. He concludes that 'there are various Christologies in the New Testament and they do not all blend or dove-tail nicely together'. Nor can we construct a 'history-of-ideas schema' where one Christology leads naturally into another. Furthermore, there is no simple graph where 'low' Christology means an early date, or 'high' is later; some of the higher accounts are very early, while some 'lower' assessments persist much later. Thus he concludes, 'perhaps the model of the sun with various beams radiating out from it is more apt than the linear development model' (p. 227).

[22] Christopher Tuckett, *Christology and the New Testament: Jesus and his Earliest Followers* (Louisville, KY: Westminster/John Knox Press, 2001).

[23] Ben Witherington III, *The Many Faces of the Christ: The Christologies of the New Testament and Beyond* (New York: Crossroad, 1998).

So, after this extensive survey, we are back to the basic shift in this essay's title – 'From Titles to Stories: A Narrative Approach to the Dynamic Christologies of the New Testament'. The work of biblical critics on Christology within the New Testament has shifted away from concentrating upon the titles to the 'narratives' about Jesus contained in, or presumed by, the various books of the New Testament. Furthermore, the variety of such narratives within the canon means that we should no longer talk of New Testament Christology as a single entity, but look at the diversity of attempts to understand the person of Jesus within these different texts.

The Gospels as Ancient Biographies

Let us return for a moment to the image of texts as windows and/or mirrors. We suggested above that both approaches tend to view the text merely as an instrument, either through which we can look for historical reconstruction or in which we can reflect upon our various concerns. Neither approach handles the question of what kind of glass we have here – window, mirror, or something else? This raises the crucial issue of genre, which we need to determine with regard to any text.[24]

A proper understanding of genre is central to the interpretation of any communication. Communication theory looks at the three main aspects of transmitter, message and receiver. In written works, this becomes author, text and audience or reader. Immediately the importance of discerning the kind of communication is clear. If the sender is transmitting Morse code, but the receiver can only understand semaphore there will be problems! Both must use the same language and so correct interpretation depends on a correct identification of the genre. One does not listen to a fairy story in the same way as to a news broadcast. Thus genre is a key convention guiding both composition and interpretation. Genre forms a 'contract' or agreement, often unspoken or unwritten, or even unconscious, between author and reader, by which the author writes according to a set of expectations and conventions and we interpret the work using the same conventions. Genre is identified through a wide range of 'generic features' that may be signalled in advance, or embedded in a work's formal,

[24] What follows is a brief summary of my PhD thesis, originally published as Richard A. Burridge, *What are the Gospels? A Comparison with Graeco-Roman Biography* (SNTSMS, 70; Cambridge: Cambridge University Press, 1992); this has now been substantially revised and updated in a new edition, published by Eerdmans, 2004.

structural composition and content. Taken together, such features communicate the 'family resemblance' of a work – its genre.

Therefore, before we can read the gospels we have to discover what kind of books they might be. Differing understandings of their genre will have differing implications for their interpretation. For much of the ancient and mediaeval periods, the gospels were interpreted on several levels: the literal, allegorical, moral and anagogical or mystical readings. The Reformers rejected all readings except for the literal, and on this basis the gospels were interpreted as history – the stories of Jesus, even biographies. This led to their being used as a basis for the production of romantic 'Lives' such as Ernest Renan's *Life of Jesus* (1863). However, during the nineteenth century, biographies began to explain the character of a person by considering his or her upbringing, formative years, schooling, psychological development and so on. The gospels began to look unlike such biographies.

During the 1920s, scholars such as Karl Ludwig Schmidt and Rudolf Bultmann rejected any notion that the gospels were biographies: the gospels have no interest in Jesus' human personality, appearance or character, nor do they tell us anything about the rest of his life, other than his brief public ministry and an extended concentration on his death. Instead, the gospels were seen as popular folk literature, collections of stories handed down orally. Far from being biographies, the gospels were described as 'unique' forms of literature.[25] Furthermore, the development of form-critical approaches to the gospels meant that they were no longer interpreted as whole narratives. Instead, they concentrated on each individual pericope, and the focus for interpretation moved more to the passage's *Sitz im Leben* in the early Church.

Redaction criticism concentrated on each gospel's theological interests and the development of theories about the communities that produced them. Once the gospels were seen as a type of 'community' document, then their interpretation focused on the development of groups such as the Johannine or Matthean communities (see, for example, the work of R. E. Brown). However, redaction critics also saw the writers of the gospels as theologians and the development of new literary approaches to the gospels viewed them as conscious literary artists. This reopened the question of the genre of the gospels and their place within the context of first-century

[25] R. Bultmann, *The History of the Synoptic Tradition* (Oxford: Blackwell, rev. edn, 1972), 371–74.

literature, with scholars such as Talbert and Aune beginning to treat the gospels as biographies.[26]

A generic comparison of a group of different works from different authors will illustrate the nature of any genre. I undertook this exercise with ten examples of ancient biography: Isocrates' *Evagoras*, Xenophon's *Agesilaus*, Satyrus' *Euripides*, Nepos' *Atticus*, Philo's *Moses*, Tacitus' *Agricola*, Plutarch's *Cato Minor*, Suetonius' *Lives of the Caesars*, Lucian's *Demonax* and Philostratus' *Apollonius of Tyana*. This is a diverse group deliberately chosen to include the origins of biography in fourth-century BC rhetorical encomia through to third-century AD forerunners of the novel and hagiography. These form a diverse and flexible genre, yet still one with a recognizable family resemblance in both form and content. Many of them were known as 'Lives', βίοι or *vitae*; the word 'biography' itself does not appear until the fifth-century work of Damascius, preserved in the ninth-century writer Photius. Bultmann's statement that the gospels are not biography was a result of comparing them with modern examples and ideas of biography. This is a category error; when using the word 'biography' of both the gospels and ancient 'Lives', we must avoid modern connotations, and compare them with one another to ascertain their shared generic features.

From the formal or structural perspective, they are written in continuous prose narrative, between 10,000 and 20,000 words in length – the amount on a typical scroll of about 30–35 feet in length. Unlike modern biographies, Graeco-Roman lives do not cover a person's whole life in chronological sequence, and have no psychological analysis of the subject's character. They may begin with a brief mention of the hero's ancestry, family or city, his birth and an occasional anecdote about his upbringing; but usually the narrative moves rapidly on to his public debut later in life. Accounts of generals, politicians or statesmen are more chronologically ordered, recounting their great deeds and virtues, while lives of philosophers, writers or thinkers tend to be more anecdotal, arranged topically around collections of material to display their ideas and teachings. While the author may claim to provide information about his subject, often his underlying aims may be apologetic, polemic or didactic. Many ancient biographies cover the subject's death in great detail, since

[26] Charles H. Talbert, *What is a Gospel? The Genre of the Canonical Gospels* (Philadelphia: Fortress Press, 1977; London: SPCK, 1978); David E. Aune, *The New Testament in Its Literary Environment* (Philadelphia: Westminster Press, 1987; Cambridge: James Clarke & Co., 1988); David E. Aune (ed.), *Greco-Roman Literature and the New Testament: Selected Forms and Genres* (SBL Sources for Biblical Study, 21; Atlanta: Scholars Press, 1988).

here he reveals his true character, gives his definitive teaching, or does his greatest deed. Finally, detailed analysis of the verbal structure of ancient biographies reveals another generic feature. While most narratives have a wide variety of subjects, it is characteristic of biography that attention stays focused on one particular person with a quarter to a third of the verbs dominated by the subject, while another 15 per cent to 30 per cent occur in sayings, speeches or quotations from the person.

Like other ancient biographies, the gospels are continuous prose narratives of the length of a single scroll, composed of stories, anecdotes, sayings and speeches. Their concentration on Jesus' public ministry from his baptism to death, and on his teaching and great deeds is not very different from the content of other ancient biographies. Similarly, the amount of space given to the last week of Jesus' life, his death and the resurrection reflects that given to the subject's death and subsequent events in works by Plutarch, Tacitus, Nepos and Philostratus. Verbal analysis demonstrates that Jesus is the subject of a quarter of the verbs in Mark's Gospel, with a further fifth spoken by him in his teaching and parables. About half of the verbs in the other gospels either have Jesus as the subject or are on his lips: like other ancient biographies, Jesus' deeds and words are of vital importance for the evangelists' portraits of Jesus. Therefore these marked similarities of form and content demonstrate that the gospels have the generic features of ancient biographies.

In the decade or so since I published my thesis, quite a lot of debate has taken place about the biographical hypothesis for the genre of the gospels, including discussions at the British New Testament Conference, the international meeting of the Society of Biblical Literature, and at the annual gatherings of the American Academy of Religion and Society of Biblical Literature.[27] Increasingly, biblical scholars are recognizing a shift of paradigm away from the Bultmannian *sui generis* approach towards understanding the gospels as some form of ancient biography. This is demonstrated by various dictionary articles which draw upon my work to argue for this new consensus,[28] and by other scholars writing about the

[27] For a full analysis of the debate over the last decade, see the revised edition of *What are the Gospels? A Comparison with Graeco-Roman Biography* (Grand Rapids: Eerdmans, 2004), chapter 11.

[28] See, for example, Henry Wansbrough, 'The Four Gospels in Synopsis', in John Barton and John Muddiman (eds.), *The Oxford Bible Commentary*, (Oxford: Oxford University Press, 2001), 1001–2; Christopher Tuckett, 'Introduction to the Gospels', in J.D.G. Dunn and J.W. Rogerson (eds.), *The Eerdmans Commentary on the Bible* (Grand Rapids: Eerdmans, 2003), 989–99, especially 990–93.

biographical genre of the gospels.[29] Therefore, to answer our question about these texts as windows and mirrors, the sort of glass which they most resemble is stained glass: here the crucial issue is not to look *through* them to what lies behind or on the other side, not at what is reflected back at us *from* them – but rather at the picture of the person portrayed *in* the glass through this biographical focus.[30]

Reading the Gospels as Christological Narratives

Therefore, if the gospels are a form of ancient biography, composed by their authors and received by their first audiences within the conventions of Graeco-Roman *bioi*, then we must study them today with the same biographical concentration upon their subject, to see the particular way each evangelist portrays an understanding of Jesus. This means that the gospels are nothing less than Christology in narrative form and so their entire accounts of Jesus become relevant for our Christological reconstruction, rather than just certain titles or passages.

One implication of the biographical hypothesis is that the gospels are about a person, more than theological ideas. Therefore the hermeneutical key for understanding them is not to be found in presumed problems in their hypothetical communities, but rather in their Christology. Every passage must be interpreted in the light of the biographical genre of the whole: what this story tells us about the author's understanding of Jesus. This Christological approach can be illustrated easily by considering the notorious problem of Mark's depiction of the disciples as lacking in faith. Despite the suggestion that the disciples are given the secret (μυστήριον) of the Kingdom of God (4.11), they fail to understand, and Jesus gets increasingly frustrated with them especially in the three boat scenes (4.40–41; 6.50–52; 8.14–21); James and John want the best seats in heaven (10.35–45), while they all fail to understand the Passion predictions (8.32–33; 9.32; 10.32–41). Eventually, they fall asleep in Gethsemane and desert Jesus, leaving Judas to betray him and Peter to deny him (14.37–50, 66–72). It is not only scholars who find this picture rather

[29] Dirk Frickenschmidt, *Evangelium als Biographie. Die vier Evangelien im Rahmen antiker Erzählkunst* (Tübingen: Francke Verlag, 1997); see also, Hurtado, *Lord Jesus Christ*, chapter 5, 259–347, especially 279 (n. 45) and 281–82.

[30] I first used this image of the gospels as stained glass in a paper for the Society for the Study of Theology when Colin Gunton was President of that Society in 1994, so I am glad to repeat it here; see also my chapter 'About People, by People, for People: Gospel Genre and Audiences', in Richard Bauckham (ed.), *The Gospels for All Christians* (Grand Rapids: Eerdmans, 1998), 113–45; see especially 124.

harsh; even Matthew and Luke 'improve' it, so that Matthew turns Mark's 'no faith' (Mk 4.40) into 'men of little faith' (Mt. 8.26), while in Luke the disciples ask Jesus to 'increase our faith' (Lk. 17.5).

Form-critical and redaction-critical approaches seek to solve this problem by relating it to certain groups in the early Church. Thus, Weeden's account is actually entitled *Mark: Traditions in Conflict*; he sees the slow-witted disciples as standing for other leaders, particularly those with a *theios aner* Christology, to whom Mark is opposed.[31] Quite apart from the fact that there are problems over the concept of *theios aner*, such an approach does not do justice to the positive material about the disciples in Mark: Jesus continues to explain things to them (e.g. 7.17–23; 8.34–38; 10.23–31; 11.20–25; 13); he has pity on their exhausted sleep (14.38); and Peter has at least followed Jesus into danger after the others fled, as he promised (14.29). If the disciples represent the wrong leaders, why does Jesus promise to meet them in Galilee (14.28; 16.7)?

Once we read the gospels through the genre of ancient biography, then the Christological key can be used to interpret such passages. The point of each passage is not to tell us about the disciples, but about the biography's subject – namely, Jesus of Nazareth – in this case, that he is someone who is hard to understand and tough to follow. Given both the positive and the negative aspects of the disciples' portrayal, the readers should not be surprised if they find discipleship difficult; yet it is such struggling disciples whom Jesus calls and teaches, despite the difficulties. Thus, reading the gospels in their biographical genre has immediate benefit for their interpretation.

Traditional form-critical approaches to the gospels saw them as a collection of individual pericopae, separated or 'cut off' (περι-κόπτω) from their contexts, strung together like beads on a string with little overall coherence. Redaction critics looked at the evangelists' theological treatment of each story, thus bringing back the author, while narrative critics have redirected our attention back to the story as a whole. Studies such as those by Rhoads and Michie on Mark, Kingsbury on Matthew, Tannehill on Luke–Acts and Culpepper on John have analysed the plot lines throughout each gospel, looking at how the characters develop, how repetition and reference back or forward in the narrative can lead to irony, and how the main themes are resolved in a climax.[32]

[31] T.J. Weeden, *Mark: Traditions in Conflict* (Philadelphia: Fortress Press, 1971).

[32] David Rhoads and Donald Michie, *Mark as Story: An Introduction to the Narrative of a Gospel* (Philadelphia: Fortress Press, 1982); Jack Dean Kingsbury, *Matthew as Story* (Philadelphia: Fortress Press, 1986; 2nd edn, 1988); Robert C. Tannehill, *The Narrative*

The biographical genre for the gospels takes this another step forward, leading us to expect the depiction of one person, the subject, as understood by another person, the author, leading up to the climax of the subject's death. Instead of a form-critical approach to the gospels as Passion narratives preceded by disjointed pericopae strung together, biographical-narratological readings show how each evangelist traces his various themes through the gospel to be resolved at the Passion.

In my book which followed the publication of my doctoral thesis, *Four Gospels, One Jesus?*, I attempted to provide such a biographical narrative reading of each gospel, using the traditional images found in books such as the Book of Kells, but using them as 'images of the Son of God' (as Irenaeus put it, in *Against the Heresies* III.11.8–9) rather than of the evangelists.[33] Thus Mark depicts Jesus like a lion who appears almost from nowhere (1.9), who then rushes around, being misunderstood by everybody, including his family and friends and the authorities (3.19–35). The descriptions of Jesus as an enigmatic wonder-worker who binds people to secrecy, the eschatological prophet who will suffer and die in Jerusalem as both Son of God and Son of Man, are held together in complementary tension in a biographical narrative, rather than explained as deriving from different historical traditions. Jesus finds Jerusalem and the Temple as barren as the fig-tree and prophesies their destruction 11–13. He suffers and dies alone in dark desolation: 'my God, my God, why have you forsaken me?' (15.34) as the Passion brings to a climax all Mark's themes. Even the ending is full of enigma, fear and awe (16.1–8).

In Matthew, however, we have Jesus' Jewish background, genealogy and birth (1–2). He is another Moses, who teaches from mountains (5.1) and fulfils the law and the prophets, giving his teaching in five great blocks like the Pentateuch (5–7, 10, 13, 18, 24–25). Unfortunately, this brings him into conflict with the leaders of Israel. In the Passion, the cry of abandonment is answered by an earthquake as *everyone* realizes this was truly the Son of God (27.51–54; cf. Mk 15.39). Finally, the Resurrection continues with further divine earthquakes and a new Israel on a mountain

---

Unity of Luke–Acts: A Literary Interpretation 2 vols. (Philadelphia and Minneapolis: Fortress Press, 1986 and 1990); R. Alan Culpepper, *Anatomy of the Fourth Gospel: A Study in Literary Design* (Philadelphia: Fortress Press, 1983). See also, Mark Stibbe, *John as Storyteller: Narrative Criticism and the Fourth Gospel* (SNTSMS, 73; Cambridge: Cambridge University Press, 1992); Mark Allen Powell, *What is Narrative Criticism? A New Approach to the Bible* (Minneapolis: Fortress Press, 1990; London: SPCK, 1993).

[33] Richard A. Burridge, *Four Gospels, One Jesus? A Symbolic Reading* (Grand Rapids: Eerdmans; London: SPCK, 1994); 2nd revised edn 2005.

commissioned to go to the Gentiles (28.1–20).[34] Again, the climax resolves all the themes of the Gospel.

Luke begins with a Greek periodic Preface (Lk. 1.1–4) and sets Jesus within the history of both Israel and contemporary Roman rule (Lk. 1.5–80; 2.1; 3.1). Jesus is concerned for the poor, the lost, outcasts, women, Samaritans and Gentiles. He is also the man of prayer (11.1–4). At the Passion he cares for women (23.27–31) and prays for the soldiers and the penitent thief (23.34, 43), committing himself in trust to his Father (23.46). After the resurrection, history looks forward from Israel's past to the world's future (24.44–47). The Gospel ends as it began 'in Jerusalem with great joy', with the disciples 'in the Temple blessing God' (24.51–53; cf. 1.5–23). Such a clear balanced biographical narrative reflects a single author and purpose.

John begins before all time, in the beginning, with God (Jn 1.1–18). Jesus is constantly centre stage and he is characterized as the author interweaves 'signs' and discourse, revealing the effect of meditation and theological reflection upon the person of Jesus. Opposition from 'the Jews' develops through the first half (2–12); at the climax, Jesus gathers his disciples, washes their feet and explains what will happen (13–17). The 'hour of glory' is also the Passion: throughout, Jesus is serenely in control, directing events (19.11), organizing his mother and disciple (19.26–27), fulfilling scripture (19.28) until finally 'it is accomplished' (19.30). After the resurrection he appears as he wishes to comfort Mary (20.14), challenge Thomas (20.26) and restore Peter (21.15–19). Once again, we have a clear portrait of the ministry of Jesus culminating in his death and resurrection.

These four individual accounts, each concerned with the resolution of their particular themes, were composed by four writers, each portraying a particular view of Jesus in the manner of ancient biography. The fact that the Fathers chose to keep four separate accounts in the canon, despite the problems of plurality and possible conflict,[35] demonstrates that they recognized these works as coherent single accounts of Jesus – and therefore

[34] For a good comparison of Matthew with Mark, see J.L. Houlden, *Backward into Light: The Passion and Resurrection of Jesus according to Matthew and Mark* (London: SCM Press, 1987).

[35] For the four-fold canon and plurality, see T.C. Skeat, 'Irenaeus and the Four-Fold Gospel Canon', *Novum Testamentum* 34.2 (1992): 194–99 and Oscar Cullmann, 'The Plurality of the Gospels as a Theological Problem in Antiquity', in his collection, *The Early Church: Studies in Early Christian History and Theology* ed. A.J.B. Higgins (Philadelphia: Westminster Press, 1956), 37–54, translated from the original German article in *Theologische Zeitschrift* 1 (1945): 23–42; see also Richard A. Burridge, *Four Gospels, One Jesus?*, 25–27, 164–79.

they need to be read in that way today. This also raises interesting theological questions about plurality and diversity within the limits of the canon. Morgan sees this as offering both a 'stimulus' to produce more 'faith images of Jesus' as well as a 'control' upon them.[36] In his arguments for 'the illocutionary stance of biblical narrative', Wolterstorff draws upon my work on biographical genre to argue that 'the gospel narratives are best understood as portraits of Jesus',[37] while Barton similarly uses my material to reflect upon 'Many gospels, one Jesus?'[38] This demonstrates that the biographical focus upon the person of Jesus in interpreting the gospels as Christological narrative is much more productive than just concentrating upon titles alone.

The Central Christological Claim

Interpreting the gospels as biographical narratives also illustrates the part played by Christological controversy in the parting of the ways between the synagogue and early Church, especially in the light of the absence of any rabbinic biography or parallels to the gospels with Jewish literature.

Individual gospels' pericopae are often compared with rabbinic material. Thus, Rabbi Michael Hilton and Fr Gordian Marshall OP in *The Gospels and Rabbinic Judaism: A Study Guide* compare Jesus' sayings with rabbinic sources. The Great Commandment (Mk 12.28–34 and the parallels in Mt. 22.34–40 and Lk. 10.25–28) is compared with a *Sifra* passage from Rabbi Akiba on Lev. 19.18, Genesis Rabba 24.7 (on Gen. 5.1), and the famous story from the Babylonian Talmud, *Shabbat* 31A, of the different reactions from Shammai and Hillel when asked to teach the whole law to a Gentile enquirer standing on one leg: Shammai chased the questioner away, while Hillel repeated the Golden Rule as the sum of the whole Torah, with the rest as commentary, but still to be learned. Hilton concludes that 'Jesus at his most "rabbinic" engaged in lively debate and answering some of the same questions as the rabbis'.[39]

[36] Robert Morgan, 'The Hermeneutical Significance of Four Gospels', *Interpretation* 33.4 (1979): 376–88; see especially 386.

[37] Nicholas Wolterstorff, *Divine Discourse: Philosophical Reflections on the Claim that God Speaks* (Cambridge: Cambridge University Press, 1995), 249–60.

[38] Stephen C. Barton, 'Many Gospels, One Jesus?' in Markus Bockmuehl (ed.), *The Cambridge Companion to Jesus* (Cambridge: Cambridge University Press, 2001), 170–83, especially 178–79.

[39] Rabbi Michael Hilton with Fr Gordian Marshall OP, *The Gospels and Rabbinic Judaism: A Study Guide* (London: SCM Press, 1988), 34.

An international symposium on Hillel and Jesus held in Jerusalem in June 1992 devotes some 170 pages to comparisons of their sayings![40] Philip Alexander notes that 'the overriding feeling is one of astonishment at the convergence of the two traditions'.[41] Alexander has written extensively on such rabbinic writings, and how New Testament scholars should use this material.[42] He collected together some rabbinic stories to compare 'Rabbinic biography and the biography of Jesus', concluding, 'there are parallels to the individual pericopae, and at this level similarities are very strong. In terms of form, function, setting and motif, the rabbinic anecdotes are very close to the Gospel pericopae, and there can be little doubt that both belong to the same broad Palestinian Jewish tradition of story-telling.'[43]

Since Bultmann and other form critics saw the gospels as strung together like beads on a string, we might expect rabbinic stories to form similar accounts of Hillel, Shammai or others. Yet, this is precisely what we do *not* find, much to everybody's surprise. Thus Philip Alexander concludes his study of 'Rabbinic biography and the biography of Jesus' thus: 'there are no Rabbinic parallels to the Gospels as such. This is by far the most important single conclusion to emerge from this paper ... There is not a trace of an ancient biography of any of the Sages ... This is a profound enigma.'[44]

Jacob Neusner has devoted much study to this question. In his 1984 book, *In Search of Talmudic Biography*, he states that 'there is no composition of tales and stories into a sustained biography'.[45] He followed this with an analysis of *Why No Gospels in Talmudic Judaism?* The stories about sages were never compiled into biographical narratives or gospels: they are 'the compositions no one made'.[46] In *The Incarnation of God* again he stresses: 'While the two Talmuds present stories about sages, neither

[40] James H. Charlesworth and Loren L. Johns (eds.), *Hillel and Jesus: Comparative Studies of Two Major Religious Leaders* (Minneapolis: Fortress Press, 1997).

[41] P.S. Alexander, 'Jesus and the Golden Rule', in *Hillel and Jesus*, 363–88; quotation from 388.

[42] See, for example, Philip S. Alexander, 'Rabbinic Judaism and the New Testament', *Zeitschrift für neutestamentliche Wissenschaft und die Kunde der älteren Kirche* 74 (1983): 237–46.

[43] Philip S. Alexander, 'Rabbinic Biography and the Biography of Jesus: A Survey of the Evidence', in C. M. Tuckett (ed.) *Synoptic Studies: The Ampleforth Conferences of* 1982 *and* 1983 (JSNTSup, 7; Sheffield: JSOT Press, 1984), 19–50; quotation from 42.

[44] Alexander, 'Rabbinic Biography and the Biography of Jesus', 40.

[45] Jacob Neusner, *In Search of Talmudic Biography: The Problem of the Attributed Saying* Brown Judaic Studies, 70 (Chicago: Scholars Press, 1984), 2.

[46] Jacob Neusner, *Why No Gospels in Talmudic Judaism?* (Atlanta, GA: Scholars Press, 1988), 33–38.

one contains anything we might call a "gospel" of a sage or even a chapter of a gospel. There is no sustained biography of any sage.'[47] Finally, he answered the claim of similarities between the gospels and Jewish material with *Are There Really Tannaitic Parallels to the Gospels?*[48]

In the symposium on Hillel and Jesus, Gottstein notes the 'basic differences between the nature of Talmudic literature and the nature of the Gospels. We have no Talmudic Gospel of any Rabbi.' He accepts my conclusions: 'Following Burridge's discussion, the present discussion assumes Gospel writing to be a form of biography' and concludes 'One could therefore ask why we do not have any instances of rabbinic biography'.[49]

One might explore, first, possible literary reasons for this absence. After all, most rabbinic material is comprised of anecdotes, which are more about a rabbi's teaching than his actions. Many of the stories are dialogues that lead up to the actual saying, without any narrative at the start to set the scene. Thus the rabbinic material is more like Q or the *Gospel of Thomas*; that is, it has the genre of sayings, *logia*, more than biographical narrative. Philip Alexander says that the rabbinic stories have an 'intensely oral character ... against the more prosy "written" style of the gospels'. They are 'extremely compressed, allusive, witty, dramatic and learned'; more like bits from a play to be performed than a text to be read, intended for oral circulation, not in written form.[50] In *The Incarnation of God*, Neusner applies a 'taxonomy of narrative' to the material and finds 'five species of the genus narrative'.[51] The problem with this is that 'narrative' is neither a genus nor a genre in itself according to most literary theory of genres, and his five 'species' are not clearly identified as subgenres.

However, the basic point is clear, that the rabbinic anecdotes are directed more towards sayings than actions. Yet, this would not prevent their being compiled into an ancient biography. Lucian's *Demonax* has a brief preface and account of the philosopher's life, followed by a large number of anecdotes all strung together, each composed mainly of dialogue leading up to a pronouncement or decision by the great sage – yet

[47] Jacob Neusner, *The Incarnation of God: The Character of Divinity in Formative Judaism* (Philadelphia: Fortress Press, 1988), 213.

[48] Jacob Neusner, *Are There Really Tannaitic Parallels to the Gospels? A Refutation of Morton Smith* (South Florida Studies in the History of Judaism, 80; Atlanta, GA: Scholars Press, 1993).

[49] A. Goshen Gottstein, 'Jesus and Hillel: Are Comparisons Possible?' in *Hillel and Jesus*, 31–55; quotations from 34–35.

[50] Alexander, 'Rabbinic Biography and the Biography of Jesus', 42.

[51] Neusner, *The Incarnation of God*, 214.

it is still called a 'life', *bios*. In fact, the *Demonax* is more loosely structured with less integration of teaching and activity than even Mark's Gospel.[52]

Thus, although the rabbinic material is more anecdotal than are the gospels and some ancient lives, it still contains enough biographical elements (through sage stories, narratives, precedents and death scenes) to enable an editor to compile a 'life of Hillel' or whoever. Such an account would have been recognizable as ancient biography and have looked like the *Demonax*. Literary and generic reasons alone are therefore not sufficient to explain this curious absence of rabbinic biography – which brings us back to theological reasons arising from their Christological focus. Since biography directs the audience's attention to the life and character of the subject, the decision to write a biographical account of Jesus has important Christological implications. Equally, the failure to write, or even compile from the anecdotes, any biographies of the rabbis also has significant implications.

Neusner argues that this is because the individual sages are not at the centre of attention. '*Sage-stories turn out not to tell about sages at all; they are stories about the Torah personified*. Sage-stories cannot yield a gospel because they are not about sages anyway. They are about the Torah ... The gospel does just the opposite, with its focus on the uniqueness of the hero.'[53] Alexander makes the same point: 'The obvious answer is that neither Eliezer nor any other Sage held in Rabbinic Judaism the central position that Jesus held in early Christianity. The centre of Rabbinic Judaism was Torah; the centre of Christianity was the person of Jesus, and the existence of the Gospels is, in itself, a testimony to this fact.'[54] Similarly, Rabbi Michael Hilton says: 'The Gospels can thus be regarded as a kind of commentary on Jesus' life, in much the same way as the Rabbis comment on biblical texts.'[55] Similarly, Gottstein in comparing Jesus and Hillel stresses that 'Gospel writing would be the product of the particular religious understanding of the messianic, and therefore salvific, activity of Jesus. The lack of Gospels in rabbinic literature would then be a less significant issue, since no salvific claim is attached to any particular Rabbi.'[56]

Thus the literary shift from unconnected anecdotes about Jesus, which resemble rabbinic material, to composing them together in the genre of an

[52] See my discussion of the *Demonax* in *What are the Gospels?*, 166, 170–71.
[53] Neusner, *Why No Gospels in Talmudic Judaism?*, 52–53; his italics.
[54] Alexander, 'Rabbinic Biography and the Biography of Jesus', 41.
[55] Hilton and Marshall, *The Gospels and Rabbinic Judaism*, 13.
[56] Gottstein, 'Jesus and Hillel', 35.

ancient biography constitutes an enormous Christological claim. Rabbinic biography is not possible because no rabbi is that unique and is only important as he represents the Torah, which holds the central place. To write a biography is to replace the Torah by putting a human person at centre stage. The literary genre makes a major theological shift that becomes an explicit Christological claim – that Jesus of Nazareth is Torah embodied.[57] So our study of genre puts Jesus at the centre and this itself is a key Christological claim which is much more important than any individual title or theological explanation.

The Plurality of Dynamic Christologies in the New Testament

In this essay, we have concentrated on the shift from Christological titles to the biographical narratives about Jesus in the four gospels. Space does not permit detailed examination of the rest of the New Testament, but here too there has been a move away from merely considering the various titles and descriptions used about Jesus to looking at the underlying narrative that informs the author's account or is presumed by what he says.

For example, Paul's encounter with the risen Christ on the Damascus road was not just a turning point in his life, but also in his theology. From then on, the significance of Jesus' life, death and resurrection, and the implications of new life 'in Christ' are crucial for Paul's understanding of the relationship between God and human beings. Furthermore, Paul's Christology is also set in an eschatological framework. Christ is the key pivot of the ages, the means whereby the new age has broken into the present through the death and resurrection of Jesus. Thus while Paul has little of the biography of Jesus' actual earthly life or ministry, the story of the whole Christ-event has become his dominating Christological narrative. Similarly, the other New Testament books may not be in narrative genres, but they still have underlying narratives which reveal their various understandings of the person of Jesus.

Thus both the history of religions evolutionary approach and the common method of studying Christological titles have proved incorrect or unhelpful, despite the amount of material written on them over the last century. Indeed, the time has come to move away from the singular idea of New Testament Christology, for this essay has demonstrated that there are

[57] Jacobus Schoneveld, 'Torah in the Flesh: A New Reading of the Prologue of the Gospel of John as a Contribution to a Christology without Anti-Semitism', in Malcolm Lowe (ed.), *The New Testament and Christian-Jewish Dialogue: Studies in Honor of David Flusser*, (Emmanuel, 24/25; Jerusalem: Ecumenical Theological Research Fraternity in Israel, 1990), 77–93.

lots of different Christologies within the New Testament. If we go back to the image of text as stained glass, we have a whole gallery of different portraits, each of which needs to be studied in its own right, not for what we can see through it or is reflected by it, but for the picture it contains. Furthermore, these pictures are not static, but dynamic as they move and develop. They should not be combined into an overarching single narrative, still less an amalgam, but allowed to speak each for themselves, bearing in mind Witherington's warning that an early date does not necessarily equal a 'low' Christology, nor need later mean 'high'.[58]

The use of the New Testament, especially by theologians and doctrine specialists must respect this diversity of Christological portraits. This means considering the narrative of each book, taken as a whole, rather than just looking at the titles. If we do this, we will be then be confronted by the central Christological claim in all the New Testament texts, that only in Jesus is God to be understood, and by his Spirit we are able to do that.

[58] Witherington, *The Many Faces of the Christ*, 227 – see note 23 above.

Chapter 3

Christ in the Trinity: Communicatio Idiomatum

Robert W. Jenson

The collocation of topics, Christology and Trinity, is both dogmatically and historically appropriate. For the two *loci* are inextricable. Indeed, a first point to be made is that the dogmatic *locus de Christo* does not become necessary or even possible until the decisive bits of trinitarian dogma are in place – Christoph Schwöbel has repeatedly made a related normative point.[1] We can of course use the word 'Christology' in other senses: thus we may conveniently speak of 'New Testament Christology' or refer to the apologists' 'Logos-Christology'. Nevertheless, the questions that traditionally compose the dogmatic and systematic *locus* on Christology presuppose at least the ὁμοούσιος τῷ Πατρί. Indeed, one can say that Christology is born and continues as exegesis of a particular text, the first part of the second article of the Nicene-Constantinopolitan Creed. We have the nest of problems and proposed answers we put together as the *locus* labelled 'Christology', because the Fathers at Nicea produced the text they did, from which the Fathers at Constantinople did not deviate in any way important to the matter of this essay.

According to standard reconstruction, the Nicene dogmatic definitions were accomplished by inserting systematic-theological phrases into a baptismal creed. A second point to keep in mind is how different the text thus produced is from what one might have predicted, and that it is the

[1] See, for example, Schwöbel's essay, 'Christology and Trinitarian Thought', in *idem* (ed.), *Trinitarian Theology Today* (Edinburgh: T&T Clark, 1995), 113–46.

text actually devised that so quickly and urgently demanded and still demands exegesis.

For something is most remarkably missing from the Nicene-Constantinopolitan Creed: the Logos-theology developed by the apologists and perfected by Origen, that is to say, what is missing is any reference to the theological system whose problematics triggered all the controversy in the first place. Undoubtedly the Nicene Fathers had the Logos-theology in mind as they worked. But the text they actually produced bears no trace of it. 'Only Son', 'God from God', 'of one being with the Father', 'by whom all things were made', and so on, appear as a string of predicates attached to a single subject; and that subject is *not* 'one Logos, incarnate in our Lord Jesus Christ' – as most of the conciliar Fathers would surely have wanted if they had foreseen what was coming. It is simply 'one Lord, Jesus Christ'. And that it is, is surely the work of the Spirit.

Now, it is that subject phrase, *as* the subject of the attributions that follow, which immediately seemed to pose a problem, and which became and remains the assignment of Christology most properly so called. How could the subject of all those belligerently unequivocal God-predicates be the man Jesus, even if he is risen as the Christ of Israel and the acknowledged 'Lord' of his followers?

The 'one' with 'Lord, Jesus Christ' was undoubtedly part of the baptismal confession the council took as its framework, and in that context it functioned as a renunciation of other candidates to be Lord. But in the new context it makes a new assertion, whether consciously intended at the councils or not: that there is not a plurality of subjects of the following creedal statements, that there is just one. In its new context, the 'one' insists that it is indeed a single unitary person who is Jesus the Christ of Israel *and* who is just so God from God, Light from Light, and so on.

Moreover, after the inserted theologoumena the creed reverts to the usual second-article creedal narrative, which narrates of its protagonist birth from a human mother, death and burial, and does so without establishing a new subject. So now we have, as the second article of this creed, one long proposition which ascribes deity in the most uncompromising terms, *and* a definitively creaturely career of birth and death, to the same singular subject, indexed by a human proper name and by a title that is meaningful only within the particular faith and culture of Israel. However can such a proposition be true? The exegetical challenge is not posed by any of the predicates, odd as some of them are in themselves, but by the unity of the subject.

Exegesis of 'one Lord, Jesus Christ' was immediately seen as demanded and immediately became controversial. The controversy has now continued for seventeen centuries – Colin Gunton and I kept up an amicable version of it from nearly our first meeting until our last.

Attempts were early made to establish at least a few rules for the argument. These efforts met with notable success at the councils of Ephesus and Chalcedon. Chalcedon itself is the original model of a bilateral ecumenical dialogue whose participants judge they can bring a positive report: each side renounces the evil opinion of which the other side suspects it – 'Who, me? I *never* thought such a thing' – '"Two sons"? Whoever would defend that?' – 'Christ a mixture of deity and humanity?' It's six other persons who think that – and remaining disagreements are judged not legitimately church-divisive. In the decree of Chalcedon, again as in some dialogue reports, the judgment that remaining disagreements in the matter are not church-divisive appears in the form of a hole in the systematic-theological centre of the decree, where things that one might think systematically necessary to be said, but which would probably re-start an argument, are simply not said.

If I may at this point intrude a remark not immediately relevant to the argument of this essay, observation of this structural equivalence between Chalcedon and modern bilateral dialogue could be salutary in two directions. We should receive dialogue reports with the same carefully limited expectation we bring to Chalcedon, the very archetype of beneficent imprecision. In the other direction, construing Chalcedon as a dialogue report has turned out greatly to facilitate its reception by those who once rejected it as a supposed systematic document, by, for example, the Armenians, who, due to a time-overlap in getting the text, understood it as a systematic statement in rivalry with the *Henotikon*.

Now, as it has in fact come about, the formulae of Chalcedon are regarded in the West and in most of the surviving East as the Spirit-given framework of all orthodox Christology – rightly so, in my judgment. But given their character as just noted, they can be no more than that: they are precisely framework and nothing more; indeed perhaps we might better think of them as scaffolding.

According to Chalcedon, the one Lord Jesus Christ has 'two natures'. This is perhaps clear enough to be going on with – though I want strongly to urge that the *notion* of 'natures' is merely a notion of secondary reflection, and not an initial given for Christology. If the gospels' narrative is true, its protagonist must indeed have the characters natural to God and the characters natural to a member of the human race.

And these natures, Chalcedon says, are the natures of one ὑπόστασις. Again, so far so good. But it is just here that Chalcedon falls silent, and so is indeed only a scaffold. For Chalcedon does not tell us what ὑπόστασις means in this context, or how an ὑπόστασις – whatever it is – can be the protagonist of a narrative, or what difference being the natures of only one hypostasis makes to the two natures, or what difference having two natures makes to the hypostasis – or indeed anything one might want to think about if one were not trying to quell a controversy otherwise judged legitimately containable.

The *matter* for which Chalcedon proposed this framework is of course the whole of what Scripture and the wider tradition of the church's first-level discourse tells about that 'one Lord, Jesus Christ'. And that is an immense and in many ways heterogeneous collection of narrative propositions: 'Jesus saves'; God's 'only Son ... was born of the Virgin Mary and suffered under Pontius Pilate'; 'And going a little farther, he threw himself on the ground, and prayed that if it were possible, the hour might pass from him'; 'And he taught them, saying, "Blessed are the poor"'; 'He was despised and rejected', and so on and on. We have all four gospels; and we have the Old Testament, which tells of a 'man of sorrows, acquainted with grief' and of the variously envisioned Coming One; and we have the church's hymns and passions and sermons and liturgies, all telling us about that 'one Lord, Jesus Christ' and what he does 'according' – as the phrase has gone – to those two natures.

The problem posed by what Chalcedon refrains from saying about the one ὑπόστασις, the problem posed by that hole in the middle of its thinking, is that, just so, the decree gives no indication of how – so to speak – all this narrative fastens to the Chalcedonian scaffolding. It left that to subsequent thinking and controversy.

We have, as the second article of the creed, one long proposition which ascribes deity in the most uncompromising terms, and human birth and death, that is to say, creatureliness at its most uncompromised, to the same singular subject. However can such a proposition be true? And when we look to all that mass of what is said about our one Lord in the gospels and the Old Testament and the church, we observe that this pattern of the creed is not idiosyncratic, but is a pattern manifested by all the decisive items of that discourse.

If we say, 'Jesus saves', our subject is the personal name of a human person, and the predicate attributes to him what only God can do. If we say, 'And going a little further, he threw himself on the ground and prayed, "Father, if it be possible let this cup pass from me ..."' we see a man in the throes of unwanted decision, and we see him addressing God as his personal Abba; we see indeed a christological crux that stumped every theologian before Maximus the Confessor, and continues to stump all who know not Maximus. If we say, 'The Son of God was born of Mary', our subject phrase is a divine name and the predicate attributes to him what only mammalian creatures suffer. If we say – and this of course has been the chief offence – *Unus ex trinitate passus est pro nobis*, we have again a bluntly divine name as subject and as predicate suffering and death, which all the world has held impossible for god – or at least for any 100 per cent godly god.

The gospel-narrative is a compound of propositions with subjects that index a person we would expect to have one of those 'two natures in Christ' and then predicate of him a character we would otherwise expect to belong to the other, indeed in most cases to belong only to the other. Doctrines of the *communio/communicatio* of natures or attributes are attempts to recognize this fact and sort it out.

No one has sorted out the various modes and combinations so painstakingly – not to say fanatically – as the Lutheran theologians of the late sixteenth and early seventeenth centuries. A quick presentation of their positions will be useful, both for their organizing and to display where the theological choices appear. I will follow the presentation of the pioneer of this tradition, Martin Chemnitz, in his *De duabus naturis in Christo*. I will note two points at which his presentation presents a theological choice to be made.

A first rubric is for propositions that simply attribute one nature to the other, indexing each nature, as they said, 'concretely' rather than abstractly, that is, as 'a man' instead of 'humanity' or 'God' instead of 'deity'. So we have, 'This man is the Son of God', or, 'The Logos is Jesus'. These are rubricized as belonging to the 'communion of natures'.

Then propositions more properly rubricized under 'communication of attributes' fall – according to Chemnitz – into three classes, or *genera*. The first class is of propositions that predicate what is proper to one nature to the person or hypostasis, indexed by the concrete of either nature, that is, either with a proper name, an identifying description, or with the sort of expression which in English would begin with an article. This class is labelled *genus idiomatum*, simply taken.

And here we encounter the first arguable matter. We might think that of course if Christ has two natures, whatever is proper to either nature can be attributed to the one hypostasis, but that this constitutes no communication of attributes *between* the *natures*. But to those Lutherans, such propositions do state a communication of attributes among the natures also, for in their analysis the hypostasis is the only concrete reality of both natures, and further is itself nothing other than that, so that what is attributed to him is in fact attributed to both natures.

Thus in referring to the one hypostasis, I just said, 'him', and Chemnitz stipulates 'concrete' reference to the hypostasis. The tendency of Western Christology in general, however, has been to resist both modes of speaking, to take 'the hypostasis' as a sheer linguistic marker for the fact of hypostatic union, and to understand the later fact as so purely a *meta*physical event that it has no consequences at the level of τά φυσικὰ. The hypostasis thus cannot be referred to directly with concrete terms, and is certainly not a 'he'. Chemnitz's and his colleagues' invariable argument is that 'Since the hypostasis of the Son is become the hypostasis of a man, it follows that . . . ' But in the usual system of Western Christology, *nothing* follows directly from the metaphysical fact of hypostastic union.

The second class is the *genus apotelismaticum*. Here we attend directly to the actions of the one Lord as one hypostasis. All that he does as King and Priest, he does in and through both natures and their characters. This is, one may say, the uncontroversial genus. Here Leo's notorious maxim is in fact adopted by the Lutherans also: each nature of Christ is active in communication with the other, each contributing that which is proper to it.

The third *genus* is the *genus maiestaticum*, and here what is said is indeed arguable or at least has been vehemently argued. I will quote Chemnitz:

> In this third *genus* the person of Christ in his role as King and High Priest performs and carries out his divine mission . . . in, with and through the human nature. [And he does this] not only according to and through the attributes which belong to the human nature in itself . . . but also according to attributes which his nature has received and possesses above, beyond and outside its natural properties . . . as a result of the hypostastic union and the *perichoresis* of natures within it.

We may put it so: each nature of Christ is active in communication with the other, each contributing what is proper to it *and* in its own way what is proper to the other. Thus, to instance the most notoriously controversial proposition in this class: 'The man Jesus, also as man, participates in the divine transcendence of time and space.'

The third *genus*, according to the Lutheran theologians – though not according to Luther himself – is asymmetrical. If there were a pair for communications of divine attributes to the human nature, these would be communications of human attributes to the divine nature; there would be a *genus tapeinotikon*. It could be said: 'One of the Trinity suffered for us, according to his human nature and, in communion with that nature, according to his divine nature.' Luther taught such communications; the Lutherans exercised more prudence.

We return now more directly to the question of the relation between all this and the doctrine of Trinity. It seems to me we now have two questions to consider. What does the *fact* of the mutual communication of divine/human attributes mean for our understanding of the Trinity? And what is the trinitarian import of doctrines *about* the fact?

In considering the first of these questions, I will work with a minimal and I hope generally acceptable statement of the fact of the *communicatio*: the one Christ lives his life as God and as a man, divinely and humanly, and his doings and sufferings cannot be sorted out into two differing sets of doings and sufferings. You cannot do what, for example, the great Theodore of Mopsuestia did in his commentary on John's Gospel: determine of each event, 'This he did as man' or 'This he did as God'.

Thus the *role* played by Jesus in the human story is at once a divine role and a human role. Thus, to stay only with creeds, his birth is narrated – 'he became incarnate' – as one cannot narrate your birth or mine. The other way around – and this is the aspect that here interests us – the role that the Son plays in the mutual triune life is at once a divine role and a human role, and so it includes, to stay only with creeds, 'born of the Virgin Mary' and 'suffered under Pontius Pilate'. If I may press the dramaturgical language just invoked one more step, the *part* which the Son plays in the triune drama is the life and fate of the man Jesus. And this is true, by the way, independently of whether there was a *logos asarkos*; for present purposes we can with gratitude finesse that question.

The Son is ὁμοούσιος τῷ Πατρί and so with the Spirit is a *persona* of the life that is God. So far, so simply Nicene, and so far, so good. But who is this Son? Were I the Son, God would be a very different God than he in fact is, and this would be so even if, contrary to possibility, the Father and the Spirit were otherwise the same. The doctrine of the Trinity has in fact no religious import unless we can and do identify the Son.

The demand for identification of a *persona* can only be answered, in this case as elsewhere, by narrative. And the – minimally stated – fact of the *communicatio* is that the narrative of the Son is a human narrative, also as he plays his role in the divine life. The most alarming items of that human narrative became thematic in Christological debate very quickly, and the debate about them has never quite come to rest. Among more or less orthodox Christians it is often verbally put to rest, but keeps producing symptoms in church life and various reaches of theology. The aspects of the human condition that most distressed the ancient world were, of course, the famous pairing, the womb and the tomb. Can the narrative identifying a *persona* of God's life include having inhabited a woman's belly? Or having been executed?

It was indeed decreed at Chalcedon that God the Son did indeed have a human birth and so has a human mother, that Mary is rightly saluted as θεοτόκος. But the church was ripped apart in the process of decision – and I find that the more ill-educated among Protestant clergy continue to suppose that this is one of those weird and probably blasphemous things that Catholics teach.

Moreover, it was later decreed, at the second Council of Constantinople (553), that *unus ex trinitate* indeed suffered death for us. But the then Pope, Vigilius, condemned the council as heretical, and it took a reciprocal condemnation of the pope for that decree to get currency in the West, which in practice it quickly lost again. In my *rigorosum* at Heidelberg, Hans von Campenhausen asked me why the decrees of this council had so little lasting affect in the West. I did not know. Afterward, Günther Bornkamm said he did not know either, and asked Hans for the explanation. Von Campenhausen roared out, '*Sie wurden einfach vergessen*! *Ho-ho-ho*!' Bornkamm remarked that with forgetfulness of the matter so well established, perhaps my lapse too could be forgiven.

Reluctance about such propositions as the *unus ex trinitate* results from definitions of the supposed 'two natures', deity and humanity, that are posited antecedently to the gospel-narrative with all its cross-over predications. If, for central instance, God's eternity is so understood that deity and death simply exclude one another by definition, then *unus ex trinitate passus est* is not just surprising, or even perhaps paradoxical, but simply nonsensical.

So the *fact* of the *communicatio* is that the mutual plot of the divine life, the ensemble of the 'processions' as they are called, is determined by what happened with Jesus of Nazareth between his conception by the Virgin and his Ascension to the Father. And the pay-off is: *this* life is the life that creates all that is and that will fulfil all that is. If we want to know how reality is constituted, we must read the gospels.

Moreover, there is another aspect of the matter. It is to the Son that the Father, by an ancient theologoumenon, looks to know himself. Much current thinking would want to adjust that a bit, and say that the Son is the Word that the Father speaks to himself to identify himself. Either way, we may ask the question: Very well, but *what* does the Father hear – or see – when he attends to the Son? And the answer must be: the narrative of Jesus-in-Israel. That narrative is God's self-determination as the particular God he is.

Thus the events of salvation's history are not intrusions in the history of the universe; almost vice versa, the history of the universe is an incident in the story of Jesus in Israel. For the universe is the creation of the particular

God whose own life is told by that story. Here indeed is the bite of the fact that the man Jesus is one of the Trinity.

It seems to me that if preachers and liturgiologists and canonists had this fact more to the front of their minds, preaching and liturgy in our churches would be rather different than it is. We would at least hear a great deal less about making the Bible relevant to the supposed truths of this world, and a great deal more about judging the world's suppositions by the narrative of the Bible. Instead of, 'You say you make your living grinding the faces of the poor? Never mind, those biblical precepts have, after all, to be interpreted in our new and very different context', we might hear, 'You say you are baptized? Right. Now let us consider how you are in the meantime to make a living.' The Episcopal Church in my country has just consecrated as bishop a man who some years ago abandoned his wife and children, to live with a lover whom he has never married – and that the lover is of his own gender is surely the least of this malefactor's disqualifications. But if we suppose that the history of the church is one piece of the history of culture – instead of the true other way around – those who oppose such accommodations must always finally be bereft of argument.

Now – finally – what such ontologically loaded doctrines *about* the *communicatio*, like that of those Lutherans at some points, finally determine, is how *stringently* the Son's inner-trinitarian role is plotted by what happens with Jesus. Does, for a central case, the death of Jesus on the cross 'manifest' the paradoxical power of love by which God rules the universe, as it is often put; or is Jesus' dying simply God ruling the universe? Does Jesus' resurrection perhaps 'show forth' God's transcendence of time, or is it the way God goes about to transcend time? I will not conceal that I think the second statement is the true one in both cases, and would judge all similar choices the same way. Which is to say, I think those Lutherans, and even more Luther himself, got this one right – whatever else they may indeed have gotten badly wrong.

In my judgment, any less stringent doctrine of the *communicatio*, that is to say, any less stringent identification between Jesus' story and the Son's role in the triune drama, leaves the way open for the plot of triune life to be determined by other stories than the biblical story – that is for a pattern of religion which the church truly can no longer support.

Chapter 4

Reformed Varieties of the Communicatio Idiomatum

Stephen R. Holmes

There are three reasons for my choice of this, admittedly somewhat abstruse, title. The first is that, looking at the conference programme as it was taking shape, I thought we needed some technical Christology somewhere, and I was also glad of an excuse to do some reading in the area of technical Christology. The second was a desire to carry on a conversation, albeit after a significant gap. Four years ago, just before the conference we held on reconciliation, I had my PhD viva. One of the things I had argued, more or less in passing, in my thesis was that there was a novel and distinctively Reformed Christology developed within the Puritan tradition. One of my examiners, Robert Jenson, took issue with this, arguing that Reformed Christology is merely a continuation of the Catholic tradition, and does not find any distinctive expression. I continue to believe that I was right, but I am also aware that I did not convince my examiner on this point. I realize four years is a fair gap, but I hope that my attempt to pick the issue up again in this essay will go some way to explain my obstinacy.

The third reason is a desire to find an answer to a question I never got to ask Colin Gunton. All who had the privilege and pleasure of discussing theology with him will know that he had two heroes when he talked Christology. Cyril of Alexandria, whose insistence that all that is predicated of Jesus Christ is predicated of the one incarnate person of the Divine Word, and not divided up into things predicated of the human nature and things predicated of the divine nature, was much admired by Colin; and John Owen, whose demand that the humanity of the Jewish man Jesus of Nazareth was never lost sight of, Colin also strongly affirmed. As I thought through this paper, and particularly as I read some of the seventeenth- and eighteenth-century debates between Lutheran and Reformed, Colin's choice of heroes struck me as more and more right, but also more and more odd.

The reason for this is as follows: at the heart of the argument of this essay is a suggestion that the novel Christology of John Owen, taken up by several others within the Anglophone Reformed tradition, is distinctively and radically Reformed, in that it can be seen to grow out of, inform and support positions the Reformed were developing in their disputes with the Lutherans. Now, both Reformed and Lutherans mapped their Christological disputes onto the famous patristic debate between Alexandria and Antioch, and the opposing heresies it gave rise to. The mapping was done differently by each side, with the Reformed identifying themselves with the tradition declared orthodox at Chalcedon, and insisting that the Lutherans were Eutychians; and the Lutherans, by contrast, claiming that the Reformed were Nestorian and that they themselves were in fact the heirs of Chalcedon. Given this, if I am right in supposing that Owen's Christology was a radicalization of standard Reformed positions, Colin's heroes are Cyril, and someone whose theology would have appeared to at least some of his contemporaries as unquestionably Nestorian.

There is something very right about this, it seems to me, because we need in Christology to hold to the genius of both the ancient, and indeed both the early modern, schools. With Alexandria and Heidelberg, we must insist that it is of decisive importance that we confess one Lord, Jesus Christ, that the hypostatic union is no fiction or figure of speech, but that God the Son is truly *homoousios* with us, as he is *homoousios* with the Father. With Antioch and Geneva, however, we must acknowledge that it is just as decisive that there is no mingling or admixture of the natures to form a *tertium quid*, a bizarre spiritual cockatrice who hovers lost in the void between humanity and divinity. Both Nestorius and Eutyches must be condemned, and so to hold as heroes two people who grasped these two truths with profundity is appropriate. The oddness relates to how these things can be held together: the account I have sketched already gives some reason to fear that the Christologies of Cyril and Owen might prove simply incoherent, and good reason to suspect that they pull in very different directions. It is, I have argued, very desirable to hold them together, but how might it be done?

First, however, to the history, and my argument with Robert Jenson, as all the other reflections presuppose that I am right about that. I want to suggest that towards the heart of Owen's Christology is a peculiar way of understanding the philosophical underpinnings of the patristic – and indeed biblical – linguistic practice that came to be known as the communication of properties – the *communicatio idiomatum* – *idiomaton koinonia*, or *antidosis ton idiomaton*.

At the head of the Reformed tradition, Calvin defines the *communicatio idiomatum* by following the doctrine of Pope Leo:

> [the Scriptures] sometimes attribute to [Christ] what must be referred solely to his humanity, sometimes what belongs uniquely to his divinity; and sometimes what embraces both natures but fits neither alone. And they so earnestly express the union of the two natures that is in Christ as sometimes to interchange them. This figure of speech (*tropus*) is called by the ancient writers 'the communication of properties' (*Inst.* II.xiv.1).

In the following section, Calvin offers some Scriptural examples: 'God purchased the church with his blood' (Acts 20.28, margin); 'the Lord of glory was crucified' (1 Cor. 2.8); 'the Word of life was handled' (1 Jn 1.1). Calvin explains these examples thus: 'Surely God does not have blood ... But since Christ, who was true God and also true man, was crucified and shed his blood for us, the things he carried out in his human nature are transferred improperly, although not without reason, to his divinity' (*Inst.* II.xiv.2).

This account of the doctrine echoes one strand of the teaching declared orthodox at Chalcedon. Leo, in his *Tome*, had followed the same procedure of dividing up the acts and properties of the incarnate Son into those which belonged to the divine nature and those which belonged to the human nature – Calvin quotes Augustine, rather than Leo, but the Latin family resemblance is marked (*Inst.* II.xiv.4). However, there was something else going on at the council: although the Fathers proclaimed that 'Peter had spoken through Leo'[1] they did not, as the Pope had apparently expected, merely promulgate his *Tome* as their declaration of faith. Instead, they put it alongside the letters of Cyril, whose approach to this question was rather different, and, famously, wrote their own definition of what was to be regarded as orthodox belief.

The immediate reason for Calvin's choice is not hard to see. Although Calvin notes, and rebuts, the ancient Christological heresies associated with the names of Nestorius and Eutyches, his main target in his exposition of the hypostatic union is the teaching of Michael Servetus,

[1] *Acts*, Session 2.

against whom he had earlier written a lengthy treatise.[2] Servetus's account of the incarnation was rather complex, and indeed somewhat strange, but the essential problem would seem to be a conflation of divine and human activity, so that the human begetting by Mary was at the same time the divine act of generation, and so on. It is no surprise, therefore, that Calvin emphasizes those aspects of the orthodox inheritance that stressed the distinction of the two natures, rather than the unity of the person, and so regarded the *communicatio* as merely a figure of speech.

Calvin is of course careful to avoid the error of Nestorius. He both treats positively of the unity of the person, and condemns Nestorianism explicitly. On the one hand, he will assert that 'the passages that comprehend both natures at once ... set forth [Christ's] true substance most clearly of all. For one reads there neither of deity nor of humanity alone, but of both at once' (*Inst.* II.xiv.3). Calvin cites a number of passages of the form 'the Father ... has given all judgement to the Son' (Jn 5.22), arguing that the possession of the right to judge – or, variously, the power to forgive sin, to raise to life, to bestow righteousness and holiness, and so on – that possession of all these things is the prerogative only of God, but that the Son does not need to be given them by the Father, so the speaking of the gift indicates the humanity of the single mediator.

On the other hand, we read '[a]way with the error of Nestorius, who in wanting to pull apart rather than distinguish the nature of Christ devised a double Christ! Yet we see that Scripture cries out against this with a clear voice: there the name "Son of God" is applied to him who is born of the virgin, and the virgin herself is called the "mother of our Lord" (*mater Domini*)' (*Inst.* II.xiv.4). Those of us who wish to free Calvin from the taint of Nestorianism would no doubt be happier if at this point he had said *theotokos*, rather than something sounding uncomfortably like *christotokos*. When, however, we consider Calvin's slightly odd account of what calling Christ 'Lord' means, developed through a discussion of the differing states of Christ, it is clear that the phrase 'mother of our Lord', while a conscious distancing from certain extremes of Marian devotion, is a strong claim in Calvin's thought. Calvin's account of Christ's state of humiliation does not, perhaps unusually for a two-states Christology, compare it mainly to a protological pre-incarnate state of glory, but to an eschatological moment when Christ's state of humiliation will be over only because the

[2] Calvin mentions Nestorianism and Eutychianism in *Inst.* II.xiv.4, and then devotes II.xiv.5–8 to refuting Servetus. His anti-Servetian treatise, the *Defensio orthodoxae fidei de sacre Trinitate*, was written in 1554. He mentions it in II.xiv.8. It can be found in *Corpus Reformatorum* VIII. 457–644.

humiliation that he has chosen to share in common with all the children of Eve will be over.

This is discussed in *Inst.* II.xiv.3, in connection with passages that speak of the eschatological handing over of the Kingdom to the Father, which Calvin fears might be used to support some form of subordinatist or Arian position. Calvin offers an account of the state of humiliation that insists it continues until this eschatological handing over, when, with the coming of the last judgment, 'as partakers in the heavenly glory we shall see God as he is'. Until that point our union with God is mediated through the heavenly session of Christ, who presently 'reign[s], joining us to the Father as the measure of our weakness permits'; at that point, Christ, 'having discharged the office of Mediator, will cease to be the ambassador of his Father, and will be satisfied with that glory which he enjoyed before the creation of the world'.

There is much we could say about this, somewhat idiosyncratic, account, but the important point for my present discussion is that Calvin connects the title 'Lord' with the divine reign, so presently, because the reign is mediated through Christ alone, Christ alone is to be called 'Lord', but it remains a divine title, which will be reclaimed by the Father (and, we presume, the Spirit, who is noticeably absent from these sections), not to remove it from Christ, but so that Father, Son and Spirit share the Lordship in the eschatological kingdom, when 'we [shall] see his divine majesty face to face'. So, to get back to the main argument, to call the blessed virgin the 'mother of our Lord' rather than *theotokos* is not to deny that she is the mother of one who is properly called God, but rather to specify more exactly that it is the person of the Trinity who became incarnate to whom she is mother, not the Father or the Spirit. Calvin is particularly concerned to stress the unconfused and unmingled two natures of the mediator, but, properly understood, nothing he says can be taken as down-playing the unity of the person.

This concern for the distinct properties of the two natures famously spills over into Eucharistic controversy. Calvin asserts that it is of the essence of being human to be locally present in one place alone: I am here, so I am not in Albuquerque. Just so, claimed Calvin, if the body and blood – undeniably human properties – of Christ are locally present in one place, they cannot be so in another: '[f]or as we do not doubt that Christ's body is limited by the general characteristics common to all human bodies, and is contained in heaven ... until Christ return in judgment, so we deem it utterly unlawful to draw it back under these corruptible elements [i.e. consecrated bread and wine] or to imagine it to be present everywhere' (*Inst.* IV.xvii.12). Thus they cannot be on many altars simultaneously; in fact, because Christ is located 'at the right hand of the Father', his body and blood are not physically located on any altar. Thus both Roman transubstantiation and Luther's consubstantiation must be false.

(In passing, it is not clear to me that any form of the *communicatio* can be helpful for a non-Calvinist position; what is wanted for the Lutheran or Thomist account to be true is not a divine property – omnipresence – but the property of being locally present in several places at once. When Quenstedt argued that 'the majesty of the omnipresence of the Logos was communicated to the human nature of Christ in the first moment of the personal union, in consequence of which, along with the divine nature, it is now omnipresent',[3] he proved far too much, in that on this account Christ is no less present in this glass of water than on the altar, and so no more present on the altar than in this glass of water. Such a position cannot support consubstantiation, as either Luther or the Formula of Concord defines the term. Indeed, of all the disputed Reformation positions on the Eucharist, it looks closest to that of Zwingli. To support consubstantiation, an account of multiple particular local presences of the same human person must be developed, not an account of human omnipresence.)

The development of the Continental scholastic Reformed tradition retained this interest in stressing the distinct properties of the two natures of Christ, not least because it continued to form an important strand of polemic against Lutheran eucharistic doctrine. At the same time, there was a move to more careful statements that were consciously in line with Chalcedonian orthodoxy. François Turretin, for example, offers a careful treatment of the hypostatic union, in the form of three questions.[4] The first of these is headed 'Did the Son of God assume human nature into the unity of his person? We affirm against the Socinians.' There is a characteristically careful statement of the question, and a careful and orthodox account of the hypostatic union which relies on an account of the enhypostatic assumption of the full, but anhypostatic, human nature into personal union by the Logos. The union is defined as 'the intimate and perpetual conjunction of the two natures ... in the unity of person' (*Inst. Elenc. Theol.* XIII.vi.5). The next question consists of a denial of the errors associated with Nestorius and Eutyches, quoting the Chalcedonian definition as the middle way, denying both. The error of Nestorius is asserted to be the invention of two persons of the two natures of Christ; as a result of this, according to Turretin, he denied that Mary was *theotokos*; that

[3] Cited in Heinrich Schmid, *The Doctrinal Theology of the Evangelical Lutheran Church*, trans. Charles A. Hay and Henry E. Jacobs (Minneapolis: Augsburg, 3rd edn, 1961), 331.

[4] *Inst. Elenc. Theol.* XIII.6–8.

Christ was God, instead calling him a 'man possessed by God'; and that there was no union of natures other than as association and an inhabitation.

Interestingly, Turretin shows himself aware of historical questions as to whether Nestorius was actually guilty of the error that bears his name, although he offers some reasons to assume he was. Nevertheless, as he notes, 'the question is historical, of fact, not of right. This does not hinder us from rejecting as fundamental the error attributed to Nestorius' (*Inst. Elenc. Theol.* XIII.vii.4). Turretin's reasons for rejecting the Nestorian heresy are exegetical, based on three sets of passages: those which teach that 'the Son of God was born of a virgin' ('God sent forth his Son, born of a woman' Gal. 4.4); those that speak of 'one person consisting of two natures' (Rom. 1.3–4 is to the fore, the *locus classicus* in this discussion); and those that 'ascribe diverse properties and operations to the one Christ' ('the Lord of glory was crucified' 1 Cor. 2.8) (XIII.vii.5–7). He makes sense of this by appealing to the anhypostatia, which if right must deny Nestorianism, and by asserting the *communicatio idiomatum*: 'suffering and death properly and formally belong to the human nature, but denominatively to the person according to the other nature' (XIII.vii.9), before doing a certain amount of squirming around the need to affirm that the Blessed Virgin should be called 'Mother of God'.

After this conscious display of catholic orthodoxy, Turretin turns to the more immediate controversy:[5] 'Were certain properties of the divine nature formally communicated to the human nature of Christ by the personal union? We deny against the Lutherans.' Turretin asserts that the personal union affects both the human nature and the person (the divine nature, being immutable and impassible, is not changed in any way). The effects on the human nature are twofold: pre-eminence, and the habitual graces which are possessed in the highest manner possible for a human creature, but no higher. This point is perhaps best illustrated by a commonplace of Reformed prolegomena: the ecumenical distinction between *theologia archetypa* – God's own intuitive, complete and single knowledge of himself – and *theologia ectypa* – the partial, studied and complex knowledge possessed by creatures. Whereas, however, other discussions tend to assert that the higher forms of ectypal theology are the knowledge of God enjoyed by the saints and angels in the beatific vision, the Reformed prolegomena asserted that the most perfect and complete ectypal theology, which still, however, was creaturely knowledge of God, and not God's own

[5] Socinianism was an immediate controversy, of course, but I know of little evidence that there were contemporary explosions of Nestorianism or Eutychianism that Turretin was concerned to combat.

knowledge of himself, was the *theologia unionis* – the knowledge of God granted to the enhypostatic human nature of Christ by virtue of the hypostatic union.[6]

This, admittedly somewhat abstruse, set of distinctions is interesting for my purposes because it demonstrates two important points. One which I shall return to, concerning the attempt to perceive two distinct psychological centres in the one person of Christ without thereby denying the hypostatic union; the other indicating that the Reformed were prepared to ascribe every perfection possible to human being to the human nature of Christ, and that in the highest degree possible to human being; they were not, however, prepared to bridge the basic chasm between Creator and created, even in the case of that created nature which was assumed into personal union with the creative Word. Turretin quotes the fourth evangelist to the effect that 'God gives the Spirit without measure' to him (Jn 3.34) (*Inst. Elenc. Theol.* XIII.viii.1; see also XIII.viii.32), which makes the point succinctly: as the highest of all creatures, there is no limit to God's gracious gifting, but as a creature still, there is a need for it.

The effects of the hypostatic union on the person are, on Turretin's telling, threefold: the communication of attributes, of office, and of honour. In each case, he insists, the communication must be considered as only from the natures to the person, not from one nature to the other. Thus Turretin's account of the *communicatio idiomatum* relies on a distinction between communication between natures and person and communication between the two natures. Properties of each nature may be meaningfully and rightly applied to the person, but properties of the one nature may not be applied to the other. Turretin's reasons in defence of this position are numerous, and not too important for my purposes here, mainly relying on supposed logical inconsistencies in the opposing position, about half of which I find convincing. The explanation of his position is more interesting, however: Turretin's great point is that the natures are different, and for there to be a real incarnation, and not a Eutychian mixing of natures leading to a *tertium quid*, the natures must remain distinct.

[6] A useful discussion of the distinction between *theologia archtypa* and *theologia ectypa*, and of the place of the *theologia unionis* in the scheme, occurs in Sebastian Rehnman, *Divine Discourse: The Theological Methodology of John Owen* (Grand Rapids: Baker, 2002), 57–71. Rehnman indicates that, although this language for the division between God's own self-knowledge and all creaturely knowledge of God is first found in Franciscus Junius, in the early years of the seventeenth century, there are hints of the concept as far back as Aristotle and Ps.-Dionysius, and he suggests that the Reformed themselves considered that it came from medieval scholasticism, with Polanus pointing particularly to Scotus's commentary on Lombard.

What, then, is implied by the hypostatic union? Turretin's definition, already quoted, is of little help: 'intimate and perpetual conjunction' of the natures 'in the unity of the person' is an assertion of orthodoxy, but offers little explanation as to what it means. The deployment of the anhypostatic-enhypostatic distinction is, as far as I can see, only a way of denying Nestorianism – insisting that there is only one hypostasis of the incarnate Son – but it offers little or nothing in the way of positive content. Turretin's doctrine is damaged by his decision to write theology in an elenctic, or controversial, mood: he is very clear what is not to be believed, including long criticisms of the patristic heresies, the Socinians, and the Lutheran position, but he can offer little in the way of positive Christology, other than a repetition of the basic Reformed instinct that somehow the hypostatic union must preserve the integrity of the natures, particularly that of the human nature, which they believed Lutheran theology was in danger of damaging.

John Owen, and with him some others in an anglophone tradition, develops the basic anti-Lutheran Christological impulse in another way again, and one that has, I think, considerably more to say about the nature of the hypostatic union. Still the theological instinct is to protect the assertion of the full humanity of Christ, to prevent the divine nature so overwhelming the human that the humanity of Christ becomes a mere cipher, something that is asserted but carries no meaning. This becomes linked, in this tradition, with three other doctrines the Reformed were characteristically concerned about: the doctrine of sanctification; the *extra calvinisticum*; and pneumatology. The doctrine is most carefully developed in Owen, and it is his account I shall follow.

Owen, of course, says all the appropriate orthodox things, but the heart of what is distinctive about his Christology lies in his discussion of the role of the Spirit in the life of the incarnate Son, which Alan Spence discussed at an earlier conference in this series.[7] In the relevant chapters of the *Pneumatologia*,[8] Owen sets out to explain the particular works of the Holy Spirit in respect to the human nature of Christ. Before entering into the exposition, however, he feels the need to deal with an objection which, he suggests, is being urged by the Socinians; the objection being that there is no need, or indeed room, for a work of the Spirit in the life of Christ, as the hypostatic union with the Son can supply all necessary divine intervention.

[7] Alan Spence, 'Christ's Humanity and Ours: John Owen', in Colin E. Gunton and Christoph Schwöbel (eds.), *Persons Divine and Human* (Edinburgh: T&T Clark, 1991), 74–97.

[8] John Owen, *Pneumatologia: Or, a Discourse Concerning the Holy Spirit* in *Works*, vol. III (of XVI) (ed. William Goold; Edinburgh: Banner of Truth, 1965).

Owen does not pause to explain why this point was seen as an adequate disproof of Trinitarian doctrine by the Socinians – it was, after all, a position which Cyril was concerned to force upon Nestorius through the seventh of his anathemas, and so is not obviously immediately destructive to orthodox theology – but I suppose that the argument would have been exegetical: Scripture speaks of works of the Spirit in the life of Christ, so if a particular doctrine cannot find room for such works, it is shown to be false.

Owen could have turned to a series of exegetical positions developed within Lutheranism to help him here, but instead he develops a distinctive form of Reformed Christology. His argument has two parts: first he proves how little is necessarily consequent on the hypostatic union, so showing which works need not have been done by the Son; and then he argues what works are proper to the Spirit within the divine economy, so demonstrating that the works he wishes to ascribe to the Spirit are not necessarily those of the Son and are properly those of the Spirit. The argument begins with the assertion '[t]he only singular immediate *act* of the person of the Son on the human nature was the *assumption* of it into subsistence with himself'.[9] The defence of this point is exegetical, with references to some of Owen's commentaries. In these references the argument seems to be devoted to asserting the positive – that this was indeed an immediate act of the Son – rather than the negative – that there are no other immediate acts of the Son.

Second, and again quoting, 'the only *necessary consequent* of this assumption of the human nature ... is the *personal union of Christ*, or the inseparable subsistence of the *assumed nature* in the person of the Son'.[10] In passing it is worth noting that the *enhypostatia* is again to the fore, but the main point is that, again, Owen's defence is directed toward the positive case, that this is in fact a necessary consequence. The defence of both negative cases comes in the third part of the argument, devoted to proving '[t]hat all other actings of God in the *person of the Son* towards the human nature were *voluntary*, and did not necessarily ensue on the union mentioned ...'[11] Why so? Because of the form of the *communicatio idiomatum* that Owen holds to: 'for there was no transfusion of the properties of one nature into the other, nor real physical [i.e. phusis-cal; from nature to nature] communication of divine essential excellencies unto

[9] John Owen, *Works* (ed. W.H. Goold; London: Banner of Truth, 1965), III, p. 160.
[10] Owen, *Works*, III, p. 160.
[11] Owen, *Works*, III, p. 161.

the humanity'.[12] Owen's argument for this proposition is twofold: first, he rehearses in a compact form one of the standard Reformed arguments to the effect that the *communicatio* does not necessarily imply a communication from nature to nature; second he relies on an exegetical point to do with knowledge. In Mk 13.32 the 'Son does not know the day and the hour' that the Father has appointed; more strikingly, in Rev. 1.1, the revelation had to be given by the Father to the now-glorified Jesus – it was not his intuitively or by right, despite his ascension to the right hand of the Father. Owen reads both of these as references to the limited knowledge of the human nature, and so argues that communications of knowledge, and hence of other properties and perfections, between the natures were voluntary. Other, then, than the act of union and the consequent personal union, the fact of incarnation demands that nothing more be ascribed to the Son.

Other theological reasoning, common to all strands of the tradition, demands that the Spirit is 'the *immediate, peculiar, efficient cause*'[13] of all *ad extra* divine works. Owen qualifies this with a brief discussion of the doctrine of appropriation, although without naming it as such, and further asserts that, as the Spirit is the Spirit of the Son, and not just of the Father, it is appropriate to insist that '[w]hatever the Son of God wrought in, by, or upon the human nature, he did it by the Holy Ghost'.

In another work, the *Christologia*, many of the same points are made. In the chapter on the 'hypostatical union' (ch. XVIII), four heads are treated: the assumption of the human nature; the consequent union of the two natures in the single person; the 'mutual communication of those distinct natures'; and the possible predication that therefore follows. The ineffable assumption of the (anhypostatic) human nature by the divine Logos is the first and most basic act – it is an act of the Trinity, in that it is purposed by the Father, who sent his Son 'in the likeness of sinful flesh'; it is carried out by the Son, in the actual act of assumption; and it is brought to completion by the Spirit, in the framing of the human nature in the womb of the virgin – Lk. 1.35. Once again, however, the basic insistence follows: the assumption was 'the only *immediate act* of the divine nature on the human person of the Son'.[14]

The hypostatic union is the first consequence of the act of assumption. The orthodox conditions are rehearsed and respected: the union took place without any change of the divine nature; without either division or

[12] Owen, *Works*, III, p. 161.
[13] Owen, *Works*, III, p. 161.
[14] Owen, *Works*, I, p. 225.

confusion of the two natures, and substantially rather than accidentally. At this point Owen suggests that the error of Nestorius had re-appeared in his day, and offers an analysis and criticism of it. I will return to this.

The various communications of the two natures are carefully enumerated: the divine nature communicates in three ways to the human: subsistence, which is to say the enhypostatic existence of the anhypostatic nature; by filling the human nature with the fullness of grace, which, however, Owen is careful to say is not an immediate act, but '[b]y the Holy Spirit';[15] and the gift of worth and dignity. Three further points are made concerning the communion of the natures within the hypostatic union, in explicit opposition to Lutheran accounts of the *communicatio idiomatum*: each nature preserves its own properties; each nature operates in the one person according to its essential properties; and yet every act of Christ is an act of the person, not of one of the natures, because only the person subsists, and so only the person can act. However, and finally, the possibility of any particular action might be determined by reference to one or both of the natures, and so one form of possible predication concerning the incarnate Son is to follow Leo and speak improperly, although not without reason, of particular actions belonging to particular natures. It is also possible to speak – again improperly, but not without reason, across the natures, so to speak: God purchasing the church 'with his own blood' is the now-standard example. This is the *communicatio idiomatum*.

The effect of Owen's Christology is profound. Clearly the radical distinction between the two natures denies any attempt to defend the real presence of the body and blood of Christ in the elements on the altar on the basis of a real communication of attributes between the natures.[16] However, and as has been pointed out before, it also has a particular effect concerning sanctification: if one believes, as Owen did, that the only direct act of the Son was the assumption of the human nature, and that the hypostatic union was the only necessary consequence of that act, then all else – and in particular the sanctification of Christ – is a work of the Spirit in the life of a human being. Thus, the command to 'be holy as I am holy', and the ancient spiritual advice to engage in the *imitatio Christi*, can have new force: the Jewish man Jesus Christ can be imitated because he was 'like

[15] Owen, *Works*, I, p. 233.

[16] I am, of course, aware that there are other possible defences of trans- or consubstantiation, not the least being straightforward exegesis of the dominical words of institution; my argument is not about the nature of the Eucharistic celebration, but about the person of Christ.

us in every way, sin apart', and so this Christology leads directly to a robust account of sanctification, a topic of particular interest to the Reformed, and another facet of their dispute with the Lutherans. Finally, the strong insistence on the continuing distinctiveness of the two natures leads naturally to a statement of the *extra calvinisticum* which, while it was a part of catholic Western doctrine before the Reformation, nonetheless became another flash-point in disputes between Lutheran and Reformed. So I suggest that Owen's Christology can be described as a distinctively Reformed Christology because it grows out of Reformed concerns, and feeds and supports disputed Reformed positions. The question must be, however: is it orthodox?

The suspicion of Nestorian tendencies has hung around Calvin's Christology for a very long time; Turretin is careful to avoid Nestorianism, but does so by avoiding any positive teaching about the nature of the hypostatic union at all; surely when we get to Owen, and a much more radical distinction of the natures, we are faced with rampant Nestorianism, and no amount of squirming will get him off the hook. This Christology might be distinctively Reformed, but it is also straightforwardly heretical. Or so the charge will go. It would, I think, not be difficult to show that Owen's doctrine lies within the bounds of Chalcedonian orthodoxy, but it might also not be helpful: the history of the Eastern churches, and particularly the Eastern monasteries, after Chalcedon is eloquent testimony to a widespread suspicion that the Council gave too much to the Nestorians in opposing Eutyches, particularly in its acceptance of Leo's *Tome*. Indeed, in the *Bazaar*, Nestorius himself seems happy with the Chalcedonian definition, and it is not obvious that this is merely a political move, although it certainly is that. So instead let me turn to Cyril himself, which will in any case be necessary to make the point concerning Colin Gunton's Christological intuitions with which I began.

Nestorius's great complaint against Cyril, and indeed Apollinarius, was that for the former to say that God the Son was born, or the latter to say that God the Son 'accepted sufferings',[17] was to make a category mistake; he held (as indeed did Cyril and Apollinarius) that God, being immutable and impassible, could not be born or suffer. Christ could suffer, and be born – the Virgin could be honoured as *christotokos* – but only because Christ had a human nature of which birth and suffering could properly be

[17] *Nestorius: The Bazaar of Heracleides* (trans. G.R. Driver and L. Hodgson; Oxford: Clarendon, 1925), I.i.48 (p. 39) for the quotation, and II.i (p. 148) for the point about God the Son being born.

predicated.[18] Behind this refusal to use the language lies a more basic issue. Nestorius finally refused to give any significant ontological depth to the union of natures in the incarnation, arguing only for a union of *prosopa*, which in his ontology more or less correspond to the medieval idea of accidents, in that they are the empirical *qualia* that attach to a thing, but not the thing itself.[19] Because of this, Nestorius would not accept that the Church could correctly speak of the divine Son as the possessor or agent of human properties or actions, nor would he accept the converse, speaking of the Jewish man Jesus as the possessor or agent of divine properties or actions. The Christ, as the complex interweaving of the two sets of *qualia*, of properties and actions, could be spoken of in either sense, but the Christ, as such an interweaving and nothing more, was not an ontologically significant being. The classical criticisms of Nestorius in undergraduate textbooks, that he described the incarnation like two stars, so close in line that they shine as one, although one is unimaginably further away from us than the other, are unfair, but they capture the essence of the problem. All that is ontologically significant for Nestorius remains two, and so we must be careful what we say – there is no real communication of properties, and so to speak as if there is must be improper.[20]

Cyril, by contrast, started from the fundamental position that the incarnate Son was one. The Christ, to whom both divine and human predicates may be applied, must be of decisive ontological significance. That aspect of Cyril's thought that Colin found so appealing, the flat refusal to divide up the actions of Christ into divine and human actions, instead insisting they all flow from the one incarnate Son, a single actor, grows from this starting-point.

> Moreover, we do not allocate the statements of our Savior in the Gospels either to two *hupostaseis* or indeed to two persons, for the one and only Christ is not twofold, even if he be considered as from two entities and they different, which had been made into an inseparable unity ... Therefore, to one person must all the

[18] *Bazaar* I.iii (p. 99).

[19] *Bazaar* I.i.57–68 (pp. 53–63), and see also the editors' comments on pp. 411–18.

[20] This becomes clear in the later development of the Nestorian tradition, wherein ousia and hypostasis are not separated (as they were not at Nicaea, of course), and so the incarnation is described as a personal union of two hypostaseis, as by Babai the Great in the first half of the seventh century.

> statements in the Gospels be ascribed, to the one incarnate *hupostasis* of the Word ...[21]

Cyril's Christology invites explication through the anhypostatic and enhypostatic elements of the human nature: the 'one incarnate subject of the Word' is a 'single person': Cyril's usual phrase is *mia phusis*, but this is already unhappy in his own writing, in that he also uses *phusis* for the divine and human natures that are united in the incarnate Son, and he clearly does not mean the same thing by the word in both cases, as he denies the obvious and inevitable result of such usage, that the incarnate Son is neither divine nor human but a *tertium quid*.[22] In the later conciliar language, the one hypostasis of the Divine Son becomes incarnate; because the incarnate Son is one person and one hypostasis, his human nature is necessarily anhypostatic, has no independent subsistence, but because there is a real human existence of the incarnate Son, the human nature is also enhypostatic, subsists truly in and through the particular subsistence of the Divine Son.

Given this, the Cyrillian and conciliar understanding of the *communicatio idiomatum* is as follows: all that is said of the incarnate Son is properly predicated of the Divine Son – necessarily, as the humanity of Christ is anhypostatic – but it is said only of the Divine Son in his incarnate state. The qualification is decisive for Cyril – it is almost the entire content of his second letter to Nestorius, for instance. Hence, again, the infamous twelfth anathema from the third letter: 'Whoever does not acknowledge God's Word as having suffered *in the flesh*, being crucified *in the flesh*, tasted death *in the flesh*, and been made first-born from the dead because as God he is Life and life-giving shall be anathema' (my emphasis). Cyril, like the Fathers of Chalcedon, wants to affirm divine impassibility strongly,[23]

[21] *Ep.* 17:13–14, in John I. McEnerney (trans.), *St Cyril of Alexandria: Letters* 1–50 (Fathers of the Church, 76; Washington, DC: Catholic University of America Press, 1987), 87. The Greek can be found in T.H. Bindley, *The Oecumenical Documents of the Faith* (rev. F.W. Green; London: Methuen, 1950).

[22] This would seem to be what Nestorius understood Cyril to mean; Cyril's denials should have been clear enough, but his language did perhaps invite the confusion.

[23] 'We confess that he, the Son begotten of God the Father, and only begotten God, though being incapable of suffering according to his own nature, suffered in his own flesh for our sake, according to the Scriptures, and that he made his own the sufferings of his own flesh in his crucified body impassibly ...' (*Ep.* 17.11 [p. 85]); 'Thus we say that he also suffered and rose again, not that the Word of God suffered in his own nature, or received blows, or was pierced, or received the other wounds, for the divine cannot suffer since it is incorporeal. But since his own body, which had been born, suffered these things, he himself is said to have suffered them for our sake. For he was the one, incapable of suffering, in the body which suffered' (*Ep.* 4.5 [p. 40]). Many other examples could be offered.

while also being able to say that God the Son suffered, in his incarnate state.

Although all this invocation of the anhypostatic-enhypostatic formula is anachronistic in discussing Cyril, it seems to me that it is very helpful. That the Jewish man Jesus Christ subsists only in the divine nature of the Word and, concomitantly, that the doings and sufferings of that Jewish man are the doings and sufferings of the Word, in his incarnate state, is almost the sum total of Cyril's claims. Given that, I hope it is now obvious from my preceding exposition of Owen's Christology, and his continual insistence on the anhypostatic-enhypostatic subsistence of the human nature, that his Christology is not incompatible with Cyril's; indeed, that it might even be described as very compatible.[24] As usual, Colin Gunton's theological intuition was spot on.

One last point, however: even if it can be reduced to the same dogmatic formulae, there is that about Owen's Christology that feels Nestorian to us; can we explain this, and then explain it away? I think we can: Owen's great insight is to investigate what is necessary to hypostatic union; and his answer, like the answers to the successive patristic versions of the same question, was 'certainly nothing that involves the confusion or diminution of the natures'. So, to take the most counter-intuitive moment of the patristic development, can there still be hypostatic union if there is more than one volitional centre in Christ? Yes, comes the orthodox answer, not least because to deny the presence of a human will with the monothelites would be to damage the human nature irreparably. Owen's key move turns not on willing, but on knowing: to put the point in Cyril-like rhetoric, the omniscient divine Son is, in his human nature, simply ignorant of certain facts, and needs to have them revealed to him by the Father through the Spirit.

The great point here, and it is a point which I think Cyril's own repeated example, of the Word's impassible suffering in the human nature, also confirms, although I have no time to show how here, is that the

[24] The ninth anathema of Cyril might appear to exclude Owen's positions, but in fact does not: 'If anyone says that the one Lord Jesus Christ has been glorified by the Spirit, and the Lord was using the power which was through the Spirit as if it belonged to someone else, and says the Lord received from the Spirit the power to act against unclean spirits, and to complete among men the miracles, and does not rather say that *the Spirit is his very own through whom he has performed miracles*, let him be anathema' (my emphasis). As can be seen, Cyril's concern is not to anathematize those who – like Owen – believe that the miracles of the Incarnate One were performed in the power of the Spirit; indeed, the anathema explicitly affirms this in the words I have italicized. Rather, the idea that the Spirit is foreign to Christ, 'belonged to someone else', and is not 'his very own', is the concern.

hypostatic union does not require a single psychological centre. A denial of theopaschitism, opposition to monothelitism, and an affirmation of Owen's point about ignorance, all point in this direction. In our culture which conflates the personal and the psychological, this is difficult to grasp, but it is surely also necessary to grasp. Trinitarian dogma would make the same point, after all, albeit in a different direction – in the Godhead is one will, one working, one activity, one energy, and so on, as John Damascene insists, but there are three persons. In the hypostatic union there is one person of the Word incarnate, but two willings, two knowings, two workings, and so on. And so the Reformed and catholic emphasis on the transcendent freedom of the Word even in the incarnation – the *extra calvinisticum* – and the distinctively Reformed emphasis on the true humanity of the incarnate Word, growing, learning new things, able to act, and to be holy, only as empowered by the Spirit, are in simple continuity not just with Chalcedon, but with Ephesus, Cyril and the anathemas.

What prevents this from being Nestorian is the hypostatic union, the single person of the incarnate Word. In conciliar Christology the union is hypostatic, not psychological, however, and what establishes the person as one is not psychology but ontology. Ownership is perhaps a helpful way of looking at this:[25] Cyril's demand is not that the Divine Word suffers, *simpliciter* – he knows this to be impossible – but that he suffers in his human nature. The decisive point is that the sufferings are his, and not another's. And with Owen, the omniscient Word knows the thoughts of the Jewish man Jesus Christ just as he knows my thoughts and yours. But, uniquely and decisively, he knows the thoughts of Jesus to be his own, in his human nature, and not another's. Such an understanding allows the necessary concerns of both Antioch and Alexandria, both Reformed and Lutheran, to be held together.

[25] And, indeed, one suggested by the quotations from Cyril in n. 23 above.

Chapter 5

Person and Nature: A Critique of the Necessity-Freedom Dialectic in John Zizioulas

Douglas Farrow

John Zizioulas's preoccupation with the dialectic of necessity and freedom is not absent in the patristic sources he prizes, such as the Cappadocians, but it is more prominent in the existentialism that provides the immediate background to his theological project. Zizioulas lays hold of this dialectic and extends it to us as the very branch by which we may escape from the vortex of existentialist thought, and from the assorted intellectual debris which has been gathering around it over the last seventy years.[1] That is, he employs it in the service of an ecclesiology which dares to present itself as an ontology of personhood, an ontology which has at its heart what even the most optimistic existentialism does not, viz., a concept of freedom through love: freedom through being as an act of *koinonia* with God in which all necessity is transcended.

When the church is viewed in this way – that is, as the divine answer to the challenge to human personhood posed by necessity, by nature, by finitude – it is immediately obvious that ecclesiology will rescue ontology, both from the doldrums into which it has fallen in Western thought and from the attack of the sceptical existentialists.[2] This orientation of

[1] See already 'Human Capacity and Incapacity', *Scottish Journal of Theology* 28 (1975): 401–47.

[2] In *The Beauty of the Infinite* (Grand Rapids: Eerdmans, 2003) David Hart makes a quite different rescue attempt that relies on a different way of reading the Cappadocians.

Zizioulas's ecclesiology to ontology is one of the reasons why Western theologians find it both foreign and fascinating. For the church is not viewed merely as an instrument of divine grace in the face of human sin, or as a sign of divine sovereignty in human history, or as a model for renewed forms of human sociality. Still less is it viewed merely as an institution, however great or humble. It is viewed rather as an anthropic – and indeed a cosmic – sine qua non. In a period of Western uncertainty about the church, and about its place in the modern world, Zizioulas offers us an ecclesiology that is nothing less than ontology, indispensable ontology, but an ontology attuned, for all its patristic trappings, to modern questions and difficulties.[3]

Neither the ecclesiology, nor the dialectic that serves it, is unproblematic however. Metropolitan John will forgive me, I'm sure, if I explore these things, in an appreciative but critical vein. I begin, as is necessary, by rehearsing what is already well rehearsed.[4]

Personhood as Freedom from Necessity

In the Cappadocians, claims Zizioulas, the being of God is identified with the Father, hence with a hypostatic or personal mode of existence. The Father is the self-grounding ground of God's existence and the principle of divine unity. God therefore is not bound by any necessity of substance, but lives in and from the freedom of the Father's self-determination *as* Father.[5] God's being as Father – as the one who readies himself for communion by lovingly begetting the Son and breathing the Spirit, without any compulsion whatever – is a transcendence of the necessity which otherwise must characterize that being in its sheer absoluteness. It is in view of the ontological priority of the Father, hence of *hypostasis* over *ousia*, that we can make the ontological equation: being = communion = freedom.[6] Authentic being is personal being, which means also inter-personal being, or

[3] Some might suggest that it is attuned too much to modern questions, or at least charge that Zizioulas misreads his patristic sources in such a way as to favour his own project. That may be the case (see, e.g., Lucian Turcescu's '"Person" versus "Individual", and Other Modern Misreadings of Gregory of Nyssa', *Modern Theology* 18.4 (2002): 527–39, but it does not follow that his project is the worse for it. The Cappadocians may be wrong where Zizioulas is right.

[4] My task can only be performed by thinking simultaneously (as he does) theologically and Christologically, as well as ecclesiologically, about the nature of personhood. This means covering some familiar ground.

[5] The Father-person's being is in his self-disposal for *koinonia* with the Son and the Spirit, and so in his causing and communing with Son and Spirit, and this is God's being in freedom.

[6] *Being as Communion* (Crestwood: St. Vladimir's Seminary Press, 1985), 40ff. The equation is also epistemological, of course: being = communion = freedom = truth.

being free even from oneself. And if this is true where God is concerned, then creaturely being (which depends upon God) will have also to be considered in the same light. Persons and personhood and the event of communion will have conceptual priority over being or substance or nature.

Now personhood is something which Zizioulas expounds by employing the term *ekstasis* alongside *hypostasis*. The former indicates freedom for the other, and indeed the investment and discovery of one's own being in the other. The latter (when paired with *ekstasis*) indicates freedom for the whole, which is also freedom for oneself in one's own particularity as bearer of the whole.[7] The two terms thus work together to delineate a concept of personhood, and of communion, which posits a perichoretic capacity for catholicity. This notion of the person as 'catholic' is a complex one, about which more will have to be said; it is directly linked, of course, to an ecclesial anthropology. But why has Zizioulas tagged the entire discussion of personhood to the problem of necessity?

For Zizioulas, as for many existentialists, necessity is the ultimate threat or challenge to personhood. The truly authentic person is the one who exists in uncompromised freedom, who is determined in his existence by no necessity whatever. Zizioulas, citing Gregory of Nyssa,[8] follows through with this logic. The truly authentic person is uncaused and uncreated, and (not being bound even by himself) has his being in communion. He is in fact the Father, apart from whom we ourselves would have no capacity for freedom, no knowledge of personhood, and hence no intuition of the threat to personhood posed by the interpretation of our being in impersonal (i.e. substantialist or even mechanistic) terms. That we do have such an intuition is the moment of truth in existentialism. Moreover, as everyone knows, creaturely freedom *is* threatened by necessity, and not merely by a necessitarian world-view. Our being, that is to say, is threatened by non-being, which presents itself in the form of the demands of biological existence. These demands are reminders of death, in all its inevitability, and come to us as debilitating distractions from the authentically personal mode of existence which constitutes real being.

Perhaps some further elaboration is in order, though we are still on familiar territory. Because of the Father, God the Son and God the Spirit are true persons also. Though they are not themselves uncaused, they belong to the Father's own being as a being-in-communion; as such they are eternal. If they are caused, their cause (and its consequence) is freedom

[7] Hence it does double duty, indicating both freedom for and freedom from oneself.
[8] Great Catechism 5 (Zizioulas, 'Human Capacity and Incapacity', 428).

itself.[9] The human person, however, is both caused and *created*. Since he belongs to the creaturely, which is not eternal, he is bound by all manner of creaturely mechanisms of cause and effect. He is bound indeed by his finitude, by his biological nature, by the necessities of his body, and by the self-centredness which all of this inevitably entails. If he is to be free at all, if his personhood is to be realized, he must overcome his natural or biological hypostasis, and all that it stands for. This he does by way of his baptismal or ecclesial hypostasis, which he gains through the liberating communion of the church, through its corporate participation in the freedom of the divine persons. That is how he too gains authentic personhood. For him personhood is a vocation, a process, a destiny. It is ecclesial in nature, liturgically accessed, and eschatologically consummated. Personhood, properly speaking, is the result of deification.[10]

Zizioulas thus takes up the concern of the existentialists – reversing the traditional association of real being with necessity – but also takes his leave of them, so that he may continue in the company of the fathers. His ontology of personhood may be tagged to the problem of necessity but it is made to rest on the doctrines of the Trinity and of the incarnation; on the claim that the incarnate Son becomes the conduit for human beings of the personalizing power of the Father and the liberating effects of the Spirit. Viewed eschatologically as the church, the incarnation is itself the complete overcoming of nature, necessity and death, *via* the advent of free and authentic human personhood. It is the personalization of the not yet personal. And through the church the cosmos as a whole is destined to become an act of communion, participating thus with man in the eternity of God. For the priestly ministry of redeemed humanity is such as to enable nature to be in freedom.[11]

[9] The *aitea* concept obviously undergoes alteration here, since where the Trinity is concerned what is caused partakes fully in the freedom of its cause (the Father). This alteration may be worth exploring. We may nevertheless have to ask whether it is possible, on this scheme, to understand the Son and the Spirit as personal in the same sense as the Father. Do the Son and the Spirit require, as we do, to be personalized, and thus also to be made to be? If so, are they as authentically personal as the Father is? And are we to regard the Father's personhood as something (logically) prior to his communion with the Son and the Spirit?

[10] Deification is a trinitarian event, as Irenaeus long ago taught. It rests first of all on the fact that the uncreated Son becomes a human being, linking God and man in his own person. It rests also upon the work of the Spirit, who reconstitutes us (in the church) as one corporate hypostasis with Christ, so that we may participate in his uncreated nature and in his eternal freedom as the Father's Son. Ultimately, of course, it rests upon the Father, who is freedom and who gives freedom.

[11] See *Being as Communion*, 101ff.

In sum, nature spells necessity but deification spells freedom from necessity, through the overcoming of nature in a personalizing act which produces the church. Ecclesiology, then, is the (philosophical) antidote Zizioulas offers to existentialist anxiety and despair about authentic existence. For ecclesiology is precisely an analysis of the transformation of the stuff of necessity into the stuff of freedom; which is also to say, it is an analysis of the eucharist. In the eucharistic *synaxis* and *koinonia*, in the Great Thanksgiving, the conditions are created for creaturely nature to transcend itself and to conquer every necessity – to have its being in the liberty of God, whose synactic principle of unity is the Father, and whose own being as triune communion is a joyful transcendence of all necessity.[12]

Catholicity and Personhood

The free or authentic person, we have said, is the catholic person: the person who lives *katholou*, which is possible only in and through the church. A catholic person is free because he has room for the other – indeed for all others – in himself. The other is no longer a source of conflict or of compulsion, but rather an opportunity for communion.[13] The catholic person, as a unique and unrepeatable source of this communion, is capable of bearing human nature in its entirety, of making it *be*.[14]

Now one is not mistaken to see a variety of influences in the background here. The Romantics, Hegel, Heidegger, Buber, *et al.*, have contributions to make. But obviously there are older resources in Christian neoplatonism which are less likely to lead in a non- or even anti-ecclesial direction. The best such resources are Denys and Maximus, to whom Zizioulas frequently appeals. What we find in Maximus especially is a concept of catholicity that takes up the microcosm/macrocosm dialectic of Greek philosophy, reinventing it on a Christological and liturgical template. Zizioulas arguably goes beyond this, however, in developing the catholicity of human personhood in terms of the *imago Trinitatis*, and in terms of personhood as such. I have elsewhere expressed certain reservations about

[12] Understood as act rather than object, and more particularly as an act of the Holy Spirit – celebrated by the people of God together with their episcopal *eikon* of the Father – the eucharist constitutes the church in its true being.

[13] The catholic person is undivided internally (for he is given his integrity from without) or externally (since in the Spirit difference does not mean division).

[14] Hence the church is reconstituted, in some quite fundamental sense, with each baptism, while remaining itself.

Maximus's model, which do not apply to that of Zizioulas.[15] Nevertheless there are questions which must be put to the latter as well.

We have seen that the Father (with the Son and the Spirit) makes divine being be, not by necessity of substance or nature, but in freedom; that is, personally, by love. Likewise Christ (with you and me) makes human being be, not by necessity but by love; not as a self-possessed something, or series of somethings, but as persons in communion, as church. He does so by overcoming the Fall: that inversion of our personhood which turns our difference from God, and from one another, into distance or division; which fractures and de-personalizes us, reducing us to thinghood, subjecting us to necessity, and so ultimately to *non*-being.[16] But how does he do so? How does Christ generate the free, the catholic, the existing person?

The answer is twofold. First, he does so by the power of his own prior personhood, that is, by virtue of the eternal relation (*schesis*) to the Father which constitutes him as a person. His personhood enables him to cause his human nature to be (viz., to be in communion), even as the Father's personhood enables the divine nature to be. Second, he generates the free or catholic person by sharing with him or her the same *schesis* that is constitutive of his own person.[17] This sharing (which requires the cross and the descent into hell) is effected in the Spirit, by sacramental means, through the baptismal and eucharistic liturgies. It has a visible structure, but it remains a mystery which is not fully susceptible to analysis. It is the mystery of the existence of Christ, who is both one and many.[18]

Each part of this twofold answer requires cross-examination. The first raises a question we might not otherwise think to put to a devoted disciple of Maximus, but we must enquire whether the Christology in play here is sufficiently Chalcedonian. It is evident enough that the line Zizioulas is

[15] Douglas Farrow, *Ascension and Ecclesia* (Edinburgh: T&T Clark, 1999), 140ff.

[16] The alternative to necessity is not construed in terms of freedom of choice (which implies division) but in terms of love (which implies unity in difference). Zizioulas does want to speak, however, of freedom of choice as a dimension of personhood which enables us to refuse personhood, that is, to deny 'the difference between person and nature' and so to reject our own existence by collapsing into individuality, into thinghood ('Human Capacity and Incapacity', 428f.) – in short, to fall away from God rather than to ascend to God by overcoming nature.

[17] See 'Human Capacity and Incapacity', 435ff.

[18] When Zizioulas speaks of Christ as 'one' he means Christ as a particular, which philosophically speaking correlates with the many; when he speaks of Christ as 'many' he refers to Christ as church, that is, to a concept of unity or of the one. The latter, whatever its philosophical colouring, is coloured also by Zizioulas's reliance ('Human Capacity and Incapacity', 408, n. 3) on the notion of 'corporate personality' drawn from H.W. Robinson and A.R. Johnson.

following requires a firm rejection of any Nestorian inclination or procedure. If personhood is prior to nature, and if it involves a form of freedom which can only have its source in God, then we are not going to take two natures as our starting-point and run the risk of implying two persons. We are going to begin instead with one Person, who invests his divine freedom in his human nature. But what of Eutychianism? In his programmatic article, 'Human Capacity and Incapacity' Zizioulas remarks that he wants to 'avoid the dilemma "divine *or* human person" as well as the curious composition "divine *and* human person"'.[19] This can be done, he believes, by observing that 'one and the same "schesis" is constitutive of Christ's being, both with regard to his humanity and with regard to his divinity'. But is this right? Can we say, *simpliciter*, that the eternal relation of Father and Son constitutes either the being or the person of Jesus Christ? Unless we were willing to abandon the distinction between immanent and economic Trinity, what this would imply is that the incarnation – the event which makes the eternal Son to be the Son also in time, to be the Davidic 'son' – has no ontological significance, and no bearing on Christ's personhood. And this in turn would require us after all to adopt the view that Christ is a divine person with a human nature but is *not* a human person, which would certainly tend to Eutychianism,[20] or to take the view that personhood, regarded in itself, is indifferent to the distinction between divinity and humanity.

Neither of these options seems to suit Zizioulas, I hasten to add.[21] But would it not be more accurate, then, to say that the Son, in taking to himself a creaturely nature so as to be the Christ, becomes also a human

[19] The phrase 'divine and human person' has (for Zizioulas) Nestorian overtones. See 'Human Capacity and Incapacity', 435f. We must avoid the conclusion that two natures means two persons, and we can do so only by recognizing that personhood is not a product of nature, but rather it is the person which allows the nature to be – in this case, which allows both natures to be. (In a cryptic argument, based partly on the vaguely Aristotelian premiss that 'there is no nature "in the nude"', Zizioulas concludes that 'it is his person that makes divine and human natures to be that particular being called Christ'.) The phrase in question, however, appears to lead from nature to person and so tends towards the Nestorian error.

[20] 'My God is not of like nature with me! He is not an individual man, but only man by nature. He does not have *soma anthropou* but *anthropinon*', insists Eutyches. Cf. D. Bonhoeffer, *Christ the Center* (New York: Harper & Row, 1978), 86; J.N.D. Kelly, *Early Christian Doctrines* (London: A. & C. Black, 1985), 332. For Eutyches, Christ is not *homoousios* with us in the patristic sense; that is, in Irenaeus' words, as 'a man among men'.

[21] On the other hand, how exactly shall we read the following statement? 'The natural qualities are not extrinsic to the identity ... but by being "enhypostasized" these qualities become dependent on the hypostasis for their being; the hypostasis is not dependent on them.' Zizioulas, 'On Being a Person', in *Persons, Divine and Human* (eds. C. Gunton and C. Schwöbel; Edinburgh: T&T Clark, 1992), 43. Do such statements about 'the mystery of personhood' not imply a certain indifference of person to nature? Cf. 'Human Capacity and Incapacity', 440.

person without ceasing to be a divine person? That he is in fact a divine and a human person? Of course it would not be more accurate unless it were pointed out with Chalcedon that there is no doubling of persons, as there is of natures; that the incarnate one is the divine person *as* a human person.[22] Nevertheless we should be clear that there is here a human person, one whose personhood is delineated both by the eternal relation of the Father to the Son *and* by a temporal relation of the same Son to the Father,[23] and to us. This 'and' (or rather, both these 'and's) will have to be taken into consideration when we examine the second part of Zizioulas's twofold answer.

Let us explore further the difficulty with the first part, however, by querying the way in which Zizioulas understands personhood, which he says is a *schesis*. This (as far as it goes) may seem unobjectionable, but plainly we cannot simply equate the person with the *schesis*, as Zizioulas appears to do. Can we say of the Father that his person is constituted by his fatherly relation to the Son? Undoubtedly, but when we go on to speak of his relation to the Spirit we make clear (unless we adopt a radical filioquist stance) that there is more to the Father than this fatherly *schesis*. Likewise, *mutatis mutandis*, with the Son. It is this 'more' which makes possible a repetition *cum* alteration in *schesis* without destroying the unity of his person. It is this 'more', in other words, which makes possible his incarnation. In the incarnation a divine person and a human person are one and the same person; and yet this one person is related to the Father as son

[22] Here we may appeal to 'anhypostasis' and 'enhypostasis'. The point of the former, as of the latter, is not to deny the concreteness of the Son's humanity – hence also his human personhood – but to affirm it, by denying that it belongs to another. Rightly regarded, these doctrines serve to clarify that, while the personhood of the incarnate Son is subject to consideration from the standpoint of temporal as well as eternal relations, and of a human as well as a divine nature, the Son is but one person. This is not because, as a person, he is somehow independent of these relations or these natures, nor yet because only one set of relations (the eternal) and only one nature (the divine) are really his. Certainly it is not because his person can be regarded as the sum of both the eternal and the temporal relations, or as the product of both the divine and the human natures; no such sum and no such product exist. The incarnate Son is but one person because, as has just been said, he is the divine person being a human person. Cf. Karl Barth, *Church Dogmatics* 1.2, 147ff., 159ff.; Aquinas, *Summa Theologiae* III. 2.4.

[23] When we ask about this temporal relation from the perspective of the Father, who does not himself become temporal or creaturely, it can only be replied that it is mediated internally by the Son. Any other reply is likely to result in Nestorianism, and to imply a breach between the immanent and the economic Trinity. Colin Gunton's attempt in *The Christian Faith* to bypass this point pneumatologically leads to an inverse form of monothelitism, for which reason it must be rejected. See Gunton, *The Christian Faith* (Oxford: Blackwell, 2002), 109f.

in two distinct ways, as God to God and as man to God.[24] We ought therefore to deny that personhood is a *schesis* – even if it is necessary to think in terms of particular constitutive relations in order to think of persons and personhood at all – for there is no third or archetypal *schesis* behind these two, to hold them together. And these two really are two, just as Christ's natures are two, without Christ being two persons.[25] The danger in Zizioulas's construct is that it cannot fail to undermine either one or the other of these claims.

Now with every sentence of such a discussion we are in danger of using words and concepts to mediate between God and man rather than letting the mediator mediate. That is, we are in danger of failing to take into account that terms such as person and nature and *schesis* must not be employed in a purely univocal way. The person–nature relation is one thing for God and another for man; to be a person is one thing for God and another for man; to *be* at all, even as an act of mutual communion, is one thing for God and another for man.[26] For just this reason we must not fail to say – not if we intend to take seriously Chalcedon's double *homoousios* – that the incarnate Son is both a divine and a human person, and we have already seen that we must not appeal to a single *schesis* or to 'the mystery of personhood' as a way of avoiding this.[27]

[24] Persons exist in and through personal relations, not as these relations, though they do not exist apart from these relations. Relations can therefore be altered, even if constitutional. The point of Chalcedon is that, God being God, the alteration which is the incarnation does not undo the intra-divine or constitutional relation. The eternal Son does not cease to be who he is in taking on human nature; nor does he become another person in addition to himself. He does, however, enter into a new and different relation to the Father in which he is constituted as a man. In this new and different relation it is perfectly appropriate to speak of him as a human person, though for fear of adoptionism the tradition has been hesitant to do so (but cf. Barth, *Church Dogmatics* 1.2, 164f.).

[25] Two natures does not mean two persons, but it does mean two ontologically distinct ways of being personal. For if natures cannot be abstracted from persons – we may agree that there is no nature 'in the nude' – neither can persons be abstracted from natures – there is no person 'in the nude' either. Therefore we cannot speak, as Zizioulas asks us to, of a person who 'makes divine and human natures to be that particular being called Christ'. We can only speak of a divine person who becomes and is a human person, while noting that this statement is not reversible: the human person is, but does not become, the divine person.

[26] If God, and only God, is his own nature (Aquinas, *Summa Theologiae* 1.39.1; cf. III.2.2), all of this follows.

[27] Could we not get round the whole problem, however, by observing that from Zizioulas's point of view Christ is not so much one person in two natures as a person, whose nature is to be personal (and so to be), assuming an impersonal or individualistic nature for the very purpose of personalizing it (making it be)? Would this not also permit us to answer Schleiermacher, who rejects the doctrine of the *assumptio* in part because he supposes that it must lead back to docetism, since 'the human nature in this way can only become a person in

But why are we pursuing this line of questioning? That we cannot make the equation, person = *schesis*, and that we must speak of the incarnate Son as personally related to the Father (as also to the Spirit) in two distinct ways, becomes still more crucial when we turn from consideration of Christ as one to a consideration of Christ as many; that is, when we turn to the second part of Zizioulas's answer, the thesis that Christ generates the free or catholic person by sharing the same *schesis* that is constitutive of his own being. The questions that arise here amount to an enquiry about the hypostatic nature of the church in its unity with the Son and, conversely, about the hypostatic nature of the incarnate Son in his unity with the church. They bring us to a consideration of Zizioulas's ecclesiology along with his Christology.

We ought, I think, to agree with Zizioulas that Christ generates the free or catholic person by sharing the same filial relation that is constitutive of his own personhood or being.[28] But it is only by not making the aforementioned equation that we can do so without implying or asserting that all are one person in Christ. Miroslav Volf, for example, thinks that this is what Zizioulas does imply. The *hypostasis*, the 'particularity and uniqueness and therefore ultimate being', of each and all cannot be 'constituted through the same filial relationship which constitutes Christ's being', as Zizioulas claims, for there would be no principle of differentiation here.[29] In making this charge Volf does not do justice, however, either to Zizioulas's way of relating nature and freedom, or to his understanding of catholicity and of the corporate Christ. For Zizioulas himself does not really want to reduce the person to the *schesis*. As there is room for distinct persons in God, so there is room for distinct persons in Christ, that is, in deified or personalized humanity. To be personal *is* to be distinct, but to be distinct for the sake of unity. What renders us personal is our participation in Christ's sonship, in his filial *schesis*, in his being *for* the Father. We become Christ, not by ceasing to be ourselves, but by finding ourselves in Christ by being for the Father as he is for the Father. As for our distinctness, it is a function both of our created individuality and of the deification which overcomes it – that is, of freedom *in*, as well as freedom from, necessity. This Volf appears to overlook, while shying away

the sense in which this is true of a person in the Trinity' (F.D.E. Schleiermacher, *The Christian Faith* [E.T. eds. H.R. MacKintosh and J.S. Stewart; Edinburgh: T&T Clark, 1976], §97.2; cf. §96.1)? On the contrary, the problem would not be solved but at best postponed.

[28] See, e.g., Heb. 2.10f.

[29] Cf. Zizioulas, 'Human Capacity and Incapacity', 438, and M. Volf, *After Our Likeness* (Grand Rapids: Eerdmans, 1998), 87.

from the (right-minded) claim that all human personhood is mediated by Christ, and so involves a form of deification or participation in God.

There is nonetheless a problem here, which Volf has highlighted for us by carrying his criticism through into ecclesiology. According to Volf, the particularity and distinctness of the church is threatened just as that of the person is threatened.[30] In the eucharist, the church (however peculiar and distinct as this or that local church) *is* Christ, and Christ the church. And as the distinction (or rather the 'gap', to use Zizioulas's own expression) between the two collapses, so does the unique heavenly ministry of Christ, while the local church takes on a universal authority and an eschatological weight which do not properly belong to it.[31] Once again Volf does not do Zizioulas justice, in my opinion – and cannot, perhaps, for reasons to be debated elsewhere, of which Volf's sacramental nominalism is but one. But the difficulty to which he points can certainly be felt in reading *Being as Communion*, in which (to approach the problem from the other side) it is often semantically impossible to substitute the name 'Jesus' where Zizioulas has the title 'Christ'.[32] That this is the case invites us to consider whether there is not in fact a Eutychianizing process at work here, a process introduced by Zizioulas's failure to distinguish adequately between *schesis* and *schesis*, that is, between Christ as God and Christ as man. Christ as man means Christ as church, Christ as *imago Trinitatis*; and

[30] 'Just as through baptism human beings are constituted into persons anhypostatically in Christ, so also does the church exist in the Eucharist anhypostatically and acquire its entire identity from the identity of Christ. This paralleling of personhood and ecclesiastical being is not fortuitous. Any distance between Christ and the church would simultaneously mean the individualization of Christ, and the possibility of the deindividualization of human beings would be lost .... Yet just as in the constituting of a person the particularity of that person is lost and the individual is absorbed into Christ, so also the church itself is threatened with being absorbed into Christ' (Volf, *After Our Likeness*, 100). This formulation fails to acknowledge the enhypostatic aspect of Zizioulas's doctrine of personhood – 'the cause of being is the particular, not the general' ('On Being a Person', 43) – and its ecclesiological implications.

[31] Cf. Volf, *After Our Likeness*, 98ff., and Zizioulas, *Being as Communion*, 110ff. (for whom the eucharist is the Christ-event in its fullness). In such matters we may share something of Volf's concern, it seems to me, without colluding in his non-Christological approach to human personhood, which subverts Zizioulas's strength as well as his weakness.

[32] To offer examples from *Being as Communion*,: 'Christ Himself becomes revealed as truth not in a community but as a community' (115). Or: 'The whole Christ, the catholic Church, was present and incarnate in each eucharistic community' (157). It does not obviate this particular difficulty to say that the *Christus totus* is, after all, a familiar theologoumenon. And the difficulty is only deepened when we hear that the church, as eucharistic event, mediates between 'the historical Jesus and the eschatological Christ' (206), making them one reality. Should we not say rather that the eucharistic event mediates between Jesus Christ, in his eschatological mode of existence, and the historical reality of the people of God? Or might both statements be true?

this *imago* is itself understood in divine terms. Like the Godhead, it is a perichoretic reality.[33]

Now I do not wish to withdraw from the term 'deification'. Nor do I wish to argue against the notion that humanity, fully achieved, is ecclesial, or that ecclesial humanity is *imago Trinitatis*.[34] But I do think that we must stop short of identifying human personhood, or human catholicity, or the ecclesial mode of being, as a form of the divine perichoresis. The 'de-individualization' and deification of the human person, as a bearer of the Spirit together with Jesus, does not mean that the human person is a person in the same sense or in the same way that a divine person is a person. We must not allow (as Zizioulas does) a univocal use of the word 'person' in reference to both God and man, whether in Christology or in ecclesiology.[35]With respect to divine persons, it is true to say that the other divine persons are co-inherent in each, and therefore that the whole of God is in each. With respect to human persons, however, it is not true to say that the others are co-inherent in each, or that the whole of man is in each. It is not true to say that Jesus Christ is the church, or that each communicant is Christ and the church.[36] It *is* true to say that every member of the church is 'in' Christ in a way that is ontologically determinative for that member, and so also for the whole church, and indeed for Christ.[37] In other words, I do not wish to withdraw either from Zizioulas's notion that each Christian person makes ecclesial humanity to be in a new and unique way. But if this implies a form of perichoresis it

[33] It does appear that for Zizioulas the term 'Christ' has become synonymous with 'Church', and that both terms have become analogous to 'God' or 'Trinity' (the former indicating Jesus, Mary, John, etc., in their being as communion, just as the latter indicates Father, Son and Spirit in their being as communion).

[34] We need to be careful here, however, for this claim requires us to admit that Jesus is the express image of the invisible God only in and with his church, and not without it.

[35] 'The perfect man is ... only he who is authentically a person ..., who possesses a "mode of existence" which is constituted as being, in precisely the manner in which God also subsists as being' (*Being as Communion*, 55, emphasis his; see 54ff.). This univocity makes it difficult to assign ontological weight to the Jesus of history: 'the real hypostasis of Jesus was proved to be not the biological one, but the eschatological or trinitarian hypostasis' (*Being as Communion*, n. 49). And this in turn leads to formulations which underestimate Christ's human particularity and undermine the pneumatology that Zizioulas wants to encourage.

[36] See *Being as Communion*, 60f. With respect to God, we may say that in and with the Father (or the Son or the Spirit) the Godhead is. Respecting the church, however, things are otherwise. Here we can say 'in and with Jesus Christ the church is' – if that is what Zizioulas really means – but we cannot say that 'in and with John Zizioulas', or even 'in and with Bishop John', the church is.

[37] This is where the 'and to us' comes into play, for if the personhood of Jesus Christ is the personhood of the eternal Son of God, it is for all that a personhood not independent of that of Mary, or even of Joseph.

does not imply the *divine* perichoresis, in which the God-man alone participates.[38] On the contrary, it implies a distinctly human form of perichoresis, albeit one which rests on the power of God: a perichoresis which does not make man God, but allows men to share with one another the gifts of God.

What, then, is the nub of our disagreement about catholicity, if disagreement it is? It is not a question of accepting or rejecting an ontology of communion, a eucharistic realism, or a doctrine of deification.[39] It is a question of adopting a version of this ontology, realism and doctrine which does not compromise the distinction between the divine and the creaturely – either protologically or eschatologically – and which does not present the church as a kind of *tertium quid* between God and man.[40] This would seem to be what Zizioulas himself wants, for *theosis*, he says, does not mean participation 'in the nature or substance of God, but in His personal existence. The goal of salvation is that the personal life which is realised in God should also be realised on the level of human existence'.[41] But this distinction between God's nature or substance and his 'personal life' or 'personal existence' is itself problematic; indeed it is not clear how Zizioulas can make such a distinction, or that we should follow him in doing so. And it becomes even more problematic if the latter is abstracted in such a way as to make it strictly transferable to human beings.

38 We need not be embarrassed about saying 'the God-man alone', or about the fact that we cannot say how he participates (except 'enhypostatically'). Nor should we imagine that John 17.21ff., e.g., warrants a theological extension of his unique participation to the church, though it certainly warrants an ecclesiology based on some form of *analogia communionis*. Cf. A. Torrance, *Persons in Communion* (Edinburgh: T&T Clark, 1996), 305f. 'The Word of God "did not assume human nature in general, but 'in atomo'" – that is, in an individual – as Damascene says (*De Fide Orth*. iii, 11)' remarks Aquinas; 'otherwise every man would be the Word of God, even as Christ was' (*Summa Theologiae* III.2.2). And even when we have heard Zizioulas on the subject of individuality, and taken into account that Christ and the Spirit are sent to liberate us from a false, self-enclosed form of the same, and thought out our eschatology, still we must say nothing to compromise the uniqueness of the God-man.

39 I have agreed that creaturely personhood is a gift of participation with God, who alone (as the Trinity) is personal *in se*. I have not agreed, however, that human being is communion in the same sense that God's being is communion. The difference is mediated by the God-man, not removed by the God-man. Nor are we, like the God-man, ourselves mediators of this difference.

40 Treating the *unio personalis* as something not affecting or touching the person will have such Eutychian effects.

41 On the level of human existence (*Being as Communion*, 50) it is worth noting that this concern for the integrity of the human, and for the trinitarian – especially the pneumatological – underpinnings of a theology that truly supports the human, is what bound John Zizioulas and Colin Gunton together, notwithstanding the latter's rejection of 'deification' as a concept injurious to that of creaturely integrity.

This line of criticism means, of course, that we must also question Zizioulas at a number of related points, just three of which can be mentioned here. First, does the eucharist, as his controversial maxim has it, make the church? Yes it does. The eucharist, together with baptism, makes the church because it is through these sacraments, conducted in the faith of Christ which arises from the gospel, that God joins us to Christ and renders us his body. It makes the church because this action of God in joining us to Christ is an eschatological action – the ascended Christ being an eschatological reality – which does not derive from (though it implicates) our 'here and now', but derives from his 'there and then'. That said, Christ is not the church, and the eucharist does not make the church by making Christ, as Zizioulas might be taken to imply. It makes the church rather by the Spirit's overcoming of that which separates or alienates us from Christ, just as Christ overcomes that which alienates us from God.[42]

Second, is each local church, in its synaxis or eucharistic celebration, really the church in its fullness? Without endorsing Miroslav Volf's alternative – an essentially quantitative approach to ecclesial fullness and unity? – we may again need to qualify Zizioulas's affirmative answer. The local church may be said to be the church in its fullness inasmuch as it cannot be at all without being with Christ and so with the whole church, past, present and future.[43] But if Christ is not himself the church, and if the church's communal life in Christ is not a form of, but only analogous to, the divine perichoresis, then the local church – even in its eucharistic unity with Christ and with the whole company of heaven – is not as such the universal church. It is rather, in its own way, an expression or manifestation, however perfect or imperfect, of the universal church.

Third, does the eschaton mean for the ecclesial person (as opposed to his or her human nature) *capax infiniti*, as Zizioulas suggests? Yes, if *capax infiniti* – or better, *aeterni* – means the ability to experience conjointly what cannot be experienced separately, viz., union and communion with God, and to share in its inexhaustible benefits. No, if it means the ability to contain or to become God, as the divine persons contain one another and so exist as God, in absolute freedom. For the eschatological fulfilment of the person (who cannot be abstracted from his or her nature) does not entail elimination of all creaturely limitation or all creaturely necessity, which

[42] *Pace* Zizioulas, *Being as Communion*, 110; cf. Farrow, *Ascension and Ecclesia*, 5ff., 70ff., *passim*.

[43] See *Being as Communion*, 143ff.; cf. Heb. 12.18ff.

would mean the elimination of the creaturely as such.[44] But the elimination of necessity, we may suppose, is not what Zizioulas has in mind when he talks about freedom from necessity. What he has in mind, as I have already said, is more precisely freedom *in* necessity, through creaturely communion with God.[45] Agreement and disagreement with Zizioulas on the matter of eschatology must be pursued elsewhere, however, for it is time to ask a final question.

Questioning the Necessity–Freedom Dialectic

Having expounded Zizioulas by way of reference to his nature–freedom dialectic, I have also ventured some critical remarks about the Christology he uses to control and deploy that dialectic. I have suggested that this Christology suffers from a certain Eutychian tendency, which in turn has a detrimental effect on his ecclesiology. I am happy, of course, to be found wrong, but since I have indeed ventured such an opinion it seems right to ask how far the tendency in question may be a product of the necessity–freedom dialectic, rather than merely a distorting factor in it. Is there, in other words, a danger in the dialectic itself that should command our attention? I think there is.

The danger does not so much lie (as Volf suggests) in the association of nature with necessity and personhood with freedom, but in the setting of nature and necessity over against personhood and freedom, whether theologically or anthropologically.[46] It is at this presuppositional level that an even stronger challenge to existentialism (and to Greek thought generally) needs to be mounted than Zizioulas attempts. Divine personhood should not be understood as a freedom won from, or preserved against, necessity or sheer absoluteness of nature, though the *concept* of divine personhood represents such a victory. Nor – and here is the point of contention – should human personhood be seen as a triumph over our creaturely nature and its exigencies. Which is to say, human personhood

[44] Conversely, it does not entail the dissolving of the distinction between the immanent and the economic Trinity, any more than it entails the dissolving of the difference between the two natures of Christ.

[45] It is curious that Zizioulas ('Human Capacity and Incapacity', 442ff.) does not bring the freedom and necessity dialectic explicity into this resolution – if resolution it is – so as to complete the parallel with capacity in incapacity and presence in absence. Less curious, of course, is the fact that he overlooks important aspects of human freedom (cf., e.g., Oliver O'Donovan, *Resurrection and Moral Order* [Grand Rapids: Eerdmans, 1986], 106ff.) which do not readily fit his theological construct, and that even in emphasizing bodily resurrection he shows little interest in treating it.

[46] Cf. Volf, *After Our Likeness*, 87.

and freedom do not arise in contradiction of created nature, nor are they a victory against non-being. It is not as if the creature *qua* creature must be impersonal, inasmuch as it is created *ex nihilo* and is subject (as God is not) to certain necessities. Down this path Eutychianism does indeed lie, since such a premiss makes it impossible to understand human personhood as human.

It is true, of course, that human personhood (understood in terms of the *imago dei*) cannot be explained adequately by reference to other features of creation.[47] Human personhood is *sui generis*, a gift specially given with and for the twin blessings of the incarnation of the Son and the coming of the Holy Spirit; that is, for communion with the Father, which (as its final cause) ultimately perfects our personhood. But that special gift, resting as it does on the mediation of the God-man, is not something contrary to creation or to our created nature. Creation is *for* it, and it for creation. Creaturely necessities do not inhibit creaturely personhood; in their proper place and time they enhance it. Whence arises, then, that debilitating competition between freedom and necessity which generates the quandaries of which Zizioulas (like the existentialists) takes notice? It arises not from creation but from the Fall, in which the relation of freedom and necessity is fundamentally altered. And here we must note that, while Zizioulas stresses the doctrine of the Fall, his conception of it requires clarification. At some points he speaks as I have just spoken; at others (like Maximus) he appears to conflate creation and fall.[48] Any suggestion that the Fall is somehow implicit in creation casts the necessity–freedom relation into an oppositional mode, the mode of fallen man's alienation from himself and from God. This skews the entire debate about the relation between necessity and freedom in the realization of human personhood.[49]

On the other hand, when we consider the teaching of the Scriptures and the fathers that human persons, in being made after the image of God, are destined to receive immortality – that the human person, as immortal, exists by virtue of the investment in that person of God's own immortal Spirit[50] – are we not obliged to speak of a triumph over our creaturely

[47] See Zizioulas, 'Human Capacity and Incapacity', 431.

[48] See Zizioulas, 'Human Capacity and Incapacity', 424ff., 434f., but note the word 'inevitable' on 435 (n. 2), and cf. *Being as Communion*, 49ff.

[49] It may be the case that it belongs to the nature of living creatures, including humans, to exist by facing and overcoming necessities of various kinds. But it does not follow that there must be a zero-sum game here, or that human personhood should be defined in terms of this overcoming (that is, in terms of liberation from necessity through communion).

[50] Irenaeus put this most succinctly, as I have noted in *Ascension and Ecclesia*, 59ff.

nature? And may we not speak of this triumph in terms of a necessity–freedom dialectic, as Zizioulas wishes to do, before speaking of the church as the divine form of human freedom? May we not indeed regard the church as the triumph of God over human nature, that is, over the 'individual' who seeks relief from necessity and finds it, not in existentialist courage or commitment, but in the new ecclesial hypostasis?[51] The answer to all these questions, surely, is yes. But this 'yes' still does not commit us to the kind of dialectic which presents human personhood *per se* as a triumph over our nature. For it *is* our nature to be open to the gift of immortality, as the proper realization of our personhood, except we be closed to that destiny by the Fall. And this means that the necessity–freedom dialectic is not a nature–person dialectic, but a dialectic internal to human nature as oriented to personhood. Which means in turn that it is internal to human personhood as such.

This alteration in perspective removes the temptation to adopt a Christology that tends towards the Eutychian, and an ecclesiology that tends towards Christomonism. For the function of the God-man is not to introduce personhood (a divine reality) into the impersonal (the creaturely), so that the latter might attain authentic existence.[52] His function is rather to perfect, together with the Spirit, a human *analogy* to divine personhood; that is, to secure for human personhood its essential openness to God and to the other, and so to make possible its pneumatic and ecclesial form, the form requisite to immortality.[53] Now immortality is indeed authentic existence, and authentic existence is an existence based on communion. It is personal existence.[54] But this same alteration in perspective also removes the temptation to regard personal existence for human beings as an existence that is God-like in the sense that it is a pure perichoretic communion, or a pure freedom from necessity. To take such a view would be to concede too much to the existentialists. For necessity is not the ultimate threat to personhood. Sin is the ultimate threat, and not

[51] Kierkegaard's protest against a false ecclesiality notwithstanding (see Farrow, *Ascension and Ecclesia*, 227f.).

[52] Through an extension and repetition of the hypostatic union? 'Personhood, I have argued, is the mode in which nature exists in its ekstatic movement of communion in which it is hypostasised in its catholicity. This, I have also said, is what has been realised in Christ as the man par excellence through the hypostatic union. This, I must now add, is what should happen to every man in order that he himself may become Christ . . . ' ('Human Capacity and Incapacity', 442; emphasis his).

[53] Or is this all that Zizioulas means when he speaks of our being joined to God in a dialectic of difference rather than division ('Human Capacity and Incapacity', 440)?

[54] Cf. Augustine, *De Trinitate* 13.3 (p. 12).

by the destruction of our personhood (for the gifts and calling of God are irrevocable) but by its perversion and frustration.[55]

And what does all this mean if not that Zizioulas's ecclesiology, while a gift to the Western church and to Western theologians, requires in its turn to be informed by, and reformed together with, Latin insights? The future lies in attempting an ecclesial ontology of personhood which carefully distinguishes the necessity–freedom dialectic from the sin–salvation dialectic, accommodating both within a more expansive doctrine of perfecting grace. But this latter will have to be governed by a Christological and pneumatological paradigm that has yet to be achieved.

[55] See Zizioulas, 'Human Capacity and Incapacity', 44ff. Shall we refuse to concede, then, that it is communion 'which makes beings be'? Surely it is God who makes beings be, in whatever way it is appropriate for them to be.

Chapter 6

He Came Down From Heaven: The Christology of Charles Williams

Brian Horne

It is a truth universally acknowledged, but perhaps still worthy of uttering, that a genuine Christology will arise, not out of detached speculation about the nature of divinity, the meaning of the universe, the purpose of life or, to borrow a phrase from the Stoics, to contemplate the meaning, origin and destiny of all that there is, but out of attention to a 'particularity'; from the attempt to reveal the meaning of a specific event in history.

> For we did not follow cleverly devised myths when we made known to you the power and coming of our Lord Jesus Christ, but we had been eyewitnesses of his majesty. For he received honour and glory from God the Father when that voice was conveyed to him by the Majestic Glory, saying, 'This is my Son my Beloved, with whom I am well pleased' (2 Pet. 1.16–17).

As with the author of the second letter of Peter, so with Charles Williams. Consider this:

> There had appeared in Palestine, during the government of the Princeps Augustus and his successor Tiberius, a certain being. This being was in the form of a man, a peripatetic teacher, a thaumaturgical orator. There were plenty of the sort about springing up in the newly-established peace of the Empire, but this particular one had a higher potential of power, and a much more distracting method. It had a very effective verbal style, notably in imprecation, together with a recurrent ambiguity of statement. It continually scored debating-points over its

> interlocutors. It agreed with everything on the one hand, and denounced everything on the other. For example, it said nothing against the Roman occupation; it urged obedience to the Jewish hierarchy; it proclaimed holiness to the Lord. But it was present at doubtfully holy feasts; it associated with rich men and loose women; it commented acerbly on the habits of the hierarchy; and while encouraging everyone to pay their debts, it radiated a general disapproval, or at least doubt, of every kind of property. It talked of love in terms of hell, and of hell in terms of perfection. And finally it talked at the top of its piercing voice about itself and its own unequalled importance. It said it was the best and worst thing that had ever happened or ever could happen to man. It said it could control anything and yet had to submit to everything. It said its Father in heaven would do anything it wished, but that for itself it would do nothing but what its Father in heaven wished. And it promised that when it had disappeared, it would cause some other Power to illumine, confirm, and direct that small group of stupefied and helpless followers whom it deigned, with the sound of the rush of a sublime tenderness, to call its friends.[1]

This is the high style of a master of rhetoric. The passage begins quite simply: 'There had appeared . . . '; but the movement of the prose urges the reader forward – there must be no lingering – creating its effect by the building up of antinomies, paradox upon paradox, until it culminates in that unexpected coda: 'sublime tenderness . . . ', alighting finally on the little word 'friends'. Rhetorical it certainly is, but there is much more than rhetoric here, and what that 'more' is we shall investigate presently. This description of the event out of which all Christology arises, is found in the opening pages of Charles Williams's history of the Church, *The Descent of the Dove* published in 1939. Or to be more precise – and to use the author's own description of the book – his 'Short History of the Spirit in the Church'. It is, perhaps, more a work of theology than of history; an attempt, to use Williams's words when defining theology, of 'measuring eternity in operation', of tracing the course of the 'bright cloud and the rushing wind' in creation. Is this the beginning of Williams's Christology? It is without doubt an arresting beginning but this was not the first time Williams had considered the person of Christ; this was not his first work of theology.

[1] Charles Williams, *The Descent of the Dove* (London: The Religious Book Club, 1939), 1–2.

To many of you, perhaps, the name of Charles Williams is unfamiliar; to some it will be known only as that of the author of fantastic fictions. To me it is the name of a man who possessed one of the most original theological minds of the twentieth century. But it is not as theologian that Williams himself wished to be remembered. On his gravestone in a quiet corner of a cemetery in the city of Oxford there is carved a simple inscription: 'Charles Walter Stansby Williams. Poet. Under the Mercy'. It was primarily to the art of poetry that he gave his life and energy but it may well be that his most valuable legacy will be, primarily, not his poetry, but his theology. He spent most of his life working as an editor for the Oxford University Press and then in his last few years as tutor and lecturer in the English faculty in the University of Oxford. For the first twenty-eight years of his life he published nothing but poetry, but, after that, all manner of writing poured out of him: plays and novels, reviews and biographies, history and theology. And he died at the relatively young age of fifty-eight in 1945. A close friend of C.S. Lewis, T.S. Eliot, J.R.R. Tolkien and Dorothy L. Sayers, he nonetheless stands apart from them, distinguished by the unique quality of his rhetoric and the originality of his Christian vision. Though, let it be said immediately, the claim to 'originality' was one that Williams never made; indeed, it would have seemed, to him, a kind of arrogance to strive for an originality in the exposition of the Christian faith. He believed he was doing nothing more than drawing attention to aspects of Christian orthodoxy that had received insufficient scrutiny or explication from other interpreters of the tradition. This was as true of his Christological writings as it was of his reflections on the doctrine of the Fall, or the Church, or the Atonement.

But before we move on to examine that Christology, we must be prepared to recognize what it is we are dealing with when we approach Williams's writings. There is a remarkable degree of intellectual coherence in the variegated assemblage of his works; remarkable precisely because there is such a variety of literary form. But it is a coherence that is achieved not only by the consistent application of certain theological motifs, but also by the pervasive spirit of a singular sensibility: that of the poet. Here we have a mind that moves more easily in the world of images and symbols than in the sphere of abstract concept; a mind that is as concerned about the exact shape of a line of poetry and the precise placing of a word or even a punctuation mark in a sentence than in the observation of academic conventions. (He was, for example, irritatingly vague in his referencing – strange in a man who wrote often in praise of accuracy.) And his writing has a peculiar density; a density of texture that is the feature of poetry rather than the density of the philosophical treatise. Its customary method is the method of contraction not the method of expansion; of the condensation of thought to a metaphorical expression rather than the discursive exposition of a conceptual position; its mode is allusive rather than explanatory. None of his theological essays presents any factual information or arguments that are not already well known, but Williams re-organizes these facts and arguments; presents them in new relationships; makes unexpected connections; arranges them like poetic tesserae to form the desired pattern of the verbal mosaic. The contemporary theologian, like the contemporary philosopher or historian, leaves little unsaid; he or she tends to see his or her task as one in which the investigation, argument or point of view must be presented with as much logic, openness and lack of mystery as can be achieved. Williams's writing deliberately leaves things unsaid and often depends for its effectiveness on the reader's sensitive awareness of what is beneath the surface; on his or her ability to make connections with the world beyond the confines of theological study. In short the reader is expected to exercise a different, and sometimes more difficult because more complex, attention to writing of this kind. Furthermore we shall find his Christology appearing not only where we expect to find it – in his theological essays – but in odd corners of novels, in glancing references in the lines of poetry, in passing comments in reviews of books that, superficially, have nothing at all to do with Christianity.

All that having been said, let us return briefly to that opening passage of *The Descent of the Dove*. Suspicions about Williams's orthodoxy might immediately have been aroused as ears caught the phrase of the second sentence: 'This being was in the form of a man . . . ' Only the form of a man? Not a real person? Those suspicions will not have been dissipated by the strange and insistent use of the impersonal third person pronoun throughout the passage. ' . . . it was present at doubtfully holy feasts; it associated with rich men and loose women . . . ' and so on. From the start you might have detected a distinct flavour of docetism here. In addition to this there may be the sense of an Arian reading of the incarnation: that use of the impersonal pronoun suggests a creature rather than a consubstantial Son, a lesser kind of divinity despite the talk of Fatherhood. What is going on here? Is Williams really to be judged guilty on two counts of heresy? If we were to evaluate his Christology solely on the evidence of this passage from *The Descent of the Dove*, I think that conclusion would be difficult to avoid – even when we remember that Paul in his famous passage from the second chapter of the letter to the Philippians had similarly made use of that term 'form': 'form of God', 'form of a slave', 'human form'. And I do not think it is easy to excuse him even when we remember the historical context of the book, when we see that part of his intention is to shock readers into a recognition of the explosiveness of the event of Jesus Christ. He was writing against a background of theologically liberal attempts at 'humanizing' the figure of Jesus; against efforts to empty out his terrifying strangeness. Williams had, by this time, read both Kierkegaard and Barth – had indeed been responsible, in his work at the Oxford University Press, for the first translations and publications of Kierkegaard's works in English, and had included several excerpts from Barth's *Epistle to the Romans* in his own anthology of readings, *The New Christian Year*. He even says at one point in this same volume: 'It is an alien Power that is caught and suspended in our midst' and he had little time for what he called 'immature and romantic devotions to the simple Jesus, the spiritual genius, the broad-minded international Jewish working-man, the falling-sparrow and grass-of-the-field Jesus'. And still more strikingly: 'They will not serve. The Christian idea from the beginning had believed that his Nature reconciled earth and heaven, and all things met in him, God and Man. A Confucian Wordsworth does not help here.'[2] Even so, and taking into consideration his penchant for the rhetorical flourish, which could lead him into dramatic overstatement, we might still feel, uncomfortably, that this picture stands in an uneasy relation to the formulations of the ancient creeds of the Christian Church. Nor can the particular passage that I quoted at length be excused on the grounds that it is 'poetic writing'. Only bad poetry is vague and inaccurate; good poetry can be the most precise of languages; and Williams was as aware of that as any other poet.

But, of course, it would be absurd to evaluate Williams's Christology solely on the basis of this passage. As I have said, he had already written a substantial essay on the incarnation before his history of the Spirit in the Church saw the light of day. This was the book for which, as a theologian, he is best known: *He Came Down From Heaven* (1938). It is easy to approach this work with the wrong presuppositions. The title prepares us for an essay on the incarnation – indeed I called it that a few moments ago – whereas its subject is actually reconciliation and redemption; an essay on the Atonement. But the reason why we can also see it as a substantial work of Christology is that Williams, like many of the early Greek Fathers, chose to focus his interpretation of the salvific work of Christ, not on the cross but the Word made flesh. That having being said, it will be observed that one of the characteristics of his theology is that he never, even for the purposes of organizational convenience, allows the separation of the

[2] Williams, *The Descent of the Dove*, 53.

categories of Incarnation and Atonement in his theological system. It will further be observed that his particular way of explicating the dogmas of Christianity is determined by a mind and an imagination that are rooted in a belief in the supernatural and its constant penetration into the world of everyday experience. Just as in *The Descent of the Dove* he describes theology as 'the measurement of eternity in operation', so here in *He Came Down From Heaven* he describes religion as 'the definition of the relationship between earth and heaven'.[3] And, as it is primarily treatise on the Atonement, we would do well to approach its Christology via the theory of the Atonement he proposes.

The first chapters contain an exposition of the Fall and its consequences for the human race, the prime consequence of which is to introduce into human nature what Williams calls 'the actual schism in reason'. The chapter that examines the Genesis story is entitled: 'The Myth of the Alteration of Knowledge'. '... they (Adam and Eve) knew good; they wished to know good as evil. Since there was not ... anything but the good to know, they knew good as antagonism. All difference consists in the mode of knowledge.'[4] He is uncomfortable with the Old Testament language of 'covering' and 'forgetting' sin on the grounds that facts cannot be erased from history, cannot be made not to have been. As man has chosen to know good as evil there is the inescapable fact of evil and the fact cannot simply be forgotten. And he remarks: if the High and Holy One is prepared to forget what has been is he not 'only finding felicity by losing fact'?[5] The consequences of the Fall cannot be put aside, undone in a miraculous action of the restoration of Edenic innocence; they can only be transformed, changed from within human nature itself. Evil must be known as good; death known as life. In the fourth chapter, 'The Precursor and the Incarnation', he introduces phrases from Julian of Norwich and Augustine to support his interpretation.

> All is most well; evil is 'pardoned' – it is known after another manner; in an interchange of love, therefore as a means of the good. *O felix culpa* – pardon is no longer an oblivion but an increased knowledge, a knowledge of all things in a perfection of joy.[6]

[3] Charles Williams, *He Came Down From Heaven* (repr.; London: Faber & Faber, 1950 [1938]), 12.
[4] Williams, *He Came Down From Heaven*, 21.
[5] Williams, *He Came Down From Heaven*, 39.
[6] Williams, *He Came Down From Heaven*, 59.

Yet how is this transformation to take place? If the facts are inescapable it must be accomplished from that place in which the facts are experienced, that is, from within the life of humanity, and yet it cannot be done by humanity; our reason is in schism and our life is one of impotence. The answer is the paradox of the Incarnation. We may already be hearing echoes of *Cur Deus Homo*, but our expectations will be disappointed if we are looking for a version of Anselm's arguments. The forensic framework of Anselm's theory is totally absent from these pages; instead of the language of debt, Williams employs the language of substitution. In God, as man, an act of substitution can be observed – indeed, it is the supreme act of substitution to which all other acts of exchange are related and from which they derive their meaning.

In a book review for the periodical *Time and Tide*, entitled 'Anthropotokos' published in the same year as *He Came Down From Heaven*, the summary of his position on the Incarnation stresses the centrality of the concept of exchange – a concept closely related to that of substitution. And he does this by means of the use of the symbol of the city – always, for him, the symbol of the redeemed life.

> What is the characteristic of any city? Exchange between citizens. What is the fact common to both sterile communication and vital communion? A mode of exchange. What is the fundamental fact of men in their natural lives? The necessity of exchange. What is the highest level of Christian dogma? Exchange between man and God, by virtue of the union of Man and God in the Single Person, who is by virtue of that Manhood, itself the City, the foundation and the enclosure ... This office of substitution did not need Christendom to exhibit it ... Christendom declared something more; it declared that this principle of substitution was at the root of the supernatural, of universal life, as well as of natural.[7]

Exchange is defined as part of the nature of the Godhead. It is seen as the root principle of all existence, divine as well as human; and the operation of exchange, already known in the life of the Trinity as the co-inherent relationship of the three Persons, is embodied in an earthly counterpart as the co-inherence of divine nature and human nature in the person of Jesus Christ. There is no docetism in this articulation of his Christology. Over and over again Williams adverts to one of his favourite Christological formulations – from the, so-called, Athanasian creed – a document that he referred to more than once as 'that great humanist Ode': 'One not by

[7] Ann Ridler (ed.), *The Image of the City* (London: Oxford University Press, 1958), 112.

conversion of the Godhead into flesh but by taking of the Manhood into God'. There is, similarly, no Arianism here either. What there is, of course, is a strong sense of deification, though he nowhere uses this term – although he does once use the rather odd word 'divinitized'; of the natural world being supernaturalized by the entry of the second person of the Trinity into the particularity of a human life. This is not to say that Williams did not argue powerfully for the reality of the human flesh of Christ; the sight of that was never to be lost – despite what he had written in the opening pages of *The Descent of the Dove*. In that same review article for *Time and Tide* he comments on the Nestorian controversy: 'Such remote Christological quarrels in the slums and boulevards of the Near East are not without interest today. It was the real nature of Perfection as credible and discoverable by men that was then in question, and it is still perfection that we are at', and then in a remark critical of what he sees as the victory of Alexandrian Christology in the conflicts of the fifth century, he says: 'The loss of (the title of the Virgin) "anthropotokos" has damaged Christendom; the Middle Ages attempted to recover it by fables, but in general it has been left too much to the revolts against Christendom to demand what should be one of the splendours of Christendom.'[8] 'Anthropotokos' – bearer of the anthropos, man; such insistence would hardly indicate a Christology that saw humanity subsumed into divinity, a subsumption that might be hinted at by too strong an attachment to that phrase from the Athanasian creed: 'the taking of the Manhood into God'. One of 'the revolts against Christendom'? It seems as if he has Nestorianism in mind and this movement of his thought, which might be read as a certain sympathy with what was condemned at the Council of Ephesus is, at first, somewhat surprising; for I would suggest that his formulation of the person of the incarnate Lord in terms of an exchange between humanity and divinity would make Monophysitism more attractive to his vision of the incarnate Word; but this is not, actually, the case. In fact, his rejection of both Nestoriansim and Eutycheanism is spelled out in a quite different, and unexpected, part of Williams's writings: in a novel, *The Greater Trumps*.

I can think of no modern novelist, perhaps no novelist in the history of prose fiction, who would place a scene involving the singing of the Athanasian creed at the centre of the plot. But so it is with this novel published in 1932. Three of the characters are attending Morning Prayer in a village church on Christmas Day; and, as anyone familiar with the

[8] Ridler (ed.), *The Image of the City*, 111.

rubrics of the Book of Common Prayer will remember, Christmas Day is one of the days in the Church's calendar on which the Athanasian creed is appointed to be sung at Morning Prayer.

> All the first part went on in its usual way; she knew nothing about musical settings of creeds, so she couldn't tell what to think of this one. The men and the boys exchanged metaphysical confidences, they dared each other, in a kind of rapture ... to deny the Trinity or the Unity; they pointed out, almost mischievously, that though they were compelled to say one thing, yet they were forbidden to say something else exactly like it ... All this Nancy half-ignored. But the second part ... for one verse held her ... the words ... sounded to her full of sudden significance. The mingled voices of men and boys were proclaiming the nature of Christ – 'God and man is one in Christ'; then the boys fell silent, and the men went on, 'One, not by conversion of the Godhead into flesh but by taking of the manhood into God.' On the assertion they ceased, and the boys rushed joyously in, 'One altogether, not' – they looked at the idea and tossed it airily away – '*not* by confusion of substance, but by unity' – they rose, they danced, they triumphed – 'by unity, by unity' – they were silent, all but one, and that one fresh perfection proclaimed the full consummation, each syllable rounded, prolonged, exact – 'by unity of person'.[9]

Thus does Williams present his Chalcedonian orthodoxy. Yet, in another area of his Christology he gives the appearance of being distinctly unorthodox; and we are now arrived at what may be his most original contribution to the subject.

He did not subscribe to the traditional view that the Incarnation was necessitated by the Fall, what he called the schism within the human's very being; he was drawn instead first by his intense preoccupation with the purely human aspect of creation, and, secondly, by his notion of the centrality of the principle of exchange, in the direction of the incarnational theology commonly associated with Duns Scotus and the Franciscans of the thirteenth and fourteenth centuries. That is, that the Incarnation of the beloved Son was due to the primal and absolute purpose of love foreshadowed in creation, and was in no way the result of the sin of human beings. This interpretation of the doctrine may be regarded as unconventional, as he himself remarked, but it is not forbidden to Christian belief, nor is it, of course, restricted to Duns Scotus and the Franciscan tradition or to those centuries; there are modern advocates of the

[9] Charles Williams, *The Greater Trumps* (London: Faber & Faber, paperback edn, 1954), 109–10.

theory, in addition to Charles Williams: B.F. Westcott in the nineteenth century and, more tentatively, Karl Rahner in the twentieth. Even Duns Scotus's older contemporary, Thomas Aquinas, was prepared to admit that it was possible to argue that the Incarnation was ordained from eternity and might have taken place whether the Fall had occurred or not, but was unwilling, himself, to agree that such a theological position was the most 'appropriate' in the light of what was to be apprehended in Scripture:

> ... since everywhere in the Sacred Scripture the sin of the first man is assigned as the reason of the Incarnation, it is more in accordance with this to say that the work of the Incarnation was ordained by God as a remedy for sin; so that, had sin not existed, the incarnation would not have been.[10]

But he is quick to add: 'Although the power of God is not limited to this – even if sin had not existed, God could have become incarnate.' He was quite prepared to see the Incarnation as the culmination of God's original creative act.

The long essay 'The Gospel of Creation' of 1886 by B.F. Wescott is his own apologia for the validity and appropriateness of such a view of God's action in the world.

> The belief that the Incarnation was in essence independent of the Fall has been held by men of the most different schools, in different ways and on different grounds. All however in the main agree in this, that they find in the belief a crowning promise of the unity of the Divine Order; a fulfilment, a consummation, of the original purpose of creation; a more complete and harmonious view of the relation of finite being to God than can be gained otherwise.[11]

Whether Williams knew this particular essay of Westcott, or that of any of the other scholars that Westcott cites, is impossible to say; he himself refers only to Duns Scotus, but, what we can say is that he is more daring – perhaps more foolhardy – more imaginative and, perhaps, less intellectually secure, than Westcott or any of the others.

The theory appears in a number of places, and in a variety of contexts, in his work. In his history of the Church, *The Descent of the Dove*, it is discussed briefly in a Postscript to the text. In his review of two books by Denis Saurat (*Regeneration* and *The Christ at Chartres*) for the periodical *Time and Tide* (2 November 1940), as in his essay 'Natural Goodness' printed in

[10] Thomas Aquinas, *Summa Theologica*, III. I. iii, trans of 1912 (London: Burns & Oates).
[11] Westcott, *The Epistles of St John* (London: Macmillan & Co., 2nd edn, 1886), 317–18.

Theology in 1941 (November), he speaks of it as a permissible belief for Christians and clearly leans towards it himself. Anne Ridler states categorically that he did hold the theory; an assertion which is borne out by the sequel to *He Came Down From Heaven*, the extended essay *The Forgiveness of Sins*.[12] In the opening of the third chapter of this later work he claims that 'the beginning of all this specific creation (the universe) was the will of God to Incarnate' (p. 119). He acknowledges in a footnote that he is following 'an arrangement of doctrine' which might be regarded as unusual but which he believes to be within the bounds of orthodoxy. He follows up the sentence with an assertion in which a far more unusual position is advanced.

> It is clear that this Incarnation, like all his other acts, might have been done to himself alone. It was certainly not necessary for him to create man in order that he might himself become man. The Incarnation did not involve the Creation. But it was within his nature to will to create joy, and he willed to create joy in this manner also.[13]

To postulate that the Incarnation had always been ordained by God as the goal and consummation of his creative activity is one thing; to suggest a hypothetical independence from creation is quite another. It is possible to draw a distinction between, on the one hand, the will to incarnate, and, on the other, the historical circumstances of the act, but the references of the scholars to circumstances are specifically to humanity's fallen condition. Here is Westcott again:

> ... it can fairly be maintained that we are led by Holy Scripture to regard the circumstances of the Incarnation as separable from the idea of the Incarnation, and to hold that the circumstances of the Incarnation were due to sin, while the idea of the Incarnation was due to the primal and absolute purpose of love fore-shadowed in Creation ...[14]

It is nowhere suggested that creation itself is a circumstance, a stage-set made necessary for the drama of the flesh-taking, which is precisely Williams's suggestion in this particular passage. Whereas Westcott sees creation as an action of God which culminates in the union of himself and man in the person of Jesus Christ, Williams postulates creation as a kind of by-product of God's primary intention: which is to take matter to Himself

[12] Charles Williams, *The Forgiveness of Sins* (London: G. Bles, 1942).
[13] Ridler (ed.), *The Image of the City*, 119.
[14] Westcott, *The Epistles of St. John*, 288.

in the personal union of the Son with human nature. If it were possible to establish an order of metaphysical precedence in the activity of the Uncreated, Incarnation would take precedence over creation.

From this it follows, with a kind of relentless inevitability, that Christ, the Son of the Father, must be seen as the agent of creation. The fourth Gospel's assertion: 'All things came into being through him, and without him not one thing came into being' is amplified and extended by Williams in the following way:

> He (Adam – humanity) *had* been created, of course, but according to a special order which involved the non-created ... He was the only creature (whose) flesh was in unique relationship to the sublime flesh which was the unity of God with matter. The Incarnation was the single dominating fact, and to that all flesh was related ... The Incarnation was the Original from which the lesser human images derived.[15]

So, to put it crudely, the Son is the instrument of a world which is brought into being so that He Himself, in the womb of the Virgin, takes flesh to Himself. What the Fall of Adam did was to determine the circumstances within which the purpose of God, already present to the Godhead from all eternity, to unite himself with matter, was achieved.

Why did Williams find this interpretation of the person and work of Christ so attractive; what made him so determined an advocate of so unusual a reading of it? The answer lies in his anthropology: his apprehension of what human life is for; and central to this are the twin principles of co-inherence and exchange. For him all genuine human life operates on the basis of exchange. That is simply a definition for him; an irreducible fact; an assumption basic to all his theology as well as his anthropology. And if this is true, the highest and deepest joy for human beings must lie in the exchange between themselves and their Creator. The nodal point and the source of all joy is the person of the Word made flesh. Some notion of exchange, I would suggest, will be present in all orthodox interpretations of the Incarnation and the Atonement, but, so far as I am able to ascertain, no theologian has so emphasized its centrality as Williams does. The concepts of exaltation and glory found in the language of deification of the Fathers of the early Church are surely what he means by joy, but his word is more intensely human, more closely linked to the quotidian experiences of personal love and desire than either the ecstatic language of the mystics or the more abstract, philosophical vocabulary of

[15] Williams, *He Came Down From Heaven*. 129–30.

some of the Fathers. While this vocabulary of substitution and exchange, emphatically used by Williams, might suggest a more immediate union between the natures than was propounded at Chalcedon, which would lead in the direction of the confusion of natures, monophysitism is avoided by the use of the complementary concept of co-inherence. The divine and human natures of the incarnate Lord do not merge into one another, are not confused, they co-inhere. Williams had been very impressed by G.L. Prestige's essay on co-inherence that concluded his study *God in Patristic Thought*;[16] Williams found his own theological sensibility confirmed by that work. So divinity and humanity exchange lives in that pattern of co-inherence, 'perichoresis', 'circumincessio', which is the historical Jesus. Here in the Incarnation is the utmost joy; the Fall could neither cause nor prevent it; the 'schism in reason' simply became the circumstances of its occurrence. But there is further reason, also anthropological. I can think of few other theologians who so consistently emphasize the significance of the human body as does Charles Williams; who so powerfully argues for the possibility of the revelation of the supernatural in and through the natural; who contends that human flesh, fragile and weak thought it may be, is capable of being the vehicle of divine glory. And so he writes the body 'was holily created, is holily redeemed, and is to be holily raised from the dead. It is, in fact, for all our difficulties with it, less fallen, merely in itself, than the soul.'[17] This is what attracted him to Dante's striking vision of the Resurrection in the fourteenth canto of *Paradiso*: 'Come la carna gloriosa e santa fia rivestita': 'the holy and glorious flesh'. Of these lines from the *Divine Comedy*, Williams writes:

> The brightness which her (i.e. Beatrice's) body shed directed attention to this future. The Resurrection was held in the word 'vita'; it is the whole life that here sings, of which ... the flesh has been the incident and means.[18]

But he comes to justify his contention that the human body is capable of being the vehicle of divine splendour by establishing it, not upon some quasi-pantheistic theory about the nature of matter, but upon the flesh-taking of the Divine Son.

> The principle of the Incarnation had been the unity of God and Man in the flesh; and the principle of the creation had therefore been a unity of man – soul and body – in flesh ... We have, except for the poets,

16 G.L. Prestige, *God in Patristic Thought* (London: Heinemann, 1936)
17 Ridler (ed.), *The Image of the City*, 84.
18 Charles Williams, *The Figure of Beatrice* (London: Faber & Faber, 1943), 207.

> rather lost this sense of the body; we have not only despised it too much, but we have not admired it enough.[19]

He entitled one of his last essays 'The Index of the Body', an essay in which the human body is perceived to be not merely one of the most important vehicles for the communication of heavenly beauty, but also as a microcosm of the whole created order. Human beings might distort the structure of their own existence and corrupt its forces, but they were ultimately powerless to destroy a pattern that had been decreed by the Father and embodied in its perfection by His incarnate Son. 'The Sacred Body is the plan upon which physical creation was built, for it is the centre of physical creation.'[20] (This essay was originally printed in *The Dublin Review* 1942 and suffered some censorship by nervous editors; you may think they were correct). In view of all this, it is hardly surprising that he should respond so positively to the speculations he found in Duns Scotus. 'Of course', says Williams, coming upon that text, 'if Christ in his human nature is predestined before all things, that is why the human body is as it is'.

But I should like to end with what could be his most interesting and provocative use of this theory. The reference occurs, not in a theological context, but in the third of his books of literary criticism, *Reason and Beauty in the Poetic Mind*.[21] The subject under discussion is John Milton, and, speaking of the peculiar difficulties of portraying – as Milton tries to do in *Paradise Lost* – Omnipotence and Omniscience in a work of art, Williams says, in an impudent way:

> . . . If Christianity were not true, it would have been necessary, for the sake of letters, to invent it. It is the only safe means by which poetry can compose the heavens, without leaving earth entirely out of the picture. The Incarnation, had it not been necessary to man's redemption, would have been necessary to his art; the rituals of the Church have omitted that important fact from their paeans.[22]

The Incarnation is seen as the means by which heaven and earth, the natural and supernatural, are united; the paradoxical point at which God and humanity are joined, and the Absolute presents itself in mutable and apprehensible flesh; our flesh. I used to think that Williams was not being entirely serious in making this claim – and, of course, it is presented in

[19] Williams, *He Came Down From Heaven*, 125.
[20] Ridler (ed.), *The Image of the City*, 86.
[21] Charles Williams, *Reason and Beauty in the Poetic Mind* (Oxford: Clarendon Press, 1933).
[22] Williams, *Reason and Beauty in the Poetic Mind*, 119.

jocular form – that as both aesthetics and theology it was both specious and untenable. Now I am less sure; and I wonder, now, if it is fanciful to introduce a comparison with one of the great theologians of the Byzantine tradition: John of Damascus. What is the basis of John's defence of icons? It is the fact of the Incarnation. If the Almighty had not united himself to matter in the form of the man Jesus there could be no ground for the representation of divinity in the manner of images, but because this has occurred, because Jesus had appeared in history, because he could be observed and worshipped, there was, not only no reason why matter should not be used to represent the divine, there was a positive injunction placed upon human beings to do exactly this. Icons, on this argument, become an indispensable part of the fabric of Christian worship and theology.

> In the former times, God, who is without form or body could never be depicted. But now when God is seen in the flesh conversing with men, I make an image of the God whom I see. I do not worship matter: I worship the Creator of matter who became matter for my sake, who willed to take His abode in matter; who worked out my salvation through matter ... God's body is God because it is joined to His person by a union which shall never pass away.[23]

Now I admit that, on the surface, John's argument is presented differently from Williams's: it is one which advances from a theological position on the nature of revelation to the justification of iconography. It does not seem to say: 'Here we have images, how best can we justify them? Let us work out a theory that does just that. And, behold, we have a convincing one to hand, namely, the Incarnation.' Or does it say that? A sceptical historian trying to evaluate the motives of John's work might, possibly, arrive at such a conclusion; or, at least, propose that John's justification was, psychologically speaking, more complicated in its motives than the theologian and his subsequent interpreters make out. Was Williams being as disingenuous as that? He was in love with the art of poetry, of that there is no doubt, and was persuaded of his high vocation as a poet. Was he invoking a convenient formula to provide a theological justification for this quasi-religious estimate of that calling? Perhaps not consciously; he certainly never developed his claim beyond this instance. But the instance remains interesting for a number of reasons. First, his aesthetics is based, at least in theory, not, as is usually the case in the Western theological tradition (Thomas Aquinas is the great exemplar here), on the doctrine of

[23] John of Damascus, *On the Divine Images*, trans. David Anderson (New York: St. Vladimir's Press, 1980), 23.

creation, but on the doctrine of the incarnation. There have, of course, been exceptions; notably, in our time, Hans Urs von Balthasar, at the centre of whose theological aesthetics is the figure of Jesus Christ, the form of the Word incarnate, '. . . the visible image of the Father, the sensuous sign *par excellence* of the invisible economy of the Divine Logos'.[24] This has extremely interesting consequences for aesthetic theory but, unfortunately, we have no time to pursue them here; our subject is Christology, not aesthetics. And then, it illustrates a sensibility that was incapable of separating religion from life, theology from aesthetics, Christology from art, theory from practice. (This capacity to make unexpected connections and this drive to unite beliefs, theories, practice gathered from a variety of contexts into a coherent whole is uncommon in professional theologians but it was the only way Charles Williams could do his work and live his life.) We could say, in conclusion, that, for him, a line of well-fashioned poetry was not only an aesthetic pleasure, it was a theological statement, and a doctrine precisely articulated not only offered the revelation of a divine truth, but was also an invitation to the enjoyment of intellectual delight.

[24] Quoted in Aidan Nichols, *Say It Is Pentecost* (Edinburgh: T&T Clark, 2001), 21.

Chapter 7

The Baptism of Christ

Murray A. Rae

The question I propose to address in this essay may be formulated very simply. Why did Jesus, the one who was without sin, submit to John's baptism of repentance for the forgiveness of sins? With regard to the theme of this volume we may enquire further, what is to be learned from this submission about the humanity and the divinity of Christ?

That Jesus was baptized by John the Baptist in the River Jordan is attested in all four gospels, though obliquely, it must be said, in the Gospel of John. This four-fold testimony notwithstanding, the accounts of Jesus' baptism reveal a certain reticence among the evangelists about why it is that Jesus should have been baptized. All four consider it vital to report the descent of the Spirit upon Jesus and the Father's seal of blessing and commissioning that this represents, but only Matthew remarks on the apparent incongruity involved in the one who was without sin responding to John's call to repent and be baptized. Mark, having reported that John baptizes those who stand in need of forgiveness, and having described the process whereby other baptismal candidates were required to confess their sins, says minimally of Jesus only that he was baptized by John in the Jordan. Mark makes no further comment about the baptism itself but presses on to highlight what happened after the baptism as Jesus emerged from the water. Luke too focuses his account on the descent of the Spirit and the voice from heaven and is even more cursory than Mark about the baptism: 'Now when all the people had been baptized', Luke says, 'and when Jesus also had been baptized and was praying, the heaven was opened, and the Holy Spirit descended upon him in bodily form . . . ' (Lk. 3.21–22a). Luke has earlier repeated Mark's description of John's baptism as a baptism of repentance for the forgiveness of sins, makes much more than Mark of John's condemnation of sin, but again avoids comment on the incongruity of Jesus presenting himself on John's terms to be baptized.

The reference to the baptism in John's Gospel is, as I have mentioned, oblique. That John's baptism is a baptism of repentance and forgiveness is implied but not stated, the emphasis being placed, rather, on John's baptism with water in contrast to the baptism of the Spirit that Jesus will bring. While the baptizing ministry of John is the context in which is reported the descent of the Spirit upon Jesus, it is never stated in John's Gospel that Jesus himself was baptized. We may perhaps gather that he was from the testimony of John the Baptist that 'I came baptizing with water for this reason, that he [the Lamb of God] might be revealed to Israel' (Jn 1.31), and further, 'I saw the Spirit descending from heaven like a dove, and it remained on him' (Jn 1.32), but we are unlikely, I suspect, to draw the inference that Jesus was baptized by John if we did not also know the Synoptic tradition. This kind of reticence in reporting the baptism is the kind of thing that encourages the Jesus Seminar to believe that this thing really happened, and to suppose furthermore that this is an incident that reveals who Jesus really was. On this occasion, if few others, I agree with them. The baptism does indeed reveal the true reality of Jesus as the Christ.

It is Matthew alone among the evangelists who pauses over the baptism and addresses the problem with which I am concerned. Matthew draws the same contrast as John between the baptism with water offered by John the Baptist and baptism with the Holy Spirit and with fire that will be offered by 'one who is coming after' John. Matthew also makes clear, however, that John's baptism with water is for repentance and forgiveness, and so reports John's own objection when the one without sin comes to him to be baptized. John would have prevented Jesus, Matthew tells us, and said to him, '"I need to be baptized by you, and do you come to me?" But Jesus answered him, "Let it be so for now; for it is proper for us in this way to fulfil all righteousness"' (Mt. 3.14–15). We shall return in due course to this response, for it is not clear without further consideration how it resolves our problem. For the moment, however, I want to pause at the problem itself. We have seen in Mark and Luke a certain reticence about reporting the baptism of Jesus, and in John that reticence manifests itself in the avoidance of any direct claim that such an incident took place. Only Matthew pauses at the baptism itself and acknowledges the incongruity of the event that occasioned the descent of the Spirit. John baptizes those who repent and confess their sins. What was Jesus doing then, in submitting to this baptism of John?

Matthew's Gospel is not alone in raising an objection to the prospect of Jesus submitting to John's baptism. The extra-canonical Gospel of the Hebrews places an objection to the baptism on the lips of Jesus himself. The text reads:

> Behold, the mother of the Lord and his brothers said to him: John the Baptist baptizes unto the remission of sins. Let us go and be baptized by him. But he said to them: Wherein have I sinned that I should go and be baptized by him? Unless what I have said is ignorance.[1]

Commenting approvingly on this text, and attempting to reconcile it with the canonical reports that the baptism did indeed go ahead, Jerome suggests that despite seeing no need for any act of repentance, Jesus shrank from following his conscience because he knew the united teaching of the Scriptures to the effect that no human being is free from sin.[2] Jerome's rather contrived effort at harmonization of the various witnesses leaves us either with a Jesus who was not after all without sin, thus contravening the testimony of the New Testament, or else with a Jesus who was ignorant or at least uncertain of his sinlessness and who thus submitted to baptism in two minds as to his own need of it. We have a choice between a sinful Jesus or a confused Jesus, neither possibility of which is easily reconcilable with the New Testament witness. Better, I think, simply to recognize at this point the wisdom of the Gospel of the Hebrews having been excluded from the canon.

Despite biblical and dogmatic objections, there are some commentators upon the baptism of Jesus who have supposed that Jesus did need to confess his own sins. D.F. Strauss, for example, contends that, being ignorant of who Jesus was, John the Baptist could not have consented to baptize him without the confession of sins required of all other baptismal candidates. The implausibility, in Strauss's mind, of a baptism unaccompanied by Jesus' confession and repentance leads him to conclude:

> There is then no alternative but to suppose, that as Jesus had not, up to the time of his baptism, thought of himself as Messiah, so with regard to the μετάνοια (*repentance*), he may have justly ranked himself amongst the most excellent in Israel, without excluding himself from what is predicated in Job iv. 18, xv. 15 [i.e that God puts no trust even in his holy ones].[3]

[1] Cited by W.D. Davies and Dale C. Allison, *A Critical and Exegetical Commentary on the Gospel According to Matthew*, I (Edinburgh: T&T Clark, 1998), 322.

[2] See again, Davies and Allison, *Critical and Exegetical Commentary*, 322.

[3] David Friedrich Strauss, *The Life of Jesus Critically Examined* (London: SCM Press, 1973), 239.

'There is little historical ground for controverting [the sinfulness of Jesus]', Strauss continues, 'for the words *which of you convicteth me of sin?* (John viii. 46) could only refer to open delinquencies, and to a later period in the life of Jesus. The scene in his twelfth year, even if historical, could not by itself prove a sinless development of his powers.'[4] Jesus was thus baptized, in Strauss's view, because, like all the other candidates presenting themselves at the Jordan, he too had need of the repentance and forgiveness upon which the rite was focused. That view may be correct, of course, but it sets aside the traditional doctrine of Jesus' sinlessness widely attested in the New Testament (see Acts 3.14; Jn 8.46; 2 Cor. 5.21; Heb. 7.26; 1 Pet. 1.19), and undermines the soteriology predicated upon that witness. I shall argue in contrast, below, that Jesus may indeed have offered confession and repentance on the occasion of his baptism, not however because of his own need, but because of his love for a humanity that had fallen into sin and which burden he now shoulders on our behalf.

Strauss is, of course, a rare dissenter from the orthodox defence of the doctrine of Jesus' sinlessness and from the consequent claim, found in almost every commentary on the baptism, that Jesus himself had no need of the baptism of John. Justin, in his dialogue with Trypho, offers an early testimony to the much more widespread conviction that 'Jesus did not go to the river because he stood in need of baptism'.[5] Tertullian likewise comments that, although Jesus was baptized, 'no repentance was due from Him'.[6] That claim is repeated as would be expected, through Cyril of Jerusalem, Ambrose, Chrysostom, Augustine, Bonaventura, Aquinas, Luther, Calvin, *et al.* It is confirmed too by Schleiermacher who overcomes the apparent incongruity of Jesus' baptism for repentance and forgiveness of sins by preferring the account of John over against those of the Synoptic Gospels. John's Gospel, Schleiermacher rightly observes, makes no mention of any need for repentance and confession when presenting

[4] Strauss, *Life of Jesus* 239. Strauss cites an 'heretical' apocryphal work which offers a precedent to his own view in apparently attributing to Jesus a confession of his own sins at baptism. Strauss notes, 'The author of the *Tractatus de non iterando baptismo* in Cyprian's works, Rigalt., p. 139, says (the passage is also found in Fabric. Cod. apocr. N.T., s. 790f.): *Est – liber, qui inscribitur Pauli Praedicatio. In quo libro, contra omnes scripturas et de peccato proprio confitentem invenies Christum, qui solus omnino nihil deliquit, et ad accipiendum Joannis baptisma paene invitum a matre sua Maria esse compulsum.*' Strauss, *Life of Jesus*, 238 n. 5.

[5] Justin Martyr, *Dialogue with Trypho*, LXXXVIII, 350. In *Ante-Nicene Fathers*, I, trans. and ed. A. Roberts and J. Donaldson (Peabody, MA: Hendrickson, 1994), 194–270; quotation on 243.

[6] Tertullian, *On Baptism*, ch. XII, 'Of the Necessity of Baptism to Salvation', in *Ante-Nicene Fathers*, III, trans and ed. A. Roberts and J. Donaldson (Peabody, MA: Hendrickson, 1994), 669–80; quotation on 674.

oneself for baptism in the Jordan. Schleiermacher thus contends that John's baptism is a symbolic representation of the need for sin to be abandoned if people are to enter the kingdom, but it does not itself accomplish the forgiveness of sin. To be baptized, on this account, is a ritual means of approving John's proclamation, rather like shouting 'Hallelujah' when the preacher says, 'go and give your money to the poor', while at the same time keeping one's wallet firmly closed. In participating in this symbolic rite, therefore, Jesus is merely endorsing John's message and demonstrating thereby the continuity between John's ministry and his own.[7] He does not confess his sins and repent under John's baptizing hand because, in fact, no one is required to do so. Ingenious though Schleiermacher's solution may be, it comes at the very considerable cost of discounting the synoptic testimony. For this reason, among others, it cannot be approved.

If the tradition is largely agreed that Jesus did not go to the Jordan because he stood in need of baptism himself, what reason is given for Jesus' response to John's call to repent and be baptized? A common view is that the baptism of Jesus is an event that sanctifies baptism itself. Chrysostom comments that 'In truth, Christ needed not baptism ... but rather baptism needed the power of Christ'.[8] The way in which the power of Christ sanctifies baptism has been variously conceived. Ambrose considers that 'The Saviour willed to be baptized not that He might Himself be cleansed, but to cleanse the water for us.'[9] Aquinas approves this view commenting that although water is 'subtle and penetrating in its own nature, [it is] made yet more so by Christ's blessing'.[10] And further, 'Christ ... *sanctified the waters by the touch of his most pure flesh*.'[11]

Taking a different line but holding still to the notion that Christ's baptism sanctifies baptism itself, John Calvin contends that:

> For this reason [Christ] dedicated and sanctified baptism in his own body, that he might have it in common with us, as a most firm bond of

[7] Schleiermacher's account of Jesus' baptism is found in his *The Life of Jesus*, ed. Jack C. Verheyden, trans. S. Maclean Gilmour (Miflintown, PA: Sigler Press, 1997), 136–45 (Lectures 21 and 22).

[8] Chrysostom, *Homilies on the Gospel of John*, Homily XVII. In *Nicene and Post-Nicene Fathers*, ed. Philip Schaff (Peabody, MA: Hendrickson, 1994), first series, vol. XIV, 58–62; quotation on 60.

[9] Ambrosiaster, Sermon 12.4; cited in St Thomas Aquinas, *Catena Aurea, Gospel of Matthew, Chapter* 3, vol. I (ed. John Henry Parker; London: J.G.F and J. Rivington, 1842). The same view is espoused by Chrysostom, in his 'Discourse on the Day of the Baptism of Christ'; 'He was baptised and sanctified the nature of water'.

[10] Aquinas, *Catena Aurea*.

[11] Aquinas, *Summa Theologiae* 3a, 38, 4.2. vol. 53 trans. Samuel Parsons OP and Albert Pinheiro OP (London: Blackfriars, 1971), 13.

> the union and society which he has condescended to form with us; so that Paul proves from it, that we are the children of God, because we have put on Christ in baptism.[12]

Calvin here hints at a notion that we will return to below. The baptism of Christ is indicative of the 'union and society' that Christ has condescended to form with us. The development of that notion will take us into a consideration of the nature of humanity itself.

Beyond the claim that baptism itself is sanctified by the baptism of Christ, a second reason for Christ's baptism, occurring commonly in the tradition, is that Christ is baptized in order to fulfil the Jewish law. This reasoning draws, obviously, on Matthew's reported word of Christ that he should be baptized 'in order to fulfil all righteousness' (Mt. 3.15). Chrysostom explains that Christ's promise to fulfil the law entails the observance of every aspect of it. Considering that baptism was enjoined upon the Jewish people by God, Chrysostom argues that Christ determined to fulfil that command as well, even though he had no personal need of it. The same reasoning is found in Jonathan Edwards: 'For it was a special command of God to the Jews', Edwards writes, 'to go forth to John the Baptist and be baptized by him. And therefore Christ, being a Jew, was subject to this command ... Hence the need to fulfil all righteousness.'[13] Such a view may also be represented in Calvin's assertion that Jesus was baptized so that 'he might render full obedience to the Father'.[14] While it is true in general terms that Christ renders full obedience to the Father, the interpretation of Mt. 3.15 in terms of a particular command of God to the Jews seems to me to miss the larger picture of God's righteousness which is fulfilled in the baptism of Jesus. We will return to this in due course.

A third reason commonly given for Christ's submission to the baptism of John is that offered in John's Gospel, namely that Christ might be revealed to Israel (Jn 1.31). Jesus consents to be baptized by John, it is suggested, both as an endorsement of John's proclamation – a view we have already met in Schleiermacher – and to give John an opportunity to confirm the veracity of his proclamation. Chrysostom, again, sets forth this argument:

[12] John Calvin, *Institutes of the Christian Religion*, IV, 15.6, trans. John Allen (Philadelphia: Presbyterian Board of Christian Education, 1936). Cf. *Commentary on a Harmony of the Evangelists, Matthew, Mark and Luke*, trans. William Pringle (Edinburgh: The Calvin Translation Society, 1845), I, 202.

[13] Jonathan Edwards, *A History of the Work of Redemption: Works of Jonathan Edwards*, IX, ed. John F. Wilson (New Haven: Yale University Press, 1989), 309–10.

[14] Calvin, *Commentary on a Harmony of the Evangelists*, 202.

> For very plain it is that One so pure as to be able to wash away sins of others, does not come to confess sins, but to give opportunity to that marvellous herald [John the Baptist] to impress what he had said more definitely on those who had heard his former words, and to add others besides.[15]

According to Chrysostom, the baptism affords John the opportunity to see in the flesh the one who he had heralded as the Lamb of God. The theophanic aspect of the baptism is a theme echoed in a number of other commentators including Aquinas.[16] The biblical basis for this is sound, I believe, but it is concerned primarily with what followed the baptism – the voice from heaven renders the baptism itself incidental to some other purpose, and rather glosses over the incongruity in the preceding scene of the sinless one being baptized.

The fourth reason for the baptism of Jesus that is commonly given in the tradition appears, for example, in Augustine who stresses that the submission of Christ to John's baptism shows forth the humility of Christ and sets an example for those called to humble themselves in baptism. 'But the Lord also was baptized', Augustine writes, 'so that because the Lord received the baptism of a servant, other servants might not disdain to receive the baptism of the Lord.'[17] Ambrose too sees in Jesus' condescension to be baptized the exemplary humility of 'a wise master inculcating His doctrines as much by His own practice, as by word of mouth'.[18] Gregory Thaumaturgus devotes a whole homily to this aspect of the baptism and extols at great length the humility of Christ in presenting himself to be baptized:

> O how vast is the humility of the Lord! O how vast His condescension! The King of the heavens hastened to John, His own forerunner, without setting in motion the camps of His angels, without dispatching beforehand the incorporeal powers as His precursors; but presenting Himself in utmost simplicity, in soldier like form, He comes up to His own subaltern.[19]

[15] Chrysostom, *Homilies on the Gospel of John*, Homily XVII.

[16] Aquinas, *Summa Theologiae* 3a, 38, 1.

[17] Augustine, *Tractates on the Gospel of John* 4.14, trans. J.W. Rettig (Washington DC: Catholic University of America Press), 105.

[18] Ambrose, Sermon 12.1. Cited in Aquinas, *Catena Aurea*.

[19] Gregory Thaumaturgus, 'The Fourth Homily: On the Holy Theophany, or on Christ's Baptism', in *Ante-Nicene Fathers*, VI, trans. and ed. A. Roberts and J. Donaldson (Peabody, MA: Hendrickson, 1994), 68–71; quotation on 68.

Not for his own sake, therefore, but as an example to his disciples, Jesus humbles himself by submitting to the baptism of John.

Like the three reasons previously adduced, this fourth account of why Jesus underwent baptism is not wrong, but neither is it wholly adequate in my view. Indeed, none of the reasons surveyed so far, either on their own or in combination, adequately address the apparent incongruity of the sinless one undergoing baptism for repentance and the forgiveness of sins. The claim that in doing so Christ sanctified baptism may be right but is not a sufficient reason. It is also claimed that Christ sanctified marriage by attending the wedding at Cana, but he did so without having to be married himself. It is secondly suggested that Christ was baptized to fulfil a particular command of God, but if the command to the Jews to be baptized was in reparation of human fault, what obligation is there to fulfil that command on one not guilty of the fault? That baptism afforded John the Baptist the opportunity to confirm his testimony about the coming one, is, again, not compelling on its own. John's Gospel accomplishes the same end while avoiding mention of the baptism itself. And finally, in respect of the display of exemplary humility by Jesus – if that is all there is to it – there might be some justice in a charge of dissimulation against one who went through the motions of confession and repentance merely as an example to others. My claim, let me repeat, is not that these accounts of why Jesus should have been baptized are wrong, but only that they fail, on their own, to get to the heart of the matter. In what remains of this essay, therefore, I propose to explore one further account of the matter that does better justice to the theological significance of Jesus' baptism.

I begin with Chrysostom whose considerations of the baptism of Christ are among the most extensive in the tradition and whose deliberations include all four reasons mentioned so far. Most interesting in Chrysostom, however, is the following account of why Jesus was baptized. Chrysostom writes:

> He [Christ] comes to baptism, that He who has taken upon Him human nature, may be found to have fulfilled the whole mystery of that nature; not that He is Himself a sinner, but he has taken on Him a nature that is sinful. And therefore, though he needed not baptism Himself, yet the carnal nature in others needed it.[20]

Chrysostom here links baptism to incarnation, to Christ's assumption of human flesh, and opens an avenue of inquiry, I shall argue, that leads us

[20] Cited in Aquinas, *Catena Aurea*.

ultimately to the cross. The suggestion being made here by Chrysostom is that the baptism of Christ, far from being merely exemplary, or simply an endorsement of John's ministry, is in fact to be understood as the outworking of the incarnation in which Jesus takes upon himself and fulfils the whole mystery of human nature. It is, in other words, proper to the incarnation itself that Jesus should be baptized. How is this to be understood while guarding against, as Chrysostom rightly does, any suggestion that Christ was himself a sinner?

Christian faith holds that, in becoming flesh, the Word of God and second person of the Trinity assumed a human nature, not merely in docetic fashion, but genuinely. The Word *became* flesh and was, by virtue of that becoming, fully and truly human. What the Word became according to John 1.14 was flesh – *sarx*. He took upon himself, in other words, that which had fallen prey to sin.[21] Romans 8.3 has it that God sent his own Son 'in the likeness of sinful flesh'. This theme, explicated by such as Edward Irving,[22] Karl Barth,[23] and recently Thomas Weinandy[24] is crucial to the proper understanding of the baptism of Jesus Christ. According to Irving, 'That Christ took our fallen nature is most manifest, because there was no other in existence to take.'[25] This point needs to be articulated carefully so as to avoid the impression that fallenness is of the essence of human nature, thus casting aspersions on the goodness of God's creation; but Irving is right to insist that the human nature and society into which the Son of God came was that nature and society which was distorted and corrupted by the Fall. This is the point we saw hinted at in Calvin. In agreement with Irving, Karl Barth is emboldened to say that while sin could not find any place in Him, the humanity Christ assumed is 'our own familiar humanity out and out, namely, not only with its natural problems, but with the guilt lying upon it of which it has to repent, with the judgement of God hanging over it, with the death to which it is liable'.[26] On Barth's account Christ offers himself to be baptized not on account of his own sin, of which he was completely free, but on account of

[21] I owe the observation to Martin Hengel who offered this explication of John 1.14 at a conference on John's Gospel held at St Andrews in July 2003.

[22] See *The Collected Writings of Edward Irving*, 5 vols., ed. G. Carlyle (London: Alexander Strahan, 1865), V, 115ff.

[23] See, for example, Karl Barth, *Church Dogmatics* (Edinburgh: T&T Clark, 1956–75) I.2, 13; IV.1, 131; 258–59.

[24] Thomas Weinandy, *In the Likeness of Sinful Flesh: An Essay on the Humanity of Christ* (Edinburgh: T&T Clark, 1993).

[25] Irving, *The Collected Writings*, V, 115–16.

[26] Barth, *Church Dogmatics*, I.2, 40.

the guilt that lay upon humanity as a whole, including, now, his own humanity. How is this to be understood?

In exploring this matter further we are assisted by the recent work in theological anthropology of John Zizioulas. To be human, as Christ certainly was, is to exist in personal relation with others. The person is not to be conceived along individualistic lines, but rather as one whose being is constituted in relation. Here we may see the correctness of Irving's assertion that in taking fallen human nature Christ took upon himself the only human nature there was to take. One cannot be human in isolation from others; indeed the myriad ways in which we attempt to do that is itself a manifestation of sin. To exist, not for others, but over against them, in defiant or even resigned independence, is a violation of the command to love one another, and defies God's judgment in creation that it was not good that man should be alone. If this relational ontology, recently reclaimed by theology, is correct, then the incarnation involves the assumption of a nature which, in virtue of its relational constitution, was marred and distorted by sin. That means, as Barth puts it, that the Son of God took upon himself the guilt that lies upon us all. Or we may prefer Paul's confession: 'For our sake [God] made him to be sin who knew no sin, so that in him we might become the righteousness of God' (2 Cor. 5.21). Here too is a clue to what might have been meant by Jesus in claiming that his submission to baptism will fulfil all righteousness. As promised earlier, we will treat this matter more fully below.

The relational conception of the human situation giving rise to the biblical claim that in becoming flesh – that is, in becoming what we are— Jesus took upon himself also our guilt, does not come easily to the Western mind that is commonly disposed to think of human beings in individualistic terms. But the relational conception is deeply rooted in Hebrew thought. The Old Testament tells of God's dealings with a people. While particular individuals may be called and anointed by God for a special role, they are never called apart from the people but rather for the sake of the people. Their actions are actions on behalf of Israel as a whole and may be redemptive or indeed catastrophic for the whole of God's people. It is this logic that enables Paul to say that 'just as by the one man's disobedience the many were made sinners, so by the one man's obedience the many will be made righteous' (Rom. 5.19). The relational conception of our human situation is at work again in Paul's reflections on Israel in Romans 11 where he claims that 'If the part of the dough offered as first fruits is holy, then the whole batch is holy; and if the root is holy, then the branches also are holy.' Such conclusions are not natural to the Western understanding of our human situation, even less so in

Postmodernity which drives still further in the direction of separation and fragmentation the already individualistic conceptions of the human person that were developed within Modernity.

It is helpful, therefore, to consider the point by reference to a non-Western culture that thinks more naturally in relational and corporate terms. The various Polynesian cultures in the island nations of the South Pacific and in New Zealand do not think of persons as individuals. The primary human entity is the extended family or the village so that 'individuals' are what they are only by virtue of their belonging to the family and the village. The implications of this conception are tellingly demonstrated in the Polynesian justice system, or, to put it otherwise, in the customary ways in which righteousness is fulfilled in the face of sin. Suppose that a crime has been committed, a murder perhaps. Within the relational conceptuality of Polynesian culture the guilt for that murder rests not only upon the perpetrator, but with equal weight upon the perpetrator's entire family. Responsibility for penance, therefore, also rests with the family as a whole. Such responsibility is worked out in the following way. The guilty family will go to the house of the victim's family. Then, sitting on the ground outside the house, the guilty family will begin a process of weeping and lament, of confession and of penance for the crime that has been committed. The individual perpetrator will be in their midst, but it is the family as a whole which bears the guilt, and so also the responsibility for repentance and the need for forgiveness. This process of penance will continue, perhaps for several days, until the family of the victim come out from their house, offer forgiveness to the perpetrator's family and begin thus a process of reconciliation.

This example is not analogous in every respect to the baptism of Christ but it does demonstrate the relational logic under which the whole family or race may be implicated by the sin of one of its members. It is along these lines, I suggest, in conformity with the biblical view, that we are to think of Jesus' assumption of human nature. His condescension is not restricted to the assumption of those limitations proper to our humanity within the conditions of the created order, but includes also his acceptance of the guilt that lies upon humanity as a whole. 'The Word became flesh' means that he who was without sin became sin and took our fallenness upon himself. We may note in passing here that the process of justice in the Polynesian context, or the fulfilment of righteousness, to put it otherwise, is directed towards reconciliation rather than punishment, and constitutes thus another point of contrast with most Western systems of justice, and of comparison with the biblical view.

Let us return to the gospel narratives of the baptism itself and enquire whether there are grounds there for pressing this relational view. Commentators have frequently observed that whatever else may be signified in the baptism of Jesus, the episode functions in the gospels as the inauguration of Jesus' ministry, the recognition of his Messiahship, and the acceptance by Jesus himself of a representative role in relation to Israel as a whole. G.R. Beasley-Murray writes that 'Jesus went to the baptism of John, not as a private individual, but as one convinced of His vocation to be the Messiah and therefore as a *representative person*.'[27] And Colin Gunton writes, in a recently published book of essays, 'The significance of [Jesus'] baptism is – among other things – that it signified Jesus' identification of himself with Israel under the judgement of God.'[28] That representative role is reinforced, it is commonly argued, by the words from heaven, 'This is my beloved Son with whom I am well pleased' which carry allusions to the corporate figures of the King in Psalm 2.7, and the servant in Isaiah 42.1. In the King first of all, and then later in the servant Messiah, the whole of Israel is gathered up and represented.[29] The King and the Messiah act on behalf of the people, so that Jesus' anointing at the baptism signals his representative significance. George Caird rightly argues therefore that:

> Jesus went to be baptised ... not for private reasons but as a man with a public calling. John had summoned all Israel to repentance and with Israel Jesus too must go. He dwelt in the midst of a people with unclean lips and could not separate himself from them. Rather he must be fully identified with them in their movement towards God. If he was to lead them into God's kingdom, he himself must enter it by the only door open to them. He must be their representative before he could be their king. He must be *numbered with the transgressors* before he could see the fruit of the travail of his soul (Isa. 53.11–12).[30]

It is to this baptism that Jesus came, not in confession of his own sin, but shouldering the corporate guilt of his people and offering a true repentance on their behalf, though not, as it turns out, on behalf of Israel alone, but on behalf of the whole of humanity. Luke, especially, emphasizes this point by following the baptism and temptation with the genealogy in

[27] G.R. Beasley-Murray, *Baptism in the New Testament* (London: Macmillan & Co., 1962), 56.

[28] Colin E. Gunton, *Father, Son and Holy Spirit: Toward a Fully Trinitarian Theology* (London: T&T Clark, 2003), 207.

[29] On which, see E. Earle Ellis, *The New Century Bible Commentary: The Gospel of Luke* (London: Marshall, Morgan & Scott, 1974), 91.

[30] G.B. Caird, *The Gospel of Saint Luke* (Harmondsworth: Penguin Books, 1963), 77, original italics.

which, by tracing Jesus' kinship back to Adam, Luke shows Jesus to belong to the whole race of humanity. Justin Martyr rightly notes, therefore, that:

> [Jesus] did not go to the river because He stood in need of baptism, or of the descent of the Spirit like a dove; even as He submitted to be born and to be crucified, not because He needed such things, but because of the human race, which from Adam had fallen under the power of death and the guile of the serpent ...[31]

Likewise emphasizing the point that in submitting to John's baptism Jesus humbly aligns himself with fallen humanity, Gregory Thaumaturgus preaches that:

> [Jesus] approached [John the Baptist] as one of the multitude, and humbled himself among the captives though He was the Redeemer, and ranged Himself with those under judgement though He was the Judge, and joined Himself with the lost sheep though He was the Good Shepherd who on account of the straying sheep came down from heaven, and yet did not forsake His heavens, and was mingled with the tares though He was the heavenly grain that springs unsown.[32]

It is crucial to recognize that the assumption of fallen human nature by Jesus is not merely for the sake of identification with humanity. The significance of the incarnation is not exhausted by Jesus' solidarity with sinners, crucial though this aspect is in fulfilment of God's promise that he will be with us always. The assumption of our fallen human nature involves, rather, not merely solidarity or identification but representation. In taking the burden of humanity's guilt upon himself, Jesus assumes responsibility for it. He takes responsibility for it and for us by presenting himself before God as our representative in confession and repentance. This representative confession and repentance of Christ on behalf of all humanity is taken up by Barth in volume IV.1 of his *Church Dogmatics* under the section headed, 'The Judge Judged in Our Place'.

> [Jesus Christ, Barth claims] placed Himself in the series of men who rebelled against God in their delusion that they would be as God, not in order to try to refuse or conceal or deny this, but in the place of all other men – who refuse to do so – to confess it, to take upon Himself this guilt of all human beings in order in the name of all to put God in the right against Him. In so doing he acted justly in the place of all and for the sake of all.[33]

[31] Justin Martyr, *Dialogue with Trypho*, chapter LXXXVIII, 243.
[32] Thaumaturgus, 'The Fourth Homily', 68.
[33] Barth, *Church Dogmatics* IV.1, 259.

'He acted justly', Barth continues, 'in that he did not refuse to do what they would not do. The one great sinner, with all the consequences that this involves, penitently acknowledges that He is the one lost sheep, the one lost coin, the lost son (Lk. 15:3f).'[34]

It is impossible to understand this within the individualistic conceptuality of Western thought by which it is sinfully asserted that each of us is responsible for the creation and ordering of our own being. It is foolishness indeed in contemporary Western culture to proclaim that the one decisive fact of our existence is not a fact of our own making but one that is accomplished for us, even despite us, by Jesus' confession and repentance, and ultimately by his death, on our behalf.

It is in this manner, nevertheless, that we may understand the baptism of Jesus in the River Jordan. Baptism is the beginning of Jesus' ministry in which he entered on his way as the Judge judged in our place.[35] It is the beginning, thus, of his passion. Jesus no more needed to be baptized than he needed to be crucified, but for the sake of humanity and in obedience to the Father, he put himself in the place of those who did need to confess and who deserved death. In his commentary on Luke's Gospel, John Moorman writes, 'The Baptism is … the first step in the redeeming work of Christ. It is not only the beginning of the ministry, it is also the beginning of the passion.'[36] Joseph Fitzmyer, by contrast, does not think that the Lucan text supports this interpretation[37] but the evidence seems to fall on Moorman's side. Luke himself, at 12.50, speaks of Jesus labouring at a baptism that is not yet complete. 'I have a baptism with which to be baptized', Jesus says, 'and what stress I am under until it is accomplished.' There seems little alternative here but to understand this saying as an anticipation of Jesus' crucifixion, giving warrant, therefore, to the view that the baptism in the River Jordan is to be seen in connection with the passion. Beyond Luke – and thus, admittedly, beyond the province of Fitzmyer's comment – the point is strengthened by the words of Jesus in Mark 10.38. After speaking to them about his death, Jesus then asks the disciples, 'Are you able to drink the cup that I drink, or be baptized with the baptism that I am baptized with?' It seems clear again here that to be baptized means to suffer and to die. What is represented symbolically through immersion in

[34] Ibid.

[35] See again, Barth, *Church Dogmatics* IV.1, 259.

[36] John R.H. Moorman, *The Path to Glory: Studies in the Gospel According to Luke* (London: SPCK, 1963), 39.

[37] Joseph Fitzmyer, *The Gospel According to Luke*, I–IX (New York: Doubleday, 1981), 482.

the waters of the Jordan is actualized at Calvary. Jesus bears our guilt, is made sin, and endures its consequences. He represents us before the Father for he alone among human beings can offer a true repentance and a true confession, undistorted by the propensity of all others of us to disobedience and pretence.

In this history of his, from baptism through to crucifixion, Jesus fulfilled all righteousness; not, however, the slim righteousness of obedience to the law, but rather the supererogatory righteousness of the God who will not go back on his promise to be *our* God. Righteousness here means right relationship. It denotes the faithfulness of God to the covenant relationality in which He has set himself with his people. The fulfilment of all righteousness means that once and for all humanity in Christ comes before the Father in confession and repentance and hears the verdict spoken, 'This is my beloved Son with whom I am well pleased'. In a very important sense, therefore, there is only one who is truly baptized, that is Jesus Christ. Only his baptism fulfils all righteousness and secures the relationality of love between the Father and his children. That is why, ever after, those who follow him are to be baptized into Christ, thereby passing through the waters with him, dying with him, and rising with him. It is in this way that the words of divine love are spoken for us as well. This is my beloved son, this is my beloved daughter, with whom I am well pleased.

The suggestion we met earlier in the tradition of commentary upon Matthew 3.15 that the fulfilment of righteousness denotes Jesus' obedience to a specific divine ordinance, namely, that the people of Israel should be baptized, deeply impoverishes the biblical conception of righteousness which is not reducible to the observance of any part of or even to the entirety of the law. Those who claimed to have fulfilled the law didn't generally impress Jesus who sought instead a righteousness 'exceeding that of the Pharisees' (Mt. 5.20). Although there are legal overtones, variously stressed by different biblical authors, righteousness, *s^e^daqah*, is fundamentally a relational concept. 'The righteousness of God appears in his God-like dealings with his people, i.e., in redemption and salvation (Isa. 45:21; 51:5f.; 56:1; 62:1)'[38] and refers to the kind of conduct that establishes and maintains right relationship.[39] Jesus' baptism, therefore, is not undertaken merely in fulfilment of the law, but to fulfil all righteousness, to set humanity, in other words, in right relationship with

[38] H. Seebass, 'Righteousness Justification', in *The New International Dictionary of New Testament Theology*, III (ed. Colin Brown; Exeter: Paternoster Press, 1978), 355.

[39] Seebass, 'Righteousness Justification', 357.

God, and to restore the covenant relationality with God for which we were created and into which we have been called.

What does all this mean for the person of Christ? The baptism discloses, it seems to me, that Christ does indeed fulfil the whole mystery of human nature, as Chrysostom nicely put it. But it discloses to us also the profound mystery of the divine Son of God who does not grasp at equality with God but makes himself nothing and assumes the form of a slave. To take the humanity first, my argument has been in this essay that it is impossible to make sense of the baptism of Christ on an individualistic account of human personhood. With an individualistic ontology informing our thinking we have either to say, with Strauss and others, that Christ himself had sinned, or else that the baptism is merely exemplary and serves only a pedagogical rather than a soteriological purpose. With a relational ontology, however, it becomes possible to see that in assuming human nature Christ binds himself to us. He allows his very being to be bound up with ours so that, while sinless himself, he shoulders our guilt, becomes tainted as it were with the fallenness that afflicts humanity, and, therefore, quite literally *in our place*, makes confession to the Father on our behalf. That baptismal action is brought to completion at Calvary where, again, in our place, he is made sin and meets the full consequence of that in death and descent into hell. The bitter cup that is finally drained at Calvary is first accepted by Jesus at his baptism and in his temptation in the wilderness. As Colin Gunton again puts it in the passage already quoted, the baptism 'points forward to [Jesus'] acceptance by death of the judgement of God on human sin'.[40] The full mystery of humanity thus revealed refers to the fallenness of our humanity; but it refers too to the fact that this humanity is loved by God, is reclaimed by God, and is reconstituted in relation to him through the baptism that Christ endures on our behalf.

What of the divinity of Christ? I have mentioned already that the baptism plays its part in revealing who God truly is, that is, the one who, through his Son, loves without limit and makes himself nothing for our sakes. But the baptism is also to be understood, irreducibly, as the action of the triune God. The Son acts by taking to himself the whole mystery of human nature, including its fallenness, its guilt, and its bondage to death; the Father declares the Son to be his Son, the one whom he has sent, and he confirms thereby that Jesus' action in identifying himself with his people and shouldering their guilt is indeed what it means to be God's Son, God's

[40] Colin E. Gunton, *Father, Son and Holy Spirit: Essays Toward a Fully Trinitarian Theology* (London: T&T Clark, 2003), 207.

anointed one, God's servant. Then the Spirit, finally, descends upon and remains with the Son precisely so that in his humanity, under the conditions, that is, of limitation and fallenness and guilt, he may bring to completion the baptism with which he is baptized. Immediately, thereafter, the Spirit drives Jesus into the wilderness where he is tempted by the devil. That means that with the Father's declared approval and by the Spirit's empowering, the Son goes through with his baptism and labours toward its completion. He goes beyond the symbolic encounter with sin and evil and on through that real encounter in which evil and sin are finally overcome.

I began this essay by asking why Jesus was baptized. My answer has been, following Chrysostom's lead, and in agreement with others along the way, that in this way Jesus enters into the full mystery of human nature, fallen and guilty as it is, and reconstitutes it in reconciled relation to God. This is the work of divine love and so reveals the one who does it as God's beloved Son.

Chapter 8

The Confession of the Son

Douglas Knight

We are preceded by a conversation, the conversation of Father, Son and Holy Spirit. Like any other piece of theology this essay attempts to set out some of the logic of that conversation. It will set out an account of the gospel in passages of narrative, and in axioms that I state but don't argue for. The narrative and the axioms serve one another and require one another. Along with this narrative theology, this essay also attempts to be a theology of the Word, which means broadly that God speaks and makes himself known to us. It does so by trying to show that a theology of the Word is also a theological logic of that Word and that narrative. The logic – that is, 'philosophy' – does not precede the Word – that is, the gospel – but it corresponds to it: Word and logic are constituted together, so the theology and justification for this account of it must be kept together. This will allow me to say that the Word is really word not when it is spoken, but when it is finally heard and an event is created by its hearing.[1]

The three persons of God have distinct works, yet they make one single work. Relations within the Trinity are not just about origins – sending and proceeding – but also about the reception of and response to these actions. That is to say that everything demands an audience, and nothing is what it is until it has been confirmed by the right audience. For the Son the constitutive audience is the Father, but at one point in the account we

[1] 'Logos' means, and requires that we articulate, all of the following: Word, the 'second' person of the Trinity, words, speech, an event of speech (an announcement, for example), language, grammar/logic/order, narrative, and hearing and reception (and thus a competent audience).

must be his audience too. The Son does not act alone, but is accompanied and driven in all he does by the Spirit. The Spirit distinguishes the Son and the Father from one another: he not only holds them together but he makes them free by in some measure holding them apart. The Father, not the Spirit, is finally the perfector and consummator: the Spirit is this subordinately. This Christological discussion of Word and narrative will therefore take us through the doctrine of the Spirit.

I. The Divine Speech

God comes to us. God is articulate and vocal, and he is generous and forthcoming. His speech is not a front for something beyond speech. He is his speech. The Father speaks. The Son is what the Father says; he is the speech of the Father. This is the first part-statement we must make about God. It needs three further moments of theo-logic. The next is that the Son hears the Father. The speech of the Father does not disappear into emptiness, but finds its hearer. The Son receives the speech of the Father, so it comes to its proper place, and is vindicated. The Son is the event of the Father's word's arrival and reception; in him the Father's word finds its proper audience and home. The third is that the Son does what the Father says; he carries out the instruction of the Father. The Son answers the Father – with his act. The Son is the act of obedience that hears and does the Father's word, so that it is not just word but *act*, word-act. The fourth moment is that the Father receives the Son; his is the voice the Father wants to hear and the answer the Father is looking for. Everything the Son says is acceptable to the Father.

The Father sends and the Son receives. The Son sends and the Father receives back. They do this in themselves; it is their joint act of conversation and communion. By one free act that takes place within this conversation they bring creation into being. The Father gives the Son the world, and the Son receives it and gives thanks for it. The Son cares for the world and, having brought it to completion, he brings the world to the Father. The Father approves the Son's custodial and parental work, and receives the world back from him. In this return act of conversation, creation is perfected, which means that it is initiated as a living, conversational being. Their act of conversation makes this act of institution, reception and finally of presentation to the Father again. The world is the product of these various actions, and the single vindicated act of creation is one item of the conversation of the Son with the Father.

We can also put this the other way around. The Father gives the Son to the world. God presents the world with this gift, of himself, in the person of the Son. Then, when many ages have passed, the perfected world presents the Son to the Father, by the Spirit. The Son will present the world, in the form of us, to the Father to receive his inspection and approval. But the Son also continually presents the first instalments of the future world, the perfected creation, to the Father. The *future* world is entirely present to the Father in the Son: it is created by that conversation and continuously opened by the Spirit who sustains their conversation. The future and completed world is continually given to the *present* world by the Spirit in the Church, which is the body of the Son for the world. The Spirit stands in for the future act of the world. Where the world is going to be, one day established in its own free and joyful activity, there the Spirit is now, representing it and preparing it for this future. The one-day competent world will take the action the Spirit gives it and, in the company of the Spirit, it will return it via the Son, to the Father, and in that act, the joint-act of Spirit and world, the world will become living, active and free.

The Father tells the world about his Son. He tells the Church, that particular form of the world chosen for this purpose, about his Son. In telling the world about his Son the Church is brought into being. The Church is the result of the Father's joy in his Son and the Son's joy in the world that he brings to the Father. The Son is telling those he wants to present to the Father about his Father. God is telling us about himself in the third person. This narration of God is not something outside God, but is itself a third person. The story and speech of God is himself the person of God, the Holy Spirit. We are told the story by being drawn into the story, and becoming characters in it. God draws and assembles us into his narration, so the story of God's action is both the *story* of our being brought into being within his action, and the *event* of our being brought into being within his action. The action of God in telling, hearing and receiving constitutes the whole economy in which we receive our being. The call and response of Father and Son creates a conversation, and their conversation brings into being a work also shared between them.

II. The Divine Service

The work of the Son is the work of God. The work of the Son is to make us holy. We are made holy by that act in which the Son states publicly before all powers and authorities what belongs to God, and gives thanks. The Son returns for all these powers and authorities, and also for us, thanks to God. This returning thanks-giving is the labour of the Son.

The Son gives to the Father the credit for the Father's speech and acts. By doing so the Son prevents any other power or authority from taking credit for these words and acts themselves. The Son forestalls their act of self-aggrandizement. He provides for them the speech-act that they must make to the Father, but which they first did not know how to make, and which they then refused to make, thereby falling into rebellion. The Son speaks to the Father the surrender and apology for this delayed and refused response that all powers and authorities must make for themselves. In the Son we return to the Father all the credit for his speech-acts. Only by this act of the Son are we prevented from being tempted to think that these acts of God are our acts. The Son prevents us from making fools of ourselves. He pre-empts our impulse to say something else, to hold on to and attribute to ourselves what we have received and must return.

The court of God is in session. God's people stand around and before him.[2] He hears and examines those who come before him. Those around him are struck by the expertise and insight of God's decisions, and are relieved to see that things are going to go well. His assembly praises God for the generosity and virtuosity with which he assesses and supplies what is required to assemble this people and sustain them in being.[3] The assembly lives from participation in this conversation of Father and Son, and from the work of creation and rule that freely derives from their conversation. This assembly that lives from God is expansive: the speech and life of God extends this heavenly assembly outwards to create an assembly on earth.

The speech of heaven creates a speech on earth. The words that go out from the Father, the Spirit gathers up from all corners of creation, makes fit, and returns to the Father, as the thankful speech of the creation integrated into the thankful speech of the Son. It is the speech of the Father to the Son that is heard on earth in the reading of Scripture, and it is the

[2] God has a company. The Church service is a court in session. 'For who in the skies above can compare with the Lord? Who is like the Lord among the heavenly beings? In the Council of the holy ones God is greatly feared: he is more awesome than all who surround him' (Psalm 89.6–7). See also Patrick Miller who writes, 'The assembly or members of it, whether the "divine ones" or "holy ones" or particular groups within the whole for example the seraphim are sometimes depicted as serving or worshipping the Lord, a part of the holy array that gives God glory.' Patrick D. Miller, 'Cosmology and World Order in the Old Testament: The Divine Council as a Cosmic-Political Symbol', reprinted in *Israelite Religion and Biblical Theology* (Sheffield: Sheffield Academic Press, 2000), 425. And, 'The council of the Lord is the place where the goal of all creation, praise, begins.' Ibid., 440.

[3] God provides justice and generosity, and arraigns those who do not do so. 'God presides in the assembly; he gives judgement among the "gods". How long will you defend the unjust and show partiality to the wicked? Defend the cause of the weak and fatherless' (Psalm 82).

speech of the Son to the Father that is heard in the responses sung by the earthly congregation. What we take to be the words of the Church, and so our words, is first the speech of God, and only then the speech of the company made glad by God.[4] God elects, transforms and integrates this conversation on earth into his own speech and labour.

The speech of God is the act of God. God's Word leaves nothing the same; it transforms, perfects and opens everything. It is sacramental. This speech is the *sacrament*. It is the irruption of the holiness of God into the world that makes all things holy. Word and sacrament are not two ministries. There is rather one Word of God, which sacramentalizes us, that is, it makes us holy, compatible with God. This Word comes to us and is received by God back from us again, bringing us into being and making us holy, by participation in that speech fitting us for further participation in that speech. We are the product of that antiphony, are sustained in life by regular re-inclusion within it. Their divine service holds in being the Church, the earth-bound overflow of the heavenly assembly. The Christian community exists when the connection and conversation between heaven and earth is live. In this call and response earth is picked up and connected into the speech and response of the Father and the Son, and becomes part of the reply the Son makes to the Father, part of what we may call their service or liturgy.[5]

The company of heaven accompany the Son. They are the procession that follows him. He regards this crowd as inseparable from himself, his own body, his glory, vindication and reward. The company of heaven is the one real and actual communion, the actualization of communion and plurality where before there was none. This communion actualizes itself on earth, for us, as the Church. The company of heaven is the speech-act of God, and the Church is the speech-act of this company, and therefore of God. The Church is nothing apart from God: the body is not the body apart from the head, nor the word the living Word apart from the speaking voice.[6] The Church is the speaking of the Son to the world, and it is the hearing and reception by the Spirit of the Son's word to the world. Everything that is, is because it is derived from this conversation, that creates first an assembly and communion, the Church, and then brings into being a world that

[4] See Otfried Hofius, 'Gemeinschaft mit den Engeln im Gottesdienst der Kirche', *Zeitung für Theologie und Kirche* 89 (1992): 172–96.

[5] *Leitourgia* = public service.

[6] Christoph Schwöbel writes, 'The Church is *creatura verbi divini*: the creature of the divine Word. The Church is constituted by God's action and not by any human action.' Christoph Schwöbel, 'The Church as Creature of the Word', in C.E. Gunton and D.W. Hardy (eds.), *On Being the Church* (Edinburgh: T&T Clark, 1989), 122.

sustains, and is sustained by, that communion. There is nothing more basic or irreducible than words, specifically the words spoken by the Son and the Father, whose words are acts. We are becoming part of the conversation of the Son and Father. We will become the words they use. We have no being outside their conversation: when they cease to employ us as the words with which they respond to one another, we are gone.

III. Speaking Humanity

The Father and the Son speak the Spirit. The Spirit is the language they speak. But the Spirit can speak and be many languages, without being any less the language of the Son and Father. The Spirit extends their speech to create a new language, humanity, which the Father and the Son are content to speak. They speak humanity, and humanity is one of the modes in which they speak divinity to each other. Humanity does not give divinity something that it did not have before: it is not a reduction of or addition to their divinity. The Son is the first speaker and the native speaker. He speaks humanity perfectly and is at home in the flesh, and in the flesh of humanity is perfectly at home with the Father. He is not impeded by or disguised by the flesh, for it is brought into existence by the speaking of the Son and the Father. The human entity and mode of being is spoken by that enfleshing word and utterance. Having spoken us into being they also speak *through* us: the Son replies to the Father in the flesh. Then they speak *to* us and so make first hearers and then speakers of us, able to hear, receive and respond to one another. They speak to us *one another*, giving us in this speech one another as words and gifts from God. We are to learn to speak to one another and receive one another from them, with thanksgiving.

This humanity the Son receives from the Father, by the Spirit. The Spirit takes from the materiality of the Father and gives it to us, making himself material to us (incarnation) and us to him (creation). The fleshly materiality of Jesus of Nazareth derives from, and is supplied by, the consummated materiality of the Spirit. As yet we speak humanity very badly: it is a language and a life we are scarcely acquainted with, so like any foreigner we mangle this language, not because we are native speakers of another language, but just because we are autistic, scarcely able to speak. But our bad performance of flesh does not make flesh problematic for God. The Father and Son speak the language of flesh perfectly; this language is sustained by their use of it, and they will enable us to be at home in it to them.

This account of humanity and materiality has avoided a simple contrast between material and spiritual. The Spirit extends to us some of the materiality of the relation of the Son to the Father. More spiritual means more real, more solid, more material, more lasting. Under such theological definition, spiritual and material are two terms for the single continuum of the complex act of God.[7] The Spirit intends to coax us up from the bottom of the gradient to the top, from no materiality or reality, through the very sketchy and provisional reality we have now, on to a full creaturely participation in the being of the Son, who is Reality. We must not decide therefore that Christ has *either* a spiritual body *or* a physical body, or attribute some actions to a divine nature and others to a human nature. We must say that Christ is fully present to the Father – fully embodied to him – by the Spirit. The Spirit makes the Son embodied and present to us, so the Son always has a spiritual body and is dressed, escorted and presented by the Spirit.

But we are not formatted to receive such a direct embodiment. Since we have as yet so little reality, we have nothing to receive the Son's reality with. Because we are not spiritual – not yet proficient at the life of the Son – this spiritual body in which the Son meets us must have the specific form that we do share. It must be a body in the partial and serial sense in which we are embodied and present to one another.[8] He must dress down for us, and be much more diffidently present, under-embodied, or serially embodied. The Son is dressed by the Spirit in a body constituted by all the presences (bodies) of the people of Israel who have looked forward to him. He is present to us as all the faithful of Israel, the body of witnesses that constitute the Old Testament. The Old Testament is the Son dressed down in the form of many bodies, for us.

Yet even that is too much for us. This host is too overwhelming for us to receive. So he is present as this host embodied in a single body of the man from Nazareth. He is present in this way only to a single generation of Israel by the one physical-and-spiritual body of Jesus Christ. Now because this many saw the Son, and because we have believed their reports, we may also start to receive him. We receive him first in the form of all the saints who teach our own generation, and through them in the form of all the teachers of the Church, themselves taught by the apostles, and through the apostolic witness of the scriptures, and all this through baptism in the

[7] There may be many graduations in this act and continuum, as many degrees of differentiation as are required to move us up, one at a time, one lesson after another, from level to level from bottom to top, to the full measure of Christ.

[8] The creature is constituted in instalments, delivered one after another and each integrated into the previous, to make the whole man, the new Adam. First comes the natural (partial), then the spiritual (whole). 'The spiritual did not come first, but the natural, and after that the spiritual' (1 Cor. 15.47).

Spirit. All these witnesses are held together by the Spirit to serve us as the single body of the Son to us.[9] The Spirit wraps them up to make them the whole Christ (*totus Christus*) to us.[10]

A truly theological pneumatology prevents us from setting spiritual and material in opposition. Spirit does not mean less material but more material, more real: when the Spirit integrates us into the whole body, the resurrection body, we will be real at last. But if we do not continually take steps against it, these two concepts always settle back to become opposites, for the reigning metaphysic of our society reverts all such theological statement to what it regards as the norm, its default setting. At stake is the job of distinguishing theology from the dualism often attributed to Augustine but which in fact dogs the whole tradition. This may help us to follow the discussion of Robert Jenson and Colin Gunton. Gunton insists that at bottom there are two natures, that of God and that of everything else, so duality is most basic, and that any other account would be monophysite or even monist. Jenson replies that at bottom there is one nature, that of God who is all in all: there must be a pneumatological unity because unity is eschatological, the work of God.[11] But of course both accounts must be given, for it is part of the Church's job to say both 'now' and 'not yet'. That means that we must not only put unity and duality as *co*-fundamental, first equal at top of our list of categories, but with them we must also put manyness, because for us in the *economia* of God there is the possibility and actuality of manyness, and therefore life and freedom and surprise.

It is not the case that the Son is available to us in terms of dualism, in just one of these two modes, *either* spiritual *or* physical. We must move the discussion out of our naturalistic default ontology and find a more suitable way of conceiving the relationship of spirit and material. I have used language as an alternative paradigm because language is simultaneously

[9] Augustine explains, 'Certainly we can apply the name "anointed" (*christus*) to all who have been anointed with his chrism; and yet it is the whole body, with its head, which is the one Christ.' Augustine, *City of God*, Book 17, chapter 4. This does not entail that the Son is absorbed into the Church. The Spirit has distinguished him from us, and gives him his particular body, by which he is one identifiable human at the right hand of God.

[10] The parts must be clothed by the whole. 'For the perishable must clothe itself with the imperishable and the mortal with immortality' (1 Cor. 15.51). So, we have two accounts of one act, in one of which the parts are covered by the whole (= the Head), in the other of which the many parts are integrated to make that whole (= body).

[11] Colin Gunton writes, 'In so far as Christ is risen he is for this reader (Jenson) risen into, almost as, the Church.' Colin Gunton, *Father, Son and Holy Spirit: Towards a Fully Trinitarian Theology* (London: T&T Clark, 2003), 219. Gunton quotes with disapproval Jenson, *Systematic Theology* (Oxford: Oxford University Press, 1999), I, 205 and 206.

one and many, discrete and open; it is both one language and very many utterances. So now we can say that the Son is available to us in the many modes and many dosages that he decides are required for us to learn to receive him. He can give himself to us faster, or more slowly and gently, adjusting himself to our pace. He wears the body that we can catch hold of.[12] He is present to us in the slower and more considered way that we would use in talking to a young child, with those pauses for checking, reinforcement and reassurance. He involves us in this gentle, recursive mode. He can supply us with, and build us up into, that real materiality that he intends for us, which is his and which he intends to share with us. Talk about speech and language, itself disciplined by a Word Christology, helps keep pneumatology theological.

IV. The Assembly

The Son is fully present to the Father – fully embodied to him – by the Spirit.[13] The Spirit assembles us around and within the Son. The assembly is both *in* the Son and *with* the Son. These two statements with their distinct prepositions may not be further compressed. The Son is their whole definition, and he is also distinctly present to them, as *not*-them, but as their head.[14] Jesus is accompanied by the Spirit just as any commander is accompanied by a detachment of his troops. He is he never alone, without some part of his company, though not always accompanied by his whole army at once. He sends troops out to bring his guests to him. He gives the saints a detachment for their support and protection – and yet they must

[12] Otherwise we would be, as Gregory Nazianzen has it, 'like men loaded with food beyond their strength and presenting eyes yet too weak to bear even the sun's light, risk the loss of that which was within the reach of their powers; but that by gradual additions ... the light of the Trinity might shine upon the more illuminated. For this reason it was I think that he gradually came to dwell in the disciples, measuring himself out to them according to their capacity to receive him, at the beginning of the gospel, after the passion, after the ascension, making perfect their powers, being breathed upon them and appearing in fiery tongues.' Gregory Nazianzen, *Fifth Oration on the Holy Spirit* in *Nicene and Post-Nicene Fathers* (ed. P. Schaff and H. Wace; Grand Rapids: Eerdmans, 1893), chapter 26, p. 326.

[13] See Gregory Nazianzen, Oration 41, in *On Pentecost*, XI, in *Nicene and Post-Nicene Fathers* (ed. P. Schaff and H. Wace; Grand Rapids: Eerdmans, 1893), p. 383: 'He wrought first in the heavenly and angelic powers, such as are first after God and around God. For from no other source flows their perfection and their brightness, and the difficulty or impossibility of moving them to sin, but from the Holy Ghost. And next in the Patriarchs and Prophets, of whom the former saw visions of God or knew him and the latter also foreknew the future, having their master part moulded by the Spirit and being associated with events that were yet future as if present, for such is the power of the Spirit.'

[14] We are *in* him, so not distinct from him, because he does not regard us as distinct from him. But he is distinct from us, made distinct from us by the Holy Spirit.

ask for reinforcements. His servants introduce and accompany us into being; they bring us into the public assembly. Our presence is our being surrounded and escorted by these sponsors and supporters sent by the Son, who are his company and his Spirit. Sometimes, for the benefit of those around us, his company is visible as the saints who encourage us, while at other times we have no visible accompaniment. Then for all the world it looks as though we have been left alone. But it merely looks that way to them. The Son leads the saints. Led by him they represent us in heaven, and sustain for us there what being we have. Led by him they pray us into being. They ask God that we be made complete and be given to them. They ask for us, and their asking for us, and the Father's approval of their request, is all the being we have. They not only pray us into existence, but pray us into being social and vocal. All the life we are given is the life they receive from the Son, and that life consists in looking forward to, and asking for, what is still lacking. They will make us as adept at seeking from the Son as they are.

Unless the Son and the Father utter us, there is no us.[15] They utter us as speakers who the Spirit will animate so we utter one another. You must speak me into being. I have no other existence than as something you say in reply to the Son, and in gratitude to the Son. You are brought into being as under-labourers of the Son. You, along with all the rest of company of heaven and communion of saints, are the medium made and employed by the Spirit. You bring me into being by bringing me into the assembly with you. My integration into this assembly is the event in which I am assembled and brought into being.

Synaxis

The Son calls together and assembles all the scattered elements of the cosmos. Assembly (*ecclesia*) means coming together (*synaxis*). The resulting action of this gathering is thanksgiving (*eucharist*).[16] The command of God brings this assembly into being, integrates it and gives it its duration and

[15] See Jenson who writes 'To be, we have maintained, is to be spoken of by God.' *Systematic Theology*, II, 295. And further: 'According to Luther the soul becomes what it hearkens to. Luther: "Do not be surprised that I said we must become the Word."' Ibid., 259.

[16] The synaxis is a function of the Son's thanksgiving (eucharist) to the Father. The synaxis creates thanksgiving, and in this sense perhaps we can say that the eucharist (thanksgiving) makes the Church. Gunton does not believe 'the eucharist makes the Church', insisting that the Church is the creature solely of the Word. He charges Jenson with not giving sufficient account of the present fallenness of the Church. See Gunton, *Father, Son and Holy Spirit*, 220–21. Is this perhaps because Gunton understands the eucharist as the act of the Church considered apart from its head?

identity. The Son not only calls, but he remembers (*anamnesis*). Other masters use their people until they are all used up, then abandon them, letting their bodies disappear back into the earth where no one can remember them or recover them. But the Son has not forgotten them; he has come to find them and bring them up from where they have been hidden in death.[17] The Son re-members his people, member to member. He assembles his congregation before him, and leads us out through a wilderness, he the head of the line, we the procession. He is far ahead so we do not see him, but we are led by his fire and are covered by his cloud. We follow him and imitate him, so what he does, we do; his every action ripples through us back down the column.

He is leading us to the great king.[18] Christ our spokesman has already gained admittance to the temple and palace of the great king. Our representative has gone in and now sits in conversation with the king. The whole delegation stretches back to the door of the palace and outside, where you and I are, in the queue. For our leader, this procession is one with him, even part of him. No interloper can snatch anyone away from his procession, for they are made impregnable by the protection he extends, his Spirit, who holds together and makes visible and co-present the whole train behind the Son.[19]

V. The Son Makes the Good Confession

The Spirit does not allow the communion of the Son with his whole people to be interrupted. The Spirit cuts short every alternative self-aggrandizement. He dethrones every master, taking away their reputation and power,

[17] 'I saw under the altar the souls of those who had been slain because of the Word of God and the testimony they had maintained. They called out in a loud voice, "How long, Sovereign Lord, until you judge the inhabitants of the earth and avenge our blood?"' (Revelation 6.9–10).

[18] Psalm 68 describes this procession. 'With mighty chariotry, twice ten thousand, thousands upon thousands, the Lord came from Sinai into the holy place. You ascended the high mountain, leading captives in your train and receiving gifts from people, even from those who rebel against the Lord God's abiding there. Your solemn processions are seen, O God, the processions of my God, my King, into the sanctuary – the singers in front, the musicians last, between them girls playing tambourines: "Bless God in the great congregation, the Lord, O you who are of Israel's fountain!" Because of your temple at Jerusalem kings bear gifts to you' (Ps. 68.17–29).

[19] There is, of course, a gap between the one (who alone sits with the Father) and all the rest of the column (who don't). The fact that there is a gap between the one man (ascended) and the many (not ascended) does not change the fact that the one man thinks that we are with him and is determined to bring it about that we are. It is the attitude of the Son that the gap is overcome and will be overcome that is determinative.

in order to establish the better reputation and more effective and ordered power of the Son. The liturgy of Spirit and Son takes back from us the praise we ascribe to ourselves, and returns it to the Father who is its proper source and giver. They take it back from us: they make us return praise to God. They take away our misdirected speech-acts, and readdress them so that they properly serve to call God to us. The Spirit co-opts the sounds we make to put the Son's praise of the Father in our mouths, even before we know the Son's name. He speaks for us and through us, though we may be the last to know. The praise and recognition that we grasp at is wrested away from us, in order that we be properly established as the creatures who receive their praise, with their being, from God.

The Son made the good confession. He confessed the Father as Lord.[20] The Son refused worship to every other authority.[21] He could not be made to utter any other name or enter any other plea. He withheld what every other man had conceded. He did not defer either to Nature, or Necessity, or Fate, or to any other foundation, preliminary or set of axioms. He gave no concession, showed no civility, made no deference. He raised all hackles and united all enemies against him by the insolence of his refusal. He withdrew authority from every authority in rebellion.[22] His word to all the

[20] 'Christ Jesus, who while testifying before Pontius Pilate made the good confession' (1 Tim. 6.12–13). See also Larry Hurtado who explains, 'The phrase "to call upon the name of the Lord" is derived directly from the Old Testament usage, where it functions as a technical expression designating prayer and sacrifice offered specifically to Yahweh (eg Genesis 4.26, 13.4).' Larry W. Hurtado, *Lord Jesus Christ: Devotion to Jesus in Earliest Christianity* (Grand Rapids: Eerdmans, 2003), 197.

[21] We have to give two accounts. The Son paid *no* respect to intermediary authorities. And yet the Son did also pay proper respect to intermediary authorities: he was a good son, who accepted discipline (Hebrews 5.8; 12.9–10), acted 'according to the Scriptures', and was obedient to the prophets and patriarchs, learning from them how to suffer and resist the resistance of the Gentiles and the aggressors.

[22] The confession of the Lord is the disavowing and dismissal of the old lords. Now all men must be commanded to throw over their old leaders and change sides. This trial of strength continues in every public assembly, where the new troops of the king are to confront every leader in the hearing of his own people. The Christian witnesses are to read out the accusation of God against each leader who lays hands on them, and give him one chance to confess the God of Israel. 'In each place you will be taken to the public assembly ... on account of me you will stand before governors and kings as witnesses to them ... just say whatever is given you at the time' (Mark 13.9–11). The Christians are the message and embassy of God to the authorities in each place. When these authorities fail to hear them, the Christians can go over their heads and direct their complaints straight to God: if they have to do this the authorities are convicted of failing in their office, and it is taken away from them. So Stephen (Acts 7.55) exercises the power of binding: the members of the court that arraigns him carry out judgment against themselves, by destroying Stephen, God's spokesman to them.

authorities of the world was No. The Son is the No of the Father spoken against every disobedient creaturely self-assessment.

The Son Drives Out the Interlopers

The Son's confession of the Father is simultaneously his confession against all interlopers and rivals. The liturgy is the sentence of God against all who promote, defer to, and so deify, any created force. That sentence is 'Go far from me', 'I never knew you'.[23] It is the command of God who expels and sends into oblivion the boastful and dissonant voices that make up this world.[24] The voice of God interrogates them then silences them.[25] It loosens the grip of the parasites on us and drives them off. He has ejected those hard masters and foreign spirits who impose a vicious authority but themselves acknowledge no discipline. He has driven them out from the top of the cosmos to the bottom.[26] The liturgy is the naming and driving out of those who exercise an influence on us that is undue, unaccountable and thus demonic. His liturgy the Son extends to us; so may we participate in his confession and are prevented from making iniquitous and unsustainable claims that assault his prerogative. The community caught up into his confession need no longer pray to the many gods and vainly beg to them for the justice it wants. The liturgy is God's word of exorcism and act of expulsion. At the weekly gathering of his assembly the people of the Son tell all masters that they are no gods.

[23] Thus in Matthew's Gospel we read, 'I tell you the truth, I do not know you' (25.12), and 'Depart from me, you who are cursed, into the eternal fire prepared for Satan and his angels' (25.41).

[24] The people of God, Israel, have only to use the name of the God of Israel and the strong places of other gods will come tumbling down. 'Everyone who calls upon the name of the Lord will be saved' (Joel 2.32; cf. Acts 2.21; Rom. 10.13) – from all other lords. Similarly, 'When the trumpet sounded the people shouted and at the sound of trumpet, when the people gave a loud shout, the wall collapsed; so every man charged in and they took the city' (Josh. 6.20).

[25] Thus in Mark, 'Just then a man in their synagogue who was possessed by an evil spirit cried out, "What do you want with us, Jesus of Nazareth? Have you come to destroy us? I know who you are – the Holy one of God". "Be quiet!" said Jesus sternly. "Come out of him!" The evil spirit shook the man violently and came out of him with a shriek' (Mark 1.23–25). And further, 'He got up, rebuked the wind and said to the waves "Quiet, be still"' (Mark 4.39). And then, 'But Jesus still made no reply, and Pilate was amazed' (Mark 15.5).

[26] The Son took his campaign through all levels of the cosmos, and returned victorious. 'He who descended is the very one who ascended higher than all the heavens, in order to fill the whole universe' (Eph. 4.9).

The Father confesses his Son.[27] He hears and accepts and vindicates his speech and act. He raises his Son from the dead and sits him at his right hand, far above all others. He has set him over all rulers, pretenders, authorities and principles.[28] The Son confesses that he is not the Father, and he does not allow anyone else to make such a claim to divine power either. Our life is the Son's act of distinguishing us from himself, and in his act God mercifully and generously supplies to us a not-God-ness.[29]

VI. The Son Prays

The Son speaks first. He speaks with the Father. He leads our speech, while we stand behind him and follow him, picking up his words and repeating them. We live on his words. Our speech is his speech first. He speaks, and we breathe in what he has spoken. We breathe in and out in the breath of the Son, his utterances creating the atmosphere we live in. We are the species that can exist only in the biosphere of his expiration. The breath and words of other lords cannot support us; the environments and forms of life derived from other sources we call 'death'. We are the creature of one Creator only, and having been brought into existence on his generosity we are engineered to it alone and cannot substitute the breath of our Creator with any thinner fuel.

The Father tells the Son what is still to do, and the Son tells the Father what is required on earth to do it. He asks the Father for whatever is missing. He requests and requisitions, and he teaches us how to do the same. He speaks first, and we speak after him.[30] He teaches us to speak out

[27] 'I will tell of the decree of the Lord: He said to me, "You are my son; today I have begotten you. Ask of me, and I will make the nations your heritage, and the ends of the earth your possession"' (Ps. 2.7). And, 'You are my Son whom I love; with you I am well pleased' (Mark 1.11).

[28] Thus Psalm 8.4–6: 'What is man that you are mindful of him, the son of man that you care for him? You made him a little lower than the heavenly beings and crowned him with glory and honour. You made him ruler over the works of your hands; you put everything under his feet.'

[29] Pannenberg refers to this as the Son's self-differentiation from the Father: 'The self-distinction of Jesus from the Father, which was the condition of the manifestation of the eternal Son in Jesus' obedience to the mission he received from the Father to proclaim God's lordship, can be described as his self-emptying and self-humbling along the lines of the early Christian hymn in Philippians 2.6–11.' Wolfhart Pannenberg, *Systematic Theology* (Edinburgh: T&T Clark, 1994), II, 375.

[30] Correct deployment of the name and power of the Son is the only knowledge of the Son. We only know the Son as he animates us with his ability to deploy his power in his Father's business.

for those who cannot speak for themselves, to see what is missing, and to intervene and provide what is required.

The Spirit speaks for the earth. What the Church does not yet know how to utter, the Spirit makes the inert things of the earth utter for it.[31] The Spirit coaches the earth in its proper response and speaks the earth into the shape and person of the one obedient man, the Son. The fleshly materiality of Jesus is given into our hands by the Spirit via the whole people of Israel, in order that we raise him to the Father with thanksgiving. He is the creation replying to God with its own voice, which is the voice it has from him.[32] Jesus Christ is the coming into speech of the earth, and the thankful creaturely word God wants to hear from it.

The Son Leads the Assembly in Prayer

I have said that the liturgy is the conversation of the Son with the Father, and that there is a circulation and traffic of requests (prayers) and receipts (thanksgiving) upward, and of provisions and interventions downward. The liturgy is the intercession, lament and thanksgiving of the Son. The psalms are the pleas and complaints the Son makes for the men who have no voice.[33] Those who already have their recognition, their praise *from men*, are not desperate, so no inarticulate sound calls to God from within them. The would-be autonomous man does not intend to be held to account or to remain under authority, but confesses no one but himself or whatever name will abet him. He corrects others, but he cannot take correction, and so is no true son.[34] The psalms express the misery of the son who is crushed and

[31] See Romans 8.22: 'We know that the whole creation has been groaning as in the pains of child birth but we ourselves who have the first-fruits of the Spirit, groan inwardly as we wait for our adoption as sons.' 8.26: 'In the same way, the Spirit helps us in our weakness. We do not know what we ought to pray for, but the Spirit himself intercedes for us with groans that words cannot express. And he who searches our hearts knows the mind of the Spirit, because the Spirit intercedes with the saints in accordance with God's will.'

[32] John Zizioulas points out that man was to act as priest of creation, to liberate creation from the predicament of mortality. Zizioulas, 'Preserving God's Creation: Three Lectures on Theology and Ecology', *King's Theological Review* 12 (1989), 1–5, 41–45; 13 (1990), Lecture 3, 5. In Lecture 1 Zizioulas writes, 'All ancient liturgies seem to be centred ... on the lifting up of the gifts of bread and wine to the Creator Father, the Anaphora, the lifting up, ... attaches equal centrality – if not more – to Man's act as the priest of Creation as it does to God's act of sending down the Holy Spirit to transform the offered gifts into the body and blood of Christ' (p. 4).

[33] The Son sings, for example, 'Give ear to my words, oh Lord, consider my sighing. Listen to my cry for help, my king and my God for to you I pray. In the morning you hear my voice; in the morning I lay my requests before you and wait in expectation' (Ps. 5.1–3).

[34] 'If you are not disciplined, and everyone undergoes discipline, then you are illegitimate children and not true sons' (Heb. 12.8).

abandoned, and they express the joy of the son whom God has heard and publicly vindicated. They are songs for two voices in antiphony. First they are songs of misery.[35] Those who have received nothing ask how long they must wait before God will rescue them from us. It is the failure of anyone on earth to hear and answer these cries and to intercede for these who cannot speak for themselves, that requires that the Son take action. He hears their prayers and comes to take them out of our power.[36] Those who have received nothing cry to God because we have made ourselves deaf to their voice and left them no other means of recourse. They call on God to free them from us who by our unconcern hold them there. The psalms are their charge against us. They are made for them by the Son: he sings them until the poor men can sing them for themselves. He sing them to us – against us – until we hear and react. But we must also sing these songs, for in singing them we will be transformed from the proud and autonomous man, too far away to hear, too busy to reply, into the poor man of the psalms' description. We are to sing this role until it takes us over, and we are the men of the Son who endure that misery, with him held in complete disregard by the world.[37]

The saints warn the people of the world not to give themselves away to the passions and masters who manipulate them and prey on them. Each generation of the saints must appeal to their contemporaries to be no longer passive, but to throw off their old lords. We stand in the court of appeal, and lodge petitions for those who are not yet articulate on their own account, who cannot or do not pray. It is our job to bear them to the Father for inspection and approval, just as we are ourselves borne. We bear this future people into being by presently bearing their needs to God and being their voices in his court, standing in for them until they are there with us. It is the priestly life. We speak and pray for them; they are the confession we make. We are to be demanding on their account, and to

[35] 'During the days of Jesus' life on earth he offered up prayers and petitions with loud cries and tears to the one who could save him from death, and he was heard because of his reverent submission. Although he was a son, he learned obedience from what he suffered' (Heb. 5.7–8).

[36] The Son sings, for instance, Psalm 10: 'Why oh Lord do you stand far off? Why do you hide yourself in time of trouble? In his arrogance the wicked man hunts down the weak, who are caught in the schemes he devises ... He says to himself "God has forgotten, he covers his face and never sees."' Atheism is the convenient belief that we have put ourselves out of God's range and live in a territory policed by no power.

[37] The Son will give his voice to his Church. Mark 9.25: 'You deaf and mute spirit,' he said, 'I command you come out of him and never enter him again.' We may suspect that the modern Church has a deaf and mute spirit, even that it has been made deaf and silent – by God.

request from God what he is waiting to give them, and that he gives them to us and us to them.[38] The world is the act of the Son to us. It is his act of hospitality.[39] Their job is to pass the Son on to us, and in this way make us ready to receive him. All the people who make up the world represent the Son to us. We have to take him from them. But they must give us the Son, and not withhold him from us. He must be their confession and ours.

VII. Pneumatology

The Spirit is making us participants in the speaking and answering of the Son. The Spirit erects Christ's world around him, and raises us to be part of his body, his very person, in that world. The Spirit is giving us a work, the work of presenting people, and this work will make us articulate and alive. God presents people to us, and expects us to present them back to him; so, we are made under-labourers in God's own work of making them present to himself so that they receive their life and being. We are inducted into the Son's work of confessing and presenting the world to the Father.

Christ is the whole, and he is a part of the whole. We are *in* him, and we are *with* him, so though we are part of him, he is distinct from us, and we are distinct from him and from one another. We are made distinct from him by the Holy Spirit. The Spirit empowers us to distinguish ourselves willingly and obediently from the Son and one from another, so we are not only receivers of an inert gift but active agents who joyfully confess that we are not the head, not the Lord. Then I can concede that you are more than I can make you, and that I may no longer inhibit your growth into the full stature of Christ. This being distinct is not a state of affairs with which we have nothing to do, but it is the act of the Holy Spirit in us by which we at last are enabled to say we are not him, and you are different from me. Our being distinct from him is our very own action, Spirit-enabled. By it we, for the first time, freely and really act, and we act freely and willingly precisely as we are able to say he is Lord. We are not the Lord, and so we can thank God.

[38] Thus Paul exhorts the church, 'And pray in the Spirit on all occasions with all kinds of prayers and requests. With this in mind be alert and always keep praying for all the saints' (Eph. 6.18).

[39] The Son makes the creation an image of the hospitality of the Father. 'He is the image of the invisible God, the firstborn over all creation. For by him all things were created: things in heaven as in earth, visible and invisible, through thrones or powers or rulers or authorities; all things were created by him and for him' (Col. 1.15).

Chapter 9

The Ascended Christ: Mediator of Our Worship

Sandra Fach

The Westminster Catechism teaches that humanity's chief end is to glorify God and to enjoy him for ever. In the early Church, the trinitarian nature of this praise was expressed in the mediatorial doxology, 'Glory to the Father through the Son and in the Spirit'. Due to doctrinal controversy, however, the mediatorial expression of the church's worship faded into the background. Though understandable given the circumstances, the development was detrimental. With the help of Josef Jungmann's influential work, *The Place of Christ in Liturgical Prayer*,[1] I will show how this development involved the shadowing of Christ's humanity and therefore the loss of recognition of his priestly role. The burden of this essay will be to argue for a renewed emphasis on Christ's *continuing* mediatorial role, a role performed in the unity of his person as the God-human, that is, the one who is God *as a human*. Although the fact of the ascension will be implicit throughout, its implications will be made clear in the second half of the essay. There, focus on the ascension will help us to clarify what this continuing mediatorial role looks like, this side of Christ's departure from us.

[1] Josef A. Jungmann, *The Place of Christ in Liturgical Prayer*, trans. A. Peeler (London: Geoffrey Chapman, 2nd Eng. edn, 1989).

I. Tell Me the Old, Old Story

Worship: The Story's End

Humanity's chief *end* is to glorify God and enjoy him forever. Let us use this brief but helpful articulation of 'worship' and allow the great commandment given to Israel to inform its content: 'You shall love the Lord your God with all your heart, and with all your soul, and with all your might.'[2] Heeding the warnings in both Testaments that such love can never be abstracted from love of one's neighbour,[3] and affirming that the cross does not save humanity *from* a life of obedient, sacrificial love but rather *to* such a life, let us say that *living for God and for others* is *to glorify God and enjoy him forever*.

Such love is the gift of the God who *is* love. 1 John teaches us that to abide in this love is to abide in God. It is, indeed, to know him – a knowledge given to us through his Son and in his Spirit.[4] Let us, then, understand worship as a *gift*. Through his two hands, the Father gives us what he demands. He lifts us up to participate in communion with him.[5] God revealed, and recognized because of reconciliation, can be enjoyed forever. This life of fellowship with God is to be declared by the community that participates in it, so that others may be drawn in – a mighty gathering that will make this joy complete.[6]

The Story's Pattern

'From God to God' is the parabolic pattern of the story. It is expressed in a mediatorial way: 'From the Father *through* the Son *in* the Spirit', 'to the Father *through* the Son *in* the Spirit'. Regarding the Son, the mediatorial nature of the pattern is expressed by the word, 'through'. Although this essay focuses on the Son's mediatorial role in worship, let it be clear at the outset that the Son's role can never be fully understood or carried out apart from the Spirit.

[2] Deut. 6.5 NRSV (New Revised Standard Version).

[3] See, for example, Isa. 58 and Amos 5. In the New Testament, the horizontal dimension of the Shema is explicit (Mt. 22.34–40; Mark 12.28–34; Luke 10.25–28). Paul's exhortation to 'present your bodies as a living sacrifice, holy and acceptable to God, which is your spiritual worship' (Rom. 12.1 NRSV) is, as the context suggests, to be worked out in mutual love (see Rom. 12; cf. Phil. 4.18).

[4] See 1 John 4.7–16.

[5] See James B. Torrance, *Worship, Community and the Triune God of Grace* (Carlisle: Paternoster Press, 1996), 9.

[6] See 1 John 1.1–4.

The early liturgies are evidence that the church recognized worship as a *gift*. The corporate expression of the mediatorial nature of worship was particularly evident in the anaphoras and doxologies of the church's early Eucharistic prayers. 'To the Father *through* Jesus Christ' reflects the form of the church's early doxologies.[7] Initially, then, praise was given to God *through* Christ, in recognition of the truth that 'there is one God; there is also one mediator between God and humankind, Christ Jesus, himself human'.[8]

[7] This, like later developments, is well documented in Jungmann's work, on which I am dependent in charting the path the church took. See especially *The Place of Christ*, 127–71. It should be noted that aspects of Jungmann's thesis have been challenged, particularly by Albert Gerhards who argues that while Jungmann's analysis of the West is generally accurate, his treatment of the East tends to overgeneralize. Specifically, he argues that there was always a tradition of addressing prayers to Christ, a tradition built on (high) Johannine Christology. It is important to note, however, that Gerhards does not reject Jungmann's thesis but seeks only to modify it, suggesting that the Arian controversy only provided the impetus for giving greater weight to one existing tradition over another (for a summary of Gerhards's critique, see Graham Redding, *Prayer and the Priesthood of Christ in the Reformed Tradition* [London: T&T Clark, 2003], 22–24). Gerhards's teacher, Balthasar Fischer (himself a student of Jungmann), acknowledges this development in the foreword to the second English edition of Jungmann's work. He states: '*The Place of Christ in Liturgical Prayer* represents what was a major breakthrough in liturgical theology, whose importance is not diminished by discovering that the total picture has turned out to be more nuanced than was supposed in the first flush of discovery. If anything, this is proof of the value of Jungmann's thesis, a seminal work whose fruitfulness has been confirmed by the refinements that subsequent research has brought to it' (see Jungmann, *The Place of Christ*, x). (Fischer here also reminds us of those aspects of piety, where Christ is addressed, which Jungmann never denies.) Two things are worth noting when considering the value of Jungmann's thesis. First, even if another strand ('to Christ') always existed, it is difficult to deny the strand/movement that Jungmann outlines (or that it was detrimental). Second, even if the Arian controversy gave greater weight to an existing tradition, that does not necessarily mean that the nature of prayer 'to Christ' post-controversy had the same tenor as prayer 'to Christ' pre-controversy. Jungmann, himself, in the context of discussing the prayer to Christ which he never denies, argues that such prayer is essentially mediatorial (cf. note 28 below).

[8] 1 Tim. 2.5 NRSV. Although the earliest forms exhibit a binitarian pattern (see, for example, Eph. 5.20; Col. 3.17; Rom. 1.8, 16.27), union to Christ was believed to be by the Spirit in whom Christians lived and moved. As Jungmann states: 'What is done in Christ is done also in the Holy Spirit, since it is he who pervades and animates the body of Christ. From this it was only a short step to beginning or ending the prayer: "We praise thee through our Lord Jesus Christ in the Holy Spirit", or (by taking the prayer of the Holy Spirit to ourselves in a more personal way and by ranging it alongside the service of the high priest) "We praise thee through our Lord Jesus Christ and through the Holy Spirit"' (*The Place of Christ*, 150). This explicit inclusion of the Holy Spirit is seen as early as the liturgical descriptions given by Justin Martyr (Jungmann, *The Place of Christ*, 150).

Theology itself arises from worship[9] but the gift of theological reflection, in turn, influences the practice of worship.[10] The mediatorial structure of 'to the Father through Jesus Christ in the Holy Spirit' changed with doctrinal development, to the point where Christ's mediation faded into the background or disappeared altogether.[11] The change was subtle at first. The word 'through' was retained, but the name 'Jesus Christ' was replaced by 'Son'. Then the word 'through' disappeared and instead of a mediatorial doxology, the church adopted the so-called coordinated doxology: 'Glory to the Father *with* the Son, together *with* the Holy Spirit'.[12] For clarity, the two doxologies are: the mediatorial doxology – 'Glory to the Father through Jesus Christ in the Holy Spirit'; and the coordinated doxology – 'Glory to the Father with the Son, together with the Holy Spirit'. The development represents a shift in emphasis from the economic to the immanent Trinity. With the loss of recognized mediation, the atmosphere became one of distance between worshippers and the God whom they worshipped. A retained emphasis on Christ's humanity could have prevented this gap. But before attempting to find a way forward (indeed, the way back), let us pause to gain a deeper understanding of why and how the mediatorial doxology disappeared.

[9] Because knowledge of God is through the gift of participation, theology itself arises out of worship. In other words, the initial movement (the first part of the parabola) is only recognized when the community is drawn into the second movement. That we can say anything at all of the God who freely chooses to move towards creation in reconciling love, indeed who freely chooses to create, is a result of fellowship with him. This is something that Geoffrey Wainwright has taught us well in his systematic theology. See *Doxology: The Praise of God in Worship, Doctrine and Life* (New York: Oxford University Press, 1980). Cf. Geoffrey Wainwright, 'Trinitarian Worship,' in *idem, Worship with One Accord: Where Liturgy and Ecumenism Embrace* (Oxford: Oxford University Press, 1997), 237–50 (246). See also Alan Torrance, 'Being of One Substance with the Father,' in Christopher Seitz (ed.), *Nicene Christianity: The Future for a New Ecumenism* (Grand Rapids: Brazos Press, 2001), 49–61 (56).

[10] Wainwright, *Doxology*, 54–57.

[11] For Jungmann's trace of the development, see *The Place of Christ*, 172–238.

[12] Or 'Glory to the Father *and* the Son *and* the Holy Spirit'. Catherine Mowry LaCugna provides a helpful summary of Jungmann's analysis: 'The liturgical development might be charted in this way. Initially praise was given to God through Christ; then, as the Arian controversies took hold, praise was directed to God (or Father) through Christ in the Holy Spirit (with the church); to the Father through the Son in the Holy Spirit; to the Father and the Son together with the Holy Spirit; to the Father, through Christ and in Christ, in the Holy Spirit; to the Father and the Son and the Holy Spirit' (Catherine Mowry LaCugna, *God for Us: The Trinity and Christian Life* [San Francisco: HarperSanFrancisco, 1991], 127). It should be noted that her summary primarily reflects the development in the East. See Jungmann, *The Place of Christ*, 191–200. The mediatorial pattern was retained much longer in the West, though here too it would eventually become overshadowed by an interpretation of 'who lives and reigns' that focused on Christ's divinity. See 209–11; cf. 221–24. This will be discussed below.

II. O God, Our Help in Ages Past: A Lesson from History

Misunderstood Mediation

Colin Gunton writes: 'Certain heresies are archetypal as attractive solutions to difficulties that are intrinsic to the faith and will therefore continue to appear in every generation.'[13] Arianism is one such heresy. As disastrous as the loss of the mediatorial pattern of worship was, equally bad was the mediatorial pattern misunderstood. Interpretation is everything. Just as the Arians used the same scriptures as their opponents, they also used the same doxology in worship. But for them, 'through Christ' meant something very different. The unqualified subordination[14] of the Arians saw Christ as a third thing, a *tertium quid*. The expression 'through Christ' implied that the Father was distant and unapproachable. In this conception, Jesus does not perform the work of the Father, but does his own work as the middle-person. Jesus is not the revelation of the Father's love, but the closest we can get to an unknowable God.

In reaction, Athanasius and others argued for the unity of God's action. There is one divine activity in which all three persons share. Those who did not believe in such unity could not affirm the consistency in the use of both the mediatorial and coordinated doxologies. For them, the coordinated doxology affirmed something the mediatorial doxology did not. In using the mediatorial doxology, they implicitly argued against the unity of God's action. St Basil the Great, who used both doxologies, was accused of confusion (indeed of heresy!). To his friend, Amphilochios, he writes:

> Lately while I pray with the people, we sometimes finish the doxology to God the Father with the form 'Glory to the Father *with* the Son, *together with* the Holy Spirit,' and at other times we use 'Glory to the

[13] Colin Gunton, 'And in One Lord, Jesus Christ ... Begotten, Not Made', in Christopher Seitz (ed.), *Nicene Christianity: The Future for a New Ecumenism* (Grand Rapids: Brazos Press, 2001), 35–48, (35).

[14] Gunton argues for a qualified subordination. He thinks it is necessary '... to do justice to the undoubtedly subordinationist elements of the biblical record'. For example, '... the Son is sent, is given, obeys, and, indeed expresses his eternal sonship in temporal or economic subordination'. This relates to his eternal *begottenness*. It is the Father who begets and the Son who is begotten. However, they are '... together one God in the *koinonia* of the Spirit. They are one because the Son and the Spirit are, in a sense, though as God, subordinate in the eternal *taxis* as they are in the economy. But in another sense they are not subordinate, for without his Son and Spirit, God would not be God' ('And in One Lord', 46–47). See also Colin Gunton, 'The Holy Spirit Who with the Father and the Son Together Is Worshipped and Glorified', in *idem, Father, Son and Holy Spirit: Essays toward a Fully Trinitarian Theology* (London: T&T Clark, 2003), 75–90, especially 77–78 and 82–85.

> Father *through* the Son *in* the Holy Spirit.' Some of those present accused us of using strange and mutually contradictory terms.[15]

Basil unashamedly used both doxologies. In a climate where parties were choosing one doxology over another, others were not so bold. In one particular case, a bishop (Bishop Leontius, 344–58) mumbled the final words of his prayer lest he offend those who used a different doxology.[16] The burden of Basil's argument in *On the Holy Spirit* is to show why his use of both doxologies is not a result of confusion. He argues that it is his attackers who are the confused ones.

The different prepositions in the mediatorial doxology cannot, argued Basil, be used to prove different natures.[17] The Son's activity is voluntary and out of love; it is not due to a lower nature: 'We must not think that the salvation the Son has won for us is the result of a slave's compulsory and subordinate service', Basil says. 'No, He voluntarily accomplishes His plan out of the goodness and compassion for His creation, fulfilling the Father's will.'[18] To say that the Son does the Father's will is not a comment about inequality; it is an expression of unity. Again, Basil's words help us to understand the meaning of the word 'through' found in the mediatorial doxology:

> When He says, 'I have not spoken on my own authority,' and 'As the Father has said unto me, so I speak,' and 'the word which you hear is not mine but the Father's who sent me' and 'I do as the Father has commanded me,' He does not use language of this kind because He is incapable of His own choice, or is lawless, or has to wait for a prearranged signal. *He wants to make it clear that His will is indissolubly united to the Father.* We must not think that what He calls a 'commandment' is an imperious order delivered by word of mouth by which the Father gives orders to His Son, as He would to a subordinate, telling Him what He should do. Instead, let us think in terms worthy of the Godhead, and realize that there is a transmission of will, like the reflection of an object in a mirror, which reaches from Father to Son without passage of time. 'The Father loves the Son, and shows Him all that He Himself is doing.' Everything the Father has also belongs to the Son[19] [emphasis mine].

[15] Basil, *On the Holy Spirit*, trans. David Anderson (New York: St. Vladimir's Seminary Press, 1980), 1.3.
[16] Jungmann, *The Place of Christ*, 175–76.
[17] Basil, *On the Holy Spirit*, 2.4–5.12.
[18] Basil, *On the Holy Spirit*, 8.18.
[19] Basil, *On the Holy Spirit*, 8.20.

The key point is this: it is wrong to think of mediation in terms of a chain of command through which tasks are administered or through which messages are sent. Yes, the Father's action is mediated through his Son and Spirit. But this is not the prevention of direct access to God, as if God is inaccessible.[20] It is rather the expression of God's one action.[21] Accordingly, Basil's use of 'with' and 'through' is entirely consistent.

Over-correction

We have seen, then, that there was an understanding of mediation that needed to be addressed. The 'through Christ' of the mediatorial doxology was understood by some in a way that did *not* affirm the unity of God's action. In reaction, the bold approach of Basil eventually gave way to the complete shadowing of the mediatorial doxology lest it be misunderstood. The developments that began in the fourth century are most evident in liturgical prayer after the fourth century.[22] The move away from the mediatorial to the coordinated doxology was made in order to correct the misunderstanding of mediation. But correction came with a cost. The emphasis on Christ's divinity would soon lead to the recession of his humanity into the background. As an example, Jungmann notes the trinitarian emphasis as it stood out on Monophysite soil and in the Gallic-Spanish area. He writes:

> This particular cultivation of the trinitarian theme in connexion with the anti-Arian attitude automatically implies a closer attention to the divinity in Christ, while the position of Mediator, appropriate to him

[20] To think that Jesus takes our prayers and passes them up the ladder is to conceive of 'through' wrongly. It is to conceive of a weakness in God. On the contrary, God sends his Son to assume our weakness. In his humanity, then, the Son prays with us. As Jungmann states: 'Christ exercises his office of Mediator in that he supports (ἐντυγχάνει) the prayer. We must, however, not now ourselves think of this support as an intercession of the Lord each time someone prays. In this sense John 16.26f. is probably to be understood, which, to be sure, was said chiefly for the consolation of the downcast disciples: "In that day you will ask in my name; and I do not say to you that I shall pray the Father for you; for the Father himself loves you." But the prayer of the individual who belongs to Christ, to his Church, gains only in him its full resonance before God ... He has indeed fellow-feeling with us. Likewise, the Church's prayers of praise to God gain meaning and value only because Christ as high priest stands at her head and joins in them ... He does not stand in the way, preventing a direct prayer-relationship between the creature and his creator, as a short-sighted criticism of the Mediator idea would suppose. But the prayer of the creature attains power and effectiveness when it is a prayer "in the name of Jesus", *in Christ*, and when it therefore arrives before God *through Christ*' (*The Place of Christ*, 137).

[21] See Gunton, 'The Holy Spirit', especially 85–88.

[22] See above, note 11.

> in his humanity, was in practice allowed to fall more and more into the background, as it was constantly misinterpreted by the Arians.[23]

Emphasizing the grandeur of Christ was not always in response to heresy; for example, titles for Christ such as 'King' and 'Saviour' were not new. The new thing was their frequent use.[24] What became problematic, however, was the move towards isolated prayer to Christ in *corporate* worship. The combination of the Son *with* the Father ('Glory to the Father with the Son') meant that prayer was now addressed to either, or back and forth to one and then the other even in the same prayer. This led to lack of clarity regarding the relationship between the Father and Son. It also meant the emphasis on Christ as Mediator was lost.[25] Back in 393, it had been precisely this fear that had caused the Council of Hippo to react against the confusion found at the popular level. In reaction to the confusion of the names of Christ and God, Father and Son, Canon 21 forbade *corporate* prayer addressed to Christ instead of the Father; and in the mediatorial formula, the Father was not to be named in place of Christ.[26] The 'straightforward' and 'unreflective nature' of popular piety[27] is, as those at Hippo noted, sometimes cause for concern. For them, addressing it meant forbidding certain forms of prayer in corporate worship. Corporate worship was to provide a check to private piety.[28] After the fourth century, however, the tide against heresy proved too strong. What, in 393, had

[23] Jungmann, *The Place of Christ*, 220. Other particular examples of this increasing emphasis on Christ's divinity are given. In the East Syrian liturgies, 'Christ appears simply as second Person of the Godhead together with Father and Holy Spirit. And at bottom, also, in most of the prayers which are directed to him, only this his divinity is in mind' (73). In the liturgies of the Byzantine region, the new prayers show a preference for addressing 'Christ our God'. Here the emphasis is on what he receives and sends down as God, that is, in his divinity (79). 'Thus the tendency is revealed to bring out the Godhead in Christ, to honour in him God *pure and simple*' (84). See 92–95 and 98–104 for similar tendencies in the liturgies of the Gallic type.

[24] Jungmann, *The Place of Christ*, 224.

[25] Jungmann, *The Place of Christ*, 225. For a counter-movement to this tendency, see 227.

[26] Jungmann, *The Place of Christ*, 169–70. Jungmann refers to A. Klawek's argument that the popular writings were probably Gnostic-Sabellian in nature which meant that the Father was thrust into the background (see 169).

[27] Jungmann, *The Place of Christ*, 214.

[28] Here it is interesting to note a point that Jungmann never denies: direct prayer to Christ was always part of private worship and in the form of hymns and acclamations. See *The Place of Christ*, 164–65, 170–71. Yet consider Jungmann's comment regarding such prayer up to the fourth century: '. . . the Christians of this early period were conscious of praying to Christ, the head of the Church, as the normal way of praying because it was the normal way of believing – and so much so that, even in private prayer, a prayer addressed to Christ was regarded as being addressed through Christ to God' (171). Its tenor, however, would undoubtedly change after the Arian controversy. This, I think, is an important point to keep in mind when considering recent research that seeks to refine Jungmann's thesis (see above, note 7).

been cause for concern regarding popular piety was now cause for concern in the context of corporate worship.[29]

With respect to Christ's role as High Priest of the Eucharist, here too the emphasis moved to his divinity. Christ has the power to consecrate and accept the offering by virtue of his Godhead.[30] In the West, the movement towards veneration of the host eventually resulted in reserve in taking the sacrament.[31] In this context, Christ – as the object of worship – was no longer seen as the advocate who enabled bold approach to the table.[32] With the loss of emphasis on Christ's humanity and his role as advocate, it is no surprise that the eucharistic atmosphere increasingly became one of fear. Graham Redding's summary of the liturgical development I have been charting serves as a fitting conclusion to this section. He writes (quoting Jungmann at the end):

> While these liturgical changes were perfectly understandable under the circumstances, they had a most unfortunate and unforeseen effect. Jungmann points out that, as the mediatorship and humanity of Christ faded into the background and Christ was thrust up into the majesty and grandeur of the Godhead, a gap emerged and came to yawn large in Christian thinking between the eternal God and sinful humanity. The worshipper was confronted immediately with the overwhelming majesty of the triune God. 'Stress was now placed not on what unites us to God (Christ as one of us in his human nature, Christ as our brother), but on what separates us from God (God's infinite majesty).'[33]

III. Our Hope for Years to Come: Recovering Lost Ground

The Cross Marks the End: The Problem of the Experiential Model

James Torrance argues that the most common and widespread view of worship is that it is something that 'we', that is, religious people, do. Jesus taught us and gave us an example of how to do it. God's grace is needed to help us in our efforts but it is, essentially, what *we* do before God: 'We go to church, we sing our psalms and hymns to God, we intercede for the

[29] Cf. note 25 above.

[30] Jungmann, *The Place of Christ*, 242–44.

[31] Initially, when prayer to Christ finds its way into the Eucharist, it is not the eucharistic presence of the Lord that is addressed; the eucharistic 'body of Christ' remains a third factor between the suppliant and Christ. The first indication of the movement towards veneration is the inclusion of the *Agnus Dei* during the fraction. See Jungmann, *The Place of Christ*, 258–59.

[32] Jungmann, *The Place of Christ*, 262–63. See especially 263, n. 3.

[33] Redding, *Prayer and the Priesthood of Christ*, 20. Cf. Jungmann's helpful summary, 251.

world, we listen to the sermon (too often simply an exhortation), we offer our money, time and talents to God.'[34] Such a view is unitarian, he argues, because it has no doctrine of the mediation of Christ and no proper doctrine of the Holy Spirit.[35]

The problem of separation (alluded to by Redding) is also the concern regarding worship understood in this way. Whatever form separation takes, it renders worship Pelagian.[36] The view outlined above expresses itself in an experiential model of worship, summed up as 'God and me', today.[37] This model '... emphasizes *our* faith, *our* decision, *our* response in an event theology which short-circuits the vicarious humanity of Christ and belittles union with Christ'.[38] This view requires a cross but – and this is key – no further work is recognized. Many who advocate (at least in practice) the view that worship is something that 'we' do, believe that their action is indeed grounded in what Christ *has* done. Mediation is important, indeed essential. However, here it is relegated to the past. In such a view, the ascended Christ is glorified along with the Father and Spirit, but there is no real sense in which that praise is made possible by the *continuing* action of Christ and the Spirit. Rather, the 'drawing up' into fellowship is something that is made possible by a work that is finished on the cross.[39] It is an exhausting model to inhabit, Torrance argues, because instead of proclaiming a gospel of grace it throws Christians back on themselves to make an appropriate response to God.[40] In this model, the mediatorial doxology has receded into the past along with Christ's finished work.

It can be argued that this model separates Christ's work from his person.[41] Many issues arise regarding the relationship between soteriology

[34] Torrance, *Worship*, 7.

[35] Torrance, *Worship*, 7.

[36] Separation has many disguises. Ironically, in much 'contemporary' worship, the fear that once characterized the atmosphere of worship has changed into a curious familiarity. FilmFour's *Dogma* comically expresses this all too prevalent phenomenon in the unveiling of the church's new recruitment tool – 'Buddy Christ', the mascot to replace the grim and no longer relevant crucifix. Misguided, of course. Where there is no cross, the gap remains.

[37] It is often this individualistic expression – 'God and *me*', today – that receives the brunt of much (deserved) criticism. Undoubtedly, the experiential model is usually expressed in this way. But even the communally minded can fall naïvely into a similar trap ('God and *us*', today) expressing themselves more as a contemporary collective rather than the *ekklesia*.

[38] Torrance, *Worship*, 18.

[39] Torrance, *Worship*, 16–18. Because there is mediation at one point, unitarian worship expressed in the experiential model actually fits a truncated *trinitarian* worship.

[40] Torrance, *Worship*, 7, 18.

[41] Torrance, *Worship*, 16.

and ontology.[42] We cannot enter into the various debates here. But in any attempt to hold being and act together, one must not collapse into the other. For our present concern, it must be said that the one who is who he is *continues* to act. We do not simply look to a person, we also need to pay attention to what this person is continuing to do. The Mediator continues to mediate.

It is Not Finished: The Once for All

The book of Hebrews describes Christ as a priest, like Melchizedek, who is a priest not through a legal requirement – like those according to the order of Aaron – but through the power of an indestructible life (see 7.11–17). Indeed it is the eternality of Christ's priesthood that makes him mediator of a better covenant. His 'more excellent ministry' (cf. 8.6) is carried out at the 'right hand of the throne of the Majesty in the heavens' where he is 'a minister in the sanctuary and the true tent' (cf. 8.1–2). Does this biblical picture not warrant a careful interpretation of the words that come from Jesus' mouth as he breathes his last on the cross: 'It is finished'?[43] Certainly something is *accomplished*, but it does not mark the end of his ministry.[44]

According to Calvin, resurrection completes what is begun on the cross. The glory of the resurrection does not draw us away from the cross because, though distinct, they go together inseparably.[45] The resurrection fulfils the purpose of the cross, revealing the cross as the door to life.[46] But although Calvin says that resurrection completes what is begun on the cross, he also speaks of the ascension as the completion of the new life. Paul van Buren argues that this is no contradiction because, according to Calvin, '... the whole work of Christ as our Substitute is one: His death in our place, His

[42] It could be argued that an overemphasis on ontology, or rather a view that conflates ontology and soteriology is problematic. In other words, although it must be affirmed that only the one who is fully human and fully divine can save, it could be argued that the 'events' themselves are made redundant if Jesus Christ simply *is* atonement. Now is neither the time to debate this nor decide how far James Torrance's argument may tend in this direction. Nevertheless, let it be said here, along with Douglas Farrow, that the issue is not whether '... Jesus is who [he] is as he does what he does, but ... the particular way in which this is construed' (*Ascension and Ecclesia: On the Significance of the Doctrine of the Ascension for Ecclesiology and Christian Cosmology* [Edinburgh: T&T Clark, 1999], 245, note 372).

[43] John 19.30 NRSV.

[44] See Douglas Farrow's article which argues for the ascension's inclusion in the atonement: 'Ascension and Atonement', in Colin Gunton (ed.), *The Theology of Reconciliation* (London: T&T Clark, 2003), 67–91.

[45] Paul van Buren, *Christ in Our Place: The Substitutionary Character of Calvin's Doctrine of Reconciliation* (Edinburgh: Oliver and Boyd, 1957), 81.

[46] Van Buren, *Christ in Our Place*, 84.

Resurrection for us, and His life with God as the new life of those for whom He died and rose.'[47]

The ascension, then, marks both Christ's experience of this new life with God and his enabling of this reality for us. How is this all *for us*? The cross is the door to life because, ironically, resurrection means Christ's death is eternal: once for all. Through resurrection, Christ's substitutionary death is eternally efficacious. In his commentary on Hebrews, Calvin writes:

> Christ so rose from the dead that, still, His death was not abolished but retains its efficacy for ever, as though (the author of Hebrews) had said: 'God raised up His Son, but in such a way that the blood He shed once for all in his death is efficacious after His Resurrection for the ratification of the everlasting covenant and brings forth its fruit just as if it were always flowing.'[48]

Here, in the language of Hebrews, the intrinsic connection of the distinct events of death, resurrection and ascension can be seen. New life made possible because of Christ's life lived, given up on the cross, and risen from the dead, is completed in the ascension to the right hand of God where Christ lives not only for himself but also *for us*.

Because Christ carried out these events *in the flesh*, they are truly *representative*.[49] Let us focus on the ascension and see how it is *for us*. We have seen, through Calvin, that the once for all is about making what *was*, continual. Therefore, our present communion with God is based on the continuation of Christ's ministry, that is, his life given as a continuing offering. Christ, because of his perfect offering of himself, is the firstfruits. He is already in full possession of that for which we hope. But this full possession is, in its continuation, also the basis for our being drawn into it. Christ, therefore, does not sit out merely as an example for us; as representative he is Saviour.

Christ Our Intercessor

Charles Wesley captured Christ's continuing intercession in this way: 'Five bleeding wounds he bears, received on Calvary. They pour effectual prayers; they strongly plead for me.'[50] How is it that Christ's wounds

[47] Van Buren, *Christ in Our Place*, 85–86.

[48] Quoted in Van Buren, *Christ in Our Place*, 82.

[49] To die in the flesh but rise in any other way would mean that representation stops short at the cross. If so, then we are to be pitied indeed! With reference to Ephesians (1.20; 2.5–6, 19) and Philippians (3.20), Calvin believed that not only life but also the opening of the heavens – for us – is in view. See Van Buren, *Christ in Our Place*, 87–88.

[50] From the hymn, *Arise, My Soul, Arise*, which Wesley wrote in 1742.

intercede for us? In understanding his offering as both firstfruits for him *and* the basis of assurance for us, how are we to interpret what is to be our confident approach to the inner sanctuary? Here we gain a glimpse of the mystery of the cross. We are forced to look from a variety of angles. No one statement, model or idea can contain all the truth that is there for us to grasp. Try as we might, a penal element cannot be avoided – careful as we must be in articulating it. But, as stated at the outset of this essay, the cross does not save us *from* a life of obedient, sacrificial love. It saves us *to* such a life. The cross may have been the wages of humanity's sin, which Christ vicariously took upon himself for our sake. But it was also the fullest expression of his obedience – the fullest expression of his life given up for others, a life we are called to imitate. The offering was given in an act that can be articulated as the consequence of sin. But the offering *itself* is good. And in the resurrection and ascension, it is affirmed and recognized as such. The eternal offering, then, is not simply to be understood as the eternal efficacy of Christ's death in terms of the wages of sin. It is also to be understood as the continual offering of the obedient life lived. In one sense the offering, viewed as consequence, is something we are saved from. But through the resurrection and ascension, we are also drawn into the offering as *life-giving*.

Therefore, we are to look at intercession in (at least) a twofold way. First, sin does not mark the way of those who walk in the light. The author of 1 John says: 'My little children, I am writing these things to you so that you may not sin.' But he continues: '. . . if anyone does sin we have an advocate with the Father, Jesus Christ the righteous'.[51] Jesus sits at the right hand of the Father as our eternal advocate. The offering that was given is continued as it is '. . . forever held up before God on our behalf'.[52] But second, we are drawn in to share what is offered. Christ's whole life of obedience (and is this not what we have defined as worship?) is the offering that is brought into the inner sanctuary. We are to join in this offering. This means that our worship is really a joining in Christ's worship. If we fail to look from both angles, we risk seeing a distorted picture. Without the emphasis on participating in the offering, we are left with the image of the Father

[51] 1 John 2.1 NRSV.

[52] Van Buren, *Christ in Our Place*, 89. According to Calvin, the initial offering and its continuation at the right hand of the Father comprise the two parts of Christ's priesthood (90).

averting his eyes away from us.[53] Instead the image – or should we say sound – is that of a mighty eucharistic chorus: the many, in their particularity, gathered to the one.

The Continuing Priestly Role: According to Divinity or Humanity?

In an attempt to address a modern guise of separation (arguably one of the costs of ancient over-correction), I have argued that Christ continues to mediate at the right hand of the Father. We turn now to T.F. Torrance's essay, 'The Mind of Christ in Worship: The Problem of Apollinarianism in the Liturgy',[54] in which Torrance stresses Christ's ongoing priestly role.[55] Against what we have seen as the experiential model of worship, Thomas Torrance stresses that our worship is a participation in heavenly worship.[56] By the Spirit we are joined to Christ who, as the writer of Hebrews insists, *continues* to be our *Leitourgos* – the leader of our worship. But what is important here is not simply that Christ continues to work. Understanding the 'who' of this work is essential. The mediating Christ who sits at the right hand of the Father is fully human. His humanity is essential to his

[53] This is arguably another misconstrual of mediation. Although Calvin spoke of Christ averting the Father's eyes, this was from our *sin*, not from us. The Father does look on *us*, but *in Christ* rather than *in ourselves*. This is supported by Calvin's rejection of the idea that Christ stands midway between us and the Father, begging for our deliverance. See Van Buren, *Christ in Our Place*, 90–91.

[54] T.F. Torrance, 'The Mind of Christ in Worship: The Problem of Apollinarianism in the Liturgy', in *idem, Theology in Reconciliation: Essays Towards Evangelical and Catholic Unity in East and West* (London: Geoffrey Chapman, 1975), 139–214. The last writing Colin Gunton prepared for press before his untimely death was a collection of essays including one on T.F. Torrance's doctrine of God. In it, he writes: 'As always, there are resources in Torrance's work which are waiting to be developed. One of his papers which has long continued to work in my mind is that on "The Mind of Christ in Worship. The Problem of Apollinarianism in the Liturgy"' ('Eastern and Western Trinities: Being and Person. T.F. Torrance's Doctrine of God', in Colin Gunton, *Father, Son and Holy Spirit: Essays toward a Fully Trinitarian Theology* [London: T&T Clark, 2003], 32–57 [54]). I came across Gunton's words, incidentally, while preparing this essay for publication. As a student in his research seminar, it is my hope that in honour of his memory, this essay will count as a development he would have welcomed.

[55] Torrance is also dependent on Jungmann's work, though he argues that a subtle Apollinarianism is also at the root of the loss of the mediatorial aspect in the liturgy. It is not my aim to argue the case for one or the other. However, it would undoubtedly be easier for those who affirmed a gap explicitly through liturgical expression to do so if there was no belief in a real union in the first place. Whatever the main root of the shift (and why not say both factors are at work?), what one says about the nature of the hypostatic union certainly determines what can be said about the notion of 'Christ *with* us', whether pre- or post-ascension.

[56] Torrance, 'The Mind of Christ in Worship', 139–40.

mediation. Here Torrance engages with Nicolas Cabasilas. Torrance argues that although Cabasilas, in his *Commentary on the Divine Liturgy*, affirms the mediating, priestly work of Christ on our behalf, '... he consistently assimilates the priestly and mediating activity of Christ to his divine activity, and does not show evidence of Athanasius' or Cyril [of Alexandria]'s point that as the incarnate Son comes to us *as man*, it is *as man* that he fulfils his office as Mediator'.[57] Cabasilas writes:

> [Christ] is Mediator between God and man, not by his words or prayers but in himself.... To think that his intercession is always made through the prayers of the liturgy is rank blasphemy and folly. For even if it is true that Christ performs the sacrifice, we cannot attribute everything that is said and done throughout the liturgy to him. He alone accomplishes the special work and purpose of the liturgy – the consecration of the offerings and the sanctification of the faithful; but the prayers, supplications and demands which surround these rites are the acts of the priest. The first are the works of the Lord, the rest the work of servants; the latter pray, the former answers prayer. The Saviour gives, and the priest offers thanks for what has been given; the priest offers, and the Lord accepts what is offered. Our Lord, it is true, offers too, but he offers himself to the Father, and also the gifts, when they have become his Body and Blood. It is because he offers himself that he is described both as Offering and Offerer, and as the receiver of the offering; he is as God the offerer and receiver, and as man the offering. But as regards the bread and wine, when they are still simply gifts, it is the priest who offers them and the Lord who receives. What does he do in receiving them? He sanctifies them, and turns them into his own Body and Blood; for it is the true nature of receiving to appropriate a thing to oneself, so that it becomes in a sense oneself, as we have said before. That is how Christ celebrates this sacrifice; in this his Priesthood consists.[58]

At the outset, Cabasilas says that Christ is Mediator between God and humanity *in himself*. Because he is both God and human, the two are united. Is this the ontological knot that prevents us from separating Christ's work from his person? And does this not meet any concern regarding the loss of Christ's role as a human? Here it is worth mentioning Jungmann's perceptive note regarding Cabasilas's use of 1 Timothy 2.5 ('There is one Mediator between God and men, the man Christ Jesus').

[57] Torrance, 'The Mind of Christ in Worship', 194.

[58] Nicholas Cabasilas, *Commentary on the Dirine Liturgy* 49 (trans. J.M. Hussey and P.A. McNulty; London: SPCK, 1966), cited in T.F. Torrance, *Theology in Reconciliation* (London: Geoffrey Chapman, 1975), 194–95.

When Cabasilas cites it in his explanation of the liturgy, he omits the Word 'man'.[59] In light of this and Torrance's concern over a priesthood that is only rendered by Christ in his divinity, what might Cabasilas mean when he says that '. . . [Christ] is as God the offerer and receiver, and *as man* the offering'? (emphasis mine).

Obviously, Cabasilas affirms a continuing role. It is apparent that he also affirms a continuing humanity. So what is the basis for concern? According to Cabasilas, Christ is Offerer and Offering because he offers himself, indeed himself a human. But how far does this offering of himself still include us? It only includes us once our offering (whether it be the bread and wine or our prayers) is *received* by him. Then, he appropriates it to himself and, once appropriated, it becomes part of his offering of himself. If this is a correct interpretation of Cabasilas, then the concern becomes clearer. What Torrance wants is a continuing priesthood that sees Christ alongside us, a fellow worshipper, even now in the midst of the congregation praying alongside us. This qualifies the notion of Christ offering prayer on our behalf. It cannot be an offering based on a prior receiving (in the manner of 'we give' and 'he takes'). Remember, Cabasilas says that Christ offers our gifts and prayers, but only after first receiving them and appropriating them to himself. We might want to quibble – if Christ offers our gifts and prayers and does so as a human, is there really a problem with the idea that he does so through receiving and appropriation? The problem is simply that it is not incarnational, in which he takes what we are too blind to see and incapable of giving. The problem is that, in this picture, Christ does the receiving and appropriation according to his divinity.[60] Is there not a risk here of viewing Christ's continual priesthood in a Nestorian way?

'Through' or 'With'? The Case for a Mediatorial 'With'

Before leaving Thomas Torrance, his critique of Basil should be noted. This brings us back to the discussion of the two doxologies. Again, for clarity, the mediatorial doxology as used by Basil is 'Glory to the Father through the Son in the Holy Spirit'; the coordinated doxology is 'Glory to the Father with the Son, together with the Holy Spirit'. First a bit of background. Not only is Torrance wary of the change to a solely

[59] Jungmann, *The Place of Christ*, 242, note 3.

[60] As Torrance states: 'Christ himself has been thrust up into the majesty of the Godhead in such a way that he is regarded as too exalted to be associated with the prayers of the liturgy which are "couched in language befitting servants"' ('The Mind of Christ in Worship', 195).

coordinated doxology, he is wary of a mediatorial doxology that only includes a mediatorial 'through' and not also a mediatorial 'with'.[61] So far, we have only seen the word 'with' in the context of the coordinated doxology. What, then, is meant by a mediatorial 'with'? According to Torrance, to use only the word 'through' affirms Christ's *past* role but it does not necessarily affirm his *continuing* role. To use also the word 'with' ensures that he is believed still to be amidst the congregation, offering up prayer with his brothers and sisters. The inclusion of 'with' is an antidote, if you will, to the experiential model of worship.

Here Torrance wants to add to Jungmann's analysis. He states:

> Prayer through the mediation of Jesus Christ the High Priest in the full sense, gives place to prayer on the basis of the high-priestly work of Christ ... The reason for this, however, is to be found not only, as Jungmann implies, in the Cappadocian reaction to Arianism, but in a comparatively underdeveloped understanding of the vicarious role of the incarnate Son along the line that runs from Athanasius to Cyril, together with a further development of the doctrine of the Trinity as three *hypostaseis* in one *ousia* in respect of the coequality of the Son and Spirit with the Father, which resulted in an overshadowing of the mediatorial aspect of prayer by the doxological.[62]

[61] He looks to ways in which the mediatorial and coordinated formulae were brought together. (To avoid confusion, it should be noted that where I have followed others in distinguishing between 'mediatorial' and 'coordinated', applying them both as adjectives to 'doxology', Torrance simply contrasts 'mediatorial' with 'doxological'. Thus what I have called 'coordinated' he calls 'doxological'.) He states: 'Athanasius' conclusion to the *De incarnatione* was typical of the underlying theological structure: "... Jesus Christ our Lord, *through* whom and *with* whom, to the Father *with* the Son himself in the Holy Spirit ..., be honour and power and glory for ever and ever. Amen." Variations upon this combination of the mediatorial and doxological formulae in which care is taken to retain a *mediatorial "with"* alongside of a *mediatorial "through"* and a *doxological "with"* are found throughout all the works of Cyril [of Alexandria]. Sometimes they are given a more extended form, and sometimes they are found in a more reduced or succinct form in which the "*with whom*" is clearly intended to be both mediatorial and doxological. It is usually in a succinct form that the mediatorial and doxological "*with*", together with a mediatorial "*through*", is found in the liturgies, especially those of old Alexandrian and old Roman provenance. On the other hand, the elision of the mediatorial "*with*" with the doxological "*with*" tended to have the effect of weakening the mediatorial "*through*", especially when the whole concept of praying and worshipping *with* Jesus Christ dropped out of sight. Thus the retention in a liturgy of an unambiguous mediatorial "*with whom*" along with a mediatorial "*through whom*" may well be taken as an indication that the old classical understanding of Christian worship, at least in its Athanasian-Cyrillian form, remains intact. That is surely the abiding significance of the oblatory formula of the old *Ordo Romanus*: "Through him and with him and in him is to thee God the Father almighty, in the unity of the Holy Spirit, all honour and glory"' ('The Mind of Christ in Worship', 187–88). To place this within the development charted above (cf. note 12), see Jungmann, *The Place of Christ*, 192–93, cf. 28–30.

[62] Torrance, 'The Mind of Christ in Worship', 189–90.

This is where he critiques Basil, saying that although Basil argues for a mediatorial 'through', '. . . he does not seem to be aware of a mediatorial "with" in the liturgy'.[63]

I want to offer a more sympathetic reading of Basil that will lead us into the final section of this essay – the implications of the ascension. The burden of *On the Holy Spirit* is to affirm the deity of the Holy Spirit. Therefore, any discussion of how it is that Christ is one with humanity is incidental. There are hints of it. But first, Basil's use of the preposition 'with' needs to be understood in context. According to Basil, both 'with whom' and 'through whom' are appropriate to use concerning the Son in the doxology. The first is appropriate for giving him praise, the second for giving thanks. (Here, then, Torrance's critique appears justified.) Before looking at chapter 7 where Basil makes this explicit, let us jump ahead for a moment to chapter 26 where the context is an explanation of the use of the preposition 'in' regarding the Holy Spirit. In paragraph 63, Basil states:

> The Spirit is said to dwell *in* created things in many and various ways, but as far as His relationship to the Father and the Son is concerned, it is more appropriate to say that He dwells *with* them, rather than *in* them. Those who are worthy receive His grace, and He works with*in* them. However, we cannot contemplate His pre-eternal existence and permanent presence with the Son and the Father unless we search for words which suitably express such an everlasting union. Truly precise *co-existence* can only be predicated of things which are mutually inseparable ... Whenever the union between things is intimate, natural, and inseparable, it is more appropriate to use *with* since this word suggests an indivisible union. On the other hand, in situations where the grace of the Spirit comes and goes, it is more proper to say that the Spirit exists *in* someone, even in the case of well-disposed persons with whom He abides continually.[64]

Basil is making a distinction between the relationship that the Holy Spirit has with the Father and Son, and the relationship the Holy Spirit has with us. Can we deduce anything from this regarding the Son? One could say that this very passage supports Torrance's argument. That is, we should use the word 'with' regarding our relationship to Christ because Christ united himself to humanity in the incarnation. But I do not think the objection holds. Basil would surely not deny the indivisibility of Christ's

[63] Torrance, 'The Mind of Christ in Worship', 190.
[64] Basil, *On the Holy Spirit*, 26.63; original italics throughout.

union to humanity in this sense. It is the basis on which he uses the preposition 'through'. Basil's point is that the Holy Spirit's relation to us is different from his relation to the Father and Son. Surely we *must* say this, in some sense, regarding the incarnate one. His relationship to the Father and Spirit is different from his relationship to us. That is the main point.

And here we come back to chapter 7 where the context is not that of the Holy Spirit but the Son. Yes, Basil thinks 'with whom' is appropriate for giving glory whereas 'through whom' is appropriate for giving thanks. But listen:

> Whenever we reflect on the majesty of the nature of the Only-Begotten, and the excellence of His dignity, we ascribe glory to Him *with* the Father. On the other hand, when we consider the abundant blessings He has given us, and how He has admitted us as co-heirs into God's household, we acknowledge that this grace works for us *through* Him and *in* Him.[65]

Note the last phrase – not only *through* him but also *in* him. Could not the preposition 'in' reflect the kind of dynamic, continual mediation that Thomas Torrance seeks in his plea for the preposition 'with'? Knowing why Basil opts for 'in' instead of 'with', it is at least plausible.

Basil does not – in the doxologies – use the preposition 'with' in a mediatorial sense. Nevertheless, there is certainly a dynamic feel to what he says elsewhere. He uses words to describe Christ's place in the Trinity (for example, 'Son', 'Only-Begotten', 'Wisdom', and so on) and contrasts them with words used to describe his relationship to creation (for example, 'Shepherd', 'King' and 'Physician'). These latter titles refer to how Christ satisfies the needs of creation. Listen to what he says in chapter 8 and see if there is not a sense of a dynamic, continual work:

> Those who flee to His ruling care for refuge, and through patient endurance correct their evil ways, He calls sheep, and He acknowledges Himself to be the *Shepherd* of those who hear His voice, refusing to listen to strange teachings. 'My sheep hear my voice,' He says. He is *King* of those who have risen to a higher way of life, submitting themselves to their lawful ruler. Because He leads men through the narrow gate of His commandments to the practice of good deeds, and because He securely shuts in those who through faith in Him find shelter in true wisdom, He is the *Door*. Therefore He says, 'If any one enters by Me, he ... will go in and out and find pasture.' Because He is

[65] Basil, *On the Holy Spirit*, 7.16.

a mighty fortress for the faithful, an unshaken and unbroken bullwark, He is called *Rock*.[66]

This passage reflects a dynamic relationship between Christ and his followers. That it affirms a continual mediating role is further supported by Basil's words at the outset of the paragraph from which the excerpt is taken. With reference to the Apostle Paul's use of 'through Jesus Christ' or 'through whom' (for example, Rom. 1.5, 8; 5.2), Basil says: 'He speaks here of the kindnesses which the Son has bestowed on us; *sometimes* He *carries* these good gifts of grace from the Father to us, and *other times* He *leads* us to the Father through Himself' (emphasis mine).[67]

There is one last piece of evidence I would like to use in support of Basil. It is found in chapter 28 and is already explicit in the chapter's title: 'Although Scripture describes men as reigning together *with* Christ, our opponents will not allow this word to be used concerning the Spirit'. Here Basil refers to Colossians and speaks of being alive together *with* Christ. Although Basil is not here making an argument for a mediatorial 'with', it is nevertheless explicit in the context of, and a necessary premiss for, the argument he *is* advancing. What he says here serves as a suitable transition to the final section of this essay. He writes:

> Did God give to the Church and to an entire race the gift of life *with* Christ, if the life *with* Christ has nothing to do with the Holy Spirit? If it is impious to even think such a thing, is it not reverent to confess our faith in those who are closely united by nature? What a boundless lack of common sense! These men confess that the saints are *with* Christ (since Paul most assuredly says that he would rather be away from the body and at home with Christ, and that his desire is to depart and be with Christ), yet they dare refuse the Spirit even the communion that Christ shares *with* men[68] [emphasis mine].

IV. God is Gone up on High with a Triumphant Noise

In a Manner Present and in a Manner Absent

We have been considering Christ's mediation, acknowledging the importance of expressing it in a way that recognizes its continuation. In

66 Basil, *On the Holy Spirit*, 8.17.

67 Basil, *On the Holy Spirit*, 8.17.

68 Basil, *On the Holy Spirit*, 28.69. Basil is not arguing for the deity of humankind when he says that we are 'with Christ'. Rather, he is in effect saying that if we – mere mortals – are united to Christ and express such communion as 'with Christ', then it is ridiculous not to allow 'with' to be used regarding the Spirit's relationship to Christ.

this last section, it remains to consider more carefully the nature of a mediatorial 'with'.

At the outset of his work, *Ascension and Ecclesia*, Douglas Farrow states: 'To grapple with the mystery of the [presence and absence] is indeed ecclesiology's constant challenge. Where either side of that mystery is neglected the mystery of the church itself is undone.'[69] Farrow's work guides us through the various ways in which this tension has been at best underplayed and at worst dissolved. Farrow does not deny Christ's presence, but he continually stresses that we must understand it in the context of Christ's real absence. In a battle against various abstractions, Farrow affirms a concrete context in which to make sense of the mystery: the Eucharist. The church affirms Christ's real absence through the cry: 'Maranatha!'[70] The affirmation that 'the Lord is here' is said within a prayer that also proclaims his death until he comes.

Farrow refuses to set the 'Where?' question aside. He writes: 'Carelessly asked, as at Sinai, it already betrays a fatal lack of interest in its subject. Diligently asked, it helps to elicit an answer about who that subject is, whether we should still be expecting him, and what we should be doing in the meantime.'[71] After discussing various answers that tradition has given to the 'Where?' question, Farrow offers his own:

> The answer we have been advocating is a disturbing one. It is not disturbing because, in maintaining that Jesus has gone in the flesh to the Father, it refuses to admit that 'we do not know what has happened to him.' On the contrary, it is disturbing because it states quite categorically that we do not know; that we cannot place him, spatially or temporally or materially or spiritually, *with respect to ourselves*[72] [emphasis mine].

It is this last phrase that is to be heeded. It sums up the case Farrow has set out to make, marking the end of a long journey that began with the recognition of 'Two Histories'.[73] If we are to proclaim a real presence, we will have to do so in a context that recognizes the divergence of Jesus'

[69] Farrow, *Ascension and Ecclesia*, 3.

[70] This is the burden of Farrow's argument in 'Confessing Christ Coming', in Christopher Seitz (ed.), *Nicene Christianity: The Future for a New Ecumenism* (Grand Rapids: Brazos Press, 2001), 133–48.

[71] Farrow, *Ascension and Ecclesia*, 267.

[72] Farrow, *Ascension and Ecclesia*, 267.

[73] This is the subtitle of the second section of his first chapter. Farrow, *Ascension and Ecclesia*, 7.

history from our own. Jesus stands over-against us. The ascension, then, has implications for the articulation of a mediatorial 'with'.

Christ Our King

Here, then, is where we might want to offer a nuance to Thomas Torrance's plea for a mediatorial 'with'. There is only room here for brief reflections which I hope to develop elsewhere. In arguing that the ascension is also substitutionary – that is, also *for us* – Calvin was careful to articulate this in a way that affirmed Christ's lordship. Christ is our substitute only as our Lord. Again, he is not just example but Saviour. Is this where we might want to emphasize not only Christ's priesthood but also his kingship?[74]

Psalm 110 is helpful here, for it emphasizes both offices. Here the ascension is understood in terms of enthronement.[75] When the church proclaims that 'Jesus is Lord', it – in Farrow's words – '... set[s] the alarm bells ringing in the palaces of Caesar'.[76] Such proclamation deprives all other rulers of any claim to direct authority.[77] This psalm, then, presents us with an image that helps us understand the key phrase highlighted above: 'with respect to ourselves'. Indeed, Christ stands over-against us. The psalmist also proclaims that 'God has gone up with a shout'.[78] But who is this God, and what is the nature of his triumph?

Here we look one last time at the church's liturgical development. The shadowing of the mediatorial pattern of worship did not happen in the West until about the sixth century. The shift in emphasis is evident in a particular interpretation of the 'who lives and reigns in the unity of the Spirit' that ended the Canon of the Mass. Instead of this being interpreted in terms of the transfigured God-human who lives, exalted, to make intercession for us, the phrase was increasingly taken over by those who used it in terms of his consubstantial union with the Father. The transition to understand Christ's 'reign' solely with respect to his divinity was underway.[79] The trinitarian interpretation which referred 'living and

74 Torrance does indeed recognize Christ's threefold office elsewhere. I believe he would, therefore, support my thoughts here. They are offered as a nuance to what he says in *this* context.

75 Farrow helpfully states: 'Of course, we may rightly speak of an enthronement already on the cross, for this is how Christ exercises his kingship among us. Yet on the cross he is still the king in exile. God has another and better throne for his Son than the one we devised!' ('Confessing Christ Coming', 236 n. 15).

76 Farrow, 'Confessing Christ Coming', 138.

77 Farrow, 'Confessing Christ Coming', 139.

78 Psalm 47.5 NRSV.

79 Jungmann, *The Place of Christ*, 207–10, 221–23.

reigning' to the Godhead of Christ led to small but significant changes. New endings were formed in which the 'living and reigning' was said simply of God. Jungmann summarizes: 'Parallel with the decay of prayer through Christ, or, where it was already firmly rooted, the decline in its esteem, the theme of the glorified head of the Church receded.'[80]

I have argued that Christ's kingship, along with his priesthood, must be maintained in any articulation of a mediatorial 'with'. To recognize Christ's kingship is to recognize that he stands (indeed reigns) over against us. But this recognition cannot involve a denial of his humanity.[81] Liturgical development has once again served to illustrate the dangers of articulating Christ's role outside the context of his humanity. Attention to the theme of the 'glorified head' must never recede. It helps us to take both offices into account. Christ is our head in the sense that he lives and reigns over against us. He is not just representative, he is Lord. But the head must be one with its body. In this sense, then, he is not just Lord, but representative! Therefore, in acknowledging Christ's kingship we must not see his divinity outside the context of his humanity – he is still God *as a human*.

Paul employs another of the psalmist's images: 'When he ascended on high he made captivity itself a captive.'[82] This is his triumph, a triumph *for us*, indicative in Paul's twist: 'he gave gifts to his people'.[83] Gifts can be given *because* booty has been taken. But the gifts are not equal to the booty; that is, the gifts are not booty that is simply re-distributed. By *taking* captivity captive, he *gives* us the freedom to be truly human. He transforms what has been damaged and tainted, and gives it back to us anew. His giving is therefore dependent on his *oneness* with us but also his triumph *against* all our self-claims that have made us captive.[84]

80 Jungmann, *The Place of Christ*, 222–23.

81 With reference to the 'disturbing' answer to the 'Where?' question, Farrow says: 'It is disturbing because it challenges the assumption that to talk about a human being who cannot be so placed is meaningless, and because it implies that every attempt to define him as something *other* than a human being is really an act of violence designed to force him to yield his meaning on our terms' (*Ascension and Ecclesia*, 267).

82 Eph. 4.8 NRSV (cf. Ps. 68.18).

83 Eph. 4.8 NRSV (Ps. 68.18 reads: '... and receiving gifts from people').

84 Here the context of 'giving' is kingship. Could we not also see here the other side of his *priesthood* – the God-humanward dimension which is nevertheless dependent on his being God *as a human*?

We Are 'With' Christ

When the church acknowledges the divergence of Jesus' history from its own, that is, when it refuses to place Jesus in any respect to itself, the church recognizes what the world has not: the provisionality of its existence.[85] Here, then, is the nuance I would like to offer to the discussion of a mediatorial 'with'. Instead of saying that 'Christ is with us', perhaps it would be better to say – this side of Christ's departure – that *we are with Christ*. Yes, we should look for more than 'through' *if* this word deals solely with something in the past. But our affirmation of 'with' needs to reflect divergence as well.

Does Christ pray with us or do we pray with him? It is not necessarily the same thing. The latter seeks to emphasize the upwards call of the liturgy: 'Lift up your hearts' – *sursum corda!* In Calvin's words, the one who would throw into question our hope of being in a manner present with Christ, 'nearly drags Christ down'.[86] What, indeed, is prayer? Graham Redding states: 'As the Spirit bring[s] us into personal union with Christ, so our lives are joined to his and we share in his eternal life of prayer before the Father. Prayer, therefore, is not a form of self-expression and wishful thinking. It is not a chat with God. It is nothing other than being united through the activity of the Spirit with the prayer of Christ.'[87]

It is indeed the Spirit who unites us to the absent one and makes him 'in a manner present'. Recognition is the gift of the Spirit. We recognize Christ as Lord only as we are united to him by the Spirit. In being united to him we also recognize what it means to be truly human. We learn this and become this as we are taught Christ's prayer. And we will not know Christ's prayer unless the Spirit guides us in praying it, that is, lifts us up that we might share it.

V. Conclusion: From Story to Doctrine – The Required (but Tricky) Shift from Economy to Theology

We have explored liturgical development in the early centuries, showing that it resulted in a glorifying that shifted in emphasis from the economic to the immanent Trinity. The shift brought with it an atmosphere of distance and the experience of separation. As detrimental as this was for the

85 Farrow, *Ascension and Ecclesia*, 3, cf. 268.

86 Quoted in Van Buren, *Christ in Our Place*, 88.

87 Graham Redding, 'To Whom Do We Direct Our Worship and Prayer … And Does It Matter?', *Stimulus* 9.3 (2001): 5–10 (7).

church's worship, we have seen that the shift makes sense when the doctrinal climate in which it arose is considered. But doctrinal differences aside, is this not a legitimate and even necessary shift? The economy leads us to an account of the God whose economy it is. Through the economy we come to understand that salvation can only be accomplished by the God who created and is therefore distinct from his creation. It was the conviction of both Irenaeus and Athanasius that the Son is mediator of redemption *and* creation.[88] Against those who do not see that it is necessary to make the shift,[89] Colin Gunton remained firm in his conviction that we have to move from the economic to the immanent lest the two collapse and God is no longer who he is other than in relation to his creation.[90] Creation must remain the free act of the one who is who he is apart from that which he creates.

Nevertheless, the order – from economic to immanent – is essential. If this order is not maintained, theology becomes mere speculation.[91] That is to say we can only speak *truthfully* of the immanent Trinity by means of the economic Trinity. Gunton writes: 'Our topic has to do with the eternal Trinity – with whom the Father and Son are eternally, and what their relationship may be. But once the conception breaks free from the economy, from what happens in time, the dangers of abstraction present themselves in full force.'[92] Certainly sonship is not limited to the economy, Gunton argues, but neither can it be construed apart from it.[93]

That the mediatorial pattern of worship moved to one that fully recognized the unity of the Godhead is, in and of itself, not a problem.

[88] Gunton, 'And in One Lord', 42–45.

[89] Gunton cites LaCugna as an example ('And in One Lord', 230, n. 14). For his argument, see the preface to *The Promise of Trinitarian Theology* (Edinburgh: T&T Clark, 2nd edn, 1997), xi–xxxi. His critique makes the reader aware of the overall context in which one finds LaCugna's summary of the liturgical development charted by Jungmann (see above, note 12).

[90] Gunton argues that the doctrine of the immanent Trinity also '... serves as a foundation for the relative independence and so integrity of worldly reality ..., and thus for human freedom. It is because God is a communion of love prior to and in independence of the creation that he can enable the creation to be itself' (*The Promise*, xviii).

[91] Although we cannot know 'from the inside' the nature of the Triune relations, we affirm that they are such that when opened up *ad extra*, God is revealed as he is in himself. This is not to argue that our knowledge is exhaustive, but only that it is true. For example, the Son does indeed reveal the Father, and in such a way that we come to know that there is, in the immanent Trinity, no Father but the Father of the Son and no Son but the Son of the Father. The God who opens himself to be in relationship with us is also the God who, in his very being, is relational. See Wainwright, 'Trinitarian Worship', 245–47. Cf. Gunton, 'And in One Lord', 45–47. See also Torrance, 'Being of One Substance', 50–56.

[92] Gunton, 'And in One Lord', 37.

[93] Gunton, 'And in One Lord', 40.

Indeed the Son and, as later affirmed, the Spirit are worthy of worship. But the move from economy to theology must not involve a move towards worshipping an abstract divinity. This is a concern shared by those who might otherwise disagree.[94] As Catherine Mowry LaCugna states: 'Praise is never rendered to an abstract unity of three coequal divine persons.'[95] With reference to the second person of the Trinity, Gunton states: 'The only begotten Son is also the lamb who takes away the sin of the world. The one who is the object of the worship of heaven in Revelation is the lamb bearing the marks of slaughter upon him. It is not a Logos with no relation to Jesus whom we confess.'[96] We have seen that liturgical development after the fourth century was not strong in maintaining this relation. As LaCugna summarizes: 'The one who unites us to God now becomes infinitely distant from us, taking his place "at the right hand of the Father" not as exalted Lord but as preexistent Christ.'[97]

As stated at the outset of this essay, theology arises from worship.[98] That is just another way of arguing that we move from economy to theology. We must, as argued, be on guard against abstract theology. But we must also be diligent in recognizing abstract worship.[99] For the latter betrays a vicious cycle, viz., when theology, which arises out of worship, is abstracted from the story in which that worship coheres, worship itself becomes abstract. In such a situation, we not only fail to give an appropriate account of God, we risk idolatry.

Worshipping some other God than the God who has made himself known is not gospel- or grace-centred worship. That is the issue that has occupied the heart of this essay. The Son, who rightfully comes to be recognized as consubstantial with the Father and therefore worthy of equal worship and glorification, must not be so projected into the majesty of the Godhead that his humanity *and all it means for him to be one of us* is lost. In other words, although we come to recognize that our God is *freely* and not *necessarily* related to us, it is nevertheless a fact that God *has* chosen to create *and* draw his creation to himself. The incarnation is intrinsic to this

[94] Gunton and LaCugna, for example, whose disagreement lies in whether or not, given such dangers, the move should be made.

[95] LaCugna, *God for Us*, 120.

[96] Gunton, 'And in One Lord', 44.

[97] LaCugna, *God for Us*, 126. See also Wainwright, *Doxology*, 63.

[98] See note 9.

[99] Wainwright concurs: 'The trinitarian name and doctrine is precisely *not* an abstract formula. It belongs to a living context. It must be kept firmly attached to the historical revelation through the telling and retelling of the story recounted in Scripture' ('Trinitarian Worship', 247).

free act.[100] And it is not a temporary event. God's desire was not simply that we come to some epistemic awareness. Rather, the 'content' of knowing God and recognizing who God is, is participation in his life of love. This never ceases to be the gift of the Father mediated by his Son and Spirit. The story must ever be told this way for this is the reality of the story. The ascension affirms this story and ensures that the Son's humanity is not lost but is the continuing basis of our communion with God.

How, then, can we – along with Basil – happily use both the mediatorial and coordinated doxologies? For we want to maintain that Christ is indeed one with the Father and with the Spirit. The way forward is surely to affirm continually Christ's humanity, especially as we move to a recognition of his divinity. For whenever and however we make such a move, we are not recognizing one who ceased to be human, but one who is continually the God-human, God *as a human*. His enthronement does not mark the end of his humanity, creating a gap between us and God. Rather, he continues to be *the man*[101] through whom we come to God. Indeed, by the Spirit, we are in a manner present *with him*, giving glory to the Father.

[100] It can certainly be argued that this is so regardless of whether or not creation fell subject to sin. That it did fall means that revelation entails reconciliation. But as to the importance of the distinction, see Douglas Farrow's critique of Barth in *Ascension and Ecclesia*, 296. Cf. 229–54. Farrow's critique (296) is within a discussion of 'Exaltation and Pre-existence' (Appendix B, 281–98), which deals with the question of the *logos asarkos*. Whichever side one takes in the debate, the point I am making here can be affirmed: the one through whom we come to the Father is none other than the God-human, the man Jesus Christ.

[101] I am grateful to Christina Gshwandtner who read an initial draft of this essay and made many helpful comments, one of which was a plea for inclusive language where it was lacking. My use of 'man' in this context is a deliberate attempt to affirm Christ's particularity as Jesus of Nazareth, who is not just a human, but a man. If we rob him of his particularity, we take away the possibility of the many – humanity in its particularity as male and female – being gathered, in its particularity – to the one.

Chapter 10

Christ for Us – Yesterday and Today: A Response to 'The Person of Christ'

Christoph Schwöbel

I. 'Who is Jesus Christ for us Today?'

Dietrich Bonhoeffer's question which has dominated much of the Christological discussions of the twentieth century has lost nothing of its relevance and urgency at the beginning of the twenty-first century. It is nor a question about the ongoing relevance of Christ's message, nor a question about 'what' Jesus Christ might be for us, but a question about the *identity* of Jesus who is confessed by Christians as the Christ in such an exclusive sense that the title-term 'Christ' has become a proper name in Christian worship, proclamation and discourse. The question, as Bonhoeffer phrases it, is an ontological question, a question about the *being* of the one whose identity is evoked by the name Jesus Christ. It is not a question about the function of Christ or a question about the ongoing effects of his work but a question that raises the crucial issue of being. Furthermore, the being of Christ is immediately introduced as a relational form of being: Christ is 'for us' so that in talking about the being of Jesus Christ we are automatically affected in our being by his being. Bonhoeffer pointedly puts the question in the present tense and underlines this by the temporal index 'today'. In this way it is stressed that the question about the identity of Jesus Christ is not a historical question in the sense that it is directed at a person from the past whose identity is doubtful and has to be established by critical historical research.

Bonhoeffer's question presupposes a situation of co-presence between us, the ones for whom Christ is who he is, and the present Jesus Christ.

If Bonhoeffer's question is understood as the guideline for Christological inquiry, as all of the papers in this volume implicitly do, Christology is not the analysis of an inert, lifeless and distant object that remains the passive material of experimental probing. Rather, it is the engagement with a living, active person with a specific identity whose manner of being is such that it determines our identity and our being. The urgency of Christological inquiry lies in the fact that the identity of Jesus Christ determines our identity as Christians, that the being of Christ shapes the being of God and our being as human beings created in the image of God, and that his presence is the space in which our present is constituted. This urgency, however, echoes the promise on which the enterprise of Christology is built. In understanding Jesus Christ – this is the presupposition from which Christology proceeds – we learn to understand our identity, we can gain access to understanding our being and, consequently, are enabled to live and act according to who we are by virtue of Christ. Our present is disclosed to us as the present which is shaped by the way Jesus Christ is personally present to us. The 'whence' of our present, where we come from, and the 'whither' of our being, our ultimate destination, is in this way shaped by Christ's present, yesterday, today and forever. If Bonhoeffer's question is taken as the guideline of Christological inquiry, the classical doctrines of Christology, the doctrines of the person and work of Christ and the doctrine of the two states of Christ – the state of exaltation and of humiliation – have to be understood as specifying the conditions of the actuality of who Christ is for us today and so as defining the possibilities of Christological discourse.

II. From Method to Matter: The 'Given' of Christology is the 'Self-Giving' of Christ

Much of the Christological debate of modernity is taken up by debates about the 'method' of Christology. What is the starting-point of Christology, the access to all Christological inquiry? This question is usually phrased in terms of alternatives: Should Christology proceed 'from above' or 'from below'? Should its focus be the *Christus praesens* of the experience of faith or the historical Jesus? Should Christology be developed from a soteriological perspective, because – as Paul Tillich and others claimed – 'Christology is a function of soteriology', or must soteriology be governed by Christology so that our experience of what Christ has done for us is controlled by who Christ is? These methodological issues can easily be seen as partial refractions of the reality of Jesus Christ as the subject-matter of Christology. However, they put asunder what the incarnation has joined together. If it is true that the Word was made flesh, can we still separate 'above' and 'below' as alternative starting-points? Is it not the point that the full reality of what is 'above' has been disclosed to us 'below' so that in Jesus Christ we have access to God the Father through the Spirit – on earth as it is in heaven? If it is true that Christ is the same, yesterday, today and forever, the one to whom the Father speaks eternally and who eternally responds to the Father in the communion of the Spirit, the *Christus praesens* and the Jesus of history are not alternative starting-points but aspects of the comprehensive reality of the incarnate Son who now sits at the right hand of the Father. And if it is the point that the one who is exalted on high has no other history than that of the man Jesus, any account of the presence of Christ must refer to the Jesus of history and any reconstruction of the history of Jesus has to start from his presence to the Father and the Spirit and so from our present as it is shaped by that history. And if the very being of Jesus Christ is being by the Father and in the Spirit, coequal with the Father and the Spirit, and so being for us, if the being of Jesus Christ is disclosed as grace and truth, is it not the case that soteriology cannot provide another starting-point for Christology than Christology itself, because in Christ there is no graceless being and no grace somehow distinct from his being? The disjunction between being and meaning, which was the reason why some Christological conceptions in the twentieth century focused on the existential meaning of Christ as opposed to a supposedly objectivized account of his being and which is the background for the thesis of the primacy of soteriology over Christology, seems to contradict a theological understanding of the being of Christ and the being of Christ for us. If Christ is the Son of the Father in the communion of the Spirit, the meaning of his being is rooted in these relationships, and if every created being is destined for communion with the triune God and thereby enabled to find the meaning of its existence, being can only be divorced from meaning in the act of contradicting God's will of communion by positing another meaning, another destiny for created being.

Once we understand the different 'starting-points' of Christological method not as alternative routes for doing Christology but as different but related aspects of the actuality of the person of Jesus Christ, these starting-points highlight the way in which the 'given' of Christology is the dynamic of Christ's self-giving. This turn from method to matter involves – as John Webster demonstrates in his essay – a description in which we try to trace the modes of Christ's self-giving as the subject-matter and methodological guideline for Christological reconstruction. The person of Jesus Christ as the subject-matter of Christological reflection remains the subject of the process of understanding since this understanding, that is, Christology, is a response to the way Christ gives himself to us. The methods of Christology are therefore prescribed by the manner of Christ's self-presentation for us. In this self-presentation the historical story of Jesus and the present reality of Jesus Christ are inextricably interwoven and form a dynamic unity in which the different aspects of the being of Christ are held together.

The self-presentation of Christ occurs through the means of creaturely communication. The witness of Jesus' word, work and person is continued through the word of Scripture witnessing to Christ and offering the promise of Christ. This promise contains a reference back to the story of Jesus' life and death, thereby holding fast to the identity of Jesus as it is narrated in the story of his life as the story of the constant interaction with God the Father in the Spirit. But, as every other promise, it contains a reference to the future, to the way in which Christ will hold fast to his promise and bring about its fulfilment. This promise for the future is contained in the belief that what Jesus has done and has suffered has once and for all established and disclosed the true relationship of the triune God to his creation. The Spirit who authenticates the word of Scripture as it is communicated in Christian witness to us and thereby establishes the link to the story of Jesus which occurred at a specific point in time and space is the same Spirit who is the 'perfecting cause' of all God's agency in whom God's ways with the world will achieve their ultimate goal. This goal is achieved precisely by the Spirit authenticating the word of Scripture to us and so enabling our faith which is a form of being in which we are conformed to Christ and oriented towards the future fulfilment in the Kingdom of God. Christ's *promise* is fulfilled by his *presence* in the word of preaching and in the visible words of the sacraments. Therefore the promise does not point to an outstanding fulfilment but gives us already a taste of the future consummation of God's communion with his reconciled and perfected creation. Our present is therefore the space that we inhabit between the coming of Christ and Christ's second coming to bring the fulfilment of God's communion with creation. In between Christ's coming in Jesus and Christ's second coming to judge the world in order to disclose the ultimate truth and offer the ultimate grace which is the foundation of the Kingdom of God, our present is constituted by the fact that Christ himself fills that interim by becoming present to us in the word of Scripture in proclamation and in the visible words of the sacraments. The 'given' of Christology is the self-presentation of Christ in order to constitute our present.

III. Christ in Trinitarian Context

A complete account of the self-presentation of Christ as the subject-matter of Christology already shows the open frontiers between Christology and trinitarian reflection. This not only applies to the complex interchange between Christology and the doctrine of the Trinity in the history of doctrine where the basic tenets of trinitarian dogma had to be defined in order to enable theologians to formulate the Christological problem with any precision; it also applies to the conceptual forms in which Christological issues are cast. Cutting the links that bind the doctrines of the Trinity and of the person and work of Christ together always seems detrimental for both of them. Treated in abstraction from Christology, the doctrine of the Trinity tends to become speculation on the immanent relations within the Godhead while losing touch with the concrete history of God's trinitarian self-disclosure. Similarly, Christological reflection tends to get lost in the intricacies of the relations of the two natures of Christ if the framework of the relations between the Father, the Son and the Spirit are no longer seen as that which defines the hypostatic identity and communal essence of God. It must clearly be kept in mind that the primary form in which the divinity of Christ has to be understood is the communicative relationship he has with the One he calls Father, a relationship which is mediated from the Father to the Son and from the Son to the Father by the Holy Spirit. Likewise, the primary form in which Jesus Christ's humanity must be understood is not in terms of the possession of a human nature but as the concrete story of a human life, initiated in relationship to God and ending in relationship to God and in between enacted as an ongoing conversation with God. Only when these relations are characterized as such which express the co-equality between the persons in relation, only on the presupposition of the *homoousios* do we get to the question to which the doctrine of the two natures attempts to provide an answer. But once we have arrived there it is important not to leave the questions and insights of trinitarian theology behind. A Christology that construes the actuality of the person of Christ only in terms of the relationship between the eternal Son and the incarnate Christ or exclusively in terms of an explication of the relationship of the two natures in one person is bound to run into difficulties. Christ never comes alone. The coming of Christ always occurs in the Spirit and always relates us in the Spirit through the Son to God the Father. To talk about the divinity and the humanity of Christ is always an abbreviation suffering from premature abstraction, because it obscures the fact that divinity is mediated only in the relationships to the Father and the Spirit and that humanity refers to the concrete human life of Jesus in which these relationships are enacted in the spatio-temporal events of a biography beginning and ending with God.

The whole range of Christological issues treated in the papers of this volume time and again refer to the trinitarian framework of Christology. If Christ's divinity is understood in terms of his relationship to the Father in the Spirit it must be understood concretely as Sonship to the God of Israel whom he calls Father and whose identity is accessible only in his self-identification as Israel's God which is continued, vindicated and expanded by his identification in the Son. And if Christ's humanity is the humanity disclosed in a concrete life-story, the question of Jesus' baptism which is addressed in Murray Rae's essay is indeed a very pertinent one. It shows that in living a concrete human life, in taking the place of humanity in estrangement from God the incarnate Son, although he is never a stranger to the Father, is dependent on the guidance of the Spirit; indeed receives his mission from the Father as mediated by the Spirit and completed in the Spirit. The declaration of Jesus as the Son by the Father and the descent of the Spirit upon him belong closely together and they testify that the relationship by which Christ's divinity is constituted is mediated in the forms that are constitutive for a human life. If we press the matter further we have to say that not only the act of the constitution of the person of Christ, the *unitio personalis*, effected by God the Father and mediated by the Spirit, is a trinitarian act of God, involving as the Creed resolutely maintains, the action of the Spirit in order to establish the relationship between the incarnate Son and God the Father. The unity of the person of the Son, the *unio personalis*, the ongoing personal union in which the divine and the human 'nature' are brought into union is also maintained in and through the relationships with the Father and the Son. Without the Father and the Spirit Jesus Christ is not a person.

Even the most cursory look at the New Testament witnesses in their variety provide ample evidence that the trinitarian framework of Christology in modes of discourse relating Jesus to the Father and the Spirit is much more in evidence than any unspecified talk about his divinity or his humanity. This has one important effect for the enterprise of doing Christology. Developing Christology within a trinitarian framework makes it easier to keep the development of Christological reflection close to the witnesses of Scripture.

IV. The Language of Christology: Modes of Response

If we look at the varieties of Christological discourse in the New Testament and in the Christian tradition we can see that there is Christological language in a variety of forms and on a number of interrelated levels. All modes of expression have a responsive character. They are tentative answers to the question that is raised by Jesus' life and message and by his death and resurrection: Who do you say that I am? Jesus' life is a provocation in that it offers an interpretation of God and of what it means to be human which challenges received authority. The provocation, however, consists in the fact that it is a new interpretation of what people believe they know already. It is not simply a new revelation of a different but novel way of understanding everything that is known about the same God people already believe in and whose law they observe. Therefore, the accusation of heresy or even blasphemy is never far away. But Jesus' message and the story also challenges the way people understand themselves before God. The provocation lies in the combined challenge to the understanding of God and the understanding of what it means to be human. Both are so bound up with the person of Jesus that responding to his message means taking a stance with regard to his person. The provocation does away with comfortable escape routes. That has to do with the eschatological urgency of Jesus' message. If the imminent coming of the Kingdom is the organizing centre of Jesus' message and if his proclamation is indeed part of the process of the coming of the Kingdom which has already started, then this implies that all questions raised in that connection cannot be deferred but require a response. Again it is clear that since Jesus' person is always involved in his message, responding to his message means taking a stance with regard to his person. The testimony of Jesus' life and death therefore has the form of a personal address that cannot remain unanswered. The specific authority claimed in this address is that it claims to be eschatologically ultimate in a sense in which only God's address could claim eschatological ultimacy. Therefore God is the context in which the text of Jesus' witness is to be understood. And Jesus is the context in which God becomes the text for human understanding. If one focuses on this character of Jesus' life's witness one can see how the specific characteristics are carried over from his proclamation to proclamation about him. Continuity is provided by the twofold contextualization where God is the context for understanding the text of Jesus' life and destiny and Jesus is the definitive context in which to understand the text of God's story and being. Christology in all forms is such a provoked response to the testimony of Jesus' life and death.

The forms of Christological discourse which we find in the New Testament and which, in connection with the exposition of more than a century of New Testament research, are comprehensively introduced in Richard Burridge's essay and display a variety of forms of acclamation, predication and narrative of different kinds. For a long time research focused almost exclusively on Christological predications and the use of title-terms; now, attention to narrative with special reference to the forms of ancient biographies plays a significant role. From a systematic perspective there need not be an alternative between predications and narratives since they fulfil a different function. One relatively simple way to organize Christological discourse is to see it as consisting of three levels or layers where the higher ones do not simply supersede the lower ones but provide criteria for their interpretation.

The first layer is that of the basic Christological predications, the guiding Christological metaphors, and the foundational Christological narratives. The narratives have the function of identity-definition: They respond to the question 'Who is Jesus?' They answer the question by telling scenes from Jesus' life which have a disclosive function for his identity. In telling the story the listener can grasp who Jesus is. What is characteristic about these stories is that they portray Jesus' identity as an open identity, one that is not self-referentially closed but determined by a relationship to another who is often addressed as 'Father'. The identity-defining narratives of Jesus always contain a 'God-component': they tell a story about Jesus, but in this story Jesus interprets God, obeys the will of God, addresses God in filial intimacy or abject dereliction which displays a similar familiarity, does things only God can do, that is, forgive sins, but does this not in competition to God but as a fulfilment of God's will for his creation. Who is Jesus? Jesus is the one who stands in a unique relationship to God so that through him God becomes actual in the stories that are told of Jesus. The identity-defining stories fix the referent of Christological predications.

Of this referent, Jesus, various predications are made: he is the Messiah, the Son of Man, the Son of God, the Son of David, the Saviour, the Kyrios, and so on. These predications can have the form of a second-person acclamation or a third-person predication. They answer the question: What is Jesus? But just like the identity-defining narratives they contain an important relational element in saying what Jesus is in relation to God's people of Israel, in relation to those who are in bondage and in need of liberation, those who await the coming of the Son of man, and so on. In this way Christological predications are always oblique self-predications of those who utter a Christological predication. All these predications have eschatological ultimacy. After Jesus there will not come another who is also a Messiah, and there will not be another saviour; there will be no need for another sacrifice. If he is the eschatological sacrifice, then he can also be the protological sacrifice, because what is ultimate is also what is first, before the sequence of temporal events takes its course. The eschatological ultimacy carries with it the claim of the sufficiency of what Jesus is and does. If he is the eschatologically ultimate Saviour, then salvation in him is sufficient; there is no other ground of salvation than Jesus. The eschatological ultimacy and soteriological sufficiency have a curious effect on the language that is being used. Jesus is the *Kyrios* clearly sounds metaphorical, a working with the juxtaposition of two realms of meaning. However, if Jesus and no other is the *Kyrios*, then this metaphorical character is literalized by its realistic interpretation. There is no other *Kyrios* and all the other *kyrioi* are at best *kyrioi* metaphorically, to be measured against the one through whose story the meaning of *Kyrios* is literally fixed. These two basic forms of Christological discourse, identity-defining narratives and predications employing title-terms, are clearly complementary and so the Christological predications often occur in narrative identity definitions.

The second layer of Christological discourse organizes the different predications and identity-defining narratives by retaining them and subsuming them under a 'master model' and a 'master story'. The most popular master models in early doctrinal development are 'the Son of God' and 'the Word of God' whose relationship is a complex story. The 'master story' is the story of the incarnation which can be told in a variety of ways. The master model specifies the correct use of the primary Christological predications and makes it possible to retain them in this way. The master story provides the overarching narrative which brackets all the other identity-defining narratives. It is characteristic for this second layer that it can both be used in a Christological sense, that is, in talking about the Son of God, and in a theological sense, as in discourse about God the Son. The same applies to the master story. The story of the incarnation can both be told as a story about the Logos being made man and as a story about God whose Logos who was with God and is God becomes incarnate. On this second level the crucial interaction between trinitarian and Christological discourse is located. It is important to note that this second level does not replace the first-level predications and stories. Rather, by providing a framework for their use which has a criteriological function, it helps to retain them.

The third level is the level of technical terms in Christology where the *homoousios* is located and concepts such as *ousia*, *hypostasis*, *physis*, *persona* and *natura* are employed. They seek to clarify the ontological import of Christological discourse on the first two levels. In doing so these concepts are employed to determine the ontological status of Christ in relation to God and in relation to humanity. Thereby they are placing Christ in a comprehensive framework for the interpretation of reality. Now, in Christology it has seldom, if ever, worked well to find a location for the reality of Christ in an existing ontological scheme. Rather, the reality of Christ demands strategies of conceptual re-formation which, in the case of Christian theology, has led to decisive modifications of the view of reality which are nevertheless expressed by using existing concepts but employing them in novel ways. This is not merely the playground for those with a speculative interest in technical philosophico-theological questions. Rather, it is in the field of these concepts that the reality of Christ is interpreted as constitutive for what is really real. The question of the *communicatio idiomatum* is a typical question for this level. In spite of the technical character of these questions they are not merely subject to criteria of semantic coherence and logical consistency. Rather, they have to be tested over against the reality that is first expressed in the predications and stories of the first level and then the ordering master models and master stories of the second level. This is how technical discussions remain in touch with the reality they are trying to capture conceptually. Conceptual re-formation is therefore the reflective echo of the reality of Christ's self-presentation. Douglas Farrow's reflections on the relationship between 'nature', 'freedom' and 'necessity' are a typical exercise of conceptual re-formation.

The *homoousios* is a good example of this. When it was first introduced it had a devastating demythologizing effect. By stating that Christ, the incarnate Son, is of one essence with the Father and of one essence with us, it excluded any account of Christ as a superman, divinized humanity, or as a demi-god, humanized divinity. And with the ontological precision demanded by this act of conceptual re-formation it depopulated the world of ancient mythologies. Divinity does not come in lesser degrees than the full possession of the divine essence, and humanity is not capable of a gradual ontological intensification in the direction of the Divine.

However, the question must be raised whether the enterprise of conceptual re-formation went far enough in Christology. The Chalcedonian definition provided the fundamental rules for discourse about the two natures attempting to depict the reality of the one person of the incarnate Lord, but many attempts to give these rules material content seemed to lead again along the road of heresy. Is the process of conceptual re-formation still an unfinished task when it comes to Christology?

V. *Communicatio idiomatum*: The Attributes of a Communicating God and of Responsive Humanity

The question whether the task of conceptual re-formation has gone far enough is particularly pertinent in one area of Christological reflection: the doctrine of the *communicatio idiomatum*. For a long time this doctrine was seen as a veritable theological antique, on display for those with an interest in the quaint world of Lutheran-Calvinist polemics in the sixteenth and seventeenth centuries in 'The Olde Curiosity Shoppe' of doctrinal history. The two treatments in this volume by Robert Jenson and Stephen Holmes not only demonstrate that there are still flames to be kindled from old doctrinal disputes but that the problem of the *communicatio idiomatum* is both at the heart of the question, which constructive material statements in Christology follow from the Chalcedonian Definition, and at the centre of the question of the interrelationship between Christology and the doctrine of God.

Classical Christology starts from two major premisses. The first is the conviction that only God can save. The rift between humanity and God, the estrangement that made humans the enemies of God, can only be overcome by God himself. If humans had the power to bridge the abyss between God and his fallen human creatures the creatures themselves could claim to be God-like or divine. The promise of the serpent from the narrative of Genesis 3, the counter-promise of the gospel, would have become true. If salvation consists in communion with God only God can graciously grant that communion. Salvation is therefore a gratuitous gift. The sole authorship of God in all matters pertaining to salvation and the sovereignty of God's grace belong together. We can call this the principle of sole divine authorship in salvation. The second is the conviction that if the rift between God and humanity concerns human beings in their entirety, the whole relational structure of what makes humans human, then every dimension of humanity must be healed by being reunited to God. If the alienation from God leaves no part or aspect of being human unaffected, then the whole of fallen humanity must be taken into communion with God. This second maxim was famously phrased by Gregory Nazianzen in the slogan, 'The unassumed is the unhealed'. We can call this the principle of complete assumption. If the contradiction against God pervades all aspects of being human, then salvation from the state of contradiction must embrace every aspect of what it means to be human.

If both principles are applied to the understanding of Christ, two points must be made simultaneously. On the one hand, the Saviour cannot be less than God otherwise we would not be saved. Any notion of a semi-divine mediator is in this way effectively excluded. The Saviour must be *vere Deus*, truly God and no other than God. On the other hand, salvation must comprehend the whole reality of what it means to be human. Anything other than complete assumption would leave a remainder that is not saved. Therefore the Saviour must be *vere homo*, truly human and nothing other than human.

The two principles, however, are merely abstractions from what the gospel narratives tell us. When they relate the reality of salvation in Jesus they tell the story of one who speaks God's word in granting forgiveness, who does God's work in healing the wounds of creation and who also shares everything that makes humans human – apart from sin – thereby demonstrating that being in contradiction with God does not belong to human nature so that humans can be saved without being transubstantiated into something that is not human. There is a consistent emphasis on the unbroken divine agency in Jesus' story and a respective stress on the unbroken continuity of a life lived in the conditions of human existence. Are these two emphases, represented in the gospels in unbroken relation, truly compatible or will they always tend to produce contradictory reconstructions of the person of Christ so that the emphasis on his divinity calls the authenticity of his humanity into question or that the stress on his humanity challenges whether he is truly divine. The doctrine of the *communicatio idiomatum* addresses this question within the framework of Christological conceptuality that had developed by the fourth century and that has remained normative throughout the long history of Christian thought. It is, however, important to note that stating the problem of the *communicatio idiomatum* in terms of the conceptuality of 'classical' Christology already presents us with a problem. The way in which the *communicatio idiomatum* is conventionally defined sees it as the communication of attributes of one of the two 'natures' of Christ, the divine and the human, in the unity of the one person of Christ. This, however, presupposes that we know what the divine nature and what the human nature are so that we can specify which attributes can legitimately be communicated from one to the other. This presupposition is by no means unproblematical. Can we know what the divine nature is *remoto Christo*, apart from Christ? Is not Christ the definitive disclosure of God so that speaking of what makes God God, that is, God's 'nature', cannot rely on pre-established notions of divinity but must attempt to reconstruct the understanding of God's nature and its attributes from God's self-disclosure in Christ? And can we know what it means to be human *remoto Christo*, apart from Christ? Is not Christ the definitive disclosure of the human destiny because it is in the image of Christ that we recognize what it means to be created in the image of God so that we cannot rely on pre-established notions of humanity but must try to reconstruct the understanding of human nature and its attributes from the disclosure of true humanity in Christ?

When we look a little more closely at the presupposition that we already know what a divine nature and a human nature are in reflection on how and to what extent their attributes can be communicated, we discover that it contains even more tacit assumptions. The most important of them is the assumption that divinity and humanity must be construed in terms of contrast. Divine nature must surely have the character of being impassible whereas human nature is, as we know only too well, characterized by passibility. Human nature whenever it is exemplified is surely defined by being restricted to one location in space whereas divine nature is not restricted to any one location in the created cosmos but stands in equal relation to all of them, which would constitute omnipresence. Correspondingly, human nature is clearly characterized by finitude, a restricted possession of the extension of time, whereas divine nature must be capable of transcending the temporal restrictions of created existence. Once these tacit presuppositions are spelt out it becomes clear that if the question of the *communicatio idiomatum* is defined in terms of preconceived notions of divinity and pre-established views of what it means to be human it is in danger of failing to do justice to the point of the Gospel story, namely, that it is the story of one who does the work of God and does so in living a human life. Once we apply concepts of divinity and humanity that are derived *remoto Christo* to the reality of Christ we are in danger of missing that very reality. In doing so we question the two principles that control the reflections of classical Christology, the principle of sole divine authorship in all matters pertaining to salvation and the principle of complete assumption of the conditions of human existence.

Both approaches to the question of the *communicatio idiomatum* in this volume try to avoid this pitfall. They take their starting-point from opposite sides of the confessional divide in discussing the question of the *communicatio idiomatum*. Jenson resolutely holds fast to the Lutheran position in the debates of the sixteenth and seventeenth centuries, maintaining that in all constructions of the *communicatio idiomatum* the unity of the person of Christ, the sole referent of the Gospel story, must govern what can be said about God and about humanity. Holmes, on the other hand, attempts to show that it is the specifically new contribution of Reformed Christology as presented in the theology of John Owen which enables us to hold fast to the authentic humanity of Christ without in any sense denying his full divinity. The emphases of both essays repeat the classical contrast between the Alexandrian and the Antiochene schools of Christology. Where Alexandria insisted on the integration of the two natures in the one person of Christ to the extent of talking about one 'nature' during the incarnation in the sense of one undivided concrete reality of Christ's life, Antioch stressed the integrity of the two natures. In the two essays the old controversy flares up again: Can the integration of the person of Christ be stated while maintaining the integrity of his humanity and divinity?

Both essays work within the framework of a trinitarian theology for Christology. For Jenson, doing justice to the Gospel story requires that we unhesitatingly see the story of Jesus as the life of the Son so that we have to see the statement *unus ex trinitate passus est*. The *communicatio idiomatum* is therefore not a strategy for resolving a problem raised by the Gospel story and its insistence that this story has only one referent without having to revise our notions of divinity and humanity. It is the fact that requires to govern all our Christological and trinitarian reconstructions. Jenson summarizes his point in this way: 'So the *fact* of the communicatio is that the mutual plot of the divine life, the ensemble of the "processions" as they are called, is determined by what happened with Jesus of Nazareth between his conception by the Virgin and his Ascension to the Father. And the pay-off is: *this* life is the life that creates all that is and that will fulfil all that is. If we want to know how reality is constituted, we must read the Gospels.' For Holmes, following Owen's view that 'the only singular immediate act of the person of the Son on the human nature was the assumption of it into subsistence with himself' which has the personal union of Christ as 'the only necessary consequent of this assumption', maintaining the radical distinction of the two natures opens up the way of understanding the story of Jesus as 'a work of the Holy Spirit in the life of a human being'. Both points are Christological *and* trinitarian: For Jenson, the story of Jesus is the self-identification of God the Son who has no other history than that of Jesus so that the narrative of 'Jesus-in-Israel' is 'God's self-determination as the particular God he is'. For Holmes, holding fast to a radical distinction of the two natures and restricting the immediate work of the Son on Jesus to the assumption of a human nature into subsistence with the Son and to its immediate consequent, the personal union, opens up a way of restoring the significance of the Holy Spirit to the doctrine of the person of Christ. This, in turn, points to the continuity between Christ's humanity and ours since being in communion with God the Father depends for Jesus as much as for us on the work of the Spirit. Both points are trinitarian and

Christological and both presuppose a version of the *enhypostasia* of the humanity of Christ in the person of the Son.

Let us try to rephrase these emphases a little. In the story of the Gospels the way in which Jesus relates to the God he calls Father are truly human relations *and* they are truly divine relations because it is in these and no other relations in which the relationship of the Son and the Father is exercised. This leads to the dialectical statements: (1) The ways in which God the Son relates to God the Father are truly human relations, and (2) The ways in which Jesus relates to God the Father are truly divine relations. The relationship between the Father and the Son, however, are always mediated by the Spirit. And this applies to both sides of the relationship: the Father relates to the Son in the Spirit and the Son relates to the Father in the Spirit. By rephrasing the Christological statements in this relational way we can see that what the story of the Gospel requires is to understand the divinity of Jesus in terms of his unbroken filial relationship to God the Father which is mediated in the Spirit. Jesus' divinity is his Sonship and not anything in addition to or apart from his Sonship. Where this Sonship is exercised, be it in the way the Father relates to Jesus as he is conceived by the Holy Spirit and is born of Mary, as he suffers and dies and is raised on the third day and ascended to heaven; be it in the way Jesus relates to God the Father by praying to him, by offering his forgiveness, by submitting to his will in free obedience – there is the divinity of Christ. The way this Sonship is exercised in being born like any other human being, in experiencing all the conditions of humanity, in suffering and in death and in being dependent on the action of the Father in the power of the Spirit to be raised to eternal life – there is the humanity of Christ. Both principles of classical Christology, the sole authorship in all matters pertaining to salvation, and the principle of complete assumption can be satisfied by such an account.

The difficulty for Christology arises where the divine 'nature' is understood as something other and independent of the relationships of the triune divine life. But what should divinity be apart from the communion of the Father, the Son and the Spirit? What divinity is, is constituted in these relationships and in no other way. This also applies to humanity. The difficulty only arises where we introduce a non-theological understanding of what it means to be human. But what are humans apart from their God-given destiny to be created in the image of God and of fulfilling this destiny as God's daughters and sons by the power of the Holy Spirit in communion with the triune God? For humans to attempt the task of self-definition apart from their relationship to their creator is the definition of sin. One could well speculate whether the intractability of the problems of

Christology comes from replacing the self-identification of God for humanity and the definition of humanity destined for communion with God in the story of the Gospels with the strategy of negative theology of speaking of God by denying everything that characterizes created existence. The old debate whether the finite is capable of comprehending the divine or whether it is not mirrors the logic of speaking of the infinite God by negations. What the story of the Gospels tells us neither confirms the slogan *finitum capax infiniti* nor the slogan *finitum non capax infiniti*. Rather, it tells that and how *infinitum est capax finiti*.

But what about the complementary doctrines of *anhypostasia* and of *enhypostasia* to which both essays by Jenson and Holmes refer? Here again the need for conceptual re-formation arises. Jenson reformulates the statement that the human nature of Christ has no other hypostasis than that of God the Son and, conversely, that the human nature of Christ has hypostatic identity only in the hypostasis of the Son by using the language of the theatre: '. . . the *part* which the Son plays in the triune drama is the life and the fate of the man Jesus'. Jesus' role in history is, consequently, none other than the role he plays as the Son of God in the drama of the triune life. We can also express that in the language of narrative. The point of the story of Jesus is the point of his story in the trinitarian life. Jesus' story has no other point, for example an independent point in human history, apart from this point in the divine story. This anhypostatic statement must at once be reversed into the enhypostatic form: the point of the human story of Jesus is its point in the divine story.

Following these reflections we can take up the question of the *idiomata*. What does the *communicatio idiomatum* say about the attributes of God? Simply that they are communicated and hence have to be understood in a precise Christological sense, *propter Christum*, as communicative attributes. Luther's famous discovery in the interpretation of the meaning of 'justice of God', as he describes it in the preface to the first volume of the *Opera Latina*, was that it should not be understood as the justice we acquire actively and which God then acknowledges, but that it should be understood as the passive justice through which God makes us just by faith. Luther understood this as the key to language about God's attributes in the biblical writings. The work of God is what God works in us; the power of God means our empowerment by God, God's wisdom the way in which God makes us wise and so on. The logic of the divine attributes is a logic of communication. If one asks what is the theological basis for such a view, one is inevitably directed to Christology. The logic of communication presupposes a logic of *exchange* which Brian Horne so elegantly identifies as the core of Charles Williams's Christology in his essay. The *unio hypostatica* of divinity and humanity in the person of Christ is the presupposition for the *mirabile commercium*, the wonderous exchange, between Christ and the sinner in justification in which Christ takes our place as sinners and we are invited to take his place as the one who is just, so that *propter Christum*, because of the Son, we as justified sinners are called to be God's daughters and sons. The *communicatio idiomatum* in Christology in this way becomes the key to the understanding of the attributes of a communicating God and of the attributes of a responsive humanity.

VI. Patterns of Worship and Patterns of Being in Communication

The concerns of technical Christology as they come to the fore in a discussion on the *communicatio idiomatum* and of Christological concepts such as 'nature' and 'hypostasis' are never independent from the way in which worship is celebrated in the name of the triune God. This occurs in the expectation that in worship the trinitarian God addresses us from the Father, through the Son in the Spirit so that we can direct our praise, our thanksgiving, our petitions and our laments to the Father through the Son and in the Spirit. This interrelationship between liturgical practice and the practice of theological reflection is particularly significant with regard to the person of Christ. In the early Church some of the most significant Christological innovations came from the way Christ was addressed in worship and raised questions which Christological theory attempted to answer. Conversely, one of the most significant tasks of the agreed formulae of doctrinal decisions was to regulate the practice of worship. Technical Christology is in many cases only an attempt to clarify what Christians do when they address Christ in prayer and liturgical acclamation and to spell out the implications of the practice of worship. Technical Christology is a test-case for the practice of worship and, perhaps more importantly, the practice of worship is the test-case of our Christology.

Offering a conceptual reconstruction of what happens in worship should never be reduced to giving an account of a merely human activity. One of the great points of consensus in the theology of the Reformation, thereby recapturing something that informed the practice of worship in the early Church, is that worship is, first and foremost, a service that God performs for us, a gift that is given to us in order to enable us to relate to God and to one another in the way appropriate to the way God relates to us.

In her paper 'The Ascended Christ: Mediator of our Worship', Sandra Fach retraces the steps by which the place of Christ in liturgy was conceived in such a way that his humanity seemed to lose its significance. This, in turn, led to the loss of the liturgical significance of Christ's priestly role. Against this backdrop she argues for regaining the significance of Christ's continuing mediatorial role and with it the significance of his humanity in the unity of his person. This, however, can only be achieved if the fully relational character of worship is retained or, if it is necessary, recovered in a situation where worship has become abstracted from the Gospel story. This is apparent where the glorification of the immanent Trinity is offered at the expense of the way the Trinity is disclosed in the divine economy. This inevitably means that the liturgical practice of the Church is separated from the biblical witness to God's self-identification and self-interpretation. The place of Christ in worship is a good example of this. If the divinity of Christ is exalted above his humanity, the mediatorial role of Christ tends to be forgotten. Christ's divinity is consequently understood only in terms of the possession of the coequal divine nature and not in terms of the relationship of God the Son to the Father who in his mediatorial role relates to us in such a way that we can dare to address the infinite God as Father, Christ's Father and our Father, in the power of the Spirit.

Fach's reflections illustrate a point of trinitarian theology that is Christologically central. God as God *is* in the immanent relations of the Godhead has disclosed himself to us in such a way in the divine economy that this constitutes a true self-disclosure of the triune God. Christ as Christ *is* in relation to the Father and Spirit must therefore include the way in which Christ is for us. Any Christological ontology offering an account of the being of Christ must therefore include both the relations of Christ to God, the Father and the Spirit, and the relations of God, the Father and Spirit in Christ for us. Because Christ's being for us is part of his being, Christ's self-giving is a part of the eternal life of God. Only in this way can we be certain that in encountering Christ for us we relate to the eternal Trinity. It follows that the incarnation is not an episode in the story of the trinitarian God but a continuing reality in that the humanity of Jesus in the unity of his person is now forever part of the eternal life of God. If it is forever part of the eternal life of God it cannot be an accident in the history of the trinitarian life of God, occasioned by the fact of human sin, but must be part of God's story from the beginning – a point that is also powerfully expressed in Charles Williams's Christology as Brian Horne depicts it. We can therefore offer glory to the Father *with* the Son, *together with* the Holy Spirit because we can offer glory to the Father *through* Jesus Christ *in* the Holy Spirit because God's self-giving *from* the Father *through* Jesus Christ *in* the Holy Spirit enables us to relate to God as he is in himself for us in worship and in theological thought.

This argument rests on the presupposition that worship is ontologically significant. It relates to the triune God on the basis of the way the triune God relates to us and in this way it defines the being of the communion of the Church through its acts of worship. The ontological significance therefore not only refers to the being of the triune God and, in our context, to the being of Christ, but also to our being. Worship enacts who we are: before the triune God and in relation to one another. The patterns of worship and the patterns of being in communion form a coherent whole. All conceptual re-formation must occur within the bounds of this coherence.

These reflections on the ontological import of trinitarian worship illustrate that the language of the liturgy is misunderstood if it is seen as a linguistic expression about states of affairs which also exist apart from being spoken. As the liturgy shows, word and being are not separate realms; they are intricately connected. The biblical witnesses present themselves as the record of a divine–human conversation which begins when the world is spoken into being by a God who is the Word he speaks, and by the Spirit who makes this Word understood. This is particularly significant in Christology because Christ is God's word to creation, the Word incarnate. And Christ is God's word as the Word that God is. Many of the difficulties in Christology, as in trinitarian theology, result from treating being and word in sharp contradistinction. Any way forward must understand God's being as communicative being and God's word as that which posits being and so precedes being.

In his essay, Douglas Knight offers a sketch of a complete re-formation of Christology in the paradigm of divine speech. In the framework of a trinitarian theology that proceeds from the axiom 'God is his speech', Knight reformulates the inner-trinitarian relations, the conversation which the triune God *is*, and the conversation which the trinitarian God *has* with his creation the being of which subsists in being spoken by God and which is thus enabled to respond to God in word and deed. This programmatic sketch invites being tested against the strands of the biblical traditions in which the response to God's speech is the only appropriate access to the God who is as he speaks and what he speaks. It documents that Christology is well advised to seek its orientation from the primary strata of witnessing to the triune God and of confessing Christ.

VII. The End of Christology: The Coming Kingdom

The rich diversity of approaches represented by the essays in this volume confirms the main thesis Colin Gunton defended in his study of continuities in Christology: *Yesterday and Today.*[1] After conducting a thorough-going conversation with Christologies, old and new, he concludes:

> There is continuity of approach, method and above all of object, for Jesus Christ, the same yesterday and today and for ever, is at once the true subject and the true object of Christology: the one who makes it possible, through his Spirit, and the one whose reality as truly God and truly man our human concepts strain to represent.[2]

By the eschatological horizon in which Christologies yesterday and today are placed we are reminded that the Christological efforts of yesterday and of today are only stages on the way to the Kingdom of God when the identity of Christ for us will be fully disclosed and when our Christology, we may hope, will be one of praise.

[1] Colin E. Gunton, *Yesterday and Today: A Study of Continuities in Christology* (London: Darton, Longman & Todd).

[2] *Ibid*, 209.

Index